Quotations for All Occasions

Compiled by
Catherine Frank

COLUMBIA UNIVERSITY PRESS   NEW YORK

Columbia University Press
New York   Chichester, West Sussex
Publishers Since 1893
Copyright © 2000 Columbia University Press

Library of Congress Cataloging-in-Publication Data

Quotations for all occasions / compiled by Catherine Frank.
    p. cm.
Includes bibliographical references and index.
ISBN 0–231–11290–4 (cloth : acid-free paper) — 0–231–11291–2 (pbk. : acid-free paper)
1. Quotations, English. I. Frank, Catherine.
PN6084.O3 Q68 2000
082-dc21   00-024048

∞

Casebound editions of Columbia University Press books are printed
on permanent and durable acid-free paper.
Printed in the United States of America

c 10 9 8 7 6 5 4 3 2
p 10 9 8 7 6 5 4 3 2

Also Available

The Columbia World of Quotations (CD-ROM)
General editors: Robert Andrews, Mary Biggs, Michael Seidel

Famous Lines
The Columbia Dictionary of Familiar Quotations
by Robert Andrews

The Columbia Dictionary of Quotations
by Robert Andrews

The Concise Columbia Dictionary of Quotations
by Robert Andrews

Women's Words
The Columbia Book of Quotations by Women
by Mary Biggs

Family Wisdom
The 2,000 Most Important Things Ever Said About Parenting,
Children and Family Life
by Susan Ginsberg

I Can Resist Everything Except Temptation
And Other Quotations from Oscar Wilde
by Karl Beckson

Of the People, By the People, For the People
And Other Quotations from Abraham Lincoln
by Gabor Borritt

Hitch Your Wagon to a Star
And Other Quotations from Ralph Waldo Emerson
by Keith Frome

Simplify, Simplify
And Other Quotations from Henry David Thoreau
by K. P. Van Anglen

Not Bloody Likely!
And Other Quotations from Bernard Shaw
by Bernard F. Dukor

When in Doubt, Tell the Truth
And Other Quotations from Mark Twain
by Brian Collins

Contents

Once in a Lifetime

Introduction

On the most important occasions of our lives, we often find ourselves at a loss for words. When we most want to console, celebrate, explain, inspire, or thank, we end up repeating phrases like "Words cannot express how I feel" or "I just don't know what to say." *Quotations for All Occasions* may just be the book to supply those words or inspire you to come up with some of your own.

Our failure to speak on important occasions sometimes results from a sense that it may be inappropriate to craft a fine turn of phrase in a time of great emotion. Eloquence may be misconstrued when it commemorates the loss of a friend, for example. (Turn to the section on bereavement and you will see that Samuel Johnson had something to say about the incompatibility of grief and "remote allusions and obscure opinions.") On the other hand, to read or share the comments of Plato, John Donne, or Woody Allen on the subject of death can help to put our own grief into perspective, and enable us to offer words instead of tears to console a friend.

Even on joyful occasions, *le mot juste* may not be a high priority. When you are shopping for turkey and trying to figure out how to fit your entire family around your dinner table, you may not have the energy to compose a moving statement about the meaning of Thanksgiving to set the tone for the feast. *Quotations for All Occasions* may give you the inspiration to impress your guests with a quotation from Sarah Josepha Hale, the founder of the modern celebration of the holiday, or to reassure them with Erma Bombeck's comment that on this one day everyone should be exonerated from dieting. Why come up with a toast for your child's wedding when the poet Richard Wilbur has already done the work for you? Why share with your child the intimate details of your first sexual encounter when you can let Moll Flanders, Martina Navratilova, and Holden Caulfield tell all? Why suffer alone when Florence King and Ursula Le Guin can enlighten you about the benefits of menopause, and when Betty Ford can inspire you to battle an addiction? *Quotations for All Occasions* can supply you with quotations to inspire and console you and bail you out when you just don't know what to say about death, Thanksgiving, marriage, sex, menopause, recovery, or any of the many occasions that confront us over the course of a year or over the course of a lifetime.

Quotations for All Occasions is a collection of quotations about many of the celebrations and rites of passage in the calendar year and in our personal lives. The collection contains three sections. First, there are quotations, beginning with New Year's Day and ending with New Year's Eve, about the occasions we experience *every year*. Then there are quotations about events that happen *occasionally*; they lack the inevitability of the calendar, but they are by no means unique. Finally, the third section of the collection contains quotations about those occasions that happen *once in a lifetime*, about the milestones by which we measure our development, count our gains and number our losses.

In the first section, "Every Year," there are quotations for all the important festivals and religious celebrations, for all the seasons, all the months, even the days of the week. (You may never again look quite the same way at Monday after you learn what Brenda Spencer did because she hated it, or at Tuesday after you read Elizabeth Taylor's report of how Richard Burton was wont to celebrate it.) Browsing through the quotations in this first section of the book you will notice the diverse views that writers have of these shared experiences, and perhaps come to a better understanding of how our culture and our place condition our sense of the passing year. The Chinese New Year, the Muslim New Year, and the Jewish New Year, for example, fall on days different from the Christian New Year.

The quotations included here reflect the customs associated with these different holidays and also highlight the different perspectives afforded by insiders and outsiders to a given tradition. If you have never celebrated Chinese New Year, you may regret your culture's lack of a "Kitchen God" after you read Amy Tan's description. If you do routinely commemorate this festival, you may still be impressed with the prose poem that Osbert Sitwell creates with his list of the lyrical names for different kinds of noisy fireworks. Even within a given culture, the same holiday may have different tones for different participants. American Christians reading Herman Wouk's quotation on Hanukkah, for example, may come to better appreciate that the American celebration of Christmas makes it difficult to find a niche for another December holiday. Ralph Waldo Emerson, Mark Twain, and Stephen Vincent Benét recall the ice cream and patriotic songs, the speeches and the fireworks that many Americans associate with Independence Day. Reformers like Williams Wells Brown, Frederick Douglass, and Frances Wright remind us that, for slaves or for women without the right to vote, this celebration of "liberty and justice for all" was felt as a yearly reminder of their country's hypocrisy. As you survey the quotations on Valentine's Day, note how the customs and lore of the day have changed over time. Chaucer and Shakespeare charm the reader when they recall the traditional lore about the mating of birds on this date, while modern women like Cathy Guisewhite and Helen Fielding's Bridget Jones provide a more jaded vision of the obligatory hearts, flowers, sex, and rejection. Even events that occur with regularity and seem to fall on all alike, the changing of seasons or the quicker cycle of days of the week, may look quite different to city and country dwellers (while George Herbert feels one cannot experience May in the city, William Cullen Bryant celebrates the way even a "few bright hours" can bring spring to a city garden in March), to the young and the old (witness the ongoing debate over the relative cruelty of April), and to the English and New Englanders (while Gertrude Jekyll's June is the embodiment of fresh young beauty, Oliver Wendell Holmes sees the month wearing a shawl and suffering from a head cold). The quotations here, which can confirm that even great minds are comforted by the warmth of the hearth in winter, can breathe new life into yearly rituals.

In the second section, "Occasionally," there are quotations for those occasions that do happen but not on a schedule. Indeed, the unpredictability may mark them as occasions in our lives. We don't choose when a disaster, an illness, or a separation will befall us, and the reactions of others may help us to respond. Henry Ward Beecher and C. S. Lewis may provide us with a sense of the purpose of suffering in our lives. Samuel Taylor Coleridge, Susan Sontag, and Robert McCrum describe pain and illness with an eloquence that brings dignity to those who are suffering. Other occasions, such as quitting an addiction, require will-power, and the words here may inspire the strength of character necessary to live through recovery. The quotations about quitting drinking, quitting smoking, and quitting overeating reflect both the continuing desire to change and the countervailing temptation to give in to the lure of a vice. It may be reassuring to know that everyone from Huck Finn to Wendy Cope has had trouble resisting the lure of a cigarette. Indeed, listing these attempts to "quit" under the heading "occasionally" underscores our weakness and difficulty in our efforts to over-come our bad habits. We may also regret the necessity to include proposals, weddings, and divorces in this category and to admit that they recur instead of happening "once in a lifetime." On the other hand, the reader may take some comfort or find some humor in the notion that the occasion of divorce has provided a common ground for writers as diverse as John Milton and Ann Landers (Eppie Lederer). We may also regret the regularity with which we must face unpleasant tasks like taking exams, attending meetings, writing reports, and surviving interviews. The reader may, however, gain a sense of the universality of his test anxiety when he reads that Robert Louis Stevenson could, many years out of school, still conjure up the terror of a late-night study session, or that Montaigne and William James found that most exams require the student to stuff the mind without exercising it. One may even start to appreciate some of the occasional burdens of life if they become the occasion to identify with the writers quoted here.

Finally, in "Once in a Lifetime," there are quotations for those occasions that for most of us occur no oftener than that. Sometimes the occasion is memorable because it is a first experience: first sex, first job, or first home. Harriet Beecher Stowe's commentary on setting up housekeeping on a scholar's income has special relevance to first-time homeowners on a budget, while Charlotte Perkins Gilman's definition of a home may serve as a welcome reminder to any homeowner that it is important to create a refuge for adults and children. Some of the events in this section are, in the chronology of our lives, events that we must experience at set times. We turn twenty, thirty, or forty only once. Our culture does not provide us with any standard ceremonies that shape and direct our reactions to these milestones. We may find some consolation in knowing that someone has survived such milestones before us and either that they have suffered as we are suffering – although you probably do not need a quotations book to encounter the sentiment that the second fifty years of life will never be as good as the first, you will find that sentiment expressed here – or that there are alternative ways to view the event and happy ways to celebrate it. Jimmy Buffett, for example, urges his fellow baby boomers to "reward" themselves instead of handling the "ball of snakes" of "mortality and accountability" that confronts them during their reflections on turning fifty.

In addition to these milestones without ritual, there are once-in-a-lifetime occasions that are surrounded by ceremony. Baptism, first communion, bar and bat mitzvah, graduation, and marriage all involve elaborate rituals that dictate how, as spectators and players, we speak about and participate in these events. But all of these events have also a private component, which may be intense. The ceremonies themselves may even dilute the meaning and the sense of importance that should make them turning points in our emotional lives. You will find here from Charles Lamb and John Keble some loving descriptions of the rite of baptism, while Charles Dickens reminds us that most babies are unimpressed. You will find practical information from Gertrude Stein on choosing appropriate godparents, and from Thomas Hood on the importance of choosing an auspicious name. Whether you are trying to educate yourself about a public ritual or to find insight into a particular milestone you happen to be passing, *Quotations for All Occasions* can provide guidance.

Every Year

Birthday

1 No length of time can make you
quit
Honour and virtue, sense and wit,
Thus you may still be young to me,
While I can better *hear* than *see*;
Oh, ne'er may fortune show her
spite,
To make me *deaf*, and mend my
sight.

JONATHAN SWIFT (1667–1745), Anglo-Irish author. "Stella's Birthday (1725)."

2 Through a dull tract of woe, of
dread,
The toiling year has pass'd and fled:
And, lo! in sad and pensive strain,
I sing my birth-day date again.

GEORGE CRABBE (1754–1832), English poet. "My Birth-Day."

3 In the gradual desuetude of old ob-
servances, this custom of solemniz-
ing our proper birth-day hath
nearly passed away, or is left to
children, who reflect nothing at all
about the matter, nor understand
any thing in it beyond cake and orange.

CHARLES LAMB (1775–1834), English essayist. "New Year's Eve," *London Magazine* (1821) and *Essays of Elia* (1823).

4 Good-morrow to the golden Morning!
Good-morrow to the world's
delight!
I've come to bless thy life's beginning,
That hath made my own so
bright!

THOMAS HOOD (1799–1845), English poet. "Birthday Verses."

5 What different dooms our birthdays bring!

THOMAS HOOD (1799–1845), English poet. "Her Birth," *Miss Kilmansegg and Her Precious Leg.*

6 So mayst thou live, dear! many
years,
In all the bliss that life endears,
Not without smiles, nor yet from
tears
Too strictly kept:
When first thy infant littleness
I folded in my fond caress,
The greatest proof of happiness
Was this—I wept.

THOMAS HOOD (1799–1845), English poet. "To My Daughter, On Her Birthday."

7 Maiden, when such a soul as thine
is born,
The morning-stars their ancient
music make.

JAMES RUSSELL LOWELL (1819–1891), U.S. author. Sonnet 7: "To M.W., On Her Birthday."

8 There are three hundred and sixty-
four days when you get un-birthday
presents— . . . And only *one* for
birthday presents, you know.

LEWIS CARROLL (CHARLES LUTWIDGE DODGSON) (1832–1898), English author and mathematician. *Through the Looking-Glass and What Alice Found There* (chapter 6, "Humpty-Dumpty") (1871).

9 To get back my youth I would do
anything in the world, except take
exercise, get up early, or be respectable.

OSCAR WILDE (1854–1900), Irish author. *The Picture of Dorian Gray* (chapter 19) (1891).

10 At another year
I would not boggle
Except that when I jog
I joggle.

OGDEN NASH (1902–1971), U.S. poet. "Birthday on the Beach."

11 Because time itself is like a spiral, something special happens on your birthday each year: The same energy that God invested in you at birth is present once again.

MENACHEM MENDEL SCHNEERSON (1902–1994), U.S. rabbi. *Toward a Meaningful Life : The Wisdom of the Rebbe* (chapter 2, "Birth: The Mission Begins") (1995).

12 Happy Birthday, Johnny,
Live beyond your income,
Travel for enjoyment,
   Follow your own nose.

W. H. AUDEN (1907–1973), Anglo-American poet. "Many Happy Returns."

13 I have always been intrigued at what went on in the world on my birthdays long before I was born.

ALEC GUINESS (b. 1914), English actor. *My Name Escapes Me: The Diary of a Retiring Actor* ("Monday, 24 April 1995") (1996).

14 I suppose it's possible that the Sundance Kid didn't like to make much of his birthdays—they may have struck him as just another reminder that his draw was getting slower by the year—but what if he truly liked a major celebration? What if he looked forward every year to marking the day of his birth with what they used to call in the West "a real wingding, with pink balloons and a few survivors"? I think Butch Cassidy would have arranged it.

CALVIN TRILLIN (b. 1935), U.S. author. *Travels with Alice* (chapter 15, "Special Occasion") (1989).

Describing plans for his wife's fiftieth birthday, Trillin notes that she loves "major celebrations" and remarks that the relation between Butch and Sundance is the new model for the married couple.

15 I used to anticipate my childhood birthday parties as if each were an annual coronation. Like most kids, I loved sitting at the head of the table with a crown on my head. In recent years, however, birthdays have been more like medical checkups—no fun at all but necessary if one intends to stay alive from year to year.

LETTY COTTIN POGREBIN (b. 1939), U.S. author. *Getting Over Getting Older: An Intimate Journey* (part I, "Facing Age"; chapter 3, "Happy Birthday to Me") (1996).

Pogrebin in this book describes the experience of turning fifty. She examines "croning" as a female "coming of age ceremony" that celebrates the "positive attributes of age—wisdom, knowledge, experience, caring." She describes a "ceremony" for obtaining an "escort" from the "sweet, verdant land" of youth to the "place of uncertainty and fear."

New Year

1 The weary yeare his race now
   hauing run,
The new begins his compass course
   anew;
with shew of morning mylde he
   hath begun,
betokening peace and plenty to en-
   sew.

EDMUND SPENSER (1552?–1599), English poet and courtier. *Amoretti,* sonnet 62 (1595).

2 The circling months begin this day,
   To run their yearly ring,
And long-breath'd time which ne'er
   will stay,
   Refits his wings, and shoots away,
It round again to bring.

MATTHEW PRIOR (1664–1721), English poet. "The New Year's Gift to Phyllis."

3 The new-year is the season in which custom seems more particularly to authorise civil and harmless lies, under the name of compliments. People reciprocally profess wishes, which they seldom form; and concern which they seldom feel.

PHILIP DORMER STANHOPE, FOURTH EARL OF CHESTERFIELD (1694–1773), English statesman and author. Letter, 26 December 1749 OS, *The Letters of Philip Dormer Stanhope, Earl of Chesterfield*, ed. John Bradshaw, vol. 1 (1929).

4 As the vulgar . . . are always very careful to end the old year well, so they are no less solicitous of making a good beginning of the new one. The old one is ended with a hearty compotation. The new one is opened with the custom of sending presents, which are termed New Year's Gifts, to friends and acquaintance.

JOHN BRAND (1744–1806), English antiquarian. "New Year's Day," *Observations on the Popular Antiquities of Great Britain: Chiefly Illustrating the Origin of Our Vulgar and Provincial Customs, Ceremonies, and Superstition* (vol. 1) (1848–49).

5 No one ever regarded the First of January with indifference. It is that from which all date their time, and count upon what is left. It is the nativity of our common Adam.

CHARLES LAMB (1775–1834), English essayist. "New Year's Eve," *London Magazine* (January 1821) and *Essays of Elia* (1823).

6 Ring out the old, ring in the new,
　Ring, happy bells, across the
　　snow:
　The year is going, let him go;
　Ring out the false, ring in the true.

ALFRED, LORD TENNYSON (1809–1892), English poet. *In Memoriam A.H.H.* 106 (1850).

7 Now the New Year reviving old Desires
The thoughtful Soul to Solitude retires.

EDWARD FITZGERALD (1809–1883), English author and translator. *The Rubáiyát of Omar Khayyám* (section 4) (1859).

8 Every man should be born again on the first day of January. Start with a fresh page. Take up one hole more in the buckle if necessary, or let down one, according to circumstances; but on the first of January let every man gird himself once more, with his face to the front, and take no interest in the things that were and are past.

HENRY WARD BEECHER (1813–1887), U.S. clergyman. "A Completed Year," *Plymouth Pulpit: Sermons. October 1882–April 1883* (1887).

9 Ring out the shame and sorrow
　And the misery and sin,
That the dawning of the morrow
　May in peace be ushered in.

JAMES WHITCOMB RILEY (1849–1916), U.S. poet. "Song of the New Year."

10 What can be said in New Year
　rhymes,
That's not been said a thousand
　times?

The new years come, the old years
　go,
We know we dream, we dream we
　know.

ELLA WHEELER WILCOX (1850–1919), U.S. poet. "The Year."

11 　　New Year's Day;
Nothing good or bad,—
　　Just human beings.

SHIKI (1869–1902), Japanese poet. In R. H. Blyth, trans., *Haiku*, 4 vols. (1949).

Blyth notes: "On New Year's Day, all things are once more in their original state of harmony. There is no distinction between higher and lower, respectable and criminal, men and animals. All are united in their ceaseless activity of their Buddha nature, without any distinction whatever, all happy today and happy ever after."

12 Welcome, New Year, but be more
kind
Than thy dead father left behind;
If I may kiss no mouth that's red,
Give me the open mouth instead
Of a black bottle of old wine
To gurgle in its neck and mine.

W. H. DAVIES (1871–1940), Welsh author. "To the New Year."

13 The year's doors open
like those of language,
toward the unknown.

ELIZABETH BISHOP (1911–1979), U.S. poet. "January First."

14 On New Year's Day when all the Christmas decorations were taken down, we felt sad and let down; to us our house looked drab and naked, and although the visiting back and forth would continue until winter came to an end, Christmas was over.

EDNA LEWIS (b. 1916), U.S. chef and author of cookbooks. *The Taste of Country Cooking* (1976).

15 I never liked New Year's Day anyway; it has too often felt like a day of foreboding.

ALEC GUINESS (b. 1914), English actor. *My Name Escapes Me: The Diary of a Retiring Actor* ("Sunday, 1 January 1995") (1996).

16 I do think New Year's resolutions can't technically be expected to begin on New Year's Day, don't you?

Since, because it's an extension of New Year's Eve, smokers are already on a smoking roll and cannot be expected to stop abruptly on the stroke of midnight with so much nicotine in the system. Also dieting on New Year's Day isn't a good idea as you can't eat rationally but really need to be free to consume whatever is necessary, moment by moment, in order to ease your hangover. I think it would be much more sensible if resolutions began generally on January the second.

HELEN FIELDING (b. 1958), English author. *Bridget Jones's Diary* ("Sunday 1 January") (1998).

Martin Luther King Day

1 Now listen, white folks!
In line with Reverend King down in
Montgomery—
Also because the Bible says I
must—
I'm gonna love you—*yes, I will! or
BUST!*

LANGSTON HUGHES (1902–1967), U.S. poet. "Brotherly Love: A Little Letter to the White Citizens of the South."

2 The assassination of Dr. Martin Luther King, Jr., was the occasion for one of those massive outpourings of hypocrisy characteristic of the human race. He stood in that line of saints which goes back from Gandhi to Jesus; his violent end, like theirs, reflects the hostility of mankind to those who annoy it by trying hard to pull it one more painful step further up the ladder from ape to angel. . . . Nothing could be more deceptive than the nationwide mourning. Beneath the

surface nothing has changed, except perhaps for the worst.

I. F. STONE (1907–1989), U.S. journalist and author. "The Fire Has Only Just Begun," in *I. F. Stone Bi-Weekly* (15 April 1968) and *Polemics and Prophecies 1967–1970* (1989).

3 Where in America today do we hear a voice like the voice of the prophets of Israel? Martin Luther King is a sign that God has not forsaken the United States of America. His presence is the hope of America.

ABRAHAM JOSHUA HESCHEL (1907–1972), U.S. (Polish-born) rabbi and theologian. Introduction of Dr. Martin Luther King at the 68th Annual Convention of the Rabbinical Assembly (Conservative), 25 March 1968, in *Two Jews, Three Opinions: A Collection of Twentieth-Century American Jewish Quotations*, ed. Sandee Brawarsky and Deborah Mark (1998).

King was assassinated ten days later.

4 Martin Luther King dedicated his life to love and to justice for his fellow human beings, and he died because of that effort.

ROBERT F. KENNEDY (1925–1968), U.S. attorney general and senator. In *Lend Me Your Ears: Great Speeches in History*, ed. William Safire (1992).

Speech to an African-American audience in Indianapolis two months before Robert Kennedy himself was assassinated in June 1968.

5 Injustice anywhere is a threat to justice everywhere.

MARTIN LUTHER KING JR. (1929–1968), U.S. clergyman and civil-rights leader. "Letter from Birmingham Jail" (16 April 1963).

6 Yes, if you want to say that I was a drum major, say that I was a drum major for justice; say that I was a drum major for peace; I was a drum major for righteousness. And

all of the other shallow things will not matter.

MARTIN LUTHER KING JR. (1929–1968), U.S. clergyman and civil-rights leader. 1968.

King here was responding to a question about what he would like to have included in his eulogy.

7 We must come to see that human progress never rolls in on the wheels of inevitability. It comes through the tireless efforts and persistent work of men willing to be co-workers with God, and without this hard work time itself becomes an ally of the forces of social stagnation.

MARTIN LUTHER KING JR. (1929–1968), U.S. clergyman and civil-rights leader. "Letter from Birmingham Jail" (16 April 1963).

8 There are no more Martins and never will be. . . . There is no black knight in black armor on a black horse waving a black magic wand going to come riding through the ghetto making every Black person healthy, wealthy and wise. So we are going to have to organize and go back to direct action. We have to wage aggressive peace.

JOSEPH LOWERY (b. 1921), U.S. clergyman. Reported in *Ebony*, November 1979.

Lowery is cofounder, and served as president, of the Southern Christian Leadership Conference.

9 Before deciding to back the bill [to create a national holiday], Reagan expressed concern about its cost. Federal offices close on national holidays, as do banks and many other businesses. [Senator Jesse] Helms [of North Carolina] claimed the resulting annual loss could be

12 billion dollars. The Congressional Budget Office put the figure at 18 million.

To those worried about the expense, said Senator Bob Dole (R-Kans.), "I suggest they hurry back to their pocket calculators and estimate the cost of 300 years of slavery, followed by a century or more of economic, political and social exclusion and discrimination."

Reported in *U. S. News and World Report* (17 October 1983).

10   The trouble with Martin Luther King, Jr., is that he believed more in America and in America's God than America did. He actually believed that the nation wished to be a nation under God, that it wished to live up to the moral ambition of its founding documents, that it wished to find a way to do right and to be right.

PETER J. GOMES (b. 1942), U.S. clergyman and theologian. *The Good Book: Reading the Bible with Heart and Mind* (chapter 3, "The Bible in America") (1996).

11   I proposed legislation in 1994 making the Martin Luther King holiday a day of community service and action rather than just a day off from work. Dr. King was more than just a teacher or a preacher. He was a man of action, and I suggested that we could honor his memory best by making this a duty of sharing and caring and acting on the principles of community and connection.

JOHN LEWIS (b. 1940), U.S. civil-rights leader and congressman. *Walking with the Wind: A Memoir of the Movement* (chapter 21, "Onward") (1998).

12   Martin Luther King's Dream was the American Dream. His quest is our quest: the ceaseless striving to live out our true creed. Our history has been built upon such dreams and labors. And by our dreams and labors we will redeem the promise of America in the twenty-first century.

BILL CLINTON (b. 1946), U.S. president. Inauguration speech, 20 January 1997.

13   I just never understood
How a man who died for good
Could not have a day that would
Be set aside for his recognition.

STEVIE WONDER (BORN STEVELUND JUDKINS) (b. 1950), U.S. singer and songwriter. "Happy Birthday."

Wonder, instrumental in the creaton of Martin Luther King Day, wrote this song before the holiday was established.

Chinese New Year

1   No-one, after the twelfth hour has struck, can claim a debt, or even make the slightest allusion to it. You now only hear the words of peace and good-will; everybody fraternizes with everybody. Those who were just before on the point of twisting their neighbor's neck, now twine their friendly arms about it.

E. R. HUC (1813–1860), French missionary. *Travels in Tartary, Thibet and China, 1844–1846*, trans. William Hazlitt and ed. Paul Pelliot, vol. 2. (1928).

Huc describes the misery and tension as the year winds down and people struggle to clear their accounts. He then notes the abrupt change brought about by the New Year custom of forgiveness.

2   The flower-boats, as they are commonly called, are particularly gay at new-year time with flowers of all

hues, and gaudy flags streaming from each mast and stern.

ROBERT FORTUNE (1813–1880), Scottish horticulturist. *Three Years' Wandering in the Northern Provinces of China* (1847).

3   And the crackers—the firecrackers—here is a perfect apotheosis of noise. A perfect carnival of uproar and deafening sound is produced, especially at New Year's time, by their almost continuous discharge, for at that joyous season a perfect pandemonium reigns rampant.

J. DYER BALL (1847–1919), British civil servant in Hong Kong. *Things Chinese: Being Notes on Various Subjects Connected with China* (1893).

Ball takes a rather condescending view of the Chinese as a supremely "noisy people" and then uses the firecrackers as an example.

4   She spoke of the New Year's gifts she had lately sent us, explaining that the flowers were symbolical of happiness and long life, that the tea had medicinal virtues, and that the bon-bons were a Chinese dainty, of which she herself was very fond.

LADY SUSAN TOWNLEY (1868–?), English author. *My Chinese Note Book* (1904).

The author describes a Chinese New Year interview between the Empress Dowager and the "Ladies of the *Corps Diplomatique.*"

5   At New Year time, solitary dwellers in remote districts leave their homes and seek some follow-creatures with whom to rejoice, and eat boiled pork; while village dwellers often flock into towns on account of the more numerous excitements there available.

J. R. CHITTY. *Things Seen in China* (1918).

6   Anyone who is able to do so returns about this time to his home.

New year is the feast of the family. The parents and the children reunite.

RICHARD WILHELM (1873–1930), author. *The Soul of China* (1928).

7   Even the sky seems to proclaim the arrival of the New Year, as the old calendar scrolls toward the last page, to say nothing of the villages and towns lying expectantly underneath. Pallid clouds loom overhead, intermittently brightened by flashes of firecrackers set off to bid farewell to the Hearth God.

LU XUN (1881–1936), Chinese author. "The New Year Sacrifice," translated by and quoted in Carol Stepanchuk and Charles Wong, *Mooncakes and Hungry Ghosts: Festivals of China* (1991).

8   [The firecrackers] were ricocheting in every direction, and with many subtle modulations of sound, so that, had I been the possessor of a properly trained ear, I should, in all probability, have been able to differentiate between the bang and hiss of the numerous varieties . . . and to distinguish Small Boxes, Flower Pots, Lanterns of Heaven and Earth, Fire and Smoke Poles, Silver Flowers, Peonies Strung on a Thread, Lotus Sprinkled with Water, Golden Plates, Falling Moons, Grape Arbours, Flags of Fire, Double-Kicking Feet, Ten Explosions Flying to Heaven, Five Devils Noisily Splitting Apart, Eight-Cornered Rockets, and Bombs for Attacking the City of Hsiang Yang, one from another.

OSBERT SITWELL (1892–1969), English author. *Escape with Me!: An Oriental Sketch-Book* (1939).

9   I am sorry to say that the New Year customs are gradually dying out. I

cannot but regret it. It may be better to be practical rather than formal, but how few really joyful times one has in one's life! Looking back on the New Year Festivals of my childhood I find them very precious. What a business they were! But what pleasure and good fellowship they gave!

CHIANG YEE (1903–1977), Chinese author, of a series called the *Silent Traveller* books. *A Chinese Childhood* (1952).

10   The Chinese New Year, even in communities so thoroughly Americanized as our Chinatowns, is a big event. . . . This is more than just a show for the visitors. New Year's day is the last and strongest link that unites the Chinese-American spiritually with his old home in Kwangtung province (for it is from this one province that the vast majority of Chinese Americans come).

WOLFRAM EBERHARD (1909–1989), German sociologist and folklorist. *Chinese Festivals* (1952).

11   Indeed, it is difficult for us Westerners to grasp the full significance of the Chinese New Year. Our Christmas, our Easter, and whatever national holiday we celebrate, all taken together really mean less to us than *the* great festival of their calendar does to the hardworking Chinese. Socially, it signifies re-union. Morally, it represents the idea of resurrection, the re-birth of the year. . . . Materially, it stands for rejuvenation both in the home and in the market place. Personally and commercially, men turn over a new leaf, strive to pay off old debts in money and loyalty, and start with a clean sheet on which they hope to

write better success and greater happiness.

JULIET BREDON and IGOR MIRRO-PHANOW. *The Moon Year: A Record of Chinese Customs and Festivals* (1927).

12   He is not Santa Claus. More like a spy—FBI agent, CIA, Mafia, worse than IRA, that kind of person! And he does not give *you* gifts, you must give *him* things. All year long you have to show him respect—give him tea and oranges. When Chinese New Year's time comes, you must give him even better things— maybe whiskey to drink, cigarettes to smoke, candy to eat, that kind of thing. You are hoping all the time that his tongue will be sweet, his head a little drunk, so when he has his meeting with the big boss, maybe he reports good things about you. This family has been good, you hope he says. Please give them good luck next year.

AMY TAN (b. 1952), U.S. author. *The Kitchen God's Wife* (1991).

In this passage a Chinese mother explains to her daughter and son-in-law the need to appease the Kitchen God, an integral figure in many Chinese New Year celebrations, and explains some methods of appeasement.

13   We weren't to sweep or empty the trash on New Year's, since we might inadvertently throw out our luck. We weren't to cry, because it would bring a sad year. We weren't to wash our luck away by washing our hair. For us children, New Year's meant our parents were not supposed to yell at us lest discord follow throughout the year.

ELLEN BLONDER (b. 1950) and ANNABEL LOW, authors. *Every Grain of Rice: A Taste of Our Chinese Childhood in America* (1998).

14 Chinese New Year is like a combi-
    nation of Thanksgiving and Easter
    that celebrates the sacredness of the
    family and presents a time of re-
    newal.

    GRACE YOUNG, U.S. author of cookbooks.
    *Wisdom of the Chinese Kitchen: Classic Family
    Recipes* (1995).

Valentine's Day

1   For this was on seynt Valentynes
    day,
    Whan every foul cometh there to
    chese his make,
    Of every kynde that men thynke
    may,
    And that so huge a noyse gan they
    make
    That erthe and eyr and tre and
    every lake
    So ful was, that unethe was there
    space
    For me to stonde, so ful was al the
    place.

    GEOFFREY CHAUCER (C. 1340–1400),
    English poet. *The Parlement of Foules.*

2   . . . since the solemn time allows
    To choose the object of our vows,
    Boldly I dare profess my flame,
    Proud to be yours by any name.

    CHARLES, DUKE OF ORLEANS (1391–
    1465), French poet and soldier. 1415. In *The
    Valentine and Its Origins* (1969).

    After the Battle of Agincourt (1415), in which
    he commanded troops, Charles was impris-
    oned in the Tower of London, from which he
    sent this poem to his wife Dorinda. The date of
    the poem is circa 1415. For 25 years Charles
    lived in England, where he composed courtly
    poetry in both French and English.

3   Win her with gifts, if she respect
    not words.

    WILLIAM SHAKESPEARE (1564–1616),
    English poet and dramatist. *The Two Gentle-
    men of Verona* 1.88.

The speaker does not specifically celebrate
Valentine's Day, but his advice applies.

4   Saint Valentine is past;
    Begin these woodbirds but to cou-
    ple now?

    WILLIAM SHAKESPEARE (1564–1616),
    English poet and dramatist. *A Midsummer
    Night's Dream* 4.1.139–40.

    Birds were supposed to have chosen their
    mates on St. Valentine's day.

5   Good morrow! 'tis Saint Valentine's
    Day
    All in the morning betime.
    And I a maid at your window
    To be your Valentine.

    WILLIAM SHAKESPEARE (1564–1616),
    English poet and dramatist. *Hamlet* 4.5.48–55.

    The first part of a song sung by Ophelia during
    her final descent into madness.

6   Oft have I heard both Youths and
    Virgins say,
    Birds chuse their Mates, and couple
    too, this day:
    But by their flight I never can di-
    vine
    When I shall couple with my Valen-
    tine.

    ROBERT HERRICK (1591–1674), English
    poet and clergyman. "To his Valentine, on S.
    Valentines Day."

7   Yestreen at the valentines' dealing,
       My heart to my mou gied a sten,
    For thrice I drew ane without fail-
    ing,
       And thrice it was written "Tam
       Glen!"

    ROBERT BURNS (1759–1796), Scottish
    poet. "Tam Glen."

    Mou is *mouth. Sten* is *leap.* Burns describes a
    custom whereby young people fill one bag
    with men's names and another with women's.
    If one draws the same name three times, one
    has named his or her future mate—here, Tam
    Glen.

8   Love darts
      Cleave hearts
    Through mail shirts.

SIR WALTER SCOTT (1771–1832), Scottish novelist and poet. *The Fair Maid of Perth, or Saint Valentine's Day* (chapter 3).

An armourer named Henry Smith tries to win the favor of Catharine Glover, the Fair Maid of Perth, by inscribing this message on a "small purse made of links of the finest work in steel." The purse holds a "small ruby cut into the form of a heart, transfixed with a golden arrow." The armourer is "much satisfied with his composition, because it seemed to imply that his skill could defend all hearts saving his own."

9   Sure, of all days that ever were
      dated,
      Valentine's Day is the fullest of
      news;
    Then ev'ry lass expects to be mated
      And Cupid goes round collecting
      his dues!
    And levies a door-rate, like parish
      or poor-rate,
      By getting the Postman to stand
      in his shoes.

THOMAS HOOD (1799–1845), English poet. "Valentine's Day."

10 This is the day on which those charming little missives, ycleped Valentines, cross and inter-cross each other at every street and turning. The weary and all forespent two-penny postman sinks beneath a load of delicate embarrassments, not his own.

CHARLES LAMB (1775–1834), English essayist. "Valentine's Day," *The Examiner* (14–15 February 1819) and *Essays of Elia* (1823).

11 Good morrow to my Valentine, sings poor Ophelia; and no better wish, but with better auspices, we wish to all faithful lovers, who are not too wise to despise old legends, but are content to rank themselves humble diocesans of old Bishop Valentine, and his true church.

CHARLES LAMB (1775–1834), English essayist. "Valentine's Day," *The Examiner* (14–15 February 1819) and *Essays of Elia* (1823).

12 On the 14th of February the windows fill with pictures for the most part odious, and meant for some nondescript class of males and females, their allusions having reference to Saint Valentine's Day, the legendary pairing time of the birds. The festival is a sad mockery, for there are no spring birds here to pair, but it reminds us that there is a good time coming.

OLIVER WENDELL HOLMES (1809–1894), U.S. author and physician. "The Seasons," *Pages from an Old Volume of Life: A Collection of Essays, 1857–1881* (1891).

13 Never sign a walentine with your own name.

CHARLES DICKENS (1812–1870), English author. *The Pickwick Papers* (chapter 33, "Mr. Weller the Elder Delivers Some Critical Sentiments Respecting Literary Composition; and, Assisted by His Son Samuel, Pays a Small Installment of Retaliation to the Account of the Reverend Gentleman with the Red Nose") (1837).

Sam Weller struggles through the composition of a valentine for his sweetheart Mary, as his father warns him against becoming too poetical. He ends up signing with a bit of rhyme: "Your love-sick / Pickwick."

14 More than when first I singled thee,
      This only prayer is mine,—
    That, in the years I yet shall see,
      As, darling, in the past, thou'lt
      be
    My happy Valentine.

JAMES RUSSELL LOWELL (1819–1891), U.S. author. "A Valentine."

15 With kindly lips of welcome, and
      with pleased
      Propitious eyes benign,
   Accept a kiss of homage from your
      least
      Last Valentine.

   CHRISTINA ROSSETTI (1830–1894),
   English poet. "Valentine to My Mother 1876."

16 Since the receipt of the missive in
   the morning, Boldwood had felt the
   symmetry of his existence to be
   slowly getting distorted in the direction of an ideal passion.

   THOMAS HARDY (1840–1928), English
   author. *Far from the Madding Crowd* (chapter
   14, "The Effect of the Letter—Sunrise") (1874).

   Farmer Boldwood reacts passionately to a valentine sent as a joke (and sealed with the
   words "Marry Me") by the impulsive Bathsheba.

17 Somebody's sent a funny little val-
      entine to me.
   It's a bunch of baby-roses in a vase
      of filigree,
   And hovering above them—just as
      cute as he can be—
   Is a fairy cupid tangled in a scarf of
      poetry.

   JAMES WHITCOMB RILEY (1849–
   1916), U.S. poet. "Her Valentine."

18 Very fine is my valentine.
   Very fine and very mine.

   GERTRUDE STEIN (1874–1946), U.S.
   author. "A Very Valentine," *A Valentine to
   Sherwood Anderson.*

   Anderson was an American writer (1876–
   1941) and one of the expatriate authors among
   Stein's circle in Paris.

19 Any valentine that is *written*
   Is as the *vendange* to the *vine.*

   MARIANNE MOORE (1887–1972), U.S.
   poet. "Saint Valentine."

   "Vendange" refers to the grape harvest.

20 I love you more than a wasp can
      sting,
   And more than the subway jerks,
   I love you as much as a beggar
      needs a crutch,
   And more than a hangnail irks.

   OGDEN NASH (1902–1971), U.S. poet.
   "To My Valentine."

21 Love with his gilded bow and crys-
      tal arrows
   Has slain us all. . . .

   ELIZABETH BISHOP (1911–1979), U.S.
   poet. "Three Valentines."

22 Poor old Valentine, a third century
   priest who was clubbed and be-
   headed on February 14th, in the
   year 270, would certainly be surprised to find himself a lovers'
   saint.

   HOWARD V. HARPER (b. 1904), U.S.
   author and Episcopal priest. *Days and Customs
   of All Faiths* (1957).

23 I bought sultry lingerie but I'm too
   embarrassed to wear it. I bought a
   suggestive card, but I'm too embarrassed to give it. I thought of rent-
   ing a sexy movie, but I'm too embarrassed to go pick one out and
   even if I did, I'd be too embarrassed to admit I had it. I'm beginning to understand why red is the
   color of Valentine's Day.

   CATHY GUISEWHITE (b. 1950), U.S.
   cartoonist. "Cathy" comic strip, quoted in Jack
   Santino, *New Old-Fashioned Ways: Holidays
   and Popular Culture* (1996).

24 My time and my eternity
   My cigarette, my nicotine
   My coffee, tea, and whole cuisine
   My loaf of bread, my jug of wine
   All this and more sweet Valentine!

JOYCE MAYNARD (b. 1953), U.S. author. *At Home in the World: A Memoir* (1998).

Maynard includes a valentine written by her father to her mother.

25 Valentine's Day tomorrow. Why? Why? Why is entire world geared to make people not involved in romance feel stupid when everyone knows romance does not work anyway.

HELEN FIELDING (b. 1958), English author. *Bridget Jones's Diary* ("Monday 13 February") (1998).

February 29

1 Ther's allus been leap years, but I doubt if any o' us ever knowed a case where any girl ever actually took advantage o' th' privilege an' asked any feller point blank t' marry her. Ther's allus been a lot o' hintin' an' beatin' around th' bush an' hypnotizin' an' vampin', but I don't believe any girl ever blurted out a straight proposal. But now that we've been emancipated, I look fer a lot o' radical changes.

KIN HUBBARD (1868–1930), U.S. humorist. Speech by Miss Mame Moon to the local (all-women) Shakespeare Club, in *The Best of Kin Hubbard: Abe Martin's Sayings and Wisecracks, Abe's Neighbors, His Almanack, Comic Drawings,* ed. David S. Hawes (1984).

Miss Mame Moon is one of many small-town characters Hubbard created to espouse this kind of rural "wisdom."

2 Sweet February Twenty Nine!—
This is our grace-year, as I live!
Quick, now! this foolish heart of mine:
 Seize thy prerogative!

WALTER DE LA MARE (1873–1956), English poet. "February 29."

3 In Scotland, it was required that a woman who was thinking of taking advantage of the leap year privilege must let her intentions be known by wearing a scarlet flannel petticoat. The edge of the petticoat must be clearly visible in order to give the wary male a sporting chance to get out of the way. This is obviously a man-made rule.

HOWARD V. HARPER (b. 1904), U.S. author and Episcopal priest. *Days and Customs of All Faiths* (1957).

Harper includes this comment after explaining that the origin of the "women's special privilege of doing the proposing in leap years" goes back to an exchange between St. Bridget and St. Patrick. St. Bridget noted that women too often remained single because they could not propose to men. They negotiated the time when women would be allowed to make a request, and St. Bridget immediately proposed to St. Patrick. He had taken a vow of celibacy, so he turned her down. He did, however, offer her a kiss and a silk gown to compensate.

4 Well, it has happened again. The Earth has circled four times around the sun, astronomers have designated this a leap year and anxious bachelors won't answer their telephones until midnight.

DAVID O'REILLY, U.S. journalist. *Philadelphia Inquirer* (29 February 1984).

St. Patrick's Day

1 The Shamrock is said to be worn by the Irish upon the anniversary of this Saint, for the following reason. When the Saint preached the Gospel to the Pagan Irish, he illustrated the doctrine of the Trinity by showing them a trefoil, or three-leave grass with one stalk, which operating to their conviction, the Shamrock, which is a bundle of this

grass, was ever afterwards worn
upon this Saint's anniversary, to
commemorate the event.

JOHN BRAND (1744–1806), English antiquarian. "St. Patrick's Day," *Observations on
the Popular Antiquities of Great Britain: The
Origin of Our Vulgar and Provincial Customs,
Ceremonies, and Superstitions* (vol. 1) (1848–
49).

2   St. Patrick's day no more we'll keep
         his color can't be seen,
    For there's a bloody law agin'
         the wearin' of the green.

ANONYMOUS, "Wearin' of the Green."

This poem appears in *The Fireside Book of Favorite American Songs* (1952), edited by Margaret Bradford Boni. She notes: "No one can
place the authorship of this Irish song of 1798.
It is an inspired street ballad born of the sorrow and the bitterness of the people—an elo-
quent arraignment of England's Irish policy of
the time."

3   No wonder that those Irish lads
         Should be so gay and frisky,
    For sure St. Pat he taught them
         that,
         As well as making whiskey.

    . . . .
    So success attend St. Patrick's fist,

         For he's a saint so clever;
    O, he gave the snakes and toads a
         twist
         And bothered them forever!

HENRY BENNETT, Irish author and per-
former. In *Famous Single and Fugitive Poems*,
ed. Rossiter Johnson (1890).

According to Rossiter Johnson, this song,
which some regard simply as a traditional ballad, was written by Bennett and a man from
the county of Cork "who sang it in alternate
lines at a masquerade in that city in the winter
of 1814–1815."

4   But wherefore lament o'er those
         glories departed?

Her star will yet shine with as vivid
    a ray!
For ne'er had she children more
    brave or true-hearted
Than those she sees on St. Patrick's
    Day.

M. J. BARRY (D. 1889), Irish poet. In *The
Well-Known Songs of Ireland* (n.d.).

Barry is said to have composed these words to
be sung to an old tune. "She" is Ireland.

5   The Irish people would be willing
    to give up a good many things be-
    fore they would give up their cele-
    bration of St. Patrick's Day.

J. WALKER McSPADDEN (1874–1960),
U.S. author and editor. *The Book of Holidays*
(1917).

6   Craving the good saint's forgive-
    ness, I ask you to rise and drink, in
    uncharitable ice water, to the im-
    mortal memory of Saint Patrick.

JOSEPH B. ROGERS, U.S. jurist. Speech on
St. Patrick's day, 17 March 1920, before the
Friendly Sons of St. Patrick. Quoted in Jack
Santino, *All Around the Year: Holidays and
Celebrations in American Life* (chapter 3,
"Winter into Spring") (1994).

Rogers, president of the Friendly Sons of St.
Patrick, made his comments during the Prohi-
bition era (1919—33), when federal law pre-
vented the manufacture and distribution of alcoholic beverages.

7   It's a great day for the Shamrock
    for the flags in full array.
    And as we go a-swinging,
    ev'ry Irish heart is singing:
    It's a great, great day.

ROGER EDENS (1905–1970), U.S. composer. "It's a Great Day for the Irish," from the
musical *Little Nellie Kelly* (1940).

8   The observance of St. Patrick's Day
    is almost as old in America as the

Irish themselves. And some say they arrived in the sixth century.

John F. Kennedy (1917–1963), U.S. president.

This remark was attributed to Kennedy by President Bill Clinton in a speech at a St. Patrick's Day reception, 17 March 1995.

9   Patrick found a way of swimming down to the depths of the Irish psyche and warming and transforming Irish imagination—making it more humane and more noble while keeping it Irish.

Thomas Cahill (b. 1940), U.S. author and historian. *How the Irish Saved Civilization* (1995).

10   Outside Ireland there is a compulsion to "show the flag" and be seen to be celebrating on Saint Patrick's Day which does not exist at home. At home, ironically, it still feels like a new Bank Holiday, held at an awkward time of year, on which, unless you intend to get well and truly plastered, or stay slumped in front of the television absorbing the relentlessly Irish flavour which dominates the day's programming, it is difficult to think of anything much to do.

Alannah Hopkin (b. 1949), Irish journalist and author. *The Living Legend of St. Patrick* (1989).

Hopkins notes that the Irish in America take the celebration of the holiday much more seriously than do the Irish themselves, who celebrate quietly unless they want to put on a show for tourists.

11   The St. Patrick's Day parade, once a defiant show of strength against Protestant power, gradually declined into a pointless annual march of aging suburbanites and drunken collegians staggering along in funny hats.

John Leo, U.S. journalist and commentator. "Of Famine and Green Beer," *U.S. News and World Report* (24 March 1997).

Leo comments on attempts to reconnect Irish celebrations with the truth of Irish history.

April Fool's Day

1   The First of April, some do say,
     Is set apart for All Fools' Day,
     But why the people call it so,
     Nor I nor they themselves do know.

Anonymous, *Poor Robin's Almanac*, quoted in A. R. Wright, *British Calendar Customs: England*, vol. 2 (1938).

2   The oldest tradition affirms that such an infatuation attends the first day of April as no foresight can escape, no vigilance can defeat. Deceit is successful on that day out of the mouths of babes and sucklings. Grave citizens have been bit upon it: usurers have lent their money on bad security: experienced matrons have married very disappointed young fellows: mathematicians have missed the longitude: alchymists the philosopher's stone: and politicians preferment on that day. What confusion will not follow if the great body of the nation are disappointed of their peculiar holiday! This country was formerly disturbed with very fatal quarrels about the celebration of Easter. . . . If our clergy come to be divided about Folly's anniversary, we may well expect all the mischiefs attendant on religious wars.

John Brand (1744–1806), English antiquarian. "All Fools' Day," *Observations on the Popular Antiquities of Great Britain* (1848–49).

Brand here quotes a "late ingenious writer in the World (No. 10)," whom he believes to be the "late Earl of Oxford"

3 *April 1.* This is the day upon which we are reminded of what we are on the other three hundred and sixty-four.

MARK TWAIN (SAMUEL CLEMENS) (1835–1910), U.S. author. *Pudd'hhead Wilson* ("Pudd'nhead Wilson's Calendar" at chapter 21) (1894).

4 APRIL FOOL, n. The March fool with another month added to his folly.

AMBROSE BIERCE (1842–?1914), U.S. author. *The Devil's Dictionary* (1881–1911).

5 The origin of this custom has been much disputed, and many ludicrous solutions have been suggested, e. g. that it is a farcical commemoration of Christ being sent from Annas to Caiaphas, from Caiaphas to Pilate, from Pilate to Herod, from Herod back again to Pilate, the crucifixion having taken place about the 1st of April.

"April Fool's Day," *Encyclopedia Britannica,* vol. 1, 11th ed.

6 Among the numerous means employed in celebrating the custom, the following may be mentioned: the loose shoe lace; the something out of your pocket; the empty egg-shell inverted in an egg-cup; the envelope enclosing a blank sheet; the pencil with a rubber point; the note for delivery to a false address; the non-existent bus-terminus; . . . the pigeon's milk; the memory powder.

A. R. WRIGHT (1862–1932), *British Calendar Customs: England,* vol. 2 (1938).

7 What pleasanter task for All Fools' Day than going over all the things that you have done before
   And don't want to do again
never no more, never no more,
never no more?

OGDEN NASH (1902–1971), U.S. poet. "Raven, Don't Stay Away from My Door—A Chant for April First."

8 A writer in the *London Public Advertiser* for March 13, 1769, advanced the idea that Noah started the whole thing. It was, said this writer, on the first day of the Jewish month that corresponds to April that Noah mistakenly sent out the dove from the ark to find out if the waters had gone down. . . . When the dove returned without having found any dry land, Noah thereupon became the first "April Fool."

HOWARD V. HARPER (b. 1904), U.S. author and Episcopal priest. *Days and Customs of All Faiths* (1957).

9 Look out! Behind you there's a rat.
He's hiding now behind the stool.
He's going to jump up on your hat.
Look out! Watch out! Oh dear,
   what's THAT!
It's only you, you April fool!

MARNIE POMEROY (b. 1932), U.S. author. "April Fools' Day."

10 Generally, . . . April Fools' Day is a day when we can lie to our friends and cause them great anxiety, as long as we justify our actions by exclaiming "April fool!"

JACK SANTINO (b. 1947), U.S. folklorist and sociologist. *All Around the Year: Holidays and Celebrations in American Life* (chapter 3, "Winter into Spring: Celebrating Rebirth and Renewal") (1994).

11   As occasion rife with artifice and subterfuge, April Fools' Day furnishes an appropriate trope for modern celebrations as tricks of trade.

LEIGH ERIC SCHMIDT (b. 1961), U.S. historian. *Consumer Rites: The Buying and Selling of American Holidays* (Epilogue, "April Fools? Trade, Trickery, and Modern Celebration"; chapter titled "Mother's Day Bouquet") (1995).

Schmidt explains: "Over the course of the nineteenth and twentieth centuries, suspicion and disbelief increasingly shadowed modern rituals: What, critics asked, were 'cunning' stationers and booksellers putting over on people with all those fancy billets-doux for St. Valentine's Day? What were Christmas and Easter but occasions for merchants to sell things, to entice the credulous and to enrich themselves? What were Mother's Day and Father's Day but the most blatant humbug, the respective fantasies of florists and menswear retailers?"

Easter

1   Most glorious Lord of lyfe, that on
    this day
    Didst make thy triumph over death
    and sin,
    And having harrowed hell, didst
    bring away
    Captivity thence captive, us to win:
    This joyous day, deare Lord, with
    joy begin.

EDMUND SPENSER (1552?–1599), English poet and courtier. *Amoretti,* sonnet 68 (1595).

2   Rise, heart; Thy Lord is risen. Sing
    his praise
        Without delays,
    Who takes thee by the hand, that
    thou likewise
        With him mayst rise;
    That, as His death calcinèd thee to
    dust,
    His life make thee gold, and, much
    more, just.

GEORGE HERBERT (1593–1633), English poet and Anglican priest. "Easter."

3   Death, and darkness get you pack-
    ing,
    Nothing now to man is lacking,
    All your triumphs now are ended,
    And what Adam marred, is
    mended.

HENRY VAUGHAN (1622–1695), Welsh-born English poet. "Easter-Hymn."

4   See from his head, his hands, his
    feet,
    Sorrow and love flow mingled
    down;
    Did e'er such love and sorrow
    meet?
    Or thorns compose so rich a
    crown?

ISAAC WATTS (1674–1748), English clergyman and hymn writer. "When I Survey the Wondrous Cross."

5   Enthronèd in thy sovereign sphere
    Thou shedd'st thy light on all the
    year:
    Sundays by thee more glorious
    break,
    An Easter Day in every week:

    And week-days, following in their
    train,
    The fulness of thy blessing gain,
    Till all, both resting and employ,
    Be one Lord's day of holy joy.

JOHN KEBLE (1792–1866), English clergyman and poet. "Easter Day," *The Christian Year* (1827).

6   Though dead, not dead;
    Not gone, though fled;
    Not lost, not vanished.
    In the great gospel and true creed,
    He is yet risen indeed;
        Christ is yet risen.

ARTHUR HUGH CLOUGH (1819–1861), British poet. "Easter Day II."

7   Spring bursts to-day,
For Christ is risen and all the
    earth's at play.

CHRISTINA ROSSETTI (1830–1894), English poet. "An Easter Carol."

8   . . . how still the Landscape stands!
How nonchalant the Hedge!
As if the "Resurrection"
Were nothing very strange!

EMILY DICKINSON (1830–1886), U.S. poet. "A Lady red—amid the Hill."

9   . . . all alone, alone, alone,
He rose again behind the stone.

ALICE MEYNELL (1847–1922), English poet. "Easter Night."

10   . . . there's the Lenten lily
That has not long to stay
And dies on Easter Day.

A. E. HOUSMAN (1859–1936), English poet. "The Lent Lily."

11   Loveliest of trees, the cherry now
Is hung with bloom along the
    bough,
And stands about the woodland
    ride
Wearing white for Eastertide.

A. E. HOUSMAN (1859–1936), English poet. "Loveliest of Trees."

12   Well the prophecy was kept;
Christ—"first fruit of them that
    slept"—
Rose with vic'try-circled brow;
So, believing one, shalt thou.

PAUL LAURENCE DUNBAR (1872–1906), U.S. poet. "An Easter Ode."

13   I bet any Sunday could be made as
popular at church as Easter is, if
you made 'em fashion shows too.
The audience is so busy looking at
each other that the preacher might
as well recite Gunga Din.

WILL ROGERS (1879–1935), U.S. humorist. 22 April 1935, *Will Rogers Speaks: Over 1,000 Timeless Quotations for Public Speakers (And Writers, Politicians, Comedians, Browsers . . .)*, ed. Bryan B. Sterling and Frances N. Sterling (1995).

14   Myrtilla's tripping down the street,
    In Easter finery.
The Easter blooms are not more
    sweet
    And radiant-hued than she.

DOROTHY PARKER (1893–1967), U.S. author. "To Myrtilla, On Easter Day."

15   We have lost Christmas through the
commercial interest . . . and I don't
want to lose Easter. We crucified
the given Christ on His birthday.
Shall we now bury the living Lord
beneath the rabbits, the eggs, satins,
finery and thoughtlessness? We say
no. We want to celebrate Easter in
religion from now on.

C. LLOYD LEE, U.S. clergyman. Quoted in Leigh Eric Schmidt, *Consumer Rites: The Buying and Selling of American Holidays* ("Raining on the Easter Parade") (1995).

Lee was a Methodist clergyman in White Plains, N.Y. He and his congregation wrote a report bemoaning the commercialization of Easter.

16   The story of Passion-Tide and Easter is the story of the winning of
that freedom and of that victory
over the evils of Time. The burden
of the guilt is accepted ("He was
made Sin"), the last agony of alienation from God is passed through
(*Eloi, lama sabachthani*); the temporal Body is broken and remade;
and Time and Eternity are reconciled in a Single Person. There is no

retreat here to the Paradise of primal ignorance; the new Kingdom of God is built upon the foundations of spiritual experience. Time is not denied; it is fulfilled. "I am the food of the full-grown."

DOROTHY L. SAYERS (1893–1957), English author. "Strong Meat," *Creed or Chaos?* (1949).

Sayers argues that Christianity, while stressing the value of innocence and a pure heart, is in fact a religion for "adult minds."

17 I can remember the pastors of my youth who on Easter Sunday would let out a year's accumulated bile against the "twicesters," as those who came but twice a year were called. One of them went so far as to welcome them at Easter by wishing them a Happy Memorial Day, a Glorious Fourth of July, a Good Labor Day, a Peaceful Veterans' Day and a Gracious Thanksgiving, and by wishing them as well a Happy Mother's Day, Happy Father's Day, Happy Children's Day, and Happy Birthdays for the year.

PETER J. GOMES (b. 1942), U.S. clergyman and theologian. *The Good Book: Reading the Bible with Mind and Heart* (chapter 16, "The Bible and Mystery") (1996).

18 The resurrection is God's way of getting our attention.

PETER J. GOMES (b. 1942), U.S. clergyman and theologian. "When Life Begins," *Sermons: Biblical Wisdom for Daily Living* (1998).

Passover

1 And this day shall be unto you for a memorial; and ye shall keep it a feast to the Lord throughout your generations; ye shall keep it a feast by an ordinance forever. Seven days shall ye eat unleavened bread; even the first day ye shall put away leaven out of your houses; for whosoever eateth leavened bread from the first day until the seventh day, that soul shall be cut off from Israel. And in the first day there shall be an holy convocation, and in the seventh day there shall be an holy convocation to you; no manner of work shall be done in them, save that which every man must eat, that only may be done by you. And ye shall observe the feast of unleavened bread; for in this very same day have I brought your armies out of the land of Egypt; therefore shall ye observe this day in your generations by an ordinance forever.

Exodus 12.14–17.

2 Pesach has come to the Ghetto
again.
The lore-laden words of the Seder are said,
And the cup of the Prophet Elijah awaits,
But the Angel of Death has intruded, instead.

BINEM HELLER, "Pesach Has Come to the Ghetto Again (Warsaw, April 19, 1943)," in *"Jewish Life" Anthology, 1946-56*, trans. (from Yiddish) Max Rosenfeld.

Heller observes that the Holocaust transforms the meaning of the Passover holiday.

3 Among the many meals of the spiritual year, the evening meal of the Passover at which the father of the household gathers together all his family is the meal of meals. It is the only one that from first to last has the character of worship; hence the Seder (Order) is, from first to last, liturgically regulated. From the very

start the word "freedom" sheds its light upon it.

FRANZ ROSENZWEIG (1886–1929), German philosopher. *Franz Rosenzweig: His Life and Thought* (1953).

4 Passover dishes are probably the most interesting of any in the Jewish cuisine because of the lack of leaven and the resulting challenge to fine cooks. There are all kinds of torten and almond cakes and puddings, and an infinity of uses for mazzah or matzos: matzo klos, or dumplings, cakes and puddings of the matzo meal. Everything is doubly rich, as if to compensate for the lack of leaven, and clarified goose and chicken fat, and beef drippings, carefully excluding suet, are used most artfully.

M. F. K. FISHER (1908–1992), U.S. food expert and author. "K is for Kosher," *An Alphabet for Gourmets* (1949).

5 The bread of freedom is a hard bread. The contrast between bread and matzo possibly points to the contrast between the lush Nile civilization that the Jews left behind them on the first Passover and the gray rubbled desert in which they came into their identity.

HERMAN WOUK (b. 1915), U.S. author. *This is My God: The Jewish Way of Life* (chapter 5, "The Nature Festivals") (1988).

6 Grandmother Hannah comes to me
    at Pesach
and when I am lighting the sabbath
    candles.
The sweet wine in the cup has her
    breath.
The challah is braided like her long,
    long hair.

MARGE PIERCY (b. 1936), U.S. poet. "A candle in a glass," *The Art of Blessing the Day: Poems with a Jewish Theme* (1999).

7 The Jewish day is delineated by a schedule of prayers; the Jewish year is freighted with time-bound obligations—six days to fast, eight days to eat unleavened bread on Passover, eight days to light candles on Hanukkah, seven weeks to "count the omer," enumerating the days between the Israelites' liberation from slavery in Egypt and the giving of the law on Mount Sinai. Counting is a way of noticing and anticipating: it reminds us that a day counts or it doesn't. Counting imputes meaning; we rarely count what we do not value.

LETTY COTTIN POGREBIN (b. 1939), U.S. author. *Getting Over Getting Older: An Intimate Journey* (chapter 4, "Time Is All There Is") (1996).

8 Passover remains relevant and contemporary, while at the same time a ritual several thousand years old. The sanction of thousands of years of tradition is retained because the ritual form is retained. The content—at least some of it—is flexible and determined by the participants at specific celebrations. Thus, the holy day is still meaningful to younger generations, because it allows for creative input and participation. It breathes.

JACK SANTINO (b. 1947), U.S. folklorist and sociologist. *All Around the Year: Holidays and Celebrations in American Life* (chapter 3, "Winter into Spring: Celebrating Rebirth and Renewal") (1994).

9 Memory insinuated itself into every nook and cranny of the festivities, from the recitation of the Hagga-

dah, a ritualized exercise in collective memory, to the physical appearance of the seder table. Assembled over time and place from a variety of sources—Grandmother's cupboard, Aunt Sadie's basement—the items displayed on the table served as tangible, physical embodiments of family history and collective memory. As much an opportunity for the display of family history as of elegance, the seder fostered a unique aesthetic.

JENNA WEISSMAN JOSELIT, U.S. author. *The Wonders of America: Reinventing Jewish Culture 1880–1950* (chapter 6, "The Call of the Matzoh") (1994).

10 As for the bitter herbs, it may be that they were instituted in order to remind people of the bitterness of the suffering of the Israelites. . . . when I began to give my own Seders with my husband . . . we instituted cutting up a horseradish root into thin slices and giving everyone a taste, to really get the effect of the strength of the herb. To see everyone with tears coursing down their faces, laughing and gasping at the same time, is fun and also makes the point—bitter herbs must be *really* bitter to experience the suffering at all.

JULIA NEUBERGER (b. 1950), English author and rabbi. *On Being Jewish* (chapter 1) (1995).

11 What does spring cleaning and clearing the house of crumbs have to do with freedom and history, anyway? Is it an artificial and self-serving way to attach importance to a housewife's ritual? Is it investing the everyday with spirituality? Do ceremony, excitement, and special

food simply serve to lock ritual into a child's mind, securing it for the future? Without the meal and the commotion, the tradition of remembering the Exodus would certainly have died.

ELIZABETH EHRLICH, U.S. author. *Miriam's Kitchen* ("May: Ironing the Kitchen") (1997).

Islamic New Year

1 In Jewish legend the world was created on New Year's day. No cosmological significance attaches to the First of Muharram, the official opening of the Muslim year. . . . These contradictory computations of the New Year are an instructive illustration of the sometimes rather casual coexistence of Islamic patterns of behavior. The best the theologians could do was to suggest a tie connecting the pagan survival with an incident of Muslim history or legend.

GUSTAV EDMUND VON GRUNEBAUM (1909–1972), Austrian author and Orientalist. *Muhammadan Festivals* (chapter 3, "Ramadân") (1951).

Von Grunenbaum notes the variety of dates and customs for celebrating Islamic New Year. He says that in "India and Indonesia the day is set aside for the dead," and that in Egypt "it is believed that on New Year, the Lotus-Tree at the Boundary of Paradise is shaken so that the leaves inscribed with the names of those who will die during the year will fall." Persians, and Muslims in Iraq, Syria, and Egypt celebrate in the spring and commemorate it with a sprinkling of water which signifies the good omen of rain and purification.

2 Muharram was designated as the first month in the Islamic year by Umar, the second Caliph. At the beginning of a new year, Muslims set aside the sins of the past and determine to make a new start. . . .

Awwal Muharram is the Islamic New Year celebration. . . . The day commemorates the flight of Muhammad from Mecca to Medina in 622 C.E. Muhammad's journey, called the Hijrah, came about as a result of hostility toward his teachings and the sparsity of converts in Mecca. In Medina, Muhammad was welcomed, and Islam gained a solid following.

In *Religious Holidays and Calendars,* 2d ed., ed. Karen Bellenir (1998).

3   According to the Qur'an, Allah created the universe with an exact number of days, months, and years so mankind might be able to calculate time conveniently. However, because the Muslim calendar is totally lunar, and is not adjusted to the sun, it moves backwards through the years, making a complete retrograde cycle about once every thirty-two and a half years. . . . The Islamic New Year is a religious event, occurring on the first day of the first lunar month, Muhàrràm, with prayers for peace and prosperity, but its secular traditions include the exchange of good wishes and coins, which are supposed to bring good luck.

In *The Folklore of American Holidays,* 2d ed., ed. Hennig Cohen and Tristram Potter Coffin (1991).

Ramadan

1   The month of Ramadân in which was revealed the Qur'ân, a guidance for mankind, and clear proofs of the guidance, and the Criterion (of right and wrong). And whosoever of you is present, let him fast the month, and whosoever of you is

sick or on a journey, (let him fast the same) number of other days. Allah desireth for you ease; He desireth not hardship for you; and (He desireth) that ye should complete the period, and that ye should magnify Allah for having guided you, and that peradverture ye may be thankful.

Qur'an 2.185; *The Glorious Koran: An Explanatory Translation by Marmaduke Pickthall* (1930; reprint 1992).

2   Eat and drink until the white thread becometh distinct to you from the black thread of the dawn.

Qur'an 2.187; *The Glorious Koran: An Explanatory Translation by Marmaduke Pickthall* (1930; reprint 1992).

3   Thirty days make up the month,
   and yet, as God's Qur'án doth tell,
In degree the *Night of Merit* doth a
   thousand months excel.

ASADÍ ABÚ NASR AHMED (*fl.* 11th cent.), Persian poet. "Asadí's Strife-Poem Between Night and Day," *A Literary History of Persia,* ed. Edward G. Browne, vol. 2 (1928).

The "Night of Merit" is the night when the Qur'an was revealed to Muhammad and is the most sacred night in this very holy month. All prayers are to be answered on this night.

4   It is affirmed [in the 97th chapter of the Qur'an] to be "better than a thousand months"; and the angels are believed to descend, and to be occupied in conveying blessings to the faithful from the commencement of it until daybreak. Moreover, the gates of heaven being then opened, prayer is held to be certain of success. Salt water, it is said, suddenly becomes sweet on this night.

EDWARD WILLIAM LANE (1801–1876), English explorer and Arabic scholar. *An Account of the Manners and Customs of the Modern Egyptians* (1860).

Lane describes the "Leylet-el-Kadr," the "Night of Power," or of the Divine decree. It is the night Muhammad is said to have received the Qur'an, usually the twenty-seventh day of the month of fasting.

5 As Queequeg's Ramadan or Fasting and Humiliation, was to continue all day, I did not choose to disturb him till towards night-fall: for I cherish the greatest respect towards everybody's religious obligations, never mind how comical, and could not find it in my heart to under-value even a congregation of ants worshipping a toad-stool.

HERMAN MELVILLE (1819–1891), U.S. author. *Moby-Dick; or, The Whale* (chapter 17, "The Ramadan") (1851).

Ishmael's condescending attitude toward this holiday is characteristic of many Western writers on the subject of Islamic customs.

6 Like the Italian, the Anglo-Catholic, and the Greek fasts, the chief effect of the "blessed month" upon True Believers is to darken their tempers into positive gloom. . . . The mosques are crowded with a sulky, grumbling population, making themselves offensive to one another on earth whilst working their way to heaven.

RICHARD F. BURTON (1821–1890), English explorer, linguist, and author. *Personal Narrative of a Pilgrimage to al'Madineh and Meccah*, vol. 1 (1893).

7 Ramathán, the fasting month, was nearly in, which kindles in Moslem spirits, even of the wild Arab, a new solemnity of religion; the Beduins, aping the town guise, which they had seen at Medina, now stood out from the byût at the hours, and making ranks, they rehearsed the formal prayer, bowing the empty

foreheads and falling upon the petticoated knees together.

CHARLES M. DOUGHTY (1843–1926), English author. *Travels in Arabia Deserta*, vol. 1 (1923).

The "byût" is the Arab home, in this case the tent of the Nomads with whom Doughty traveled. He writes of the hardships of trying to carry out the strict fasts while navigating through the desert heat and notes that the Qur'an does not require those who are traveling to follow the injunctions of the prophet. While he describes the hardships these people suffer for their faith, this quotation indicates that he is not wholly sympathetic with nor understanding of the complexity of their religious practices.

8 When the new moon has been seen, the news passes like wild fire through the town, and soon it seems as though all the noise suppressed for a whole month has concentrated itself within one night.

C. SNOUCK HURGRONJE (1857–1936), Dutch scholar of Arabic culture. *Mekka in the Later Part of the 19th Century*, trans. J. H. Manahan (1931).

The fast of Ramadan is broken when the new moon is seen.

9 A person walking in the lanes of Mecca on a Ramadan morning hears voices chanting the Koran in nearly every house. Many do their chanting in the cloisters of the Haram. Thus, with sleeping, reading and praying, the Muslims spend the long slow hours until sunset.

E. RUTTER, English travel writer. *The Holy Cities of Arabia*, vol. 2 (1928).

During the month of Ramadan, in which the prophet Muhammad is supposed to have received the Qur'an, many people try to read the scriptures in their entirety in order to bring themselves closer to the religious ideal. The Haram is the large mosque in Mecca.

10 There is clearly an ascetic aspect in the multiple dimensions of the

practice of the Ramadan fast; to savour the poverty of the poor, their
hunger, to fast, to share with them,
to expiate one's own sins, to forgive
others theirs, to renew contact with
one's nearest and dearest, to tame
one's passions, to counter Satan at
every turn.

ABDELHAI DIOURI, anthropologist. "Of
Leaven Foods: Ramadan in Morocco," in *Culinary Cultures of the Middle East*, ed. Sami Zubaida and Richard Tapper (1994).

Mother's Day

1   She openeth her mouth with wisdom, and in her tongue is the law
of kindness.
    She looketh well to the ways of
her household, and eateth not the
bread of idleness.
    Her children rise up, and call
her blessed; her husband also, and
he praiseth her.

Proverbs 31.26–30.

This is the portrait of a virtuous woman taught
to King Lemuel by his mother.

2   My heart had fully transferred to
her person the homage that it gave
to her beauty at first, and whatever
change she underwent, as long as
she always remained herself, my
feelings could not change. . . . I
loved her neither out of duty nor
out of interest nor out of convenience; I loved her because I was
born to love her.

JEAN-JACQUES ROUSSEAU (1712–
1778), French author. *Confessions* (book 4)
(1781); trans. Christopher Kelly (1990).

3   A fond mother, though, in pursuit
of praise for her children the most
rapacious of human beings, is likewise the most credulous; her demands are exorbitant; but she will
swallow anything.

JANE AUSTEN (1775–1817), English novelist. *Sense and Sensibility* (chapter 21) (1811).

Said of Lady Middleton, who cheerfully accepts the false praise of the flattering Miss Steele.

4   All-Gracious! grant, to those that
bear
    A mother's charge, the strength
and light
To lead the steps that own their
care
    In ways of Love, and Truth, and
Right.

WILLIAM CULLEN BRYANT (1794–
1878), U.S. poet and editor. "The Mother's Hymn."

5   Men are what their mothers made
them.

RALPH WALDO EMERSON (1803–
1882), U.S. author. "Fate," *The Conduct of Life* (1860).

6   Youth fades; love droops; the leaves
of friendship fall;
A mother's secret hope outlives
them all.

OLIVER WENDELL HOLMES (1809–
1894), U.S. author and physician. "The Mother's Secret," in *Over the Tea Cups* (1891).

7   The angels, whispering to one
another
Can find, among their burning
terms of love,
        None so devotional as that of
"Mother "

EDGAR ALLAN POE (1809–1849), U.S.
author. "To My Mother."

Poe writes here to Maria Clemm, his mother-in-law, shortly after the death of his wife Virginia. Because Virginia was 14 years younger than Poe and only 13 when he married her, there has been much speculation about the nature of the relationship among the three. Poe frequently addressed Maria as "my own darling mother" or "my dear dear Muddy."

8 Mother is the name for God in the lips and hearts of little children.

WILLIAM MAKEPEACE THACKERAY (1811–1863), English novelist. *Vanity Fair* (chapter 37) (1847).

This quotation ends: "and here was one who was worshipping a stone!" It is in reference to Rebecca Sharp Crawley, the least maternal of women.

9 She loves me when I'm glad er sad;
She loves me when I'm good er
   bad;
An', what's a funniest thing, she
   says
She loves me when she punishes.

JAMES WHITCOMB RILEY (1849–1916), U.S. poet. "A Boy's Mother."

10 It was easy to know them, fluttering about with extended, protecting wings when any harm, real or imaginary, threatened their precious brood. They were women who idolized their children, worshiped their husbands, and esteemed it to be a holy privilege to efface themselves as individuals and grow wings as ministering angels.

KATE O'FLAHERTY CHOPIN (1851–1904), U.S. author. *The Awakening* (chapter 4) (1899).

These are the reflections of Edna Pontellier, a woman in rebellion, contrasting herself with the perfect "mother-women" who surround her in the resort of Grand Island.

11 The souls of little children are marvellously delicate and tender things, and keep for ever the shadow that first falls on them, and that is the mother's or at best a woman's. There was never a great man who had not a great mother—it is hardly an exaggeration.

OLIVE SCHREINER (1855–1920), South African author. *The Story of An African Farm* (part 2, chapter 4) (1883).

12 No ordinary work done by a man is either as hard or as responsible as the work of a woman who is bringing up a family of small children; for upon her time and strength demands are made not only every hour of the day but often every hour of the night.

THEODORE ROOSEVELT (1858–1919), U.S. president. "The American Woman as a Mother," *The Mother's Anthology: In Tribute to Mothers*, ed. William Lyon Phelps (1976).

13 It is the nightly custom of every good mother after her children are asleep to rummage in their minds and put things straight for next morning, repacking into their proper places the many articles that have wandered during the day.

J. M. BARRIE (1860–1937), English author. *Peter Pan* (chapter 1, "Peter Breaks Through") (1911).

14 If I were damned of body and soul, I know whose prayers would make
   me whole,
Mother o' mine, O mother o' mine!

RUDYARD KIPLING (1865–1936), English author. "Mother o' Mine."

15 Washington's Birthday is for the "Father of our Country"; Memorial Day for our "Heroic Fathers"; 4th of July for "Patriot Fathers"; Labor Day for "Laboring Fathers"; Thanksgiving Day for "Pilgrim Father[s]"; and even New Year's Day is for "Old Father Time."

ANNA JARVIS (1864–1948), founder of the Mother's Day movement. Quoted in Leigh Eric Schmidt, *Consumer Rites: The Buying and Selling of American Holidays* (section 1, "Anna Jarvis and the Churches: Sources of a New

Celebration"; chapter 5, "Mother's Day Bouquet") (1995).

Schmidt notes that this examination of the "patriarchy of the American calendar" was one of Anna Jarvis's "favorite devices . . . in defense of Mother's Day." He notes that churches found the celebration of Mother's Day reassuring even as early as the 1910s and 1920s because it affirmed traditional women's roles of "self-sacrificing domesticity and sentimental piety." Jarvis herself would have been excluded from the honors of the day because she "remained unmarried and childless."

16 Mother's Day, it's a beautiful thought, but it's somebody's hurtin' conscience that thought of the idea. It was someone who had neglected their mother for years, and then they figured out: I got to do something about Momma. And knowing Momma was that easy, they figured, "we'll give her a day, and it will be all right with Momma." Give her a day, and then in return Momma gives you the other 364. See?

WILL ROGERS (1879–1935), U.S. humorist. 12 May 1935, *Will Rogers Speaks: Over 1,000 Timeless Quotations for Public Speakers (And Writers, Politicians, Comedians, Browsers . . .)*, ed. Bryan B. Sterling and Frances N. Sterling (1995).

17 Oh, my dark children, may my
   dreams and my prayers
Impel you forever up the great
   stairs—
For I will be with you till no white
   brother
Dares keep down the children of
   the Negro mother.

LANGSTON HUGHES (1902–1967), U.S. poet. "The Negro Mother."

18 From the dawn of civilization mothers, as a class, were held in reasonably high regard until Mother's Day was established, with the purpose of compelling every

man, under pain of social ostracism, to declare that his mother was the greatest woman who ever lived, and to give proof, in consumer goods, of his tremulous adoration of her. In consequence a lot of men,—just to show that their souls are their own and without any ill-will toward the authors of their being—kick and buffet their mothers all over the house on Mother's Day, although during the other 364 days of the year they take them to the movies, buy them bags of nut fudge, and provide them with lacy shawls and crime-story magazines.

ROBERTSON DAVIES (1913–1995), Canadian author. "Of Compulsory Affection," *The Table Talk of Samuel Marchbanks* (1949).

19 It is . . . Mothering Sunday, the florists' commercial delight—a far cry from the ancient practice of visiting a cathedral or the mother church of the diocese.

ALEC GUINESS (b. 1914), English actor. *My Name Escapes Me: The Diary of a Retiring Actor* ("Sunday, 17 March 1996") (1996).

Mothing Sunday is a different date in England, but many people in this country share Guiness's cynicism about the involvement of the florists in engineering this tribute.

20 A person can choose his friends and select a wife, but he has only one mother, I always say. The trouble with many of us is that we don't appreciate our mothers. I think that a certain day should be set aside each year and dedicated to mothers. It could be called "Mother's Day."

MAX SHULMAN (b. 1919), U.S. author. *Barefoot Boy With Cheek* (chapter 1) (1943).

Asa Hearthrug, a bombastic young man preparing to go off to college, celebrates his mother and reveals his ignorance about the yearly commemoration.

21 Certainly the mother serves the interests of patriarchy: she exemplifies in one person religion, social conscience, and nationalism. Institutional motherhood revives and renews all other institutions.

ADRIENNE RICH (b. 1929), U.S. author. *Of Woman Born: Motherhood as Experience and Institution* (chapter 2, "The Sacred Calling") (1976).

Memorial Day

1 Slowly and sadly we laid him down,
   From the field of his fame fresh
      and gory;
   We carved not a line, and we raised
      not a stone,
   But we left him alone with his
      glory.

CHARLES WOLFE (1791–1823), Irish poet and curate. "The Burial of Sir John Moore at Corunna."

Wolfe's poem implies the importance of remembering soldiers who died in the field without a proper memorial.

2 Spirit, that made those heroes dare
   To die, and leave their children
      free,
   Bid Time and Nature gently spare
   The shaft we raise to them and
      thee.

RALPH WALDO EMERSON (1803–1882), U.S. author. "Concord Hymn: Sung at the Completion of the Battle Monument, July 4, 1837."

3 Your silent tents of green
   We deck with fragrant flowers;
   Yours has the suffering been,
   The memory shall be ours.

HENRY WADSWORTH LONGFELLOW (1807–1882), U.S. poet. "Decoration Day."

4 Hushed are their battle-fields,
   ended their marches,
   Deaf are their ears to the drumbeat
      of morn,—
   Rise from the sod, ye fair columns
      and arches!
   Tell their bright deeds to the ages
      unborn!

OLIVER WENDELL HOLMES (1809–1894), U.S. author and physician. "Hymn For the Celebration at the Laying of the Corner-Stone of Harvard Memorial Hall, Cambridge, October 6, 1870."

5 It is rather for us to be here dedicated to the great task remaining before us—that from these honored dead we take increased devotion to that cause for which they gave the last full measure of devotion—that we here highly resolve that these dead shall not have died in vain—that this nation, under God, shall have a new birth of freedom—and that government of the people, by the people, for the people, shall not perish from the earth.

ABRAHAM LINCOLN (1809–1865), U.S. president. Gettysburg Address (19 November 1863).

6 In the beauty of the lilies Christ
   was born across the sea,
   With a glory in His bosom that
      transfigures you and me;
   As he died to make men holy, let us
   die to make men free.

JULIA WARD HOWE (1819–1910), U.S. social reformer and author. "The Battle Hymn of the Republic" (stanza 5) (1861).

7 No more shall the war-cry sever
   Or the winding rivers be red;
   They banish our anger for ever,
   When they laurel the graves of
      our dead!
   Under the sod and the dew

Waiting the judgment day;—
Love and tears for the Blue,
Tears and love for the Gray.

FRANCIS MILES FINCH (1827–1907),
U.S. lawyer and poet. "The Blue and the
Gray."

Some editions of the poem carry this headnote:
"The women of Columbus, Mississippi, had
shown themselves impartial in the offerings
made to the memory of the dead. They
strewed flowers alike on the graves of the Con-
federate and of the National soldiers."

8   A monument for the Soldiers!
        Built of a people's love,
And blazoned and decked and pan-
        oplied
        With the hearts ye build it of!
And see that ye build it stately,
        In pillar and niche and gate,
And high in pose as the souls of
        those
        It would commemorate!

JAMES WHITCOMB RILEY (1849–
1916), U.S. poet. "A Monument for the Soldiers."

9   So, with the singing of paeans and
        chorals,
        And with the flag flashing high
            in the sun,
Place on the graves of our heroes
        the laurels
        Which their unfaltering valor has
            won!

PAUL LAURENCE DUNBAR (1872–
1906), U.S. poet. "Ode for Memorial Day."

10   One sure certainty about our Me-
        morial Days is that as fast as the
        ranks from one war thin out, the
        ranks from another take their place.
        Prominent men may run out of
        Decoration Day speeches, but the
        world never runs out of wars. Peo-
        ple talk peace, but men give up
        their life's work to war.

WILL ROGERS (1879–1935), U.S. humorist. 31 May 1929, *Will Rogers Speaks: Over
1,000 Timeless Quotations for Public Speakers
(And Writers, Politicians, Comedians, Browsers
. . .)*, ed. Bryan B. Sterling and Frances N. Sterling (1995).

11   Now we spread roses
     Over your tomb—
     We who sent you
     To your doom.

LANGSTON HUGHES (1902–1967), U.S.
poet. "Poem to a Dead Soldier."

12   The stone statues of the abstract
        Union Soldier
        grow slimmer and younger each
            year—.

ROBERT LOWELL (1917–1977), U.S.
poet. "For the Union Dead."

13   I am so sorry about all them lying
     dead on the hill, the trooper from
     the First Minnesota and all the old
     women and the farmers . . . and I
     wish my speech had been great, just
     as I wish I could bring them all
     back to life, but it's over and now
     summer can begin. School can let
     out. Baseball gets going and the
     sweet corn begins to get serious.

GARRISON KEILLOR (b. 1942), U.S. au-
thor and radio personality. "How I Came to
Give the Memorial Day Address at the Lake
Wobegon Cemetery This Year," *We Are Still
Married* (1989).

Father's Day

1   A wise son maketh a glad father;
     but a foolish son is the heaviness of
     his mother.

Proverbs 10.1.

2   The glory of a man is from the
        honour of his father.

Ecclesiasticus 1.7.

3 The father's obligations to his son are: he must circumcise him, redeem him, teach him Torah, teach him a trade, and help him secure a wife.—some also say, teach him to swim.

Tosefta Kiddushin 1.11, in *The Talmudic Anthology: Tales and Teachings of the Rabbis*, ed. Louis I. Newman (1947).

4   Why, 'tis a happy thing
To be the father unto many sons.

WILLIAM SHAKESPEARE (1564–1616), English poet and dramatist. *Henry VI, Part III* 3.2.104–105.

Spoken by King Edward.

5 It is a wise father that knows his own child.

WILLIAM SHAKESPEARE (1564–1616), English poet and dramatist. *The Merchant of Venice* 2.2.70.

6 Fathers that wear rags
    Do make their children blind,
But fathers that bear bags
    Shall see their children kind.

WILLIAM SHAKESPEARE (1564–1616), English poet and dramatist. *King Lear* 2.4.47–50.

Spoken by the Fool, these lines expose the truth of Lear's mistreatment by his daughters, who ignore his needs now that they possess his wealth.

7 Greatness of name in the father ofttimes helps not forth but overwhelms the son; they stand too near one another, the shadow kills the growth. So much, that we see the grandchild come more and oftener to be heir.

BEN JONSON (1573–1637), English poet and dramatist. *Timber; or, Discoveries Made upon Men and Matter* (1641).

8 One father is enough to governe one hundred sons, but not a hundred sons one father.

GEORGE HERBERT (1593–1633), English poet and Anglican priest. *Outlandish Proverbs*, no. 404 (1640).

9 One father is more than a hundred Schoolemasters.

GEORGE HERBERT (1593–1633), English poet and Anglican priest. *Outlandish Proverbs*, no. 686 (1640).

10 It is impossible to please all the world and one's father.

JEAN DE LA FONTAINE (1621–1695), French author. *Fables* (book 3, Fable 1) (1668).

11 As for myself, I know what trouble I've given you at various times through my peculiarities, and as my own boys grow up, I shall learn more and more of the kind of trial you had to overcome in superintending the development of a creature different from yourself, for whom you felt responsible.

WILLIAM JAMES (1842–1910), U.S. philosopher and psychologist. Letter to his father, 14 December 1882, in *Letters of a Nation: A Collection of Extraordinary American Letters*, ed. Andrew Carroll (1997).

Henry James Sr. died before he received his son's farewell letter. It was read at the funeral by Henry James Jr.

12 Only a dad but he gives his all
To smooth the way for his children small,
Doing with courage stern and grim,
The deeds that his father did for him,
This is the line that for him I pen,
Only a dad, *but the best of men.*

EDGAR A. GUEST (1881–1959), U.S. author. "Only a Dad."

13 A Father's Day would call attention to such constructive teachings from the pulpit as would naturally point out: The father's place in the home. The training of children. The safeguarding of the marriage tie. The protection of womanhood and childhood. The meaning of this, whether in the light of religion or of patriotism is so apparent as to need no argument in behalf of such a day.

MRS. J. B. DODD. In *Father: An Anthology of Verse*, ed. Margery Doud and Cleo M. Parsley (1931).

Mrs. Dodd, of Spokane, Wash., wanted to create a tribute for her father, William J. Smart, who had reared his children without the help of a mother. In 1910, Mrs. Dodd asked for and got the support of the Spokane Ministerial Association to publish this statement. Local YMCAs and newspapers also supported the idea, and before long the holiday was celebrated nationwide.

14 For the great heart of him hurries
    At the call of help from you.
He will help us mend the broken
    Heart of ours or hope or toy,
And the tale may bide unspoken—
    For he used to be a boy.

JAMES W. FOLEY. "Daddy Knows" (1913), in *Father: An Anthology of Verse*, ed. Margery Doud and Cleo M. Parsley (1931).

15 Father's Day was comical in part because fathers seemed so out of place or uncomfortable in this holiday world of sentimental gifts and domestic flattery. The "little remembrances" of flowers, cards, and novelties became funny when showered on Father; they opened up a line of humor that played on the gendered incongruities of holiday gift giving. As one editorial writer on the holiday put the matter in 1925, fathers have "no talent for the fribbles and frabbles and furbelows with which Mother signalizes well-being."

LEIGH ERIC SCHMIDT (b. 1961), U.S. historian. *Consumer Rites: The Buying and Selling of American Holidays* (section 4, "The Invention of Father's Day: The Humbug of Modern Ritual"; chapter 5, "Mother's Day Bouquet") (1995).

Schmidt notes that the founder of Mother's Day, Anna Jarvis, saw Father's Day as a "poorly disguised plot of 'some necktie, tobacco, whiskey and lottery promoters.'" Schmidt further comments: "The snide perception that the holiday was an inane hoax and that merchants were responsible for putting it over on people found ample expression. Father's Day, more than any other celebration up to that time, demonstrated the corrosive cynicism that had come to hedge in modern rituals in a world of advertising and promotion."

16 What Mother's Day did for the florist industry, Father's Day did for the necktie industry. Along with tobacco, shirts, and other typically masculine gifts, neckties appeared on the earliest Father's Day greeting cards, and retailers wasted no time in turning the holiday to their advantage.

Holiday Symbols, ed. Sue Ellen Thompson (1998).

Independence Day

1 The new Governments we are assuming in every Part will require a Purification from our Vices, and an Augmentation of our Virtues, or they will have no Blessings. The people will have unbounded Power. And the people are extremely addicted to Corruption and Venality, as well as the Great.

JOHN ADAMS (1735–1826), U.S. president. Letter to his wife Abigail Adams, 3 July 1776, in *Letters of a Nation: A Collection of Extraordinary American Letters*, ed. Andrew Carroll (1997).

2   The Fourth of July has been celebrated in Philadelphia in the manner I expected. The military men,
and particularly one of them, ran
away with all the glory of the day.
Scarcely a word was said of the so-
licitude and labors and fears and
sorrows and sleepless nights of the
men who projected, proposed, defended and subscribed the Declaration of Independence.

BENJAMIN RUSH (1746–1813), U.S.
statesman, delegate to the Continental Congress, and signer of the Declaration of Independence. Letter to John Adams, 20 July 1811,
in *Letters of a Nation: A Collection of Extraordinary American Letters*, ed. Andrew Carroll
(1997.)

The "particular" military man Rush refers to is
George Washington, considered by Rush to be
a kind of tyrant over the American people.

3   Dating, as we justly may, a new era
in the history of man from the
Fourth of July, 1776, it would be
well—that is it would be useful—if
on each anniversary we examined
the progress made by our species in
just knowledge and just practice.
Each Fourth of July would then
stand as a tidemark in the flood of
time by which to ascertain the advance of the human intellect, by
which to note the rise and fall of
each successive error, the discovery
of each important truth, the gradual melioration in our public institutions, social arrangements, and,
above all, in our moral feelings and
mental views.

FRANCES (FANNY) WRIGHT (1795–
1852), U.S. (Scottish-born) reformer. Speech,
New Harmony, Ind., 4 July 1828, in *Lend Me
Your Ears: Great Speeches in History*, ed. William Safire (1992).

4   Yet America is a poem in our eyes;
its ample geography dazzles the

imagination, and it will not wait
long for metres.

RALPH WALDO EMERSON (1803–
1882), U.S. author. "The Poet," *Essays, Second Series* (1844).

5   We grant no dukedoms to the few,
    We hold like rights and shall;—
Equal on Sunday in the pew,
    On Monday in the mall.
        For what avail the plough or
            sail,
        Or land or life, if freedom fail?

The noble craftsman we promote,
    Disown the knave and fool
Each honest man shall have his
    vote,
        Each child shall have his
            school.
        A union then of honest men,
        Or union nevermore again.

RALPH WALDO EMERSON (1803–
1882), U.S. author. "Boston, *sicut patribus, sit
Deus nobis. Read in Faneuil Hall, on December 16, 1873, on the Centennial Anniversary of
the Destruction of the Tea in Boston Harbor.*"

While Emerson was not delivering an Independence Day speech and was speaking specifically of Boston, his sentiments express the
ideal vision of American life.

6   We give thy natal day to hope,
    O Country of our love and
        prayer!
Thy way is down no fatal slope,
    But up to freer sun and air.

    · · · · · · · · · · · · · · · ·

A refuge for the wronged and poor,
    Thy generous heart has borne
        the blame
That, with them, through thy open
    door,
        The old world's evil outcasts
            came.

JOHN GREENLEAF WHITTIER (1807–
1892), U.S. poet. "Our Country (Read at
Woodstock, Conn., July 4, 1883)."

7   I know that upon 4th of July, our
    4th of July orators talk of Liberty,
    while three million of their own
    country men are groaning in abject
    Slavery. This is called "the land of
    the free and the home of the
    brave"; it is called the "asylum of
    the oppressed"; and some have
    been foolish enough to call it the
    "Cradle of Liberty." If it is the "cra-
    dle of liberty," they have rocked the
    child to death. It is dead long since,
    and yet we talk about democracy
    and republicanism, while one-sixth
    of our countrymen are clanking
    their chains upon the very soil
    which our fathers moistened with
    their blood.

    WILLIAM WELLS BROWN (1815?–
    1884), U.S. abolitionist. "A Lecture Delivered
    Before the Female Antislavery Society Of Sa-
    lem, Massachusetts, [14 November] 1847," in
    *The Narrative of William Wells Brown, a Fugi-
    tive Slave* (1969).

8   The rich inheritance of justice, lib-
    erty, prosperity and independence,
    bequeathed by your fathers, is
    shared by you, not by me. The sun-
    light that brought light and healing
    to you, has brought stripes and
    death to me. This Fourth of July is
    yours, not *mine*. *You* may rejoice, *I*
    must mourn.

    FREDERICK DOUGLASS (c.1817–1895),
    U.S. abolitionist. "The Meaning of July Fourth
    for the Negro," 5 July 1852, in *The Life and
    Writings of Frederick Douglass*, ed. Philip S.
    Foner, vol. 2 (1950–75).

9   It is the fourth of Seventh-month,
    (what salutes of cannon and
    small-arms!)

    WALT WHITMAN (1819–1892), U.S.
    poet. *Song of Myself*, section 15.

10 The President, throned behind a ca-
    ble locker with a national flag

spread over it, announced the
"Reader," who rose up and read
that same old Declaration of Independence which we have all listened
to so often without paying any attention to what it said; and after
that the President piped the Orator
of the Day to quarters and he made
the same old speech about our national greatness which we so religiously believe and so fervently ap-
plaud. Now came the choir into
court again, with the complaining
instruments, and assaulted "Hail
Columbia"; and when victory hung
wavering in the scale, George returned with his dreadful wild-goose
stop turned on and the choir won,
of course. A minister pronounced
the benediction, and the patriotic
little gathering disbanded. The
Fourth of July was safe, as far as the
Mediterranean was concerned.

MARK TWAIN (SAMUEL CLEMENS)
(1835–1910), U.S. author. *The Innocents
Abroad* (chapter 10) (1869).

The narrator here describes a group of American tourists creating a taste of home in the
midst of foreign surroundings.

11 *July 4.* Statistics show that we lose
    more fools on this day than in all
    the other days of the year put to-
    gether. This proves, by the number
    left in stock, that one Fourth of July
    per year is now inadequate, the
    country has grown so.

    MARK TWAIN (SAMUEL CLEMENS)
    (1835–1910), U.S. author. *Pudd'head Wilson*
    ("Pudd'nhead Wilson's Calendar" at chapter
    17) (1894).

12 We [Americans] are the lavishest
    and showiest and most luxury-lov-
    ing people on the earth; and at our
    masthead we fly one true and hon-

est symbol, the gaudiest flag the world has ever seen.

MARK TWAIN (SAMUEL CLEMENS) (1835–1910), U.S. author. "Diplomatic Pay and Clothes" (1899).

13 The business of the Fourth of July is not perfect as it stands. See what it costs us every year with loss of life, the crippling of thousands with its fireworks and the burning down of property. It is not only sacred to patriotism and universal freedom but to the surgeon, the undertaker, the insurance offices—and they are working it for all it is worth.

MARK TWAIN (SAMUEL CLEMENS) (1835–1910), U.S. author. Speech, London, at a dinner of the American Society, 4 July 1899, in *Lend Me Your Ears: Great Speeches in History*, ed. William Safire (1992).

14 Sing in the tones of prayer,
    Sing till the soaring soul
    Shall float above the world's con-
        trol
In Freedom everywhere!
Sing for the good that is to be,
Sing for the eyes that are to see
The land where man at last is free,
    O sing for Liberty!

JAMES WHITCOMB RILEY (1849–1916), U.S. poet. "Liberty: New Castle, July 4, 1878."

15 There'll be ice-cream and fireworks
    and a speech
By Somebody the Honorable Who,
The lovers will pair off in the kind
    dark
And Tessie Jones, our honor-gradu-
    ate,
Will read the Declaration.
That's how it is. It's always been
    that way.
That's our Fourth of July, through
    war and peace,
That's our Fourth of July.

STEPHEN VINCENT BENÉT (1898–1943), U.S. author. "Listen to the People: Independence Day, 1941."

16 That rugged individualism that is the personification of our American sense of freedom, and which we celebrate on the Fourth of July and in our popular myths and heroes, also contributes to the breakdown of the social fabric that has always provided a secure context for our freedoms. Freedom "from" has not yet yielded to an appropriate freedom "for."

PETER J. GOMES (b. 1942), U.S. clergyman and theologian. *The Good Book: Reading the Bible with Heart and Mind* (chapter 3, "The Bible in America") (1994).

Labor Day

1 Who first invented work, and
    bound the free
And holyday-rejoicing spirit down
To the ever-haunting importunity
Of business in the green fields, and
    the town—
To plough, loom, anvil, spade—and
    oh! most sad,
To that dry drudgery at the desk's
    dead wood?

CHARLES LAMB (1775–1834), English essayist. "Work" (1819).

Lamb did not have the opportunity to celebrate Labor Day, but he expresses the weariness of many different types of workers. This poem originally appeared in the *Examiner* on 29 August 1819.

2 Toiling,—rejoicing,—sorrowing,
    Onward through life he goes;
Each morning sees some task begin,
    Each evening sees it close;
Something attempted, something
    done,
    Has earned a night's repose.

HENRY WADSWORTH LONGFELLOW (1807–1882), U.S. poet. "The Village Blacksmith."

3 In spite of oppressors, in spite of false leaders, in spite of labor's own lack of understanding of its needs, the cause of the worker continues onward. Slowly his hours are shortened, giving him leisure to read and to think. Slowly his standard of living rises to include some of the good and beautiful things of the world. Slowly the cause of his children becomes the cause of all. His boy is taken from the breaker, his girl from the mill. Slowly those who create the wealth of the world are permitted to share it. The future is in labor's strong, rough hands.

MOTHER JONES (MARY HARRIS) (1830–1930), U.S. labor organizer. *The Autobiography* (concluding passage) (1925).

4 Eight hours for work, eight hours for rest,
Eight hours for what we will.

I. G. BLANCHARD (b. 1835), U.S. author. "Eight Hours" (c. 1868).

These lyrics appear in *The Fireside Book of Favorite American Songs* (1952), edited by Margaret Bradford Boni. She notes: "The campaign for an eight-hour work day, begun in earnest after the Civil War, resulted in the passage of an eight-hour law by Congress on June 25, 1868. It proved ineffectual. Blanchard's song, written during the original campaign, was revived in the 80's, when labor worked for a more effective law. It became the official song of the movement." The music for the song was composed by Rev. Jesse H. Jones.

5 Two important features of Labor Day are, first, that the various unions shall lay aside any differences that they may have; and second, that employers are asked to meet with the workers to discuss matters relating to the welfare of the laboring classes.

J. WALKER MCSPADDEN (1874–1960), author and editor. *The Book of Holidays* (1917).

McSpadden carefully traces the work of labor unions in creating this holiday.

6 Master, I've filled my contract, wrought in Thy many lands;
Not by my sins wilt Thou judge me, but by the work of my hands.
Master, I've done Thy bidding, and the light is low in the west,
And the long, long shift is over . . .
Master, I've earned it—
Rest.

ROBERT W. SERVICE (1874–1958), Canadian poet. "The Song of the Wage-Slave."

7 You load 16 tons and what do you get?
Another day older and deeper in debt.
. . . .
St. Peter, don't you call me 'cause I can't go
I owe my soul to the company store.

MERLE TRAVIS (1917–1983), U.S. singer and songwriter. "Sixteen Tons," *Rise Up Singing: The Group-Singing Song Book*, ed. Peter Blood Patterson (1988).

8 Workin' nine to five
what a way to make a livin',
barely gettin' by
It's all takin' and no givin'

DOLLY PARTON (b. 1946), U.S. singer and songwriter. "9 to 5," in Peter Seeger and Bob Reiser, *Carry It On: A History in Song and Picture of the Working Men and Women of America* (1985).

9 Americans were supposed to pause yesterday to praise working men and women and contemplate the

role of labor unions in the nation's history. . . . But just as Memorial Day has largely become a time to gather 'round the barbecue and welcome the beginning of summer, so Labor Day has largely become a day to give the season a good send-off.

SAM HOWE VERHOVEK, journalist. "Holiday for the Workers?" in the *New York Times* (6 September 1988).

10 Frankly, I don't believe people think of their office as a workplace anyway. I think they think of it as a stationery store with Danish. You want to get your pastry, your envelopes, your supplies, your toilet paper, six cups of coffee, and you go home.

JERRY SEINFELD (b. 1954), U.S. comic. *SeinLanguage* (1993).

Rosh Hashanah

1 And the Lord spoke unto Moses, saying, Speak unto the children of Israel, saying, In the seventh month, in the first day of the month, shall ye have a sabbath, a memorial of blowing of trumpets, an holy convocation. Ye shall do no servile work therein: but ye shall offer an offering made by fire unto the Lord.

Leviticus 23.23–25.

2 Sing aloud unto God, our strength; make a joyful noise unto the God of Jacob. Take a psalm, and bring hither the timbrel, the pleasant harp with the psaltery. Blow up the trumpet in the new moon, in the time appointed, on our solemn feast day. For this was a statute for Israel, and a law of the God of Jacob.

Psalm 81.1–4.

3 R. Judah says: "Man is judged on New Year and his doom is sealed on the Day of Atonement."

Tractate Rosh Hashanah 16a (Talmud), in *The Rosh Hashanah Anthology*, ed. Philip Goodman (1973).

4 All good things come to Israel through the Shofar. They received the Torah with the sound of the Shofar. They conquered in battle through the blast of the Shofar. They are summoned to repent by the Shofar, and they will be made aware of the Redeemer's advent through the Great Shofar.

Elihahu Zuta 22, in *The Talmudic Anthology: Tales and Teachings of the Rabbis*, ed. Louis I. Newman (1947).

5 On New Year Sarah, Rachel and Hannah were remembered on high [and they conceived]; on New Year Joseph went forth from prison; on New Year the bondage of our ancestors in Egypt ceased.

Tractate Rosh Hashanah 10b-11a (Talmud), in *The Rosh Hashanah Anthology*, ed. Philip Goodman (1973).

6 Rabbi Johanan said: "The fate of men of perfection is sealed on Rosh ha-Shanah; they are either to be aided in accumulating more Mitzwot; or they are to enjoy Paradise.

"The fate of men of complete wickedness is also sealed on Rosh ha-Shanah; they are either to receive opportunity to add to their wickedness, or they are to depart for Purgatory.

"The fate of the rank and file of men is left open, however, until Yom Kippur. If they repent they receive another chance to do good."

Rosh ha-Shanah 16b (amplified), in *The Talmudic Anthology: Tales and Teachings of the Rabbis*, ed. Louis I. Newman (1947).

7 It has been said that omens are of significance; therefore, a man should make a regular habit of eating, at the beginning of the year, pumpkin, fenugreek, leek, beet, and dates [as these grow in profusion and are symbolic of prosperity].

Horayot 12a, in *The Rosh Hashanah Anthology*, ed. Philip Goodman (1973).

8 Three books are opened [in heaven] on New Year, one for the thoroughly righteous, and one for the intermediate. The thoroughly righteous are forthwith inscribed definitively in the book of life; the thoroughly wicked are forthwith inscribed definitively in the book of death; the doom of the intermediate is suspended from New Year till the Day of Atonement; if they deserve well, they are inscribed in the book of life; if they do not deserve well, they are inscribed in the book of death.

Tractate Rosh Hashanah 16b (Talmud), in *The Rosh Hashanah Anthology*, ed. Philip Goodman (1973).

9 "May you be inscribed and sealed for a good year" or "May your name be inscribed in the book of life."

Traditional Rosh Hashanah greeting, first mentioned in the work of Rabbi Jacob Milin, also known as Maharil (1360–1427), in *The Rosh Hashanah Anthology*, ed. Philip Goodman (1973).

10 Some of the townspeople stood on the wooden bridge reciting the *Tashlikh*; others lined the river's banks. Young women took out their hankerchiefs [sic] and shook out their sins. Boys playfully emptied their pockets to be sure that no transgression remained. The village wits made the traditional *Tashlikh* jokes. "Girls, shake as hard as you want, but a few sins will remain." "The fish will get fat feeding on so many errors."

ISAAC BASHEVIS SINGER (1904–1992), U.S. (Polish-born) author. "Tashlikh" (1962), trans. Singer and Cecil Hemley, in *The Rosh Hashanah Anthology*, ed. Philip Goodman (1973).

Singer describes a scene from his Polish boyhood and the custom of *Tashlikh*. Following the afternoon Rosh Hashanah services, sins are symbolically cast into running water and witnessed by fish, whose eyes, like God's, are always open.

11 The blowing of the shofar, the ram's horn, is an alarm, as it was for the tribes of Israel in the desert when the enemy approached, and for the armies of David and Solomon in the Holy Land; an alarm waking the soul to Judgment. The enigmatic words, "a day of remembrance," with which the Torah describes the first of Tishri, become clear; God reviews the deeds of the year, and men recall with dread that all acts come at last to an accounting.

HERMAN WOUK (b. 1915), U.S. author. *This is My God: The Jewish Way of Life* (chapter 6, "The High Holy Days") (1988).

12 On the eve of Rosh Hashanah, the last day of that accursed year, the whole camp [Buna] was electric with the tension which was in all our hearts. In spite of everything,

this day was different from any other. The last day of the year. The word "last" rang very strangely. What if it were indeed the last day? . . .

Once, New Year's Day had dominated my life. I knew that my sins grieved the Eternal; I implored his forgiveness. Once, I had believed profoundly that upon one solitary deed of mine, one solitary prayer, depended the salvation of the world.

This day I had ceased to plead. I was no longer capable of lamentation. On the contrary, I felt very strong. I was the accuser, God the accused. My eyes were open and I was alone—terribly alone in a world without God and without man.

ELIE WIESEL (b. 1928), U.S. (Romanian-born) author and Holocaust survivor. *Night* (fifth section), trans. (from French) Stella Rodway (1960).

13   Every *Rosh Hashannah*, the Jewish New Year, Jews say a prayer that I have been saying to myself more and more as I grow older. . . . "Blessed art thou O Lord our God, King of the universe," the prayer begins, "who has given us life and kept us safe and allowed us to reach this season." It is the right prayer for a new century, a blessing for a new "season."

ELI N. EVANS, U.S. historian and foundation president. *The Provincials* (chapter 26, "Looking Ahead") (1997).

Evans is president of the Charles H. Revson Foundation.

14   The High Holy Days of my childhood . . . embodied the very essence of new beginnings; for autumn, not spring, was when everything was new: my clothes, my classroom, books, pencil box, teachers—and Jewish chronology, which decreed a fresh start, a clean slate, a chance to improve on the past.

LETTY COTTIN POGREBIN (b. 1939), U.S. author. "The High Holy Days," chapter 5 in *Deborah, Golda, and Me: Being Female and Jewish in America* (1991).

15   These year's-end holidays have in them the quality of transition that we find in other festivals of the new year, no matter when they are celebrated. Yom Kippur marks the end of the solemn days and the beginning of the regular days of the new year. The Ten Days, during which the gates of heaven are open, are a time out of time, a period of liminality during which people can shape their destinies, retract vows and right wrongs. In short one can make oneself over for the new year, in a way that recalls, however dimly, the custom of New Year's resolutions.

JACK SANTINO (b. 1947), U.S. folklorist and sociologist. *All Around the Year: Holidays and Celebrations in American Life* (chapter 5, "Autumn into Winter: Celebrating Death and Life") (1994).

16   The Jewish New Year, . . . like all New Year celebrations, projects and tries to satisfy the human need for periodic regeneration. That's why the New Year is followed by a day of atonement, Yom Kippur, a day on which we purify ourselves of sin, cast out the accumulated imperfections of the past so as morally to make ourselves as new, as pure, as the coming year itself.

ALAN SHAPIRO (b. 1952), U.S. poet. *The Last Happy Occasion* ("In Awkward Reverence") (1996).

Yom Kippur

1 And thou shalt number seven sabbaths of years unto thee, seven times seven years; and the space of the seven sabbaths of years shall be unto thee forty and nine years. Then shalt thou cause the trumpet of the jubilee to sound on the tenth day of the seventh month, in the day of atonement shall ye make the trumpet sound throughout all your land.

Leviticus 25.8–9.

2 And ye shall have on the tenth day of this seventh month an holy convocation, and ye shall afflict your souls; ye shall not do any work therein; But ye shall offer a burnt offering unto the Lord for a sweet savor: one young bullock, one ram, and seven lambs of the first year; they shall be unto you without blemish.

Numbers 29.7–8.

3 On the Day of Atonement, eating, drinking, washing, anointing, putting on sandals, and marital intercourse are forbidden. A king or a bride may wash their faces and a woman after childbirth may put on sandals.

Tractate Yoma 8.1 (Mishnah), trans. Herbert Danby, in *The Yom Kippur Anthology*, ed. Philip Goodman (1971).

4 Just as if a nut falls into some dirt you can take it up and wipe it and rinse it and wash it and it is restored to its former condition and is fit for eating, so however much Israel may be defiled with iniquities all the rest of the year, when the Day of Atonement comes it makes atonement for them, as it is written, *For on this day shall atonement be made for you, to cleanse you* (Leviticus 16.30).

Song of Songs Rabbah 6.11, in *The Yom Kippur Anthology*, ed. Philip Goodman (1971).

5 Things between thee and God are forgiven in Yom Kippur. Things between thee and thy fellowman are not forgiven thee, until he has forgiven thee.

Sifra to Ahare, in *The Talmudic Anthology: Tales and Teachings of the Rabbis*, ed. Louis I. Newman (1947).

6 Next year in Jerusalem!

Traditional answer given by the congregation at the blowing of the shofar, which ends the Yom Kippur liturgy at sunset.

7 And may atonement be granted to the whole congregation of Israel and to the stranger who lives among them, for all have transgressed unwittingly.

The High Holyday Prayer Book: Rosh Hashanah and Yom Kippur, trans. and ed. Ben Zion Bokser (1959).

From the Kol Nidre, a prayer chanted three times as a prelude to Yom Kippur services.

8 O my God, before I was created I was nothing, and now that I have been created, what am I? In life I am dust, and more so when I fall prey to death. When I measure my life in Thy presence, I am confused and I am ashamed. Help me, O God and God of my fathers, to steer clear of sin. And as for my past sins, purge me of them in Thy great mercy, but, I pray, not through severe and painful disease.

The High Holyday Prayer Book: Rosh Hashanah and Yom Kippur, trans. and ed. Ben Zion Bokser (1959).

Part of confession recited ten times in the course of the Yom Kippur liturgy.

9 Accept Thou with favor my prayer for forgiveness, my confession which I make before Thee. May the words of my mouth and the meditation of my heart be acceptable before Thee, my Rock and my Redeemer. Amen.

The Union Prayerbook for Jewish Worship (1962).

Concluding sentences of a Reform prayer for Yom Kippur.

10 It was meet and right when everything has shown abundance as they would have it, and they enjoy a full and perfect measure of goodness, that amid this prosperity and lavish supply of boons, they should by abstaining from food and drink remind themselves of what it is to want, and offer prayers and supplications, on the one hand to ask that they may never really experience the lack of necessities, on the other to express their thankfulness because in such wealth of blessings they remember the ills they have been spared.

PHILO OF ALEXANDRIA (C. 20 B.C.– A.D. 45), Jewish philosopher. *The Special Laws* 2.20, in *Philo* (Loeb Classical Library), vol. 7, trans. F. H. Colson (1937).

11 It is the day on which the master of the prophets descended [from Mt. Sinai] with the second set of tablets of the Law and communicated to the people forgiveness for their great sin. This day became forever a day of repentance and true worship. On it are forbidden all corporeal pleasure; every burden and care of the body; that is to say, work is not done. Only confessions are permitted so that one will confess his sins and repent of them.

MAIMONIDES (MOSES BEN MAIMON) (1135–1204), Jewish (Spanish-born) philosopher, rabbi, jurist, and physician. *Guide for the Perplexed* 3.43.

12 I . . . do not know what to do, and how much to do, and how to achieve the purpose of the holy men who first uttered these prayers. That is why I take the book of our blessed Master Luria and keep it open before me while I pray, that I may offer it to God with all its fervor, ecstasy, and secret meaning.

MARTIN BUBER (1878–1965), Austrian philosopher. "The Prayer Book," a short story trans. Simon Chasen, in *The Yom Kippur Anthology*, ed. Philip Goodman (1971).

A rabbi explains why, though he doesn't look at the words, he keeps a prayer book open during the Day of Atonement.

13 With all its pleasures, Passover was only nice. Yom Kippur was weird, monumental. Imagine not eating for a whole day to prove something or other to God, or yelling at God in the synagogue as the bearded old men did in their white shawls, their heads thrown back, their Adam's apples tearing at their skinny throats.

KATE SIMON (1912–1990), U.S. travel writer. "Battles and Celebrations," in *Bronx Primitive* (1982).

14 Since the fall of Jerusalem any gaiety that was in Yom Kippur has faded. Our Atonement Day is a time of mordant grieving melodies, of bowed heads and wrung hearts. No one who has heard the *Kol Nidre* chanted at sunset when the holy

day begins can doubt that the worshippers are carrying out literally a law many thousands of years old, and afflicting their souls.

HERMAN WOUK (b. 1915), U.S. author. *This Is My God: The Jewish Way of Life* (chapter 6, "The High Holy Days") (1988).

15 Yom Kippur. The Day of Atonement.

Should we fast? The question was hotly debated. To fast would mean a surer, swifter death. We fasted here the whole year round. The whole year was Yom Kippur. But others said that we should fast simply because it was dangerous to do so. We should show God that even here, in this enclosed hell, we were capable of singing His praises.

ELIE WIESEL (b. 1928), U.S. (Romanianborn) author and Holocaust survivor. *Night* (fifth section), trans. Stella Rodway (1960).

Wiesel describes how existence in a Nazi prison camp challenged his understanding of Jewish religious practices.

16 In moments of weakness
We do not remember
Promises of Atonement Day.
Look past forgetfulness,
Take only from our hearts;
Forgive us, pardon us.

ZEEV FALK, "Kol Nidre," trans. Stanley Schachter, in *The Yom Kippur Anthology*, ed. Philip Goodman (1971).

17 The New Year is a great door
that stands across the evening and
Yom
Kippur is the second door. Between
them
are song and silence, stone and clay
pot
to be filled from within by myself.

MARGE PIERCY (b. 1936), U.S. poet. "Coming Up on September," *The Art of Blessing the Day: Poems with a Jewish Theme* (1999).

18 Flawed humans though we are, come Yom Kippur we have a moment to turn God's mirror on ourselves, if there is a God. Or it is a moment to think about something larger than everyday life, to contemplate obligations to other people, to regret our failures, to renounce our shallowness. . . . Within all the nattering activity, this day is a silent space.

ELIZABETH EHRLICH, U.S. author. *Miriam's Kitchen: A Memoir* ("September: Longing") (1997).

Halloween

1 From Ghoulies and ghosties and
. long-leggety beasties
And things that go bump in the
night,
    Good Lord, deliver us.

Cornish prayer.

2 Now it is the time of night
That the graves, all gaping wide,
Every one lets forth his sprite,
In the church-way paths to glide.

WILLIAM SHAKESPEARE (1564–1616), English poet and dramatist. *A Midsummer Night's Dream* 5.1.379–82.

Puck is not specifically referring to Halloween, but the sentiment conjures up the imagery of the holiday.

3   The Hag is astride,
        This night for to ride;
The Devill and shee together:
        Through thick, and through
        thin,
        Now out, and then in,

Though ne'r so foule be the
weather.

ROBERT HERRICK (1591–1674), English
poet and clergyman. "The Hag."

4   I believe that men are generally still
a little afraid of the dark, though
the witches are all hung, and Christianity and candles have been introduced.

HENRY DAVID THOREAU (1817–
1862), U.S. author. *Walden* ("Solitude"), vol. 2
(1854).

5   There was . . . a serious and weird
feeling, on Hallow E'en night, not
felt so much on any other night;
witches and evil spirits were believed to be more numerous than
usual; fairies were believed to be
unusually active; ghosts were supposed to make their appearance on
this night; and a full-dress performance of the watch in the church-
porch on that night was capable of
teaching the watchers that the Angel of Death is sometimes nearer
than they imagine.

A. R. WRIGHT (1862–1932), *British Calendar Customs, England*, vol. 3 (1940).

6   Midnight has come, and the great
Christ Church Bell
And many a lesser bell sound
through the room;
And it is All Souls' Night,
And two long glasses brimmed with
muscatel
Bubble upon the table. A ghost may
come;
For it is a ghost's right,
His element is so fine
Being sharpened by his death,
To drink from the wine-breath
While our gross palates drink from
the whole wine.

WILLIAM BUTLER YEATS (1865–1939),
Irish poet. "All Souls' Night: Epilogue to 'A Vision.'"

7   The evening of October thirty-one
is Hallowe'en or Nut Crack Night.
It is clearly a relic of pagan times
but it is still very popular. It is a
night set apart for walking about
and playing harmless pranks, such
as placing the hotel omnibus on
top of the Baptist church or plug-
ging the milkman's pump.

KIN HUBBARD (1868–1930), U.S. humorist. *The Best of Kin Hubbard: Abe Martin's
Sayings and Wisecracks, Abe's Neighbors, His
Almanack, Comic Drawings,* David S. Hawes
(1984).

8   At the very glimpse of a Jack-o'-
lantern
I've got one foot on the bus to
Scranton.
When Halloween next delivers the
goods,
You may duck for apples—I'll duck
for the woods.

OGDEN NASH (1902–1971), U.S. poet.
"Trick or Trek."

9   This Hallowe'en you come one
week.
You masquerade
as a vermilion, sleek,
fat, crosseyed fox in the parade
or, where grim jackolanterns leer,

go with your bag from door to
door
foraging for treats.

W. D. SNODGRASS (b. 1926), U.S. poet.
Heart's Needle (section 8) (1959).

10 It was Halloween that did me in,
that single day when your children
turn to you for imagination and

creativity, the one day of the year when you must transcend fantasy.

ERMA BOMBECK (1927–1996), U.S. humorist and newspaper columnist. "Halloween Challenges 'No Talent' Mother" (30 October 1979), in *Forever, Erma: Best Loved Writing from America's Favorite Humorist* (1996).

Bombeck comments on the "shame" of being a mother who sends her children out with costumes that consist of grocery bags over their heads, while every other mother in the neighborhood dresses her children in elaborate costumes "right out of the wax museum."

11 I'm always in town for Halloween. Even if I didn't happen to enjoy walking in the Village Halloween parade in my ax murderer's mask, I would feel it my duty to be there because of the long-established role of a father in passing on important cultural traditions to the next generation.

CALVIN TRILLIN (b. 1935), U.S. author. *Third Helpings* ("Spaghetti Carbonara Day") (1983).

12 Halloween was a time of candy corn, jack-o'-lanterns, candy kisses, peanut-butter cups, bubble gum, Fig Newtons, soapy windows. I tried to tell about Halloween and what it represented to me—a great ritual of childhood when the world for a single night opened its doors and its coffers of candy and fun and happiness.

PAT CONROY (b. 1945), U.S. author. *Conrack* (1972).

Conroy, a young white teacher on the South Carolina sea island of Yamacraw, tries to persuade his class of isolated African-American students to get permission to celebrate Halloween on the mainland in Beaufort, S.C.

13 There was mystery here; there was mystery in the black cats and walking skeletons and living scarecrows that we saw decorating school windows, mystery in the grinning gargoyles and jack-o-lanterns on all the porches. I loved Halloween.

JACK SANTINO (b. 1947), U.S. folklorist and sociologist. *All Around the Year: Holidays and Celebrations in American Life* (chapter 5, "Autumn into Winter: Celebrating Death and Life") (1994).

14 Altho' outside it teems and pours
The boys about sixteen
Are busy runnin' rappin' doors
With turf—at Halloween.

B. M. TEGGART. Quoted in Jack Santino, *The Hallowed Eve: Dimensions of Culture in a Calendar Festival in Northern Ireland* (1998).

Santino notes that this is one of many "local poems" for Halloween, and that the genre "indexes Halloween food, pranks, and belief customs." He comments that such rhyming was part of the Irish Halloween tradition.

15 Those seemingly interminable dark walks between houses, long before street-lit safety became an issue, were more adrenalizing than the mountains of candy filling the sack. Sadly Halloween, with our good-natured attempts to protect the little ones, from the increasingly dangerous traffic and increasingly sick adults, has become an utter bore.

LAUREN SPRINGER, U.S. journalist. In *The Undaunted Garden* ("The Arrival of Fall") (1994), and reprinted in *The Writer in the Garden*, ed. Jane Garmey (1999).

16 I think there's a magic in Halloween that allows people to suspend things and allow certain fantasies and let their own wishes come true. So I don't know if that would work on a Tuesday afternoon in the middle of "reality."

FRED. Quoted in Jack Kugelmass, *Feasts and Celebrations in North American Ethnic Communities* ("Imagining Culture: New York City's Village Halloween Parade") (1995).

Fred is a man who had dressed as a good fairy in the Greenwich Village Halloween parade and felt that in the touch of his magic wand there was a healing power. He was interviewed by Jack Kugelmass.

Veterans Day

1   God bless the Flag and its loyal defenders,
     While its broad folds o'er the battle-field wave,
Till the dim star-wealth rekindle its splendors,
     Washed from its stains in the blood of the brave!

OLIVER WENDELL HOLMES (1809–1894), U.S. author and physician. "God Save the Flag."

2   [The American soldier] is not only brave but he is generous; and when he has fought for a principle and won, he has no desire to crush his foe, but is eager to abide by the old Latin maxim of "live and let live;" and he forgets and forgives, and lends a helping hand when a disposition to do the right thing is shown.

CLARA BARTON (1821–1912), U.S. nurse and philanthropist. Letter to Jessie L. Gladden, 7 November 1898, in *Letters of a Nation: A Collection of Extraordinary American Letters*, ed. Andrew Carroll (1997).

Barton founded the American Red Cross.

3   Soldiers and saviors of the homes we love;
Heroes and patriots who marched away,
And who marched back, and who marched on above—
     All—all are here to-day!

JAMES WHITCOMB RILEY (1849–1916), U.S. poet. "Soldiers Here To-Day."

4   Underneath the autumn sky,
Haltingly, the lines go by.
Ah, would steps were blithe and gay,
As when first they marched away,
Smile on lip and curl on brow, —
Only white-faced gray beards now
Standing on life's outer verge,
E'en the marches sound a dirge.

PAUL LAURENCE DUNBAR (1872–1906), U.S. poet. "The Veteran."

5   Ay, War, they say, is hell; it's heaven, too.
It lets a man discover what he's worth.
It takes his measure, shows what he can do,
Gives him a joy like nothing else on earth.
It fans in him a flame that otherwise
Would flicker out, these drab, discordant days;
It teaches him in pain and sacrifice
Faith, fortitude, grim courage past all praise.

ROBERT W. SERVICE (1874–1958), Canadian poet. "Wounded."

6   The soldier above all other people prays for peace, for he must suffer and bear the deepest wounds and scars of war.

DOUGLAS MACARTHUR (1880–1964), U.S. general. Speech to West Point Cadets, 12 May 1962, in *Lend Me Your Ears: Great Speeches in History*, ed. William Safire (1992).

7   War demands real toughness of fiber—not only in the soldiers that must endure, but in the homes that must sacrifice their best.

DWIGHT D. EISENHOWER (1890–1969), U.S. general and president. Letter, 16

April 1944, *Letters to Mamie*, ed. John S. D. Eisenhower (1978).

8 Men who have offered their lives for their country know that patriotism is not the *fear* of something; it is the *love* of something. Patriotism with us is not the hatred of Russia; it is the love of this republic and of the ideal of liberty of man and mind in which it was born, and to which this Republic is dedicated.

ADLAI STEVENSON (1900–1965), U.S. politician. Speech to an American Legion convention, Madison Square Garden, New York City, 27 August 1952, in *Lend Me Your Ears: Great Speeches in History*, ed. William Safire (1992).

Stevenson was governor of Illinois and the Democratic nominee for president in 1952 and 1956.

9 If your names on this wall make it harder to send guys half way around the world to die, then maybe it wasn't a total waste.

JOHN "SOUP" CAMPBELL, Vietnam War veteran. Letter to Eddie Van Every, 8 June 1985, in *Letters of a Nation: A Collection of Extraordinary American Letters*, ed. Andrew Carroll (1997).

Van Every was a soldier who served in Campbell's company in Vietnam and was killed. Campbell left his letter at the Vietnam Veterans Memorial ("The Wall") in Washington, D.C.

Thanksgiving

1 Thou that hast giv'n so much to me,
Give one thing more, a gratefull heart.

GEORGE HERBERT (1593–1633), English poet and Anglican priest. "Gratefulnesse."

2 Now therefore I do recommend and assign Thursday, the twenty-sixth of November next, to be devoted to the service of that great and glorious Being . . . for the kind care and protection of the people of this country, previous to their becoming a nation; for the signal manifold mercies, and the favorable interpositions of his providence, in the course and conclusion of the late war . . . for the peaceable and rational manner in which we have been enabled to establish Constitutions of Government for our safety and happiness, and particularly the national one now lately instituted.

GEORGE WASHINGTON (1732–1799), U.S. general and president. Proclamation of 1789, in Jack Santino, *All Around the Year: Holidays and Celebrations in American Life* (chapter 5, "Autumn into Winter: Celebrating Death and Life") (1994).

3 Gluttony and surfeiting are no proper occasions for thanksgiving.

CHARLES LAMB (1775–1834), English essayist. "Grace Before Meat," in *London Magazine* (November 1821) and *Essays of Elia* (1823).

4 We should love our native land were it a sterile rock; but we love it better when to our cultivation it yields an ample increase; and the farmer, instead of sighing for foreign dainties, looks up to heaven, and depends on his own labours; and when they are crowned with a blessing, he thanks God, as tens of thousands throughout our State are doing this day. Let us join our voices with theirs.

SARAH JOSEPHA HALE (1788–1879), U.S. author and editor. *Northwood, or Life North and South* (chapter 8, "Thanksgiving Dinner") (1852).

Hale persuaded President Lincoln to set aside a national day of thanksgiving. In her novel, she describes a feast that includes roasted turkey, a sirloin of beef, goose, ducklings, and chicken pie, in addition to "the celebrated pumpkin pie, an indispensable part of a good and true Yankee Thanksgiving; the size of the pie usually denoting the gratitude of the party who prepares the feast." In this quotation, an American defends the Thanksgiving custom as a celebration of the bounty of American agriculture, which does not value or require the introduction of foreign delicacies.

5 Our Thanksgiving Day, becoming the focus, as it were, of the private life and virtues of the people, should be hallowed and exalted, and made the day of generous deeds and innocent enjoyments, of noble aspirations and heavenly hopes.

SARAH JOSEPHA HALE (1788–1879), U.S. author and editor. Editorial, *Godey's Lady's Book* (1865), and reprinted in Jack Santino, *All Around the Year: Holidays and Celebrations in American Life* (chapter 5, "Autumn into Winter: Celebrating Death and Life") (1994).

Since 1827, Hale had worked to establish Thanksgiving Day. She was instrumental in getting Lincoln to create the national celebration.

6 I awoke this morning with a devout thanksgiving for my friends, the old and the new. Shall I not call God the Beautiful, who daily showeth himself to me in his gifts?

RALPH WALDO EMERSON (1803–1882), U.S. author. "Friendship," *Essays, First Series* (1841).

7 Ah! on Thanksgiving day, when from East and from West,
From North and from South come the pilgrim and guest,
When the gray-haired New Englander sees round his board
The old broken links of affection restored,
When the care-wearied man seeks his mother once more,
And the worn matron smiles where the girl smiled before,
What moistens the lip and what brightens the eye?

What calls back the past, like the rich Pumpkin pie?

JOHN GREENLEAF WHITTIER (1807–1892), U.S. poet. "The Pumpkin."

8 I . . . invite my fellow-citizens in every part of the United States, and also those who are at sea and those who are sojourning in foreign lands, to set apart and observe the last Thursday of November next as a day of thanksgiving and praise to our beneficent Father who dwelleth in the heavens.

ABRAHAM LINCOLN (1809–1865), U.S. president. National Thanksgiving Proclamation (3 October 1863), in Ralph and Adelin Linton, *We Gather Together: The Story of Thanksgiving* (1949).

Lincoln issued this proclamation at the suggestion of Sarah Josepha Hale, editor of *Godey's Lady's Book*. She had started a national campaign for a Thanksgiving holiday. Lincoln's initiative superseded Washington's 1789 proclamation and was undertaken as the Civil War was being fought. Lincoln noted that there had been "blessings of fruitful fields and healthful skies" despite "needful diversions of wealth and of strength from the fields of peaceful industry to the national defense." Franklin Roosevelt later changed the date from the last to the third Thursday in November because merchants wanted a longer Christmas shopping season.

9 Our honest Puritan festival is spreading, not as formerly, as a kind of opposition Christmas, but as a welcome prelude and adjunct, a brief interval of good cheer and social rejoicing, heralding the longer season of feasting and rest from labor in the month that follows.

OLIVER WENDELL HOLMES (1809–1894), U.S. author and physician. "The Seasons," *Pages from an Old Volume of Life: A Collection of Essays, 1857–1881* (1891).

10 *Thanksgiving Day.* Let us all give humble, hearty, and sincere thanks,

now, but the turkeys. In the island of Fiji they do not use turkeys; they use plumbers. It does not become you and me to sneer at Fiji.

MARK TWAIN (SAMUEL CLEMENS) (1835–1910), U.S. author. *Pudd'nhead Wilson* ("Pudd'nhead Wilson's Calendar" at chapter 18) (1894).

11 [Thanksgiving] as founded by th' Puritans to give thanks f'r bein' presarved fr'm th' Indyans, an' we keep it to give thanks we are presarved fr'm th' Puritans.

PHILIP DUNNE (1867–1936), U.S. humorist. "Thanksgiving," *Mr. Dooley's Opinions* (1901).

12 Folks is go'gin' me wid goodies,
   an' dey's treatin' me wid caih,
An' I's fat in spite of all dat I kin do.
I's mistrus'ful of de kin'ness dat's erroun' me evahwhaih,
Fu' it's jest' too good, an' frequent, to be true.

PAUL LAURENCE DUNBAR (1872–1906), U.S. poet. "Soliloquy of a Turkey."

13 From pestilence, fire, flood, and sword
We have been spared by thy decree,
And now with humble hearts, O Lord,
We come to pay our thanks to thee.

PAUL LAURENCE DUNBAR (1872–1906), U.S. poet. "A Thanksgiving Poem."

14 Thanksgiving Day! In the days of our founders, they were willing to give thanks for mighty little, for mighty little was all they expected.
   . . . Those old boys in the Fall of the year, if they could gather a few pumpkins, potatoes and some corn for the Winter, they was in a thanking mood.

But if we can't gather in a new car, a new radio, a new tuxedo and some Government relief, we feel like the world is agin us.

WILL ROGERS (1879–1935), U.S. humorist. 28 November 1934, *Will Rogers Speaks: Over 1,000 Timeless Quotations for Public Speakers (and Writers, Politicians, Comedians, Browsers . . .)*, ed. Bryan B. Sterling and Frances N. Sterling (1995).

15 When the gales of coming winter
   outside your window howl,
When the air is sharp and cheery so
   it drives away your scowl,
When one's appetite craves turkey
   and will have no other fowl,
   It's Thanksgiving time!

LANGSTON HUGHES (1902–1967), U.S. poet. "Thanksgiving Time."

16 What we're really talking about is a wonderful day set aside on the fourth Thursday of November when no one diets. I mean, why else would they call it Thanksgiving?

ERMA BOMBECK (1927–1996), U.S. humorist and newspaper columnist. "No One Diets on Thanksgiving" (26 November 1981), in *Forever, Erma: America's Best-Loved Writing from America's Favorite Humorist* (1996).

17 Thanksgiving, if there is to be any at all, must begin and end with God. Once we have been able to liberate Thanksgiving from the clutches of the Pilgrim mystique as well as from the countercultural clutches of the protesters, and once we have been liberated from the "count-your-many-blessings-name-them-one-by-one" routine, we will have made a significant step in that process of redeeming the familiar.

PETER J. GOMES (b. 1942), U.S. clergyman and theologian. "Redeeming the Familiar," *Sermons: Biblical Wisdom for Daily Living* (1998).

The protesters Gomes refers to were protesting against the displacement of American Indians by European settlers.

18 On Thanksgiving at our house we like variety, so we don't have turkey every year. Last year we had a swan. It was nice; everyone got some neck.

GEORGE CARLIN (b. 1937), U.S. comic. "Gobble This," *Brain Droppings* (1997).

19 I happen to be on record with an explanation of why we can't have our Thanksgiving Day that much earlier: Americans all begin their Christmas shopping on the day after Thanksgiving, and if they started their Christmas shopping in the middle of October they'd run out of money sometime in November. The people who are hard to shop for wouldn't get any presents at all.

CALVIN TRILLIN (b. 1935), U.S. author. *Family Man* (chapter 8, "Thanksgiving Wanderings") (1998).

This comment appears in an essay about Trillin's distaste for Thanksgiving and particularly for turkey, which he would like to replace with spaghetti carbonara. He notes that he has proposed a switch to the Canadian Thanksgiving date in October, and offers the explanation above for general resistance to the idea.

Hanukkah

1 The commandment to light the Hanukkah lamp is an exceedingly precious one, and one should be particularly careful to fulfill it, in order to make known the miracle, and to offer additional praise . . . to God for the wonders which He has wrought for us. Even if one has no food to eat except what he receives from charity, he should beg—or sell his garment to buy—oil and lamps, and light them.

MAIMONIDES (MOSES BEN MAIMON) (1135–1204), Jewish (Spanish-born) rabbi, philosopher, jurist, and physician. Megillah and Hanukkah (Mishneh Torah), in *The Hanukkah Anthology*, ed. Philip Goodman (1976).

2 Mighty, praised beyond compare,
        Rock of my salvation,
    Build again my house of prayer,
        For thy habitation!

"Maoz Tzur" ("Rock of Ages"), trans. Solomon Solis Cohen, in *The Hanukkah Anthology*, ed. Philip Goodman (1976).

One of the most popular hymns of the Ashkenazic Jews and a traditional part of Hanukkah celebrations, it is attributed to the 13th-century writer Mordecai.

3 I have a little dreidel,
    I made it out of clay;
    And when it's dry and ready
    Then dreidel I shall play.

Traditional song, arranged by Samuel S. Grossman and Samuel E. Goldfarb, in *The Hanukkah Anthology*, ed. Philip Goodman (1976).

4 You don't go to *heder* for eight days in a row, you eat pancakes every day, spin your dreidel to your heart's content, and from all sides Hanukkah money comes pouring in. What holiday could be better than that?

SHOLOM ALEICHEM (BORN SOLOMON J. RABINOWITZ) (1859–1916), Russian author writing in Yiddish. "Hannukah Money," *The Old Country*, trans. Julius and Frances Butwin (1946).

The author explains here why Hannukah is the best holiday for children.

5 When we light the Hanukkah candles
    let us remember the grave choices freedom illuminates for us.

RUTH F. BRIN (b. 1921), U.S. poet, fiction writer, and interpreter of Jewish liturgy. "An Interpretation of Hannukah," *Interpretations for the Weekly Torah Reading* (1965).

6   One must never forget. . . . Hanukkah is the celebration of our war, the celebration of the war of God. In the present war we have forgotten the war of the living God, we have forgotten Matthias, the high priest.

AVIGDOR HAMEIRI, Israeli author. "The Living Menorah" (*The Jewish Spectator*, December 1946), trans. Shlomo Katz; in *The Hanukkah Anthology*, ed. Philip Goodman (1976).

These are the words of a soldier who during the Second World War was made into a "living menorah" by having his hands dipped in hot tar by a sadistic superior.

7   Hanukkah commemorates and celebrates the first serious attempt in history to proclaim and champion the principle of religio-cultural diversity in the nation. The primary aim of the Maccabees was to preserve their own Jewish identity and to safeguard for Israel the possibility of continuing its traditional mission.

THEODOR HERZL GASTER (1906–1992.), Anglo-American folklorist and religion scholar. *Festivals of the Jewish Year: A Modern Interpretation and Guide* (1976).

8   Hannukkah is the Festival of Lights. It commemorates an ancient Jewish rebellion against oppression, during which the Temple in Jerusalem was miraculously recaptured from pagan hellenizers and rededicated to the worship of God. The candles of Hanukkah celebrate that rededication. They also help brighten the long winter nights. . . . I also want another miracle. But if it does not come, we will make a human miracle. We will give the world the special gift of our Jewishness. We will not let the world burn out our souls.

CHAIM POTOK (BORN HERMAN HAROLD) (b. 1929), U.S. author. "Miracles for a Broken Planet," *McCalls* (December 1972).

Potok quotes his father on the eighth night of Hanukkah 1938. The father tries to console the son, who wishes that God would stop the Nazi persecution of the Jews just as he allowed the Maccabees to recapture the Temple of Jerusalem from pagan hellenizers.

9   A lack of clear and satisfying religious identity hurts American Jews most in December. . . . It is a good thing that Hanuka is then at hand. . . . The tale of the Feast of Lights, with its all-too-sharp comment on our life nowadays, is very colorful. It is of the greatest use in giving the young a quick grasp of the Jewish historic situation. The gifts win their attention. The little candles stimulate their questions. The observance seems tooled to the needs of self-discovery.

HERMAN WOUK (b. 1915), U.S. author. *This is My God: The Jewish Way of Life* (chapter 7, "The Minor Holy Days") (1988).

10   "Jewish Christmas"—that's what my gentile friends called Chanukah when I was growing up in Michigan in the thirties and forties. Anachronistic, yes, but they had a point. Observing the dietary laws of separating milk and meat dishes was far easier for the handful of Jewish families in our little town than getting through December without mixing the two holidays.

FAYE MOSKOWITZ, U.S. essayist and teacher. *And the Bridge Is Love: Life Stories* (1991).

11 Those candles were laid out,
friends invited, ingredients bought
for latkes and apple pancakes,
that holiday for liberation
and the winter solstice

when tops turn like little planets.

MARGE PIERCY (b. 1936), U.S. poet.
"My mother's body," *The Art of Blessing the
Day: Poems with a Jewish Theme* (1999).

12 Millions of kids before me had
spun the dreidl on this holiday and
millions more would do so in many
years to come. I saw myself as a
passing bridge, a peon, a crucial
component in an infinite chain.
The accident of my Hispanic birth
had only added a different cultural
flavor to the already plentiful gallery of childhood smiles. I was, all
Jewish children are, time-travelling
Maccabees reenacting a cosmic festival of self-definition. This thought
made me stronger, a superhero of
sorts, a freedom-fighter with a mission: to smile was to remember, to
insert myself in history.

ILAN STAVANS (b. 1960), U.S. (Mexcian-
born) author and teacher. *The Riddle of Catin-
flas: Essays on Hispanic Popular Culture*
(1988).

Kwanzaa

1 The fact is that there is nowhere on
the African continent a holiday
named Kwanzaa. . . . Kwanzaa is an
Afro-American holiday which by its
very definition reflects the dual
character of the identity and experience of the Afro-American people.

MAULANA KARENGA (b. 1941), U.S.
professor of African-Amerrican studies. *The African American Holiday of Kwanzaa: A Celebration of Family, Community, and Culture*
(1988).

Karenga is the creator of Kwanzaa, which was
first celebrated in 1966.

2 It's an African holiday created by
African people. It speaks to me in a
way it can't speak to people outside
our culture. We honor and affirm
our family, community, and culture.

MAULANA KARENGA (b. 1941), U.S.
professor of African-American studies. Quoted
in Aldore Collier, "The Man Who Invented
Kwanzaa," *Ebony* (January 1988).

3 To be sure, celebrating Kwanzaa is
not an end in itself. Neither is having an Africa medallion swinging
from your neck, wearing a kente
cloth hat, or giving your children
African names. Medallions, clothes,
and newly created rites should remind us of our collective strength,
and of the fact that this strength is
manifest only through individual
effort. What we are doing with
Kwanzaa and "Afrocentricity" in
general is using our culture as an
ideal that each of us tries to live up
to.

ERIC V. COPAGE, U.S. author and editor.
*Kwanzaa: An African-American Celebration of
Culture and Cooking* (1991).

4 Every day of the year we must apply and practice the Nguzo Saba
sincerely and faithfully to harvest
success. If you wanted to sing like
Whitney Houston, would you think
of your music only once a week?
. . . If you wanted to be a champion athlete like Michael Jordan,
would you abuse your body, neglect
your meals, and skip routine practice?

DOROTHY WINBUSH RILEY (b. 1946), U.S. educator. *The Complete Kwanzaa: Celebrating Our Cultural Harvest* (1995).

5 Like Christians at Christmas, African-Americans now have a choice. They can ignore the inevitable commercialization of Kwanzaa and keep the home candles burning. Or they can celebrate Kwanzaa in the old-fashioned American way—by commodifying it.

KENNETH L. WOODWARD and **PATRICE JOHNSON**, U.S. journalists. "The Advent of Kwanzaa: Will Success Spoil an African-American Fest?" *Newsweek* (11 December 1995).

The authors include this comment as part of a story about the trend whereby businesses, such as McDonald's fast-food restaurants and Hallmark greeting cards, now market Kwanzaa.

6 The seven principles of Kwanzaa—unity, self-determination, collective work and responsibility, cooperative economics, purpose, creativity and faith—teach us that when we come together to strengthen our families and communities and honor the lessons of the past, we can face the future with joy and optimism.

BILL CLINTON (b. 1946), U.S. president. "Kwanzaa Greetings," *Jet* (30 December 1996).

7 We ask you to imagine a world where African people all sing the same songs, all dance to the same music, all dream the same dreams, and all work for the same goals. This is the true purpose of Kwanzaa: to put us all on one accord. There will always be diversity in our songs, but we should strive to always make beautiful music.

DAVID HALL (b. 1950), U.S. educator. Quoted in Barbara Eklof, *For Every Season:*

The Complete Guide to African American Celebrations, Traditional to Contemporary (1997).

From Hall's greeting to the first National Kwanzaa Celebration, held on Jekyll Island, Ga., 27 December 1990.

8 Kwanzaa's success depends on exacerbating consciously or unconsciously, black people's sense of alienation from Christmas. With its fat white man who delivers toys and gifts to children, Christmas simply confirms many African Americans' perception that everything in American society reinforces the idea of white supremacy.

GERALD EARLY (b. 1952), U.S. professor of African and African-American studies. Quoted in "Dreaming of a Black Christmas," *Harper's* (January 1997).

Christmas

1 I sing the birth was born tonight,
The Author both of life and light,
　The angels so did sound it;
And like the ravished shepherds said,
Who saw the light, and were afraid,
　Yet searched, and true they found it.

BEN JONSON (1572–1637), English poet and dramatist. "A Hymn on the Nativity of My Saviour."

2 Kindle the Christmas Brand, and then
　Till Sunne-set let it burne;
Which quencht, then lay it up agen,
　Till Christmas next returne.

ROBERT HERRICK (1591–1674), English poet and clergyman. "The Ceremonies for Candlemasse day."

3 What sweeter musick can we bring,
Then a Caroll, for to sing

The Birth of this our heavenly
King?

ROBERT HERRICK (1591–1674), English
poet and clergyman. "A Christmas Caroll, sung
to the King in the Presence at White-Hall."

4   The shepherds sing; and shall I silent be?
    My God, no hymne for thee?
My soul's a shepherd too; a flock it
feeds
    Of thoughts, and words, and
    deeds.
The pasture is thy word; the
streams, thy grace
    Enriching all the place.

GEORGE HERBERT (1593–1633), English
poet and Anglican priest. "Christmas."

5   They talke of Christmas so long,
that it comes.

GEORGE HERBERT (1593–1633), English
poet and Anglican priest. *Outlandish Proverbs*,
no. 840 (1640).

6   How shall we celebrate the day,
When God appear'd in mortal clay:
    The mark of worldly scorn:
When the Archangels heavenly
Lays,
Attempted the Redeemer's Praise
    And hail'd Salvation's Morn.

THOMAS CHATTERTON (1752–1770),
English poet. "A Hymn for Christmas Day."

7   Each age has deem'd the new-born
year
The fittest time for festal cheer

· · · · · · · · · · · ·

And well our Christian sires of old
Loved when the year its course had
roll'd
And brought blithe Christmas back
again,
With all his hospitable train.
Domestic and religious rite

Gave honour to the holy night;
On Christmas eve the bells were
    rung;
On Christmas eve the mass was
    sung;
That only night in all the year,
Saw the stoled priest the chalice
    rear.

SIR WALTER SCOTT (1771–1832), Scottish novelist and poet. *Marmion* (introduction
to canto 6).

8   He who can turn churlishly away
from contemplating the felicity of
his fellow-beings and can sit down
darkling and repining in his loneliness when all around is joyful may
have his moments of strong excitement and selfish gratification, but
he wants the genial and social sympathies which constitute the charm
of a Merry Christmas.

WASHINGTON IRVING (1783–1859),
U.S. author. "Christmas," *The Sketch Book of
Geoffrey Crayon, Gent.* (1819–20).

9   Now Christmas is come,
        Let us beat up the drum,
And call all our neighbors together,
        And when they appear,
        Let us make them such cheer,
As will keep out the wind and the
    weather.

WASHINGTON IRVING (1783–1859),
U.S. author. "Christmas Eve," *The Sketch Book
of Geoffrey Crayon, Gent.* (1819–20).

Cited as a "good old Christmas song" sung by
Simon Bracebridge.

10   But it is a cold, lifeless business
when you go to the shops to buy
something, which does not represent your life and talent, but a
goldsmith's.

RALPH WALDO EMERSON (1803–
1882), U.S. author. "Gifts," *Essays, Second Series* (1844).

11 Rise, happy morn, rise, holy morn;
    Draw forth the cheerful day from
      night;
    O Father, touch the east, and
      light
The light that shone when Hope
    was born.

ALFRED, LORD TENNYSON (1809–1892),
English poet. *In Memoriam A.H.H.* 30 (1850).

12 Happy, happy Christmas, that can
win us back to the delusions of our
childish days; that can recall to the
old man the pleasures of his youth;
that can transport the sailor and
the traveller, thousands of miles
away, back to his own fire-side and
his quiet home!

CHARLES DICKENS (1812–1870), En-
glish author. *The Pickwick Papers* (chapter 28,
"A Good-Humoured Christmas Chapter, Con-
taining an Account of a Wedding and Some
Other Sports Beside: Which Although in Their
Way, Even as Good Customs as Marriage Itself,
Are Not Quite so Religiously Kept Up in These
Degenerate Times") (1836–37).

13 Christmas was close at hand, in all
his bluff and hearty honesty; it was
the season of hospitality, merriment, and open-heartedness; the
old year was preparing, like an ancient philosopher, to call his friends
around him, and amidst the sound
of feasting and revelry to pass
gently and calmly away.

CHARLES DICKENS (1812–1870), En-
glish author. *The Pickwick Papers* (chapter 28,
"A Good-Humoured Christmas Chapter, Con-
taining an Account of a Wedding, and Some
Other Sports Beside: Which Although in Their
Way, Even as Good Customs as Marriage Itself,
Are Not Quite so Religiously Kept Up in These
Degenerate Times") (1836–37).

14 It was deemed a disgrace not to get
drunk at Christmas; and he was regarded as lazy indeed, who had not
provided himself with the necessary

means, during the year, to get
whisky enough to last him through
Christmas.

FREDERICK DOUGLASS (C. 1817–
1895), U.S. abolitionist. *Narrative of the Life
of an American Slave* (chapter 10) (1845).

In this part of his narrative, Douglass describes
the way slaveholders used holidays as "safety-
valves, to carry off the rebellious spirit of en-
slaved humanity."

15 What can I give Him
    Poor as I am?
If I were a shepherd
    I would bring a lamb;
If I were a wise man,
    I would do my part,—
Yet what I can give Him
    Give my heart.

CHRISTINA ROSSETTI (1830–1894),
English poet. "A Christmas Carol."

16 There was a good deal of laughing
and kissing and explaining, in the
simple, loving fashion which makes
these home-festivals so pleasant at
the time, so sweet to remember
long afterward, and then all fell to
work.

LOUISA MAY ALCOTT (1832–1888),
U.S. author. *Little Women* (1868–69).

Alcott describes a Christmas celebration during
hard times, when members of the March family give homemade gifts whose value is in the
loving labor they invested in them.

17   Now 'tis Christmas morn;
Here's to our women old and
    young,
    And to John Barleycorn!

THOMAS HARDY (1840–1928), English
author. "The Dead Quire."

18 The magi, as you know, were wise
men—wonderfully wise men—who
brought gifts to the Babe in the
manger. They invented the art of

giving Christmas gifts. Being wise, their gifts were no doubt wise ones, possibly bearing the privilege of exchange in case of duplication.

O. HENRY (WILLIAM SYDNEY POR-TER) (1862–1910), U.S. short-story writer. "Gifts of the Magi."

19 Alas! how dreary would be the world if there were no Santa Claus! It would be as dreary as if there were no Virginias. There would be no childlike faith then, no poetry, no romance to make tolerable this existence. We should have no enjoyment, except in sense and sight. The eternal light with which childhood fills the world would be extinguished.

Editorial, *New York Sun* (21 September 1897).

Part of the response to 8-year-old Virginia O'Hanlon, who had asked, "Is there a Santa Claus?" She was confidently answered by the editors of *The Sun*: "Yes, Virginia, there is a Santa Claus."

20 Home shall men come,
To an older place than Eden
And a taller town than Rome.
To the end of the way of the wandering star,
To the things that cannot be and that are,
To the place where God was homeless
And all men are at home.

G. K. CHESTERTON (1874–1936), English author. "The House of Christmas."

21 This is the good news of Christmas. He who stands by you and helps you is alive and present! It is he who was born that Christmas Day! Open your eyes, open your ears, open your heart! You may truly see, hear, and experience that he is here,

and stands by you as no one else can do!

KARL BARTH (1886–1968), Swiss theologian. "He Stands By Us," sermon before Christmas Communion service, 1958, in *Lend Me Your Ears: Great Speeches in History*, ed. William Safire (1992).

22 The Dickensian Christmas-at-Home receives only perfunctory lip-service from a press which draws a steady income from the catering and amusement trades. Home-made fun is gratuitous, and gratuitousness is something which an industrialized world cannot afford to tolerate.

ALDOUS HUXLEY (1894–1963), English author. "New Fashioned Christmas," *The Olive Tree and Other Essays* (1936).

23 To perceive Christmas through its wrapping becomes more difficult with every year.

E. B. WHITE (1899–1985), U.S. author. "The Distant Music of the Hounds," *The Second Tree from the Corner* (1954).

White in this essay comments that, despite all the distractions and commercialization of the modern observance of Christmas, the holiday remains a miracle because it has "an essential simplicity that is everlasting and triumphant, at the end of confusion."

24 No love that in a family dwells,
No carolling in frosty air,
Nor all the steeple-shaking bells
Can with this single Truth compare—
That God was Man in Palestine
And lives to-day in Bread and Wine.

JOHN BETJEMAN (1906–1984), English poet. "Christmas."

25 Santa Claus, this psychiatrist says, is a dangerous sentimental father-figure, who is expected to satisfy "unreasonable wants," and who by that

very expectation delays the "necessary adjustment of the preadolescent child to the world of reality."

ALISTAIR COOKE (b. 1908), English journalist. "Christmas Eve" (no. 3) (1952).

Originally broadcast in Britain as part of Cooke's "Letter from America" program.

26 A barn with cattle and horses is the place to begin Christmas; after all, that's where the original event happened, and that same smell was the first air that the Christ Child breathed.

PAUL ENGLE (1908–1991), U.S. author. *Prairie Christmas* ("An Iowa Christmas") (1960).

27 It's comin' on Christmas
They're cutting down trees
They're putting up reindeer and
  singing songs of joy and peace
Oh, I wish I had a river I could
  skate away on.

JONI MITCHELL , singer and songwriter. "River" (1971), in Jack Santino, *New Old-Fashioned Ways: Holidays and Popular Culture* (1976).

28 The true Christmas bathes every little thing in light and makes one cookie a token, one candle, one simple pageant more wonderful than anything seen on stage or screen.

GARRISON KEILLOR (b. 1942), U.S. author and radio personality. *Lake Wobegon Days* ("Winter") (1985).

29 Christmas is a conspiracy to make single people feel lonely.

ARMISTEAD MAUPIN (b. 1944), U.S. author. *Tales of the City* (1978).

30 I have been investigating the science of Christmas for more than a decade. When I first began to take an

interest in the subject, I was unprepared for the breadth and depth of the insights that would eventually emerge. Take those flying reindeer, Santa's red and white color scheme, and his jolly disposition, for example. They are all probably linked to the use of a hallucinogenic toadstool in ancient rituals.

ROGER HIGHFIELD (b. 1958), U.S. author. *The Physics of Christmas: From the Aerodynamics of Reindeer to the Thermodynamics of Turkey* (chapter 1, "Christmas and the Scientist: An Introduction") (1988).

New Year's Eve

1 For auld lang syne, my dear,
    For auld lang syne,
We'll tak a cup o' kindness yet
    For auld lang syne!

ROBERT BURNS (1759–1796), Scottish poet. "Auld Lang Syne."

2 And ye, who have met with Adversity's blast,
    And been bow'd to the earth by
      its fury;
To whom the Twelve Months, that
  have recently pass'd,
    Were as harsh as a prejudiced
      jury,—
Still, fill to the Future! and join in
  our chime,
    The regrets of remembrance
      to cozen,
And having obtained a New Trial of
  Time,
    Shout in hopes of a kindlier
      dozen!

THOMAS HOOD (1799–1845), English poet. "Anacreontic: For the New Year."

3   The year
Has gone, and, with it, many a glorious throng

Of happy dreams. Its mark is on
each brow,
Its shadow in each heart. In its
swift course,
It waved its sceptre o'er the beautiful,—
And they are not.

GEORGE DENISON PRENTICE (1802–
1870), U.S. poet. "The Closing Year."

4   Good-by, Old Year!
   Good-by!
We have seen sorrow—you and I—
   Such hopeless sorrow, grief and
    care
That now, that you have come to
   die,
   Remembering our old despair,
'Tis sweet to say, "Good-by—
   Good-by, Old Year!
    Good-by!"

JAMES WHITCOMB RILEY (1849–
1916), U.S. poet. "Good-By, Old Year."

5   My pipe is out, my glass is dry;
   My fire is almost ashes too;
But once again, before you go,
   And I prepare to meet the New:
Old Year! a parting word that's
   true,
   For we've been comrades, you
    and I—
I thank God for each day of you;
There! bless you now! Old Year,
   good-bye!

ROBERT W. SERVICE (1874–1958), Canadian poet. "The Passing of the Year."

Days of the Week

1   Monday's child is fair of face,
Tuesday's child is full of grace,
Wednesday's child is full of woe,
Thursday's child has far to go,
Friday's child is loving and giving,

Saturday's child has to work for its
living,
But a child that's born on the Sabbath day
Is fair and wise and good and gay.

In *The Oxford Dictionary of Nursery Rhymes*,
ed. Iona Opie and Peter Opie (1952).

2   Solomon Grundy,
Born on a Monday,
Christened on Tuesday,
Married on Wednesday,
Took ill on Thursday,
Worse on Friday,
Died on Saturday,
Buried on Sunday:
This is the end
Of Solomon Grundy.

In *The Oxford Dictionary of Nursery Rhymes*,
ed. Iona Opie and Peter Opie (1952).

3   You know that Munday is Sundayes
   brother;
Tuesday is such another;
Wednesday you must go to church
   and pray;
Thursday is half-holiday;
On Friday it is too late to begin to
   spin;
The *Saturday is half* -holiday agen.

"Divers Crab-Tree Lectures" (1639). Quoted in
John Brand, *Observations on the Popular Antiquities of Great Britain*, vol. 2 (1848–49).

4   That all those that marry on Tuesdays and Thursdays, shall be happy.
. . . Those that begin journies upon
a *Wednesday* shall run through
much danger.

"Rare tract called the Animal Parliament,
1707," quoted in John Brand. *Observations on
the Popular Antiquities of Great Britain*, vol. 2
(1848–49).

5   When through the Town, with slow
   and solemn Air,

Led by the Nostril, walks the mu-
    zled Bear;
Behind him moves majestically dull,
The Pride of *Hockley-hole*, the surly
    Bull;
Learn hence the Periods of the
    Week to name,
Mondays and *Thursdays* are the
    Days of Game.

JOHN GAY (1685–1732), English dramatist
and poet. *Trivia: Or, the Art of Walking the
Streets of London* (book 2) (1716).

6   When fishy Stalls with double Store
    are laid;

. . . .

Wednesdays and *Fridays* you'll observe from hence,
Days, when our Sires were doom'd
    to Abstinence.

JOHN GAY (1685–1732), English dramatist
and poet. *Trivia; Or, The Art of Walking The
Streets of London* (book 2) (1716).

7   And if I loved you Wednesday,
      Well, what is that to you?
    I do not love you Thursday—
      So much is true.

EDNA ST. VINCENT MILLAY (1892–
1950), U.S. poet. "Thursday."

8   Last Monday nite
    I saw a fight
    Between Wednesday and Thursday
    Over Saturday nite
    Tuesday asked me what was going
    on
    I said "Sunday's in the meadow
    And Friday's in the corn."

JOHN PRINE, U.S. singer and songwriter.
"Quiet Man" (1971).

Sunday

1   Remember the sabbath day, to keep
    it holy. Six days shalt thou labor
and do all thy work; But the seventh day is the sabbath of the Lord
thy God; in it thou shalt not do any
work, thou, nor thy son, nor thy
daughter, thy manservant, nor thy
maidservant, nor thy cattle, nor thy
stranger that is within thy gates: For
in six days the LORD made heaven
and earth, the sea, and all that in
them is, and rested the seventh day;
wherefore, the LORD blessed the
sabbath day, and hallowed it.

Exodus 20.8–11.

2   O day most calm, most bright,
    The fruit of this, the next worlds
      bud,
    Th'indorsement of supreme delight,
    Writ by a friend, and with his
      bloud;
    The couch of time; cares balm and
      bay:
    The week were dark, but for thy
      light.

GEORGE HERBERT (1593–1633), English
poet and Anglican priest. "Sunday."

3   The Country Parson, as soon as he
    awakes on Sunday morning, pres-
    ently falls to work, and seems to
    himselfe so as a Market-man is,
    when the Market day comes, or a
    shopkeeper, when customers use to
    come in. His thoughts are full of
    making the best of the day, and
    contriving it to his best gaines.

GEORGE HERBERT (1593–1633), English
poet and Anglican priest. "The Parson on Sundays," *A Priest to the Temple, or The Country
Parson* (1632).

4   Of all the days that's in the week
      I dearly love but one day—
    And that's the day that comes be-
    twixt
      A Saturday and Monday;

For then I'm dressed all in my best
    To walk abroad with Sally;
She is the darling of my heart,
    And she lives in our alley.

HENRY CAREY (c.1687–1743), English poet and musician. "Sally in Our Alley."

5   [Sunday] should be different from another day. People may walk, but not throw stones at birds. There may be relaxation, but there should be no levity.

SAMUEL JOHNSON (1709–1784), English author. Quoted in James Boswell, *Journal of a Tour to the Hebrides*, 20 August 1773 (1785).

6   There is something delightful in beholding the poor prisoner of the crowded and dusty city enabled thus to come forth once a week and throw himself upon the green bosom of nature. He is like a child restored to the mother's breast; and they who first spread out these noble parks and magnificent pleasure grounds which surround this huge metropolis have done at least as much for its health and morality as if they had expended the amount of cost in hospitals, prisons, and penitentiaries.

WASHINGTON IRVING (1783–1859), U.S. author. "A Sunday in London," *The Sketchbook of Geoffrey Crayon, Gent.* (1819–20).

Irving opens up his description by calling the city on Sunday a "gigantic monster . . . charmed into repose" when the "intolerable din and struggle of the week are at an end."

7   He goes on Sunday to the church,
    And sits among his boys;
He hears the parson pray and preach,
    He hears his daughter's voice,
Singing in the village choir,
    And it makes his heart rejoice.

HENRY WADSWORTH LONGFELLOW (1807–1882), U.S. poet. "The Village Blacksmith."

8   In calm and cool and silence, once again
I find my old accustomed place among
My brethren, where, perchance, no human tongue
Shall utter words; where never hymn is sung,
Nor deep-toned organ blown, nor censer swung,
Nor dim light falling through the pictured pane!

JOHN GREENLEAF WHITTIER (1807–1892), U.S. poet. "First Day Thoughts."

The use of the term "First Day" and the description of the meeting reflect Whittier's Quaker background.

9   My father and mother were both of the old-fashioned orthodox school, with minds formed on Jeremy Taylor, Blair, South, and Secker, who thought it their duty to go diligently to church twice on Sunday, communicate four times a year (their only opportunities), after grave and serious preparation, read a sermon to their household on Sunday evenings, and watch over their children's religious instruction, though in a reserved, undemonstrative manner.

CHARLOTTE M. YONGE (1823–1901), English novelist. *Chantry House* (chapter 2, "Schoolroom Days") (1889).

Taylor, Blair, South, and Secker were all royalists and theologians with a distaste for Puritanism.

10   Some keep the Sabbath going to Church—
I keep it, staying at Home—
With a Bobolink for a Chorister—
And an Orchard, for a Dome—

EMILY DICKINSON (1830–1886), U.S. poet. "Some keep the Sabbath going to Church."

11 They have three Sundays a week in Tangier. The Muhammadans' comes on Friday, the Jews' on Saturday, and that of the Christian Consuls on Sunday.

MARK TWAIN (SAMUEL CLEMENS) (1835–1910), U.S. author. *The Innocents Abroad, or The New Pilgrims Progress* (chapter 9) (1869).

12 . . . The laziest of all days—
To git up any time—er sleep—
Er jes' lay round and watch the haze
A-dancin' crost the wheat, and keep
My pipe a-goern laisurely.

JAMES WHITCOMB RILEY (1849–1916), U.S. poet. "Uncle Dan'l In Town Over Sunday."

The speaker here, a country man, complains of "city ways," which create a lot of noise and activity but nothing of substance to do.

13 Lie still and rest, in that serene repose
That on this holy morning comes to those
Who have been burdened with the cares which make
The sad heart weary and the tired heart ache.

ELLA WHEELER WILCOX (1850–1919), U.S. poet. "Poems of the Week."

14 Cease from unnecessary labours,
Saunter into the green world stretching far,
Light a long cigar,
Come, enjoy your Sunday
While yet you may!

ROBERT GRAVES (1895–1985), English author. "Come, Enjoy Your Sunday."

15 But Sunday was a gala day
When, in their best attire,
They'd listen, with rejoicing hearts,
To Sermons on Hell Fire,
Demons I've Met, Grim Satan's Prey,
And other topics just as gay.

STEPHEN VINCENT BENÉT (1898–1943), U.S. author. "Pilgrims and Puritans."

16 Eternity resembles
One long Sunday afternoon.

DONALD JUSTICE (b. 1925), U.S. poet. "Nostalgia and Complaint of the Grandparents."

17 Hate Sunday night. Feels like homework night.

HELEN FIELDING (b. 1958), English author. *Bridget Jones's Diary* ("Sunday 14 May") (1998).

*M*onday

1 It is a custom in Ireland, among shoemakers, if they intoxicate themselves on Sunday, to do no work on Monday; and this they call making a Saint Monday or keeping Saint Crispin's day. Many here adopted this good custom from the example of the shoemakers.

MARIA EDGEWORTH (1767–1849), Irish author. "Tomorrow," *Popular Tales* (chapter 6; footnote dated August 1803) (1837).

"Tomorrow" is the story of Basil, a young man who longs for genius but ruins his life with procrastination. Presumably the shoemakers indicate the institutional popularity of his bad habits.

2 MONDAY, n. In Christian countries, the day after the baseball game.

AMBROSE BIERCE (1842–?1914), U.S. author. *The Devil's Dictionary* (1881–1911).

3   Poverty compels me
        To face the snow and sleet,—
    For pore wife and children
        Must have a crust to eat.—
    The sad wail of hunger
        It would drive me insane,
    If it wasn't for Blue-Monday
        When I git to work againe!

JAMES WHITCOMB RILEY (1849–
1916), U.S. poet. "'Blue Monday' at the Shoe
Shop (In the Early Seventies)."

4   "As Monday goes, so goes the
        week," dames say.
    Refreshed, renewed, use well the
        initial day.
            And see! thy neighbour
            Already seeks his labour.

ELLA WHEELER WILCOX (1850–1919),
U.S. poet. "Poems of the Week."

5   Blue Monday, how I hate blue
        Monday
    Have to work like a slave all day

DAVE BARTHOLOMEW (b. 1920), U.S.
trumpeter, bandleader, and songwriter, and
ANTOINE (FATS) DOMINO (b. 1928),
U.S. singer and songwriter. "Blue Monday"
(1957), in *The World's Greatest Fake Book*, ed.
Chuck Sher (1983).

6   Red beans were traditionally cooked
    while the Monday wash was drying
    on the line, and since New Orleans
    humidity made that an all-day job,
    the beans cooked for many hours.

RIMA COLLIN and **RICHARD COLLIN**,
U.S. food writers and professors. *The New Or-
leans Cookbook* (1992).

7   Hangin' around
    Nothing to do but frown
    Rainy days and Mondays always get
        me down.

ROGER NICHOLLS and **PAUL WIL-
LIAMS** (b. 1940), U.S. songwriters. "Rainy
Days and Mondays" (1971).

The song was a hit for the brother-and-sister
act The Carpenters.

8   Tell me why I don't like Mondays,
    I wanna shoo-oo-oo-oo-oo-oot
    The whole day down.

BOB GELDOF (b. 1954), Irish singer and
songwriter. "I Don't Like Mondays" (1980).

Geldof and his group The Boomtown Rats
based this refrain for their song on a news
story about a 16-year-old high school student,
Brenda Spencer, who used her father's gun to
shoot into a crowd at her high school. She injured eight students and killed the school principal and custodian. When asked what had
prompted her, she replied, "I don't like Mondays."

9   It's just another manic Monday
    I wish it was Sunday
    'Cause that's my fun day
    My I don't have to run day.

**PRINCE NELSON (CHRISTOPHER AL-
EXANDER, THE ARTIST FORMERLY
KNOWN AS PRINCE)** (b. 1958), U.S.
singer and songwriter. "Manic Monday"
(1986).

The song was a hit for the female singing
group The Bangles.

Tuesday

1   Richard doesn't like to give presents
    when you're supposed to give pres-
    ents. Christmas and birthdays go
    right by. But when he goes out and
    buys something, say, because it's a
    Tuesday, he's terribly excited.

ELIZABETH TAYLOR (b. 1932), American (English-born) actress. *Elizabeth Taylor: An
Informal Memoir* (chapter 7) (1965).

The recipient of one of Richard Burton's gifts
might also be terribly excited—he was famous
for lavishing Taylor with expensive gems.

2   Tuesday had always been our day
    together. Most of my courses with
    Morrie were on Tuesday, he had of-
    fice hours on Tuesdays, and when I

wrote my senior thesis . . . it was on Tuesdays that we sat together. . . . We're Tuesday people.

MITCH ALBOM (b. 1958), U.S. memoirist. *Tuesdays with Morrie: An Old Man, A Young Man and Life's Greatest Lesson* (1997).

Wednesday

1 My Wednesday nights came regularly round, our quartette parties came regularly off, my violincello was in good tune, and there was nothing wrong in my world—or if anything not much—or little or much, it was no affair of mine.

CHARLES DICKENS (1812–1870), English author. *Dombey and Son* (chapter 53, "More Intelligence") (1848).

Mr. Morfin here comments on his ability and desire to take care of his duties for Mr. Dombey, an exacting businessman—to "let everything about me go on, day by day, unquestioned, like a great machine," and to "take it for granted and consider it all right."

2 Half-way unto the end—the week's high noon.
The morning hours do speed away so soon!
And, when the noon is reached, however bright,
Instinctively we look toward the night.

ELLA WHEELER WILCOX (1850–1919), U.S. poet. "Poems of the Week."

3 Why don't you come up and see me sometime? Come up on Wednesday, that's amateur night.

MAE WEST (1892–1980), U.S. actress. In *The Penguin Book of Women's Humor*, ed. Regina Barreca (1996).

Friday

1 The housewife should kindle the Sabbath candles with a joyous heart

and good will, for it is a great privilege accorded to her. It brings her the merit of holy sons, who will be Lights of the World in Torah, and who will increase peace on earth. It also merits her to give long life unto her husband. Therefore she should be careful in the observance of this Mitzwah.

Zohar 1.48b, in *The Talmudic Anthology: Tales and Teachings of the Rabbis*, ed. Louis I. Newman (1947).

2 Some days . . . are commonly deemed unlucky; among others, Friday labours under that opprobrium; and it is pretty generally held that no new work or enterprise should commence on that day. . . . A respectable merchant of the city of London informed me that no person there will begin any business, i. e. open his shop for the first time, on a Friday.

JOHN BRAND (1744–1806). *Observations on the Popular Antiquities of Great Britain*, vol. 2 (1848–49).

3 Midst the wealth of facts and fancies
That our memories may recall,
Thus the old school-day romances
Are the dearest, after all!—
When some sweet thought revises
The half-forgotten tune
That opened "Exercises,"
On "Friday Afternoon."

JAMES WHITCOMB RILEY (1849–1916), U.S. poet. "Friday Afternoon: To William Morris Pierson, [1868–1870]."

4 From feasts abstain; be temperate, and pray;
Fast if thou wilt; and yet, throughout the day,

Neglect no labour and no duty
    shirk:
Not many hours are left thee for
    thy work.

ELLA WHEELER WILCOX (1850–1919),
U.S. poet. "Poems of the Week."

5   I shall never forget Shabbat in my
town. When I shall have forgotten
everything else, my memory will
still retain the atmosphere of holiday, of serenity pervading even the
poorest houses: the white table-
cloth, the candles, the meticulously
combed little girls, the men on
their way to the synagogue. When
my town shall fade into the abyss of
time, I will continue to remember
the light and the warmth it radiated
on Shabbat.

ELIE WIESEL (b. 1928), U.S. (Romanian-
born) author and Holocaust survivor. *A Jew Today* (part 1, "Words and Memories: To Be a
Jew") (1978).

6   It was a nice way to remember, to
gather those scattered Friday nights
of candles strewn over childhood's
inconsistent terrain. A token of
memory, and also of history, the
collective remembrance far beyond
memory's reach.

ELIZABETH EHRLICH, U.S. author. *Miriam's Kitchen* ("October: Diaspora") (1997).

Ehrlich describes her return to the ritual of
lighting Sabbath candles on Friday nights.

Saturday

1   When dirty Waters from Balconies
    drop,
And dextrous Damsels twirle the
    sprinkling Mop,
And cleanse the spatter'd Sash, and
    scrub the Stairs;

Know *Saturday's* conclusive Morn
    appears.

JOHN GAY (1685–1732), English dramatist
and poet. *Trivia: Or, the Art of Walking the
Streets of London* (book 2) (1716).

2   With regard to Saturday afternoons,
perhaps men who live by manual
labour, and have families to support
by it, cannot spend them better
than in following the several call-
ings in which they have employed
themselves on the preceding days of
the week. For industry will be no
bad preparation for the Sabbath.

JOHN BRAND (1744–1806). *Observations
on the Popular Antiquities of Great Britain*, vol.
2 (1848–49).

3   The evening of the last day of the
week was always celebrated by what
is styled on board of English ves-
sels, "The Saturday-night bottles."
Two of these were sent down into
the forecastle, just after dark; one
for the starboard watch, and the
other for the larboard.

HERMAN MELVILLE (1819–1891), U.S.
author. *Omoo* (chapter 12, "Death and Burial
of Two of the Crew") (1847).

4   The common failings in that part
of the country amongst the poor
were Saturday-night drunkenness
and looseness in the relations between young men and young
women. Mrs. Caffryn's indignation
never rose to the correct boiling
point against these crimes.

MARK RUTHERFORD (1831–1913), English author. *Clara Hopgood* (chapter 12)
(1896).

Mrs. Caffryn is a shop owner who refuses to be
as upset by her neighbor's drunkenness as she
is by the squalor in which they must live.

5 Saturday night is the loneliest night
     in the week,
   'Cause that's the night
   that my sweetie and I
   used to dance cheek to cheek.

   SAMMY CAHN (1913–1993), U.S. lyricist.
   "Saturday Night" (1996), in *The World's Greatest Fake Book*, ed. Chuck Sher (1983).

   Music for the song was composed by Jules
   Styne.

6 . . . Saturday morning,
   all my tiredness gone away.
   Got my money and my honey,
   and I'm out on the stem to play.

   DAVE BARTHOLOMEW (b. 1920), U.S.
   trumpeter, bandleader, and songwriter, and
   ANTOINE (FATS) DOMINO (b. 1928),
   U.S. singer and songwriter. "Blue Monday"
   (1957), in *The World's Greatest Fake Book*, ed.
   Chuck Sher (1983).

7 Come Saturday morning
   I'm going away with my friend.
   We'll Saturday spend till the end of
     the day.

   DORY PREVIN (b. 1936?), U.S. lyricist.
   "Come Saturday Morning" (1969).

   The song, with music by Fred Karlin, is associated with the film *The Sterile Cuckoo*, starring
   Liza Minelli.

8 A congregation of Jews that reads
   from the Torah every Saturday, that
   includes babies and grandparents,
   the memories of Holocaust survivors and the enthusiasm of converts, will show you that you need
   not live and die on your own island
   of time. You are part of an extended family whose memories
   stretch back past Mount Sinai.

   PAUL COWAN (1940–1988), U.S. journalist and author. *Mixed Blessings: Marriage Between Jews and Christians* (1987).

January

1 Two-headed Janus, opener of the
   softly gliding year, thou who alone

of the celestials dost behold thy
back, O come propitious to the
chiefs whose toil ensures peace to
the fruitful earth, peace to the sea.

OVID (43 B.C.–c. A.D. 18), Roman poet.
Fasti 1.63, in *Ovid in Six Volumes* (Loeb Classical Library), vol. 5, trans. James George Frazer (1989).

2 A Drunkard cannot meet a Cork
   Without a Revery—
   And so encountering a Fly
   This January Day
   Jamaicas of Remembrance stir
   That send me reeling in—
   This moderate drinker of Delight
   Does not deserve the spring—

   EMILY DICKINSON (1830–1886), U.S.
   poet. "A Drunkard cannot meet a Cork."

3 I do not like January very much. It
   is too stationary. Not enough happens. I like the evidences of life,
   and in January there are too few of
   them.

   **VICTORIA (OR VITA) SACKVILLE-
   WEST** (1892–1962), English novelist and
   poet. *Country Notes* ("January") (1940).

4 In the South we go in quest of
   spring as soon as Christmas is past
   and the new year begins. The first
   days of January find us searching
   among the last fallen leaves for purple violets and white hyacinths and
   the yellow buds of winter aconite.

   ELIZABETH LAWRENCE (1904–1985),
   U.S. landscape architect. "The Onset of
   Spring," *The Home Garden* (February 1943),
   and reprinted in *The Writer in the Garden*, ed.
   Jane Garmey (1999).

February

1 Our Roman fathers gave the name
   of *februa* to instruments of purification. . . . The month is called af-

ter these things, because the Luperci purify the whole ground with
strips of hide, which are their instruments of cleansing, or because
the season is pure when once
peace-offerings have been made at
the graves and the days devoted to
the dead are past. Our sires believed
that every sin and every cause of ill
could be wiped out by rites of pur-
gation.

OVID (43 B.C.—C. A.D. 18), Roman poet.
Fasti 2.19 ff., in *Ovid in Six Volumes* (Loeb
Classical Library), vol. 5, trans. James George
Frazer (1989).

The Luperci were a group of priests who lived
near the Palatine Hill in Rome and engaged in
rituals of cleansing. They attempted to ensure
the fertility of the women and agriculture of
the country.

2   February makes a bridge and
    March breaks it.

GEORGE HERBERT (1593–1633), English
poet and Anglican priest. *Outlandish Proverbs*,
no. 739 (1640).

3   The most serious charge which can
    be brought against New England is
    not Puritanism but February. . . .
    Spring is too far away to comfort
    even by anticipation, and winter
    long ago lost the charm of novelty.

JOSEPH WOOD KRUTCH (1893–1970),
America author and educator. *The Twelve Sea-
sons* (1949); in *The Writer in the Garden*, ed.
Jane Garmey (1999).

*M*arch

1   It is now March, and the northern
    wind drieth up the southern dirt.
    The tender lips are now masked for
    fear of chapping, and the fair hands
    must not be ungloved. Now riseth
    the sun a pretty step to his fair
    height, and Saint Valentine calls the
    birds together where nature is

pleased in the variety of love. . . . I
hold it the servant of nature and
the schoolmaster of art, the hope of
labor and the subject of reason.

NICHOLAS BRETON (C. 1535–C. 1626),
English author. *Fantastics: Serving for a Perpetual Prognostication* (1626).

2   Remember March, the ides of
    March, remember.

WILLIAM SHAKESPEARE (1564–1616),
English poet and dramatist. *Julius Caesar*
4.3.18.

The ides in the ancient Roman calendar was
the 15th of March, May, July, and October
and the 13th of other months.

3   It is the first mild day of March:
    Each minute sweeter than before,

    . . . .

    There is a blessing in the air,
    Which seems a sense of joy to yield
    To the bare trees, and mountains
      bare,
    And grass in the green field.

WILLIAM WORDSWORTH (1770–
1850), English poet. "To My Sister."

4   Like an army defeated
    The snow hath retreated,
    And now doth fare ill
    On the top of the bare hill;
    The Ploughboy is whooping—
      anon—anon:
      There's joy in the mountains;
      There's life in the fountains!

WILLIAM WORDSWORTH (1770–
1850), English poet. "Written in March While
Resting on the Bridge at the Foot of Brother's
Water."

According to Dorothy Wordsworth's journal,
the poem was composed on a bridge at
Brother's Water, a small lake.

5   Slayer of the winter, art thou here
    again?

O welcome, thou that bring'st the summer nigh!
The bitter wind makes not thy victory vain,
Nor will we mock thee for thy faint blue sky.
Welcome, O March!

WILLIAM MORRIS (1834–1896), English author, artist, and social reformer. "The Months."

6 When coughs are changed to laughs, and when
    Our frowns melt into smiles of glee,
And all our blood thaws out again
    In streams of ecstasy,
And poets wreak their roundelay,
The Spring is coming round this way.

JAMES WHITCOMB RILEY (1849–1916), U.S. poet. "When Early March Seems Middle May."

7 March is no land of extremes. Dull as life,
It offers small flowers and minor holidays.

JOHN UPDIKE (b. 1932), U.S. author. "March: A Birthday Poem."

April

1 Some there are who grudge thee the honour of the month, and would snatch it from thee, Venus. For they say that April was named from the open (*apertum*) season, because spring then opens (*aperit*) all things, and the sharp frost-bound cold departs, and earth unlocks her teeming soil, though kindly Venus claims the month and lays her hand on it.

OVID (43 B.C.–c. A.D. 18), Roman poet. *Fasti* 4.85 ff., in *Ovid in Six Volumes* (Loeb Classical Library), vol. 5, trans. James George (1989).

2 Whan that Aprill with his shoures soote
The droghte of March hath perced to the roote,
And bathed every veyne in swich licour
Of which vertu engendered is the flour:
. . . .
Thanne longen folk to goon on pilgrimages.

GEOFFREY CHAUCER (1343–1400), English poet. General Prologue, *The Canterbury Tales* (c. 1387).

3 It is now April, and the nightingale begins to tune her throat against May. The sunny showers perfume the air and the bees begin to go abroad for honey. The dew, as in pearls, hangs upon the tops of the grass, while the turtles sit billing upon the little green boughs. . . . It were a world to set down the worth of this month, but in sum, I thus conclude: I hold it the heaven's blessing and the earth's comfort.

NICHOLAS BRETON (c. 1535–c.1626), English author. *Fantastics: Serving for a Perpetual Prognostication* (1626).

4 O, how this spring of love resembleth
The uncertain glory of an April day,
Which now shows all the beauty of the sun,
And by and by a cloud takes all away.

WILLIAM SHAKESPEARE (1564–1616), English poet and dramatist. *Two Gentlemen of Verona* 1.3.84–87.

Spoken by Proteus.

5   'Tis the merry Nightingale
       That crowds, and hurries, and pre-
         cipitates
       With fast thick warble his delicious
         notes,
       As he were fearful that an April
         night
       Would be too short for him to ut-
         ter forth
       His love-chant, and disburthen his
         full soul
       Of all its music!

SAMUEL TAYLOR COLERIDGE (1772–
1834), English poet and critic. "The Nightingale: A Conversation Poem, April 1798."

6   The April winds are magical,
     And thrill our tuneful frames;
     The garden-walks are passional
     To bachelors and dames.

RALPH WALDO EMERSON (1803–
1882), U.S. author. "April."

7   Sweet April! many a thought
     Is wedded unto thee, as hearts are
       wed;
     Nor shall they fail, till, to its au-
       tumn brought,
       Life's golden fruit is shed.

HENRY WADSWORTH LONGFELLOW
(1807–1882), U.S. poet. "An April Day."

8   Oh, to be in England
     Now that April's there,
     And whoever wakes in England
     Sees, some morning, unaware,
     That the lowest boughs and the
       brushwood sheaf
     Round the elm-tree bole are in tiny
       leaf.

ROBERT BROWNING (1812–1889), English poet. "Home-Thoughts from Abroad."

9   Ah, but I know, for never April's
       shine,
         Nor passion gust of rain, nor all
           her flowers

Scattered in haste, were seen so
  sudden fine
    As she in various mood, on
      whom the powers
    Of happiest stars in fair conjunc-
      tion smiled
    To bless the birth of April's dar-
      ling child.

JAMES RUSSELL LOWELL (1819–1891),
U.S. author. "An April Birthday at Sea."

10   Bare twigs in April enhance our
       pleasure;
         We know the good time is yet to
           come.

     · · · · · · · · · · · · · ·

     Bare twigs in Autumn are signs for
       sadness;
         We feel the good time is well-
           nigh past.

WILLIAM ALLINGHAM (1824–1899),
Irish author. "Winter."

11   'Tis April again in my garden, again
       the grey stone-wall
         Is prankt with yellow alyssum
           and lilac aubrey-cresses;
         Half-hidden the mavis caroleth
           in the tassely birchen tresses
     And awhile on the sunny air a
       cuckoo tuneth his call.

ROBERT SEYMOUR BRIDGES (1844–
1930), English poet. "To Francis Jammes."

12   April is the cruellest month, breed-
       ing
     Lilacs out of the dead land, mixing
     Memory and desire, stirring
     Dull roots with spring rain.

T. S. ELIOT (1888–1965), Anglo-American
poet and critic. The Waste Land ("The Burial of
the Dead") (1922).

13   It is not enough that yearly, down
       this hill,
     April

Comes like an idiot, babbling and
strewing flowers.

EDNA ST. VINCENT MILLAY (1892–
1950), U.S. poet. "Spring."

14 O April, full of blood, full of
breath, have pity upon us!
Pale, where the winter like a stone
has been lifted away, we emerge
like yellow grass.
Be for a moment quiet, buffet us
not, have pity upon us,
Till the green come back into the
vein, till the giddiness pass.

EDNA ST. VINCENT MILLAY (1892–
1950), U.S. poet. "Northern April."

May

1 I incline to think that the elders
[maiores] gave their own name to
the month of May: they considered
the interests of their own class. . . .
No slight proof of the proposed
honour is furnished by the next
month, the month of June, which is
named after young men [juvenes].

OVID (43 B.C.–c. A.D. 18), Roman poet.
Fasti 5.75, in Ovid in Six Volumes (Loeb Classical Library), vol. 5, trans. James George Frazer (1989).

2 Is not thilke the mery moneth of
May,
When loue lads masken in fresh
aray?
How falles it then, we no merrier
bene,
Ylike as other, girt in gawdy greene?
Our bloncket liueryes bene all to
sadde,
For thilke same season, when all is
ycladd
With pleasaunce.

EDMUND SPENSER (1552?–1599), En-
glish poet and courtier. "Maye," The Shephear-
des Calendar (1579).

"Bloncket liueryes" are gray coats worn by the
shepherds.

3 Then while time serves, and we are
but decaying,
Come, my Corinna! come, let's goe
a Maying.

ROBERT HERRICK (1591–1674), English
poet and clergyman. "Corinna's Going A-May-
ing."

4 Hee that is in a towne in May lo-
seth his spring.

GEORGE HERBERT (1593–1633), English
poet and Anglican priest. Outlandish Proverbs,
no. 988 (1640).

5 Hail bounteous May that dost inspire
Mirth and youth and warm desire!

JOHN MILTON (1608–1674), English
poet. "Song: On May Morning."

6 We in thought will join your
throng,
Ye that pipe and ye that play,
Ye that through your hearts today
Feel the gladness of the May!

WILLIAM WORDSWORTH (1770–
1850), English poet. "Ode: Intimations of Im-
mortality from Recollections of Early Childhood."

7 May is lilac here in New England,
May is a thrush singing "Sun up!"
on a tip-top ash-tree,
May is white clouds behind pine-
trees
Puffed out and marching upon a
blue sky.
May is a green as no other,
May is much sun through small
leaves,
May is soft earth,
And apple-blossoms,
And windows open to a South
wind.

AMY LOWELL (1874–1925), U.S. poet. "Lilacs."

8 May is a perfect time to be in Tuscany—a time when it's still not too hot for a *contessa* to spend some time next to the pool, gazing approvingly over the vineyards that surround her.

CALVIN TRILLIN (b. 1935), U.S. author. *Travels with Alice* (chapter 15, "Special Occasion") (1989).

June

1 Oh for boyhood's time of June,
Crowding years in one brief moon,
When all things I heard or saw,
Me, their master, waited for.

JOHN GREENLEAF WHITTIER (1807–1892), U.S. poet. "The Barefoot Boy."

2 The end has come, as come it must
    To all things; in these sweet June
    days
The teacher and the scholar trust
    Their parting feet to separate
    ways.

JOHN GREENLEAF WHITTIER (1807–1892), U.S. poet. "At School-Close, Bowdoin Street, Boston, 1877."

3 June comes in with roses in her hand, but very often with a thick shawl on her shoulders, and a bad cold in her head.

OLIVER WENDELL HOLMES (1809–1894), U.S. author and physician. "The Seasons," *Pages from an Old Volume of Life: A Collection of Essays, 1857–1881* (1891).

4 Too young for love?
    Ah, say not so,
While daisies bloom and tulips glow!
June soon will come with lengthened day
To practise all love learned in May.

OLIVER WENDELL HOLMES (1809–1894), U.S. author and physician. "Too Young for Love."

5 And what is so rare as a day in
    June?
    Then, if ever, come perfect days;
Then Heaven tries earth if it be in
    tune,
    And over it softly her warm ear
    lays:
Whether we look, or whether we
    listen,
We hear life murmur, or see it glisten.

JAMES RUSSELL LOWELL (1819–1891), U.S. author. "The Vision of Sir Launfal."

6 June the month of months
    Flowers and fruitage brings too,
When green trees spread shadiest boughs,
    When each wild bird sings too.

CHRISTINA ROSSETTI (1830–1894), English poet. "June."

7 How the wind howls this morn
About the end of May,
And drives June on apace
To mock the world forlorn
And the world's joy passed
    away.

WILLIAM MORRIS (1834–1896), English author, artist, and social reformer. "The End of May."

Morris here seems to make a case for seeing May and June as cruel months.

8 What is one to say about June—the time of perfect young summer, the fulfillment of the promise of earlier months, and with as yet no sign to remind one that its fresh young beauty will ever fade?

GERTRUDE JEKYLL (1843–1932), English gardener. "Rain After Drought," *Home and Garden* (1900); reprinted in *The Writer in the Garden*, ed. Jane Garmey (1999).

Jekyll is sometimes referred to as the "first lady of modern garden design."

9   Ah! how sweet to seem, love,
      Drugged and half aswoon
   With this luscious dream, love,
      In the heart of June.

JAMES WHITCOMB RILEY (1849–1916), U.S. poet. "In the Heart of June."

July

1   I know of nothing that makes one feel more complacent, in these July days, than to have his vegetables from his own garden. What an effect it has on the market-man and the butcher! It is a kind of declaration of independence.

CHARLES DUDLEY WARNER (1829–1900), U.S. author. *My Summer in a Garden* ("What I Know About Gardening: Tenth Week") (1870).

2   Between April's youthful optimism and September's mature acceptance comes July; characterized both by longing and by hope, it constitutes a sort of horticultural midlife crisis.

JOE ECK and WAYNE WINTERROWD, U.S. landscapers and authors. "July," *A Year at North Hill: Four Seasons in a Vermont Garden* (1995); reprinted in *The Writer in the Garden*, ed. Jane Garmey (1999).

August

1   It is now August, and the sun is somewhat towards his declination, yet such is his heat as hardeneth the soft clay, dries up the standing ponds, withereth the sappy leaves, and scorcheth the skin of the naked.

NICHOLAS BRETON (c. 1535–c.1626), English author. *Fantastics: Serving for a Perpetual Prognostication* (1626).

2   In these golden latter August days, Nature has come to a serene equilibrium. Having flowered and fruited, she is enjoying herself. I can see how things are going: it is a down-hill business after this; but, for the time being, it is like swinging in a hammock,—such a delicious air, such a graceful repose!

CHARLES DUDLEY WARNER (1829–1900), U.S. author. *My Summer in a Garden* ("Fourteenth Week") (1870).

3   That August time it was delight
   To watch the red moons wane to white
   'Twixt grey seamed stems of apple-trees;
   A sense of heavy harmonies
   Grew on the growth of patient night,
   More sweet than shapen music is.

ALGERNON CHARLES SWINBURNE (1837–1909), English poet. "August."

4   . . . throbbing on and on, the pulse of heat
      Increases—reaches—passes fever's height,
   And Day slinks into slumber, cool and sweet,
      Within the arms of Night.

JAMES WHITCOMB RILEY (1849–1916), U.S. poet. "August."

5   When August days are hot an' dry,
   When burning copper is the sky,
   I'd rather fish than feast or fly
   In airy realms serene and high.

PAUL LAURENCE DUNBAR (1872–1906), U.S. poet. "In August."

6   I'm as corny as Kansas in August.

OSCAR HAMMERSTEIN (1895–1960), U.S. lyricist and librettist. "A Wonderful Guy," from the musical *South Pacific* (1949).

7   . . . lucky August, best of months
    For us, as for that Roman once—
    For you're a Leo, same as me
    (Isn't it comforting to be
    So lordly, selfish, vital, strong?

    PHILIP LARKIN (1922–1985), English
    poet and critic. "Dear CHARLES, My Muse,
    Asleep or Dead."

September

1   Up from the meadows rich with
    corn,
    Clear in the cool September morn,

    The clustered spires of Frederick
    stand
    Green-walled by the hills of Mary-
    land.

    Round about them orchards sweep,
    Apple and peach tree fruited deep,

    Fair as the garden of the Lord
    To the eyes of the famished rebel
    horde.

    JOHN GREENLEAF WHITTIER (1807–
    1892), U.S. poet. "Barbara Frietchie."

2   Now thin mists temper the slow-
    ripening beams
    Of the September sun: his golden
    gleams
    On gaudy flowers shine, that prank
    the rows
    Of high-grown hollyhocks, and all
    tall shows
    That Autumn flaunteth in his bushy
    bowers.

    ROBERT BRIDGES (1844–1930), English
    poet. "The Garden in September."

October

1   Can't tell what it is about
    Old October knocks me out!—

I sleep well enough at night—
And the blamedest appetite
Ever mortal man possessed,—

JAMES WHITCOMB RILEY (1849–
1916), U.S. poet. "Old October."

2   The trees are in their autumn
    beauty,
    The woodland paths are dry,
    Under the October twilight the wa-
    ter
    Mirrors a still sky. . . .

    WILLIAM BUTLER YEATS (1865–1939),
    Irish poet. "The Wild Swans at Coole."

3   I cannot but remember
       When the year grows old—
    October—November—
       How she disliked the cold!

    EDNA ST. VINCENT MILLAY (1892–
    1950), U.S. poet. "When the Year Grows
    Old."

4   Bittersweet October. The mellow,
    messy, leaf-kicking, perfect pause
    between the opposing miseries of
    summer and winter.

    CAROL BISHOP HIPPS, U.S. garden
    writer and photographer. "October," *In a
    Southern Garden* (1995), and reprinted in *The
    Writer in the Garden*, ed. Jane Garmey (1999).

November

1   November's sky is chill and drear,
    November's leaf is red and sear.

    SIR WALTER SCOTT (1771–1832), Scot-
    tish author. *Marmion* (introduction to canto 1)
    (1808).

2   Autumn I love thy latter end to
    view
    In cold novembers day so bleak and
    bare
    When like lifes dwindld thread
    worn nearly thro

Wi lingering pottering pace and
  head bleachd bare
Thou like an old man bids the
  world adieu

JOHN CLARE (1793–1864), English poet.
"Written in November."

3   Talk not of sad November, when a
    day
      Of warm, glad sunshine fills the
        sky of noon,
      And a wind, borrowed from
        some morn of June,
    Stirs the brown grasses and the leaf-
    less spray.

JOHN GREENLEAF WHITTIER (1807–
1892), U.S. poet. "A Day."

4   This sunlight shames November
    where he grieves
      In dead red leaves, and will not
      let him shun
    The day, though bough with
    bough be over-run.

DANTE GABRIEL ROSSETTI (1828–
1882), English poet and painter. *House of Life*,
sonnet 69, "Autumn Idleness."

5   The world is tired, the year is old,
   The faded leaves are glad to die.

SARA TEASDALE (1884–1933), U.S. poet.
"November."

6   Apart from the pleasures of gardening, November has beauty of its
   own. The Saxons called it the wind-
   month, for then the fishermen drew
   up their boats and abandoned fishing till the spring; it was called the
   slaughter-month, too, when pigs
   and cattle were salted down for
   preservation throughout the winter.

VICTORIA (OR VITA) SACKVILLE-
WEST (1892–1962), English novelist and
poet. *Country Notes* ("Wind-month") (1940).

7   While November numbly collapses,
   this beech tree, heavy as death
   on the lawn, braces for throat-
   cutting ice, bandaging snow.

EDWIN HONIG (b. 1919), U.S. poet. "November Through a Giant Copper Beech."

December

1   In drear nighted December,
      Too happy, happy tree,
    Thy branches ne'er remember
      Their green felicity—
    The north cannot undo them
      With a sleety whistle through
      them,
    Nor frozen thawings glue them
      From budding at the prime.

JOHN KEATS (1795–1821), English poet.
"In Drear Nighted December."

2   The sun that brief December day
   Rose cheerless over hills of gray,
   And, darkly circled, gave at noon
   A sadder light than waning moon.

JOHN GREENLEAF WHITTIER (1807–
1892), U.S. poet. "Snow-Bound: A Winter
Idyl."

3   Yet my heart loves December's
    smile
   As much as July's golden beam;
   Then let us sit and watch the while
   The blue ice curdling on the
   stream.

EMILY JANE BRONTË (1818–1848), English author. "How Still, How Happy! Those
are Words."

Spring

1   In the spring time, the only
      pretty ring time,
    When birds do sing, hey ding a
    ding, ding.
    Sweet lovers love the spring.

WILLIAM SHAKESPEARE (1564–1616), English poet and dramatist. *As You Like It* 5.3.18–20.

Sung in the Forest of Arden by two of the banished pages of the Duke, to honor the marriage of Touchstone and Audrey.

2 Spring, the sweet Spring, is the
     year's pleasant king;
   Then blooms each thing, then
     maids dance in a ring,
   Cold doth not sting, the pretty
     birds do sing.

THOMAS NASHE (1567–1601), English poet. "Spring."

3 Sweet spring, full of sweet dayes
     and roses,
   A box where sweets compacted lie;
   My musick shows ye have your
     closes,
               And all must die.

GEORGE HERBERT (1593–1633), English poet and Anglican priest. "Vertue."

4 Now do a choir of chirping min-
     strels bring,
   In triumph to the world, the youth-
     ful spring.

THOMAS CAREW (1594–1640), English poet. "The Spring."

5 Still let my Song a nobler Note as-
     sume
   And sing th' infusive Force of
     Spring on Man;
   When Heaven and Earth, as if con-
     tending, vye
   To raise his Being, and serene his
     Soul.
   Can he forbear to join the general
     Smile
   Of Nature? Can fierce Passions vex
     his Breast,
   While every Gale is Peace, and
     every Grove
   Is Melody?

JAMES THOMSON (1700–1748), Scottish poet. "Spring," *The Seasons*.

6 The Sun does arise,
   And make happy the skies;
   The merry bells ring
   To welcome the Spring.

WILLIAM BLAKE (1757–1827), English poet and artist. "The Ecchoing Green."

7   What a strange thing,
     To be thus alive
               Beneath the cherry-
                 blossoms!

ISSA (1763–1827), Japanese poet. In R. H. Blyth, trans. *Haiku*, 4 vols. (1949).

Blyth notes: "Of all the multitude of strange [things] in this mysterious world or ours, the strangest is the simple fact of our own existence."

8 The country ever has a lagging
     Spring,
       Waiting for May to call its vio-
         lets forth,
   And June its roses.

   . . . .

   Within the city's bound the time of
     flowers
       Comes earlier. Let a mild and
         sunny day,
   Such as full often, for a few bright
     hours,
       Breathes through the sky of
         March the airs of May,
   Shine on our roofs and chase the
     wintry gloom—
       And lo! our borders glow with
         sudden bloom.

WILLIAM CULLEN BRYANT (1794–1878), U.S. poet and editor. "Spring in Town."

9 The Spring! I shrink and shudder at
     her name!
       For why, I find her breath a bit-
         ter blighter!

And suffer from her *blows* as if they came
  From Spring the Fighter.

THOMAS HOOD (1799–1845), English poet. "Spring: A New Version."

10 For thou, O Spring! canst renovate
All that high God did first create.
Be still his arm and architect,
Rebuild the ruin, mend defect;
Chemist to vamp old worlds with new,
Coat sea and sky with heavenlier blue.

RALPH WALDO EMERSON (1803–1882), U.S. author. "May-Day."

11 . . . in my breast
  Spring wakens too, and my regret
  Becomes an April violet,
And buds and blossoms like the rest.

ALFRED, LORD TENNYSON (1809–1892), English poet. *In Memoriam A.H.H.* 115 (1850).

Throughout the poem Tennyson mourns the loss of his friend and charts the progress of his grief over the course of several years of changing seasons.

12 Out of the city, far away
  With Spring to-day!
Where copses tufted with primrose
  Give me repose,
Wood-sorrel and wild violet
  Soothe my soul's fret.

WILLIAM ALLINGHAM (1824–1889), Irish author. "A Holiday."

13 A Light exists in Spring
Not present on the Year
At any other period—
When March is scarcely here

A Color stands abroad
On Solitary Fields

That Science cannot overtake
But Human Nature feels.

EMILY DICKINSON (1830–1886), U.S. poet. "A Light exists in Spring."

14 For winter's rains and ruins are over,
  And all the season of snows and sins;
The days dividing lover and lover,
  The light that loses, the night that wins;
And time remembered is grief forgotten,
And frosts are slain and flowers begotten,
And in green underwood and cover
  Blossom by blossom the spring begins.

ALGERNON CHARLES SWINBURNE (1837–1909), English poet. *Atalanta in Calydon* (first chorus).

15 Spring goeth all in white
Crowned with milk-white may:
In fleecy flocks of light
O'er heaven the white clouds stray:

ROBERT BRIDGES (1844–1930), English poet. *Shorter Poems* (book 4, poem 8).

16 Nothing is so beautiful as Spring—
  When weeds, in wheels, shoot
    long and lovely and lush;
  Thrush's eggs look little low
    heavens, and thrush
Through the echoing timber does
  so rinse and wring
The ear, it strikes like lightnings to
  hear him sing.

GERARD MANLEY HOPKINS (1844–1889), English poet. "Spring."

17 I am amazed at this spring, this conflagration
Of green fires lit on the soil of earth, this blaze

Of growing, these smoke-puffs that
  puff in wild gyration,
Faces of people blowing across my
  gaze!

D. H. LAWRENCE (1885–1930), English
author. "The Enkindled Spring."

18 I haven't seen a crocus or a rose-
    bud,
      or a robin on the wing,
    But I feel so gay in a melancholy
    way
      that it might as well be spring.

OSCAR HAMMERSTEIN (1895–1960),
U.S. lyricist and librettist. "It Might As Well Be
Spring," from the musical *State Fair* (1945).

19 Spring, of all seasons most gratui-
    tous,
    Is fold of untaught flower, is race of
    water,
    Is earth's most multiple, excited
    daughter;

    And those she has least use for see
    her best.

PHILIP LARKIN (1922–1985), English
poet and critic. "Spring."

Summer

1 Sumer is icumen in,
   Lhude sing cuccu!
   Groweth sed, and bloweth med,
   And springth the wude nu—
   Sing cuccu!

ANONYMOUS. "The Cuckoo Song" (c.
1250).

2 All-Conquering Heat, o intermit
   thy Wrath!
   And on my throbbing Temples potent thus
   Beam not so fierce! Incessant still
   you flow,

And still another fervent Flood succeeds,
Pour'd on the Head profuse. In
  vain I sigh
And restless turn, and look around
  for Night.

JAMES THOMSON (1700–1748), Scottish
poet. "Summer," *The Seasons.*

3 Rich music breaths in summers
     every sound
   And in her harmony of varied
     greens
   Woods meadows hedgrows corn-
     fields all around
     Much beauty intervenes
   Filling with harmony the ear and
   eye
     While oer the mingling scenes
     Far spreads the laughing sky

JOHN CLARE (1793–1864), English poet.
"Summer Images."

4 What is more gentle than a wind in
     summer?
   What is more soothing than the
     pretty hummer
   That stays one moment in an open
     flower,
   And buzzes cheerily from bower to
     bower?

JOHN KEATS (1795–1821), English poet.
"Sleep and Poetry."

5 Now the roses are coming into
   bloom; the azalea, wild honey-
   suckle, is sweetening the roadsides,
   the laurels are beginning to blow;
   the white lilies are getting ready to
   open; the fireflies are seen now and
   then, flitting across the darkness;
   the katydids, the grasshoppers, the
   crickets make themselves heard; the
   bullfrogs utter their tremendous
   voices, and the full chorus of birds
   make the air vocal with its melody.

OLIVER WENDELL HOLMES (1809–1894), U.S. author and physician. "The Seasons," *Pages from an Old Volume of Life: A Collection of Essays, 1857–1881* (1891).

6 Summer is coming, summer is
   coming.
     I know it, I know it, I know it.
   Light again, leaf again, life again,
     love again,
     Yes, my wild little Poet.

ALFRED, LORD TENNYSON (1809–1892), English poet. "The Throstle."

7 There is a temperate zone in the mind, between luxurious indolence and exacting work; and it is to this region, just between laziness and labor, that summer reading belongs.

HENRY WARD BEECHER (1813–1887), U.S. clergyman. "Eyes and Ears" (1866), in *Beecher as a Humorist: Selections from the Published Works*, ed. Eleanor Kirk (1887).

8 As imperceptibly as Grief
   The Summer lapsed away—
   Too imperceptible at last
   To seem like Perfidy—

EMILY DICKINSON (1830–1886), U.S. poet. "As imperceptibly as Grief."

9 . . . while you gasp and pant
   And try to cool yourself—and
     can't—
   With soda, cream and lemonade,
   The heat at ninety in the shade,—
   Just calmly sit and ponder o'er
   These same degrees, with ninety
     more
   On top of them, and so concede
   The weather now is cool indeed!

JAMES WHITCOMB RILEY (1849–1916), U.S. poet. "At Ninety in the Shade."

10 In winter I get up at night
    And dress by yellow candle-light.
    In summer, quite the other way,
    I have to go to bed by day.

ROBERT LOUIS STEVENSON (1850–1894), Scottish author. "Bed in Summer," *A Child's Garden of Verses* (1885).

11 In the good old summer time,
    In the good old summer time,
    Strolling thro' the shady lanes with
      your baby mine;
    You hold her hand and she holds
      yours,
    And that's a very good sign
    That she's your tootsey wootsey
    In the good old summer time.

RON SHIELDS, U.S. lyricist. "In the Good Old Summer Time."

12 When th' summer landscape takes on a scuffed an' faded appearance like a over exposed ten dollar suit we know we are face t' face with dog days, that midsummer season o' th' year when all livin' things jist sorter peter out an' langour rules supreme in shop an' mart an' field.

KIN HUBBARD (1868–1930), U.S. humorist. "Dog Days," *The Best of Kin Hubbard: Abe Martin's Saying and Wisecracks, Abe's Neighbors, His Almanack, Comic Drawings*, ed. David S. Hawes (1984).

13 'Tis wealth enough of joy for me
    In summer time to simply be.

PAUL LAURENCE DUNBAR (1872–1906), U.S. poet. "In Summer Time."

14 We're a couple of sports,
      The pride of the tennis courts,
    In June, July, and August,
      We look cute when we're
        dressed in shorts.

IRVING BERLIN (1888–1989), U.S. songwriter. "A Couple of Swells," as performed in the musical *Easter Parade* (1948).

15 This is summer, unmistakably. One can always tell when one sees schoolteachers hanging about the

streets idly, looking like cannibals during a shortage of missionaries.

ROBERTSON DAVIES (1913–1995), Canadian author. "Of Schoolteachers," *The Table Talk of Samuel Marchbanks* (1949).

16   Summers are the best. And I figured summer was my best time for meeting someone, too, because in the summer people are looking for someone to snuggle up with for the winter. And because in the summer I could take off my shirt.

ANDREW TOBIAS (JOHN REID) (b. 1947), U.S. author. *The Best Little Boy in the World Grows Up* (1998).

Tobias is commenting on trying to meet a man on Fire Island in New York.

𝒜utumn

1   No spring nor summer beauty hath such grace
As I have seen in one autumnal face.

JOHN DONNE (1572–1631), English poet, clergyman, and courtier. "Elegy 9: The Autumnal."

2   Autumnall Agues are long, or mortall.

GEORGE HERBERT (1593–1633), English poet and Anglican priest. *Outlandish Proverbs*, no. 148 (1640).

3   The pale descending Year, yet pleasing still,
A gentler Mood inspires; for now the Leaf
Incessant rustles from the mournful Grove,
Oft startling such as, studious, walk below,
And slowly circles thro' the waving Air.

JAMES THOMSON (1700–1748), Scottish poet. "Autumn," *The Seasons*.

4   O Autumn, laden with fruit, and stained
With the blood of the grape, pass not, but sit
Beneath my shady roof, there thou may'st rest,
And tune thy jolly voice to my fresh pipe;
And all the daughters of the year shall dance!
Sing now the lusty song of fruits and flowers.

WILLIAM BLAKE (1757–1827), English poet and artist. "To Autumn."

From the volume *Poetical Sketches* (1783).

5   Yet, in these autumn days when Nature expires,
Here, in these veiled scenes, I find more attractions;
It is a friend's sad goodbye; it is the last smile
From lips that death is going to close forever!

ALPHONSE DE LAMARTINE (1790–1869), French author. "Autumn," *Poetical Meditations*, tr. Gervase Hittle (1993).

6   O wild West Wind, thou breath of Autumn's being,
Thou, from whose unseen presence the leaves dead
Are driven, like ghosts from an enchanter fleeing,

Yellow, and black, and pale, and hectic red,
Pestilence-stricken multitudes. . . .

PERCY BYSSHE SHELLEY (1792–1822), English poet. "Ode to the West Wind."

7   The warm sun is failing, the bleak wind is wailing,
The bare boughs are sighing, the pale flowers are dying,
And the Year

On the earth her death-bed, in a
shroud of leaves dead,
   Is lying. . . .

PERCY BYSSHE SHELLEY (1792–1822),
English poet. "Autumn: A Dirge."

8   He hath his autumn ports
And havens of repose, when his
   tired wings
      Are folded up, and he content
      to look
On mists in idleness: to let fair
   things
      Pass by unheeded as a threshold
      brook.

JOHN KEATS (1795–1821), English poet.
"Four Seasons Fill the Measure of the Year."

"He" here refers to "man" in the collective
sense. Keats compares the seasons of man to
the seasons of the year, and here describes the
contentment of middle age.

9   Season of mists and mellow fruit-
fulness,
      Close bosom-friend of the ma-
      turing sun;
Conspiring with him how to load
   and bless
      With fruit the vines that round
      the thatch-eves run
To bend with apples the moss'd
   cottage-trees,
      And fill all fruit with ripeness to
      the core.

JOHN KEATS (1795–1821), English poet.
"To Autumn."

10   There the ash-tree leaves do vall
      In the wind a-blowen cwolder,
An' my childern, tall or small,
      Since last Fall be woone year
      wolder;
Woone year wolder, woone year
   dearer.

WILLIAM BARNES (1801–1886), English
poet, scholar, and clergyman. "Leaves A-Val-
len."

Barnes writes in the dialect of his native Dor-
set.

11   The gentle wind, a sweet and passionate wooer,
Kisses the blushing leaf, and stirs
   up life
Within the solemn woods of ash
   deep-crimsoned,
And silver beech, and maple yellow-
leaved,
Where Autumn, like a faint old
   man, sits down
By the wayside a-weary.

HENRY WADSWORTH LONGFELLOW
(1807–1882), U.S. poet. "Autumn."

12   Gone hath the Spring, with all its
   flowers,
      And gone the Summer's pomp
      and show,
And Autumn, in his leafless bowers,
   Is waiting for the Winter's snow.

JOHN GREENLEAF WHITTIER (1807–
1892), U.S. poet. "Autumn Thoughts."

13   The year is getting to feel rich, for
his golden fruits are ripening fast,
and he has a large balance in the
barns, which are his banks. The
members of his family have found
out that he is well to do in the
world. September is dressing herself
in show of dahlias and splendid
marigolds and starry zinnias. October, the extravagant sister, has ordered an immense amount of the
most gorgeous forest tapestry for
her grand reception.

OLIVER WENDELL HOLMES (1809–
1894), U.S. author and physician. "The Seasons," *Pages from an Old Volume of Life: A
Collection of Essays, 1857–1881* (1891).

14   The foliage has been losing its
freshness through the month of August, and here and there a yellow

leaf shows itself like the first gray
hair amidst the locks of a beauty
who has seen one season too many.

OLIVER WENDELL HOLMES (1809–
1894), U.S. author and physician. "The Seasons," *Pages from An Old Volume: A Collection of Essays, 1857–1881* (1881).

15 The air is damp, and hushed, and
  close,
    As a sick man's room when he tak-
    eth repose
      An hour before death;
  My very heart faints and my whole
  soul grieves
  At the moist rich smell of the rot-
  ting leaves.

ALFRED, LORD TENNYSON (1809–
1892), English poet. "Song [A spirit haunts the
year's last hours]."

A lyric written in Tennyson's youth at So-
mersby and published in 1830.

16 Tears, idle tears, I know not what
  they mean,
  Tears from the depth of some divine despair
  Rise in the heart, and gather to the
  eyes,
  In looking on the happy Autumn-
  fields,
  And thinking of the days that are
  no more.

ALFRED, LORD TENNYSON (1809–
1892), English poet. *The Princess,* section 4.

Lines presented as a diverting song by one of
the maidens. Tennyson wrote this lyric probably near Tintern Abbey. His friend Arthur Hallam, the subject of Tennyson's *In Memorian
A.H.H.,* was buried nearby.

17 Oh, good gigantic smile o' the
  brown old earth,
    This autumn morning! How he
    sets his bones
  To bask i' the sun, and thrusts out
  knees and feet.

From the ripple to run over in its
  mirth

ROBERT BROWNING (1812–1889), English poet. *James Lee's Wife* (section 7,
"Among the Rocks").

The speaker here conveys the message that
men must love freely while on earth, not
counting gains and losses, but opening themselves to experience, like the earth soaking up
the autumn sun.

18 Fall, leaves, fall; die, flowers, away;
  Lengthen night and shorten day;
  Every leaf speaks bliss to me
  Fluttering from the autumn tree.

EMILY JANE BRONTË (1818–1848), English author. "Fall, leaves, fall."

19 Coldly, sadly, descends
  The autumn-evening. The field
  Strewn with its dank yellow drifts
  Of wither'd leaves, and the elms
  Fade into dimness apace,
  Silent;—hardly a shout
  From a few boys late in their play!

MATTHEW ARNOLD (1822–1888), English poet and critic. "Rugby Chapel, November 1857."

Published 1867.

20 Now Autumn's fire burns slowly
  along the woods,
    And day by day the dead leaves
    fall and melt,
    And night by night the monitory
    blast
    Wails in the key-hole, telling how
    it pass'd
  O'er empty fields, or upland soli-
  tudes,
    Or grim wide wave; and now the
    power is felt
  Of melancholy, tenderer in its
  moods
    Than any joy indulgent Summer
    dealt.

WILLIAM ALLINGHAM (1824–1889),
Irish author. "Autumnal Sonnet."

21 Márgarét áre you gríeving
Over Goldengrove unleaving?
Leáves, líke the things of man, you
With your fresh thoughts care for,
    can you?

GERARD MANLEY HOPKINS (1844–
1889), English poet. "Spring and Fall."

22 This was one of those perfect New
England days in late summer where
the spirit of autumn takes a first
stealthy flight, like a spy, through
the ripening country-side, and, with
feigned sympathy for those who
droop with August heat, puts her
cool cloak of bracing air about leaf
and flower and human shoulders.

SARAH ORNE JEWETT (1849–1909),
U.S. author. "The Courting of Sister Wilby."

23 But the air's so appetizin'; and the
    landscape through the haze
Of a crisp and sunny morning of
    the airly autumn days
Is a pictur' that no painter has the
    colorin' to mock—
When the frost is on the punkin
    and the fodder's in the shock.

JAMES WHITCOMB RILEY (1849–
1916), U.S. poet. "When the Frost is on the
Punkin."

24 It almost seems as if autumn were
the true creator, more creative than
the spring, which is too even-toned,
more creative when it comes with
its will-to-change and shatters the
much too ready-made, self-satisfied
and really almost bourgeois-com-
placent image of summer.

RAINER MARIA RILKE (1857–1926),
German poet. Letter to Clara Rilke, 12 August
1904, Selected Letters: 1902–1926, trans. R. F.
C. Hull (1988).

25 There is the moon;
And white and yellow chrysanthe-
    mums;
    Autumn draws to its close.

SHIKI (1869–1902), Japanese poet. In R.
H. Blyth, trans., Haiku, vol. 3 (1949).

Blyth notes: "Surprisingly little is needed for
happiness, for the good life, for the way of
Haiku. A great deal of wisdom, and the moon
and chrysanthemums white and yellow,—and
autumn is passing, life is being lived."

26 The leaves fall early this autumn, in
    wind.
The paired butterflies are already
    yellow with August
Over the grass in the West garden;
They hurt me. I grow older.

EZRA POUND (1885–1972), U.S. poet.
"The River-Merchant's Wife: A Letter."

27 There comes a morning, always, at
this time of year when one awakes
to the realisation that one's knees
and the tip of one's nose are unex-
pectedly cold, and, still drowsy,
scrabbles to regain the blankets one
had flung off during the earlier part
of the night; then, aroused to full
consciousness, leaps from bed to
gaze out of the window. What has
happened? The familiar summer aspect has changed.

VICTORIA (OR VITA) SACKVILLE-
WEST (1892–1962), English novelist and
poet. Country Notes ("Between Two Seasons")
(1940).

28 . . . I know that Beauty must ail
    and die,
And will be born again,—but ah, to
    see
Beauty stiffened, staring up at the
    sky!
Oh, Autumn! Autumn!—What is
    the Spring to me?

EDNA ST. VINCENT MILLAY (1892–
1950), U.S. poet. "The Death of Autumn."

Winter

1   You naked trees, whose shady
        leaues are lost,
    Wherein the byrds were wont to
        build their bowre:
    And now are clothd with mosse
        and hoary frost,
    Instede of bloosmes, wherewith
        your buds did flowre:
    I see your teares, that from your
        boughes doe raine,
    Whose drops in drery ysicles re-
        maine.

    EDMUND SPENSER (1552?–1599), En-
    glish poet and courtier. "Januarye," *The She-
    pheardes Calendar* (1579).

2   . . . winter tames man, woman, and
        beast. . . .

    WILLIAM SHAKESPEARE (1564–1616),
    English poet and dramatist. *The Taming of the
    Shrew* 4.1.20.

    Grumio describes the effect of the cold on the
    hot temper of Kate, the wife of his master Pe-
    truchio and the "shrew" of the play's title.

3   Blow, blow, thou winter wind,
    Thou art not so unkind
        As man's ingratitude.

    WILLIAM SHAKESPEARE (1564–1616),
    English poet and dramatist. *As You Like It*
    2.7.174.

4   How like a winter hath my absence
        been
    From thee, the pleasure of the fleet-
        ing year!
    What freezings have I felt, what
        dark days seen!
    What old December's bareness ev-
        erywhere!

    WILLIAM SHAKESPEARE (1564–1616),
    English poet and dramatist. Sonnet 97 ("How
    like a winter hath my absence been").

5   He that passeth a winters day es-
        capes an enemy.

    GEORGE HERBERT (1593–1633), English
    poet and Anglican priest. *Outlandish Proverbs,*
    no. 864 (1640).

6   Thus Winter falls,
    A heavy Gloom oppressive o'er the
        World,
    Thro' Nature shedding Influence
        malign,
    And rouses up the Seeds of dark
        Disease.
    The Soul of Man dies in him,
        loathing Life,
    And black with more than melan-
        choly Views.

    JAMES THOMSON (1700–1748), Scottish
    poet. "Winter," *The Seasons.*

7   My bones
    Feel the quilts;
        A frosty night

    BUSON (1715–1783), Japanese poet. In R.
    H. Blyth, trans. *Haiku,* vol. 4 (1949).

    Blyth notes: "The Japanese never had and
    never seemed to desire any means of being
    comfortably warm in winter. Rich and poor
    alike shivered from the end of autumn until the
    middle of spring. Especially the poets (who
    seem to have been indigent on the whole),
    more sensitive to the cold than ordinary peo-
    ple, spent many a night of grinding wretched-
    ness trying to sleep in spite of cold feet and
    thin shanks. The way in which Buson says,
    'My bones feel the quilts' instead of 'The quilts
    touched my bones' shows the activity of the
    supersensitiveness."

8   "The sweeping blast, the sky
        o'ercast,"
        The joyless winter day
    Let others fear, to me more dear
        Than all the pride of May:
    The tempest's howl, it soothes my
        soul,
        My griefs it seems to join;
    The leafless trees my fancy please,
        Their fate resembles mine!

    ROBERT BURNS (1759–1796), Scottish
    poet. "Winter: A Dirge."

Burns commented in his *First Common Place Book* that he loved to walk on "a cloudy winter day, and hear a stormy wind howling among the trees and raving o'er the plain," and that winter "is my best season for devotion; my mind is rapt up in a kind of enthusiasm to Him who, in the pompous language of Scripture, 'Walks on the wings of the wind.'"

9   The Frost performs its secret ministry,
Unhelped by any wind. The owlet's cry
Came loud—and hark, again! loud as before.
The inmates of my cottage, all at rest,
Have left me to that solitude, which suits
Abstruser musings. . . .

SAMUEL TAYLOR COLERIDGE (1772–1834), English poet and critic. "Frost at Midnight."

Coleridge, in this "conversation poem," describes his "abstruser musings" as on a cold winter night he cares for his infant son by the "thin blue flame" of his "low-burnt fire."

10   The English winter—ending in July,
To recommence in August.

GEORGE GORDON, LORD BYRON (1788–1824), English poet. *Don Juan* (canto 13, stanza 42).

11   As an earthquake rocks a corse
    In its coffin in the clay,
So White Winter, that rough nurse,
    Rocks the death-cold Year to-day;
Solemn Hours! wail aloud
For your mother in her shroud.

PERCY BYSSHE SHELLEY (1792–1822), English poet. "Dirge for the Year."

12   The ice-bound floods that still with rigour freeze
The snow clothd valley and the naked tree
These sympathising scenes my heart can please

Distress is theirs—and they resemble me.

JOHN CLARE (1793–1864), English poet. "To a Winter Scene."

13   Announced by all the trumpets of the sky,
Arrives the snow, and, driving o'er the fields,
Seems nowhere to alight: the whited air
Hides hills and woods, the river, and the heaven,
And veils the farm-house at the garden's end.

RALPH WALDO EMERSON (1803–1882), U.S. author. "The Snow-Storm."

14   He comes,—he comes,—the Frost Spirit
    comes! Let us meet him as we may,
And turn with the light of the parlor-fire
    his evil power away;
And gather closer the circle round, when
    that firelight dances high,
And laugh at the shriek of the baffled Fiend
    as his sounding wing goes by!

JOHN GREENLEAF WHITTIER (1807–1892), U.S. poet. "The Frost Spirit."

15   When there is nothing left of the winter snow but these ridges behind the stone walls, and a dingy drift here and there in a hollow, or in the woods, Winter has virtually resigned the icicle which is his sceptre.

OLIVER WENDELL HOLMES (1809–1894), U.S. author and physician. "The Seasons," *Pages from an Old Volume of Life: A Collection of Essays, 1857–1881* (1891).

16 Here comes Winter, savage as when he met the Pilgrims at Plymouth, Indian all over, his staff a naked splintery hemlock, his robe torn from the backs of bears and bisons, and fringed with wampum of rattling icicles, turning the ground he treads to ringing iron, and, like a mighty sower, casting his snow far and wide, over all hills and valleys and plains.

OLIVER WENDELL HOLMES (1809–1892), U.S. author and physician. "The Seasons," *Pages from an Old Volume of Life: A Collection of Essays 1857–1881* (1891).

Holmes reflects a nineteenth-century image of American Indians.

17 The frost is here,
And fuel is dear,
And woods are sear,
And fires burn clear,
And frost is here
And has bitten the heel of the going year.

ALFRED, LORD TENNYSON (1809–1892), English poet. "Winter," *The Window, or, The Song of the Wrens* (published privately in 1867, with music in 1870 and in 1874).

Apparently Tennyson liked this little song but was concerned about publishing it because he felt it was too light and might diminish his reputation.

18 The best fire in winter is made up of *exercise*, and the poorest of *whiskey*. He that keeps warm on liquor is like a man who pulls his house to pieces to feed the fireplace.

HENRY WARD BEECHER (1813–1887), U.S. clergyman. In *Plain and Pleasant Talk about Fruits, Flowers, and Farming* ("Almanac for the Year: Work for January") (1859), and reprinted in *Beecher As a Humorist: Selections from the Published Works of Henry Ward Beecher*, ed. Eleanor Kirk (1887).

19 There's a certain Slant of light,
Winter Afternoons—

That oppresses, like the Heft
Of Cathedral Tunes—

Heavenly Hurt, it gives us—
We can find no scar,
But internal difference,
Where the Meanings, are—

EMILY DICKINSON (1830–1886), U.S. poet. "There's a certain Slant of light."

20 The boughs, the boughs are bare enough
But earth has never felt the snow.
Frost-furred our ivies are and rough

With bills of rime the brambles shew
The hoarse leaves crawl on hissing ground
Because the sighing wind is low.

GERARD MANLEY HOPKINS (1844–1889), English poet. "Winter with the Gulf Stream."

Hopkins describes the effects of a mild winter.

21 When will you cease, O dismal days?
    When will you set me free?
For the frozen world and its desolate ways
    Are all unloved of me!

JAMES WHITCOMB RILEY (1849–1916), U.S. poet. "Shadow and Shine."

22 Winter is icumen in,
Lhude sing Goddamm,
Raineth drop and staineth slop,
And how the wind doth ramm!

EZRA POUND (1885–1972), U.S. poet. "Ancient Music."

A parody of "Sumer is icumen in." See Summer, quotation 1.

23 Midwinter spring is its own season
Sempiternal though sodden towards sundown,
Suspended in time, between pole and tropic.

When the short day is brightest,
  with frost and fire,
The brief sun flames the ice, on
  pond and ditches,
In windless cold that is the heart's
  heat.

T. S. ELIOT (1888–1965), Anglo-American poet. "Little Gidding," *Four Quartets*.

24 I leave this year as a man leaves
  wine,
Remembering the summer, bountiful, the good fall, the months mellow and full.
I sit in the northern room, in the
  dusk, the death of a year,
And watch it go down in thunder.

WILLIAM EVERSON (1912–1994), U.S. author. "Year's End."

25 That time of year you may in me
  behold
When Christmas trees are blazing
  on the walk,
Raging against stable snow and the
  cold
And low sky's bundled wash,
  deadwhite as chalk.

DELMORE SCHWARTZ (1913–1966), U.S. author. "The Winter Twilight, Glowing Black and Gold."

Schwartz echoes Shakespeare's Sonnet 73 "That time of year thou mayst in me behold / When yellow leaves, or none, or few, do hang / Upon those boughs which shake against the cold."

Occasionally

Back to School

1 Then the whining schoolboy, with
his satchel
And shining morning face, creeping
like snail
Unwillingly to school.

WILLIAM SHAKESPEARE (1564–1616),
English poet and dramatist. *As You Like It*
2.7.145–47.

Jacques here describes the second of the seven
stages of man.

2 A little learning is a dangerous
thing;
Drink deep, or taste not the Pierian
spring;
There shallow draughts intoxicate
the brain,
And drinking largely sobers us
again.

ALEXANDER POPE (1688–1744), English
poet. *An Essay on Criticism* (lines 215–18)
(1711).

3 I should, in fact, be averse to
boarding-schools, if it were for no
other reason than the unsettled
state of mind which the expectation
of the vacations produce. On these
the children's thoughts are fixed
with eager anticipating hopes, for,
at least, to speak with moderation,
half of the time, and when they arrive they are spent in total dissipation and beastly indulgence.

MARY WOLLSTONECRAFT (1759–
1797), English author and feminist. *A Vindication of the Rights of Woman* (chapter 12, "On
National Education") (1792).

4 Well do I remember how, on the
last day of the holidays, I used always to rise early, and think that I
had got twelve more whole hours
of happiness, and how those hours
used to pass me with mercifully

slow feet. . . . Three more hours!
. . . Sixty more minutes! . . .
Five! . . .

MAX BEERBOHM (1872–1956), English
critic, essayist and caricaturist. "Going Back to
School," *More* (1899).

Beerbohm describes seeing the envy "inscribed" on the face of a "very small, pale
boy" at Victoria Station. The boy's expression
reminds him of his own fifteen trips back to
school. He expresses his relief at having "no
construe of Xenophon to prepare . . . nor any
ode of Horace to learn, painfully, by heart."

5 Life at a vile boarding school is in
this way a good preparation for the
Christian life, that it teaches one to
live by hope. Even, in a sense, by
faith; for at the beginning of each
term, home and the holidays are so
far off that it is as hard to realize
them as to realize heaven. Tomorrow's geometry blots out the distant
end of term as tomorrow's operation may blot out the hope of Paradise.

C. S. LEWIS (1898–1963), English author.
Surprised by Joy: The Shape of My Early Life
(chapter 2, "Concentration Camp") (1955).

6 On the first day of school, my children said to me, "Aren't you glad
that our education's free?"

ERMA BOMBECK (1927–1996), U.S. hu-
morist and newspaper columnist. "The Twelve
Days of School" (September 1975), in *Forever,
Erma: America's Best-Loved Writing from
America's Favorite Humorist* (1996).

The words here, which recall the Christmas
carol "The Twelve Days of Christmas," lead
into a litany of expenses—everything from
Crayolas to cameras—required by "free
schools."

7 Autumn has become my favorite
time of year. It took a while for
negative associations with the beginning of the school year to wane,
for the golden sunlight and foliage

to stop conjuring up the intestinal butterflies that went along with similarly toned school buses lurching down the street.

LAUREN SPRINGER, U.S. author and newspaper columnist. In *The Undaunted Garden* (1994), and reprinted in *The Writer in the Garden*, ed. Jane Garmey (1999).

Taking Exams

1   I should be inclined to say that as plants are stifled with too much moisture, and lamps with too much oil, so too much study and matter stifles the action of the mind, which, being caught and entangled in a great variety of things, may lose the ability to break loose, and be kept bent and huddled down by its burden.

MICHEL EYQUEM DE MONTAIGNE (1533–1589), French essayist. "Of Pedantry," book 1, essay 25 (1578–80), *The Complete Essays of Montaigne*, trans. Donald M. Frame (1976; originally published 1958).

2   Some books are to be tasted, others to be swallowed, and some few to be chewed and digested; that is, some books are to be read only in parts; others to be read, but not curiously; and some few to be read wholly, and with diligence and attention. Some books also may be read by deputy, and extracts made of them by others, but that would be only in the less important arguments, and the meaner sort of books; else distilled books are, like common distilled waters, flashy things.

FRANCIS BACON (1561–1626), English philosopher, essayist, and statesman. "Of Studies," *Essays or Counsels, Civil and Moral* (1625), and reprinted in *The Essays of Francis Bacon*, ed. John Pitcher (1985).

3   Oh! might my ill-past hours return again!
No more, as then, should Sloth around me throw
   Her soul-enslaving, leaden chain!
No more the precious time would I employ
In giddy revells, or in thoughtless joy,
A present joy producing future woe.

But o'er the midnight Lamp I'd love to pore,
I'd seek with care fair Learning's depths to sound,
   And gather scientific Lore.

SAMUEL TAYLOR COLERIDGE (1772–1884), English poet and critic. "Quae Nocent Docent."

4   . . . this cheek and brow,
Whose paleness, burnèd in with heats of thought,
Would make an angel smile to see how ill
Clay thrust from Paradise consorts with mind—

ELIZABETH BARRETT BROWNING (1806–1861), English poet. "The Student."

5   Cramming seeks to stamp things in by intense application immediately before the ordeal. But a thing thus learned can form but few associations. On the other hand, the same thing recurring on different days, in different contexts, read, recited on, referred to again and again, related to other things and reviewed, gets well wrought into the mental structure. This is the reason why you should enforce on your pupils habits of continuous application.

WILLIAM JAMES (1842–1910), U.S. philosopher and psychologist. "Memory," *Talks to*

Teachers: On Psychlogy; and to Students on Some of Life's Ideals (1892).

6   A student must be of low caliber indeed if, with printed text and written notes before him covering the entire work of the term, he cannot cram enough facts into his head and keep them there long enough to get past the examination. When he has done this, so far as his present state of mind is concerned, he seems to be through with those facts—finished; he is never going to want them again, or worry about them. The habit of forgetting, the habit of not even taking things into his consciousness except under certain extraordinary conditions, is a vicious and subtle one he is not able to shake off.

    Thomas Alva Edison (1847–1931), U.S. inventor. *The Diary and Sundry Observations of Thomas Alva Edison* ("Sundry Observations"; chapter 4, "Education and Work"; section 19, "The Habit of Forgetting" [1925]), ed. Dagobert D. Runes (1948).

7   With song elate we celebrate
    The struggling Student wight,
    Who seeketh still to pack his pate
    With treasures erudite.

    James Whitcomb Riley (1849–1916), U.S. poet. "The Poor Student."

8   People are afraid of war and wounds and dentists, all with excellent reason; but these are not to be compared with such chaotic terrors of the mind as fell on this young man, and made him cover his eyes from the innocent morning.

    Robert Louis Stevenson (1850–1894), Scottish author. "Some College Memories," written for the "Book of the Edinburgh University Union Fancy Fair" (1886).

    Stevenson describes a young man who has confidently studied all night and then goes completely blank at daybreak on the morning of the test, finding himself unable to write his own name, much less the exam.

9   To those who know, a written examination is far from being a true criterion of capacity. It demands too much of mere memory, imitativeness, and the insidious willingness to absorb other people's ideas. Parrots and crows would do admirably in examinations. Indeed, the colleges are full of them.

    Stephen Leacock (1865–1944), Canadian (English-born) humorist. "Oxford As I See It," *My Discovery of England* (1922).

10 After these years of lectures heard,
    Of papers read, of hopes deferred,
    Of days spent in the dark stacks
    In learning the impervious facts
    So well you can dispose with them,
    Now that the final day has come
    When you shall answer name and
        dates
    Where fool and scholar judge your
        fate
    What have you gained?

    James V. Cunningham (b. 1911), U.S. author. "To a Friend, on Her Examination for the Doctorate in English."

11 On students, the most immediate effect of testing is anxiety. Most families have their characteristic exam-time symptoms. The household rhythms change. Girls' parents resign themselves to the overeating or under-nourishment, the sleepiness or insomnia, the amenorrhea, the fitful tears, the furious rejection of help. Boys' parents brace themselves for the lunatic sensitivity to noise, the ritually elaborate apparatus of study, the vocabulary of grunts and snarls, the midnight car-

bohydrates and the shuddering re-
fusal of breakfast.

DONALD BARR (b. 1921), U.S. educator.
*Who Pushed Humpty Dumpty? Dilemmas in
American Education Today* (chapter D, "Test
Ban?") (1971).

Falling in Love

1   Love me little, love me long!
    Is the burden of my song:
    Love that is too hot and strong
        Burneth soon to waste.
    Still I would not have thee cold—
    Not too backward, nor too bold;
    Love that lasteth till 't is old
        Fadeth not in haste.

ANONYMOUS, "Love Me Little, Love Me
Long!" (16th century).

2   Many are of the opinion that the
    vertues of love are very many, and
    that it is of force to reduce us from
    savageness to civilnesse, from folly
    to wit, from covetousnesse to liber-
    alitie, from clownishnesse to cour-
    tlinesse, yea from all vice to all ver-
    tue. But if the effects therof bee
    rightly considered, I see not but
    that wee may more justly say, that
    the inconveniences of love bee infi-
    nite, and that it bringeth us from
    modesty to impudencie, from lear-
    nynge to lewdnesse, from stayed
    firmnes to staggering fickelnesse,
    from liberalitie to prodigalitie, from
    warinesse to wilfulnesse, from good
    beehaviour to dissolute livinge,
    from reason to rage, yea, from all
    goodnesse to all vanitie . . .

GEORGE PETTIE (c. 1548–1589), English author. "Scilla and Minos," *A Petite Pallace of Pettie His Pleasure* (1576).

3   It lies not in our power to love or
    hate,

For will in us is overrul'd by fate.

. . . .

Where both deliberate, the love is
    slight;
Who ever lov'd, that lov'd not at
    first sight?

CHRISTOPHER MARLOWE (1564–
1593), English poet and dramatist. "Hero and
Leander" (sestiad 1, lines 167–68 and 175–
76).

4   Did my heart love till now? For-
    swear it, sight!
    For I ne'er saw true beauty till this
    night.

WILLIAM SHAKESPEARE (1564–1616),
English poet and dramatist. *Romeo and Juliet*
1.5.54–64.

Romeo reacts to seeing Juliet for the first time.

5   One half of me is yours, the other
    half yours—
    Mine own, I would say; but if
    mine, then yours,
    And so all yours.

WILLIAM SHAKESPEARE (1564–1616),
English poet and dramatist. *The Merchant of
Venice* 3.2.16–18.

With this riddle, Portia responds to her suitors.

6   It is to be all made of fantasy,
    All made of passion, and all made
    of wishes,
    All adoration, duty, and observance,
    All humbleness, all patience and
    impatience,
    All purity, all trial, all observance.

WILLIAM SHAKESPEARE (1564–1616),
English poet and dramatist. *As You Like It*
5.2.89–93.

The shepherd Silvius answers the question
what it is to love.

7   I am giddy; expectation whirls me
    round.
    Th' imaginary relish is so sweet

That it enchants my sense. What
  will it be,
When that the wat'ry palates taste
  indeed
Love's thrice repured nectar? Death,
  I fear me,
Swooning destruction, or some joy
  too fine,
Too subtle, potent, tun'd too sharp
  in sweetness
For the capacity of my ruder pow-
  ers
I fear it much; and I do fear besides
That I shall lose distinction in my
  joys,
As doth a battle when they charge
  on heaps
The enemy flying.

WILLIAM SHAKESPEARE (1564–1616),
English poet and dramatist. *Troilus and Cressida* 3.2.17-28.

Troilus anticipates a meeting with Cressida, arranged by Pandarus.

8   She lov'd me for the dangers I had
      pass'd,
    And I lov'd her that she did pity
      them.

WILLIAM SHAKESPEARE (1564–1616),
English poet and dramatist. *Othello* 1.3.169–
70.

Othello describes how he told Desdemona the
story of his life and thereby won her heart.

9   I brought a heart into the room,
      But from the room I carried none
        with me:
    If it had gone to thee, I know
    Mine would have taught thine heart
      to show
        More pity unto me; but Love,
          alas,
      At one first blow did shiver it as
        glass.

JOHN DONNE (1572–1631), English poet,
clergyman, and courtier. "The Broken Heart."

10 Adieu to Liberty! adieu to Fame!
    For other gifts, for softer joys I
      pine;
    In one fair breast I wish a mutual
      flame,
    In one fair breast alone to burn
      with mine.

GEORGE CRABBE (1754–1832), English
poet. "An Elegy to Love."

11 When you lov'd me, and I lov'd
      you,
    Then both of us were born anew.

SAMUEL TAYLOR COLERIDGE (1772–
1834), English poet and critic. "The Second
Birth."

12 There's a feast undated, yet
      Both our true lives hold it fast,—
    Even the day when first we met.
      What a great day came and
        passed,
        —Unknown then but known
          at last.

ALICE MEYNELL (1847–1922), English
poet. "An Unmarked Festival."

13 "Love at first sight," some say, mis-
      naming
    Discovery of twinned helplessness
    Against the huge tug of procrea-
      tion.

ROBERT GRAVES (1895–1985), English
author. "At First Sight."

14 Don't worry about losing. If it is
    right, it happens—The main thing
    is not to hurry. Nothing good gets
    away.

JOHN STEINBECK (1902–1968), U.S.
author. Letter to his 14-year-old son Thom, 10
November 1958, in *Letters of a Nation: A Collection of Extraordinary American Letters*, ed.
Andrew Carroll (1997).

Steinbeck's son had written to say that he
might be in love.

15 Got heartburn, palpitation, indigestion, anorexia, psychasthenia, euphoria and delusions of grandeur. Hallucinations by day and insomnia by night. Got misery and ecstasy.

CHARLES DREW (b. 1921), U.S. surgeon. Letter to his fiancée Lenore Robbins, 1940, in *Letters of a Nation: A Collection of Extraordinary American Letters*, ed. Andrew Carroll (1997).

The doctor is writing as a medical student describing the painful details of new love and separation. He became a pioneer in the preservation and storage of blood to be used in emergencies.

16 I think spring is inside me. I feel spring awakening, I feel it in my entire body and soul. I have to force myself to act normally. I'm in a state of utter confusion, don't know what to read, what to write, what to do. I only know that I'm longing for something.

ANNE FRANK (1929–1945), Dutch diarist. *The Diary of a Young Girl: The Definitive Edition* (Saturday, 12 February 1944), trans. Susan Massotty (1995).

In this entry Anne describes her growing affection for Peter, one of her fellow residents in the "Secret Annex."

Breaking Up

1 And wilt thou leave me thus,
That hath loved thee so long
In wealth and woe among:
And is thy heart so strong
As for to leave me thus?

THOMAS WYATT (1503–1542), English poet and courtier. "The Lover's Appeal."

2 Since there's no help, come let us kiss and part;
Nay, I have done, you get no more of me,
And I am glad, yea glad with all my heart

That thus so cleanly I myself can free.

MICHAEL DRAYTON (1563–1631), English poet. *Idea* (sonnet 61).

3 Now thou hast loved me one whole day,
Tomorrow when thou leav'st, what wilt thou say?
Wilt thou then antedate some new-made vow?
Or say that now
We are not just those persons which we were?

JOHN DONNE (1572–1631), English poet, clergyman, and courtier. "Woman's Constancy."

4 I prethee, send me back my heart,
Since I cannot have thine;
For if from yours you will not part,
Why then should you keep mine?

HENRY LAWES (1596–1662), English poet. "I Prethee, Send Me Back My Heart."

5 'Tis not that I am weary grown
Of being yours, and yours alone;
But with what face can I incline
To damn you to be only mine?

JOHN WILMOT, EARL OF ROCHESTER (1647–1680), English author. "Upon Leaving His Mistress."

6 Let the love die. Are there not other loves
As beautiful and full of sweet unrest,
Flying through space like snowy-pinioned doves?

ELLA WHEELER WILCOX (1850–1919), U.S. poet. "Let Them Go."

7 What shall I give you, my lord, my lover?
The gift that breaks the heart in me:

I bid you awake at dawn and discover
I have gone my way and left you
free.

SARA TEASDALE (1884–1933), U.S. poet.
"The Gift."

8   Don't try to patch it up,
Tear it up, tear it up!
Wash him out,
Dry him out,
Push him out, fly him out,
Cancel him and let him go!

OSCAR HAMMERSTEIN (1895–1960),
U.S. lyricist and librettist. "I'm Gonna Wash
That Man Right Outa My Hair," from the musi-
cal *South Pacific* (1949).

Richard Rodgers composed the music for the
song.

9   The sleepless nights,
The daily fights,
The quick toboggan when you
reach the heights—
I miss the kisses and I miss the
bites
I wish I were in love again.

LORENZ HART (1895–1943), U.S. lyricist. "I Wish I Were in Love Again."

10 I am no good at love
I betray it with little sins
For I feel the misery of the end
In the moment that it begins
And the bitterness of the last good-
bye
Is the bitterness that wins.

NOËL COWARD (1899–1973), English
dramatist, composer, and actor. "I Am No
Good at Love."

11 I bet you're wonderin' how I knew
'bout your plans to make me blue
with some other guy you knew before
between the two of us guys you
know I loved you more

. . . .
I heard it through the grapevine
Not much longer would you be
mine.

NORMAN WHITFIELD (b. 1943) and
BARRET STRONG (b. 1941), U.S. song-
writers. "I Heard It Through the Grapevine," in
Earl L. Stewart, *African American Music: An
Introduction* (1998).

12 I'd like to help you in your struggle
to be free
There must be fifty ways to leave
your lover.

PAUL SIMON (b. 1941), U.S. singer and
songwriter. "50 Ways to Leave Your Lover"
(1975).

Proposals

1   She's beautiful, and therefore to be
woo'd;
She is a woman, therefore to be
won.

WILLIAM SHAKESPEARE (1564–1616),
English poet and dramatist. *The First Part of
Henry VI* 5.3.78–79.

Spoken by Suffolk of the Lady Margaret.

2   We will have rings and things, and
fine array;
And kiss me, Kate, we will be married a' Sunday.

WILLIAM SHAKESPEARE (1564–1616),
English poet and dramatist. *The Taming of the
Shrew* 2.1.320–21.

Petruchio proposes and plans his wedding in
one fell swoop, despite the reluctance of Kate,
his intended bride.

3   *Don Pedro:* Will you have me, lady?
Beatrice: No, my lord, unless I
might have another for working
days. Your grace is too costly to
wear every day.

WILLIAM SHAKESPEARE (1564–1616),
English poet and dramatist. *Much Ado About
Nothing* 2.1.310–12.

Beatrice is too "mirthful" to be well-suited to the serious Don Pedro.

4   Dear Isabel,
I have a motion much imports your
   good,
Whereto if you'll a willing ear incline,
What's mine is yours and what is
   yours is mine.

WILLIAM SHAKESPEARE (1564–1616), English poet and dramatist. *Measure for Measure* 5.1.539–42.

In wrapping up the loose ends of the play, the Duke includes this proposal.

5   I am your wife, if you will marry
   me;
If not, I'll die your maid, To be
   your fellow
You may deny me, but I'll be your
   servant,
Whether you will or no.

WILLIAM SHAKESPEARE (1564–1616), English poet and dramatist. *The Tempest* 3.1.83–86.

Miranda proposes to Ferdinand, making a move that indeed puts her in a brave new world.

6   Allow me, then, Mademoiselle, to
place today on the altar of your
charms, the offering of my heart,
which aspires to and strives after no
other glory than for the rest of its
life to be, Mademoiselle your very
humble, very obedient and very
faithful servant and husband.

MOLIÈRE (JEAN BAPTISTE POQUE-LIN) (1622–1673), French dramatist. *The Hypochondriac* (La malade imaginaire) 2.5 (1673), in *The Plays of Molière in French*, trans. A. R. Waller, vol. 8 (1926).

A physician, who is the hypochondriac father's first choice of a mate for his daughter, proposes. The doctor is not the daughter's ultimate choice.

7   My reasons for marrying are, first,
that I think it a right thing for
every clergyman in easy circumstances (like myself) to set the example of matrimony in his parish.
Secondly, that I am convinced it
will add very greatly to my happiness; and thirdly—which perhaps I
ought to have mentioned earlier,
that it is the particular advice and
recommendation of the very noble
lady whom I have the honour of
calling patroness.

JANE AUSTEN (1775–1817), English novelist. *Pride and Prejudice* (vol. 1, chapter 19) (1813).

Mr. Collins proposes unsuccessfully to Elizabeth Bennet.

8   Let men tremble to win the hand of
woman, unless they win along with
it the utmost passion of her heart!

NATHANIEL HAWTHORNE (1804–1864), U.S. author. *The Scarlet Letter* (chapter 15, "Hester and Pearl") (1850).

The narrator makes this exclamation in describing the unhappy marriage of Chillingworth and Hester.

9   Barkis is willin'.

CHARLES DICKENS (1812–1870), English author. *David Copperfield* (chapter 5) (1849–50).

Mr. Barkis is a carrier "of a phlegmatic temperament, and not at all conversational." He asks young David to convey to the kindly cook and housekeeper Peggoty his, Mr. Barkis's, interest in marriage.

10 You will be surprised that he proposed seven times once in a hack-
ney-coach once in a boat once in a
pew once on a donkey at Tunbridge
Wells and the rest on his knees.

CHARLES DICKENS (1812–1870), English author. *Little Dorrit* (book 1, chapter 24) (1855–57).

Flora describes to Little Dorrit the proposal from Mr. F. His persistence may serve as an inspiration or his lack of success as a deterrent.

11 You could draw me to fire, you could draw me to water, you could draw me to the gallows, you could draw me to any death, you could draw me to anything I have most avoided, you could draw me to any exposure and disgrace. This and the confusion of my thoughts, so that I am fit for nothing, is what I mean by your being the ruin of me. But if you would return a favourable answer to my offer of marriage, you could draw me to any good—every good—with equal force.

CHARLES DICKENS (1812–1870), English author. *Our Mutual Friend* (chapter 15, "The Whole Case So Far") (1864–65).

The unsuccessful proposal of the stern schoolmaster Bradley Headstone to the mild-mannered Lizzie Hexam.

12 You are lonely; I love you; I want you to consent to be my wife; I will wait, but I want you to promise that you will marry me—no one else.

GEORGE ELIOT (MARY ANN OR MARIAN EVANS) (1819–1880), English author. *Middlemarch* (book 2, "Old and Young"; chapter 15) (1871–72).

In a moment of youthful indiscretion, Lydgate proposes, without success, to Madame Laure, a French actress and unsuitable potential wife for the young medical student.

13 And at home by the fire, whenever you look up, there I shall be—and whenever I look up, there will be you.

THOMAS HARDY (1840–1928), English author. *Far from the Madding Crowd* (chapter 4, "Gabriel's Resolve—The Visit—The Mistake") (1874).

In this scene, Gabriel Oak offers to Bathsheba a piano, the music of his flute, a gig for mar-

ket, nice flowers, birds, a frame for cucumbers, and newspaper chronicles of the wedding and births, and concludes with this description of the security of marriage. Bathsheba turns him down, although the two are married before the novel's end.

14 My later courtship was carried on by telegraph. I taught the lady of my heart the Morse code, and when she could both send and receive we got along much better than we could have with spoken words by tapping our remarks to one another on our hands. Presently I asked her thus, in Morse code, if she would marry me. The word "Yes" is an easy one to send by telegraphic signals, and she sent it. If she had been obliged to speak it she might have found it harder.

THOMAS ALVA EDISON (1847–1931), U.S. inventor. *The Diary and Sundry Observations of Thomas Alva Edison* ("Sundry Observations"; chapter 1, "Autobiographical"; section 2 [1925]), ed. Dagobert D. Runes (1948).

Edison had been deaf since the age of 12. He saw his hearing loss as an advantage in an increasingly noisy world—an attitude reflected in his celebration of his use of Morse code as a medium for his marriage proposal.

15 I have a theory that it is always the women who propose to us, and not we who propose to women. Except, of course, in middle-class life. But then the middle classes are not modern.

OSCAR WILDE (1854–1900), Irish author. *The Picture of Dorian Gray* (chapter 6) (1891).

16 I don't see anything romantic in proposing. It is very romantic to be in love. But there is nothing romantic about a definite proposal. Why, one may be accepted. One usually is, I believe. Then the ex-

citement is all over. The very essence of romance is uncertainty.

OSCAR WILDE (1854–1900), Irish author. *The Importance of Being Earnest* (act 1) (1895).

Algernon Moncrieff comments on his friend Jack Worthing's plan to propose to Gwendolyn Fairfax.

17 Daisy, Daisy,
Give me your answer, do!
I'm half crazy,
All for the love of you!
It won't be a stylish marriage,
I can't afford a carriage,
But you'll look sweet
On the seat
Of a bicycle built for two!

HARRY DACRE (1860–1922), Anglo-American poet. "Daisy Bell."

Margaret Bradford Boni, editor of *The Fireside Book of Favorite American Songs* (1952), notes that when Dacre came to this country from England he was "astounded" at the duty charged as a result of the bicycle he had transported. According to Boni, "A chance remark of a friend, 'Lucky for you it was not built for two,' gave Dacre the idea for his famous bicycle song, 'Daisy Bell,' which started the whole cycle of bicycle songs so popular in the '90s."

18 I have nothing to offer you but my strength for your defence, my honesty for your surety, my ability and industry for your livelihood, and my authority and position for your dignity. That is all it becomes a man to offer to a woman.

GEORGE BERNARD SHAW (1856–1950), Irish dramatist and critic. *Candida* (act 3) (1898).

The minister Mr. Morell offers himself to his wife Candida, as he believes he must compete with the young poet Marchbanks for his wife's affection. Technically this is not a proposal but a sort of renegotiation of the marriage contract. While the poet offers "My weakness. My desolation. My heart's need," Candida says she will stick with her husband, whom she sees not as a defender or provider but as one who needs protection after years of having been coddled by women. In explaining the wife's role as she performs it, she says, "I build a castle of comfort and indulgence and love for him, and stand sentinel always to keep little vulgar cares out. I make him master here, though he does not know it, and could not tell you a moment again how it came to be so."

19 I thought well as well him as another and then I asked him with my eyes to ask again yes and then he asked me would I yes to say yes my mountain flower and first I put my arms around him yes and drew him down to me so he could feel my breasts all perfume yes and his heart was going like mad and yes I said yes I will Yes.

JAMES JOYCE (1882–1941), Irish author. *Ulysses* (chapter 18) (1921).

Molly accepts the sexual proposal of Leopold Bloom, being, if not a girl who can't say "no," at least a girl who can't say anything but "yes."

20 To my mind, a man must choose a wife for himself, without advice from anybody. As I said to Tony before he ever proposed to this girl: Make sure that she's *good*, and a *lady*, and *healthy*, and *intelligent*, and that she's going to get on with your friends and relations, and you with hers—and then, my dear boy, if you feel that you can afford to marry—then I suppose there's no help for it.

E. M. DELAFIELD (EDMEE ELIZABETH MONICA DASHWOOD, NÉE DE LA PASTURE) (1890–1943), English author. "Discussing the Fiancée," *As Others Hear Us* (1937).

Engagement

1 Courtship to marriage is as a very witty prologue to a very dull play.

WILLIAM CONGREVE (1670–1729), English author. *The Old Bachelor* (5.4) (1693).

2 An engaged woman is always more agreeable than a disengaged. She is satisfied with herself. Her cares are over, and she feels that she may exert all her powers of pleasing without suspicion. All is safe with a lady engaged; no harm can be done.

JANE AUSTEN (1775–1817), English novelist. *Mansfield Park* (vol. 1, chapter 5) (1814).

3 Court a gal for fun, for the luv yu bear her, for the vartue and bissness thare is in her; court her for a wife and for a mother, court her as yu wud court a farm—for the strength ov the sile and the parfeckshun ov the title; court her as tho she want a fule, and yu a nuther; court her in the kitchen, in the parlor, over the wash-tub, and at the pianner; court this way, yung man, and if yu don't git a good wife and she don't git a good hustband, the falt won't be in the courting.

JOSH BILLINGS (HENRY W. SHAW) (1818–1885), U.S. humorist. "On Courting," *The Complete Works of Josh Billings* (1899).

4 I would rather not be engaged. When people are engaged, they begin to think of being married soon, . . . and I should like everything to go on for a long while just as it is.

GEORGE ELIOT (MARY ANN *OR* MARIAN EVANS) (1819–1890), English author. *The Mill on the Floss* (book 6, "The Great Temptation"; chapter 2, "First Impressions") (1860).

Lucy Deane here cites her reluctance to make a formal engagement with Stephen Guest.

5 AFFIANCE, pp. Fitted with an ankle-ring for the ball-and-chain.

AMBROSE BIERCE (1842–?1914), U.S. author. *The Devil's Dictionary* (1881–1911).

6 To speak frankly, I am not in favour of long engagements. They give people the opportunity of finding out each other's character before marriage, which I think is never advisable.

OSCAR WILDE (1854–1900), Irish author. *The Importance of Being Earnest* (act 3) (1895).

7 What could he and she really know of each other, since it was his duty, as a "decent" fellow, to conceal his past from her, and hers, as a marriageable girl, to have no past to conceal? What if, for some one of the subtler reasons that would tell with both them, they should tire of each other, misunderstand or irritate each other? . . . [With] a shiver of foreboding he saw his marriage becoming what most of the other marriages about him were: a dull association of material and social interests held together by ignorance on the one side and hypocrisy on the other.

EDITH WHARTON (1862–1937), U.S. author. *The Age of Innocence* (book 1, chapter 6) (1920).

Newland Archer contemplates his engagement to May Welland. He aspires to "passionate and tender comradeship" with his fiancée but realizes that such a relation would require "on her part, the experience, the versatility, the freedom of judgment, which she had been carefully trained not to possess." He is not driven to wonder what qualities he would have to acquire to forge such a bond.

8 What's th' sense o' exhaustin' all th' pleasures o' life durin' th' first few months o' courtship? Why not save a few pleasures t' look forward t'

after you've satisfied th' instalment houses? Marriage at best is quite a comedown fer most any girl, 'specially if her engagement period wuz one long an' riotous dream.

KIN HUBBARD (1868–1930), U.S. humorist. *Abe Martin's Primer* ("Th' Cost o' Sparking'") (1914).

Spoken by Miss Tawney Apple.

Moving In (With a Partner)

1   Come live with me and be my love,
And we will all the pleasures prove
That valleys, groves, hills, and
    fields,
Woods or steepy mountain yield.

CHRISTOPHER MARLOWE (1564–1593), English poet and dramatist. "The Passionate Shepherd to His Love."

2   One turf shall serve as pillow for us
    both;
One heart, one bed, two bosoms,
    and one troth.

WILLIAM SHAKESPEARE (1564–1616), English poet and dramatist. *A Midsummer Night's Dream* 2.2.41–42.

Lysander tries to persuade Hermia to sleep closer to him.

3   It seems a pity that the good old phrase "living in sin" is likely to be dropped by the C of E. So many friends, happily living in sin, will feel very ordinary and humdrum when they become merely partners; or, as the Americans say, "an item." Living in sin has always sounded daring and exotic.

ALEC GUINESS (b. 1914), English actor. *My Name Escapes Me: The Diary of a Retiring Actor* ("Wednesday, 7 June 1995") (1996).

4   Thinking in terms of one
Is easily done—
One room, one bed, one chair,
One person there,

. . . .

But counting up to two
Is harder to do.

PHILIP LARKIN (1922–1985), English poet and critic. "Counting."

Quitting Smoking

1   Some sigh for this and that,
    My wishes don't go far,
The world may wag at will,
    So I have my cigar.

THOMAS HOOD (1799–1845), English poet. "The Cigar."

2   Where, though I, by sour physician,
Am debarr'd the full fruition
Of thy favours, I may catch
Some collateral sweets, and snatch
Sidelong odours, that give life
Like glances from a neighbour's
    wife;
And still live in the by-places
And the suburbs of thy graces;
And in thy borders take delight.

CHARLES LAMB (1775–1834), English essayist. "A Farewell to Tobacco."

3   Some hard smokers are great workers, as we all know; but few who have watched the effect of nicotization on will and character would deny that it handicaps a man, and often pretty heavily, in the race for distinction. It encourages revery,— the contemplation of the possible, which is a charming but unwholesome substitute for the performance of the duty next at hand.

OLIVER WENDELL HOLMES (1809–1894), U.S. author and physician. "The Human Body and Its Management," *Pages from* an *Old Volume of Life: A Collection of Essays, 1857–1881* (1891).

4 By the indulgence of a simple and harmless propensity,—of a propensity which can inflict an injury upon no person or thing except the coat and the person of him who indulges in it,—of a custom honored and observed in almost all the nations of the world,—of a custom which, far from leading a man into any wickedness or dissipation to which youth is subject, but, on the contrary, begets only benevolent silence, and thoughtful good-humored observation—I found at the age of twenty all my prospects in life destroyed.

WILLIAM MAKEPEACE THACKERAY (1811–1863), English novelist. *Fitz-Boodle's Confessions*; published originally in *Fraser's Magazine* (1841).

The speaker complains that women have a distaste for cigarettes and smoke and that he had a run-in with someone insulted by his indulgence.

5 Ernest felt now that the turning point of his life had come. He would give up all for Christ—even his tobacco. So he gathered together his pipes and pouches, and locked them up in his portmanteau under his bed where they should be out of sight, and as much out of mind as possible. He did not burn them, because someone might come in who wanted to smoke, and though he might abridge his own liberty, yet, as smoking was not a sin, there was no reason why he should be hard on other people.

SAMUEL BUTLER (1835–1902), English author. *The Way of All Flesh* (chapter 50) (1903).

6 A cigarette is the perfect type of a perfect pleasure. It is exquisite, and it leaves one unsatisfied. What more can one want?

OSCAR WILDE (1854–1900), Irish author. *The Picture of Dorian Gray* (chapter 6) (1891).

7 I should like to say that I left off smoking because I considered it a mean form of slavery, to be condemned for moral as well as physical reasons; but though I see the folly of smoking clearly now, I was blind to it for some months after I had smoked my last pipe. I gave up my most delightful solace, as I regarded it, for no other reason than that the lady who was willing to fling herself away on me said that I must choose between it and her.

J. M. BARRIE (1860–1937), English author. *My Lady Nicotine* (chapter 1, "Matrimony and Smoking Compared") (1890).

8 I know, I feel, that with the introduction of tobacco England woke up from a long sleep. Suddenly a new zest had been given to life. The glory of existence became a thing to speak of. Men who had hitherto only concerned themselves with the narrow things of home put a pipe into their mouths and became philosophers.

J. M. BARRIE (1860–1937), English author. *My Lady Nicotine* (chapter 13, "The Grandest Scene in History") (1890).

9 Open the old cigar-box, get me a
　　Cuba stout,
For things are running crossways,
　　and Maggie and I are out.

We quarrelled about Havanas—we
　　fought o'er a good cheroot,
And *I* know she is exacting, and she
says I am a brute.

. . . .

A million surplus Maggies are willing to bear the yoke;
And a woman is only a woman, but
a good Cigar is a Smoke.

RUDYARD KIPLING (1865–1936), English author. "The Betrothed."

The headnote for the poem cites a "Breach of
Promise Case, circa, 1885" in which one of
the betrothed stated: "You must choose between me and your cigar." It appears that Kipling's speaker has made his choice.

10   The nicotine addict, like the opium
fiend and the alcoholic, quickly
loses respect for observance of laws
and any personal obligations to
share in cultural or civic interests.

GRACE GEORGE (b. 1895?), U.S. social
worker. *It's Smart Not To Smoke* (1947).

In an alarming and largely unscientific way,
this short work outlines the social and health
consequences of smoking.

11   What a weird thing smoking is and
I can't stop it. I feel cosy, have a
sense of well-being when I'm smoking, poisoning myself, killing myself
slowly. Not so slowly maybe. I have
all kinds of pains I don't want to
know about and I know that's what
they're from. But when I don't
smoke I scarcely feel as if I'm living. I don't feel as if I'm living unless I'm killing myself.

RUSSELL HOBAN (b. 1925), U.S. author.
Turtle Diary (chapter 7, "William G.") (1975).

12   I like you more than I would like
To have a cigarette

WENDY COPE (b. 1945), English poet.
"Giving Up Smoking."

In *A Poem a Day* (1994), in which this poem
appears, Cope is quoted as saying: "People
who have never been addicted to nicotine
don't understand what an intense love poem it
is."

13   Smoking is, if not my life, then at
least my hobby. I love to smoke.
Smoking is fun. Smoking is cool.
Smoking is, as far as I am concerned, the entire point of being an
adult. It makes growing up genu-
inely worthwhile. I am quite well
aware of the hazards of smoking.
Smoking is not a healthful pastime,
it is true. Smoking is indeed no
bracing dip in the ocean, no strenu-
ous series of calisthenics, no two
laps around the reservoir. On the
other hand, smoking has to its advantage the fact that is a quiet pursuit. Smoking is, in effect a digni-
fied sport.

FRAN LEBOWITZ (b. 1950), U.S. author.
"When Smoke Gets in your Eyes . . . Shut
Them," *Social Studies* (1981).

14   Twelve hundred people—two
jumbo jet planeloads a day of men,
women, and children. Yes, innocent
children, denied their bright fu-
tures, those happy moments of
scoring the winning touchdowns, of
high school and college gradua-
tions, marriage, parenthood, profes-
sional fulfillment, breakthroughs in
engineering, medicine, economics,
who know *how* many Nobel Prize
winners? Lambs, slaughtered by
Nicholas Naylor and the tobacco
industry fiends he so slickly represented.

CHRISTOPHER BUCKLEY (b. 1952),
U.S. author. *Thank You for Smoking* (Prologue)
(1994).

In Buckley's novel, Naylor is a public-relations
man for the tobacco industry.

Quitting Drinking

1   If you wish to keep your affairs secret, drink no wine. For wine

causes the voice to be uplifted and secrets to be revealed.

Zohar 4.177b, in *The Talmudic Anthology: Tales and Teachings of the Rabbis,* ed. Louis I. Newman (1947).

2 All excess is ill; but drunkenness is of the worst sort. It spoils health, dismounts the mind, and unmans men. It reveals secrets, is quarrelsome, lascivious, impudent, dangerous, and mad. In fine, he that is drunk is not a man: because he is so long void of reason, that distinguishes a man from a beast.

William Penn (1644–1718), English philosopher and statesman. *Fruits of Solitude: Reflections and Maxims Relating to the Conduct of Human Life* (part 1), "Temperance," no. 72 (1693).

3 Sir, I have no objection to a man's drinking wine, if he can do it in moderation. I found myself apt to go to excess in it, and therefore, after having been for some time without it, on account of illness, I thought it better not to return to it. Every man is to judge for himself, according to the effects which he experiences.

Samuel Johnson (1709–1784), English author. Quoted in James Boswell, *Life of Johnson* ("16 March 1776") (1791).

4 Hence Burgundy, Claret, and Port,
    Away with old hock and madeira!
Too earthly ye are for my sport;
    There's a beverage brighter and
    clearer!

John Keats (1795–1821), English poet. "Hence Burgundy, Claret, and Port."

The speaker vows to eschew alcohol and instead to "drink at the eye" on sunshine.

5 See drinkers of water, their wits
    never lacking,

Direct as a railroad and smooth in
    their gaits;
But look at the bibbers of wine,
    they go tacking,
Like ships that have met a foul
    wind in the *straights.*

Thomas Hood (1799–1845), English poet. "Drinking Song: By a Member of a Temperance Society, as Sung by Mrs. Spring at Waterman's Hall."

6 Men "drink" because they like it, much more than for any good they suppose it does them, beyond such pleasure as it may afford; and this is precisely the point that all arguments fail to reach. Pleasure is the bird in the hand which foolish persons will always choose before the two birds in the bush which are to be the rewards of virtue.

Oliver Wendell Holmes (1809–1894), U.S. author and physician. "The Human Body and Its Functioning," *Pages from an Old Volume of Life: A Collection of Essays, 1858–1881* (1891).

Holmes explains why it is so difficult to persuade people to quit drinking.

7 Who hath sorrow? Who hath woe?
They who do not answer no;
They whose feet to sin incline,
While they tarry at the wine.

Carrie Nation (1846–1911), U.S. prohibitionist. Comment made circa 1893. Quoted in Carleton Beals, *Cyclone Carry* (chapter 14) (1962).

8 If ever I want to sign the pledge,
It's the morning after I've had an
    edge.

George Ade (1866–1944), U.S. humorist and journalist. "R-E-M-O-R-S-E."

9 If when you say "whisky" you mean the devil's brew, the poison scourge, the bloody monster that

defiles innocence, dethrones reason, destroys the home, creates misery and poverty, yea literally takes the bread from the mouths of little children; if you mean the evil drink that topples the Christian man and woman from the pinnacle of righteous, gracious living into the bottomless pit of degradation, and despair, and shame, and helplessness, and hopelessness—then certainly I am against it. But, if when you say "whisky" you mean the oil of conversation, the philosophic wine, the ale that is consumed when good fellows get together, that puts a song in their hearts and laughter on their lips, and the warm glow of contentment in their eyes . . . if you mean the drink that enables a man to magnify his joy, and his happiness, and to forget, if only for a little while, life's great tragedies, and heartaches, and sorrows . . . then certainly I am for it.

NOAH SWEAT, U.S. judge and politician. Campaign speech, 1948, in *Lend Me Your Ears: Great Speeches in History*, ed. William Safire (1992).

Sweat was running for state representtive in Alcorn County, Miss. Safire indicates that Sweat copyrighted the speech in 1952 because so many politicians were using it.

Losing Weight

1   Eat a third, drink a third, and leave empty in your stomach the remaining third. If anger overtakes you, there will be room for the expansion of your stomach, and you will not suffer from apoplexy.

Gittin 70, in *The Talmudic Anthology: Tales and Teachings of the Rabbis*, ed. Louis I. Newman (1947).

2   I think thou art in the habit of eating a great deal, and that thy power of restraining appetite is more slender than a hair, whilst an appetite such as thou nourishest would rupture a chain, and a day may come when it will tear thee up.

SHEIKH SA'DI (1184–1291), Persian author. *Tales from The Gulistân or the Rose-Garden of the Sheikh Sa'di of Shirâz* (story 93) (1258), trans. and ed. Richard Burton (1928).

3   But temprance teacheth this, where he keepeth schoole;
He that knoweth when he hath enough is no foole.
Feed by measure, and defie the phisition!
And in the contrarie mark this condition;
A swine over fat is cause of his own bane.

JOHN HEYWOOD (1497?–?1580), English author and musician. *The Proverbs of John Heywood* (part 2, chapter 7) (1874; originally published 1546).

4   When I was about thy years, Hal, I was not an eagle's talent in the waist; I could have crept into any alderman's thumb-ring. A plague of sighing and grief! It blows a man up like a bladder.

WILLIAM SHAKESPEARE (1564–1616), English poet and dramatist. *The First Part of King Henry IV* 2.4.326 ff.

Falstaff, known for his generous spirit, dissolute life, and corpulence, considers the issue of his weight.

5   Do I not bate? Do I not dwindle? Why, my skin hangs about me like an old lady's loose gown; I am wither'd like an old apple-john.

WILLIAM SHAKESPEARE (1564–1616), English poet and dramatist. *The First Part of King Henry IV* 3.3.2–4.

Falstaff complains of losing some of the pounds from his ample frame.

6 [Temperance.] To this a spare diet contributes much. Eat therefore to live, and do not live to eat. That is like a man, but this below a beast.

WILLIAM PENN (1644–1718), English philosopher and statesman. *Fruits of Solitude: Reflections and Maxims Relating to the Conduct of Human Life* (part 1), "Temperance," no. 59 (1693).

7 Th' great national curse t'day is over-eatin'. We do not only eat too much, but we devote too much time thinkin' about eatin'. . . . Ever'where we look there's a eatin' place. . . . Wherever ther's population enough t' fill a few stools we find a great brazen coffee urn an' a stack of buns.

KIN HUBBARD (1868–1930), U.S. humorist. "'Eats' by Dr. Mopps," *Abe Martin's Primer: The Collected Writings of Abe Martin and His Brown County, Indiana, Neighbors* (1914).

8 From the day on which she weighs 140, the chief excitement of a woman's life consists in spotting [people] who are fatter than she is.

HELEN ROWLAND (1875–1950), columnist and essayist. In *The Penguin Book of Women's Humor*, ed. Regina Barreca (1996).

9 . . . I wonder if there is a woman in the world strong-minded enough to shed ten pounds or twenty,— And say There now, that's plenty.

OGDEN NASH (1902–1971), U.S. poet. "Curl Up and Diet."

10 A big man is always accused of gluttony, whereas a wizened or osseous man can eat like a refugee at every meal, and no one ever notices his greed.

ROBERTSON DAVIES (1913–1995), Canadian author. "Avoirdupois a Cross, "*The Table Talk of Samuel Marchbanks* (1949).

The speaker describes eating lunch with a "man of generous proportions" who is "tormented unmercifully" about his weight by his fellow diners. Marchbanks comments that the man in fact eats "consideringly, without haste or greed."

11 Unnecessary dieting is because everything from television to fashion ads have made it seem wicked to cast a shadow. This wild, emaciated look appeals to some women, though not to many men, who are seldom seen pinning up a *Vogue* illustration in a machine shop.

PEG BRACKEN (b. 1918), U.S. author. *The I Hate to Cook Book* (1960).

12 As you know, there are more diet books than dieters, among them the Atkins diet, the Stillman diet, the Scarsdale diet, the Zone diet, the grapefruit diet, the Drinking Man's diet, the Eating Man's diet, the Sleeping Man's diet, the Beverly Hills diet, the Akron, Ohio diet, the Mayo Clinic diet, the Hold the Mayo diet, and the latest, the Nothing But Prunes and Kaopectate diet.

MEL BROOKS (b. 1926) and CARL REINER (b. 1922), U.S. comics. *The 2,000 Year Old Man In the Year 2000: The Book. Including How Not to Die and Other Good Tips* (chapter 35, "The 2,000 Year Old Man's Seven-Day Diet") (1997).

13 Although he has "been down," as he puts it, for fourteen years, after twenty-five years of exceptional fatness, he sees himself not as a man who weighs one hundred and sixty but as a man who is constantly in danger of weighing three hundred and twenty.

CALVIN TRILLIN (b. 1935), U.S. author. *American Fried: Adventures of a Happy Eater* (chapter 3) (1979).

Trillin refers to his friend Fats Goldberg, the pizza baron.

14 She's got this real funny idea about a diet: you don't get fat if no one sees you eating.

GLORIA NAYLOR (b. 1950), U.S. novelist. *Linden Hills* ("December 22nd") (1985).

Wedding

1 In house to kepe houshold *when folkes will needes wed,*
Moe things belong then foure bare legges in a bed.
I reckened my wedding a suger sweete spice,
But *reckeners without their host must recken twice.*
And although it were sweet for a weeke or twaine,
Sweete meate will have sowre sauce, I see now plaine.

JOHN HEYWOOD (1497?–?1580), English author and musician. *The Proverbs of John Heywood* (part 1, chapter 8) (1874; originally published 1564).

2 Let endless Peace your steadfast hearts accord,
And blessed Plentie wait vpon your bord;
And let your bed with pleasures chast abound,
That fruitfull issue may to you afford
Which may your foes confound,
And make your joyes redound.

EDMUND SPENSER (1552?–1599), English poet and courtier. *Prothalamion* (lines 101–106).

3 Wooing, wedding, and repenting is as a Scotch jig, a measure, and a cinquepace. The first suit is hot and hasty, like a Scotch jig, and full as fantastical; the wedding, mannerly-modest, as a measure, full of state and ancientry; and then comes Repentance and, with his bad legs, falls into the cinquepace faster and faster, till he sink into his grave.

WILLIAM SHAKESPEARE (1564–1616), English poet and dramatist. *Much Ado About Nothing* 2.1.67 ff.

Beatrice comments on marriage, before she is won over by the charms of Benedick.

4 Wedding is great Juno's crown,
    O blessed bond of board and
        bed!
'Tis Hymen peoples every town;
    High wedlock then be honorèd.
Honor, high honor, and renown,
    To Hymen, god of every town!

WILLIAM SHAKESPEARE (1564–1616), English poet and dramatist. *As You Like It* 5.4.140–45.

5 Honor, riches, marriage-blessing
Long continuance, and increasing,
Hourly joys be still upon you!

WILLIAM SHAKESPEARE (1564–1616), English poet and dramatist. *The Tempest* 4.1.106–108.

Lines spoken by Juno in the pageant, organized by Prospero and his minion Ariel, to celebrate the marriage of Miranda and Ferdinand.

6 I . . . chose my wife, as she did her wedding-gown, not for a fine glossy surface, but such qualities as would wear well.

OLIVER GOLDSMITH (c, 1728–1774), Anglo-Irish author. *The Vicar of Wakefield* (chapter 1, "The Description of the Family of Wakefield in Which a Kindred Likeness Prevails as Well of Minds as of Persons") (1766).

7 Timid brides, you have, probably, hitherto been addressed as angels.

Prepare for the time when you shall again become mortal.

MARIA EDGEWORTH (1768–1849), Irish author. "An Essay on the Noble Science of Self-Justification," *Letters for Literary Ladies* (1795).

Edgeworth goes on to advise brides: "Contradict, debate, justify, recriminate, rage, weep, swoon, do anything but yield to conviction."

8   A wedding is a licensed subject to joke upon, but there really is no great joke in the matter after all;— we speak merely of the ceremony, and beg it to be distinctly understood that we indulge in no hidden sarcasm upon a married life. Mixed up with the pleasure and joy of the occasion, are the many regrets at quitting home, the tears of parting between parent and child, the consciousness of leaving the dearest and kindest friends of the happiest portion of human life, to encounter its cares and troubles with others still untried and little known: natural feelings which we would not render this chapter mournful by describing, and which we should be still more unwilling to be supposed to ridicule.

CHARLES DICKENS (1812–1870), English author. *The Pickwick Papers* (chapter 28, "A Good-Humoured Christmas Chapter, Containing an Account of a Wedding, and Some Other Sports Beside: Which Although in Their Way, Even as Good Customs as Marriage Itself, Are Not Quite so Religiously Kept Up in These Degenerate Times") (1837).

Dickens describes the mixed feelings occasioned by a wedding ceremony.

9   Such days can hardly be agreeable to the man of whom it is known by all around him that he is on the eve of committing matrimony. There is always, on such occasions, a feeling of weakness, as though the man had been subdued, brought at length into a cage and tamed, so as to be made fit for domestic purposes, and deprived of his ancient freedom amongst the woods; whereas the girl feels herself to be the triumphant conqueror, who has successfully performed this great act of taming.

ANTHONY TROLLOPE (1815–1882), English novelist. *Ayala's Angel* (chapter 64, "Ayala's Marriage") (1881).

10   "It is a habit which exhibits, perhaps, the unconscious inherent cynicism of the human mind, for people who consider that they have reached the acme of mundane felicity, to distribute this token of esteem to their friends, with the object probably" (he took the knife from a waiter and went to the table to slice the cake) "of enabling those friends (these edifices require very delicate incision—each particular currant and subtle condiment hangs to its neighbour—a wedding-cake is evidently the most highly civilized of cakes, and partakes of the evils as well as the advantages of civilization!)—I was saying, they send us these love-tokens, no doubt (we shall have to weigh out the crumbs, if each is to have his fair share) that we may the better estimate their state of bliss by passing some hours in purgatory."

GEORGE MEREDITH (1828–1909), English author. *The Ordeal of Richard Feverel* (chapter 32, "Procession of the Cake") (1859).

Adrian carefully portions out a piece of cake and extravagantly analyzes its meaning for Hippias.

11   I think a wedding-day
     Looks best, as mountains do,
        some miles away,

Or squalid fishing-smacks far out to
sea,
Seen lily-sailed in sunshine and
blue haze,
Where the delicious lights are all
men chase,
And no man ever reaches.

W. H. MALLOCK (1849–1923), English
author. "A Marriage Prospect (From an Unfin-
ished Drama)."

The speaker savors the six weeks before his
wedding. After the marriage he anticipates
only the misery attendant upon having to
"consecrate" his days "In sober, sombre truth,
for good and ill, / To the one worship of a
withering face."

12 Every time I hear that march from
Lohengrin,
I am glad I'm on the outside look-
ing in.
I have heard a lot of married peo-
ple talk,
And I know that marriage is a long,
long walk.
To some people weddings mean ro-
mance,
But I prefer a picnic or a dance.

GUS KAHN (1886–1941), U.S. lyricist.
"Makin' Whoopee."

13 Of all life's ceremonies that of marriage is the most touching and
beautiful. This is the long anticipated climax of girlhood—and boyhood, too—the doorway to true
maturity, the farewell to parents as
protectors, the acceptance of responsibility.

AMY VANDERBILT (1908–1974), U.S.
author. *Amy Vanderbilt's Etiquette* (introduction, "The Ceremonies of Life") (1971).

Vanderbilt urges her readers to remember that
"the elaborateness or simplicity of the wedding
is of no real consequence. It is the spirit in
which we marry that is truly meaningful."

14 Women often weep at weddings,
whereas my own instinct is to laugh

uproariously and encourage the
bride and groom with merry
whoops. The sight of people getting
married exhilarates me; I think that
they are doing a fine thing, and I
admire them for it.

ROBERTSON DAVIES (1913–1995), Canadian author. "Of Nuptial Merriment," *The
Table Talk of Samuel Marchbanks* (1949).

15 I toast you both, good son and dear
new daughter.
May you not lack for water,
And may that water smack of
Cana's wine.

RICHARD WILBUR (b. 1921), U.S. poet.
"A Wedding Toast."

Starting a Business

1 I hired me a little shop, . . . took
small gain, kept no debt-book, gar-
nished my shop, for want of plate,
with good wholesome thrifty sentences, as "Touchstone, keep thy
shop, and thy shop will keep thee."
"Light gains make heavy purses."

GEORGE CHAPMAN (1559–1634), English author. *Eastward Hoe* (1.1.45 ff.) (c.
1605).

These are the words of the goldsmith Touchstone. Chapman collaborated on the play with
Ben Jonson and John Marston. Jonson and
Chapman were imprisoned because of the
anti-Scottish satire in the play.

2 If a man will begin with certainties,
he shall end in doubts; but if he
will be content to begin with
doubts, he shall end in certainties.

FRANCIS BACON (1561–1626), English
philosopher, essayist, and statesman. *The Ad-
vancement of Learning* 1.5.8 (1605).

Bacon's advice is not necessarily intended for
entrepreneurs, but it represents one approach
to a start-up.

3 Those that never were in business have reason to avoid it, because they do not know it. Those that have been in it, have at least as much reason to dislike it, because they do know it.

GEORGE SAVILE, MARQUIS OF HALI-FAX (1633–1695), English courtier and author. *Maxims* (1750), in *The Works of George Savile, Marquis of Halifax,* ed. Mark N. Brown, vol. 3 (1989).

4 A vigorous beginning at business carries it very near the end. A wavering at the first setting out invites and calls for a misfortune.

GEORGE SAVILE, MARQUIS OF HALI-FAX (1633–1695), English courtier and author. *Maxims* (1750), in *The Works of George Savile, Marquis of Halifax,* ed. Mark N. Brown, vol. 4 (1989).

5 Whatever business you have, do it the first moment you can; never by halves, but finish it without interruption, if possible. Business must not be sauntered and trifled with.

PHILIP DORMER STANHOPE, FOURTH EARL OF CHESTERFIELD (1694–1773), English statesman and author. Letter to his son, 5 March 1752 OS, *The Letters of Philip Dormer Stanhope. Earl of Chesterfield,* ed. John Bradshaw, vol. 2 (1929).

6 Nothing . . . will ever be attempted, if all possible objections must be first overcome.

SAMUEL JOHNSON (1709–1784), English author. *The History of Rasselas, Prince of Abissinnia* (chapter 6, "A Dissertation on the Art of Flying") (1759).

Johnson's characters are not talking about business, but their emphasis on taking a leap of faith represents one approach to starting any new enterprise.

7 The best-laid schemes o' mice an' men
    Gang aft agley.

ROBERT BURNS (1759–1796), Scottish poet. "To a Mouse."

Burns's speaker suggests the limits of planning.

8 I draw a plan and work out every detail on the plan before starting to build. For otherwise one will waste a great deal of time in makeshifts as the work goes on and the finished article will not have coherence. It will not be rightly proportioned. Many inventors fail because they do not distinguish between planning and experimenting.

HENRY FORD (1863–1947), U.S. industrialist. In *My Life and Work* (1922; reprint 1973), and reprinted in *Ford on Management: Harnessing the American Spirit* (chapter 1, "The Beginning of Business") (1991).

9 This is the strategy of "creative imitation." It waits until somebody else has established the new, but only "approximately." Then it goes to work. And within a short time it comes out with what the new really should be to satisfy the customer, to do the work customers want and pay for. The creative imitation has then set the standard and takes over the market.

PETER F. DRUCKER (b. 1909), U.S. businessman and writer. *The Executive in Action* ("Innovation and Entrepreneurship: Practice and Principles"; section 3, "Entrepreneurial Strategies"; chapter 17, "Hit Them Where They Ain't") (1996).

Drucker gives the example of IBM's "perfection" of the Apple company's personal computer.

10 Start with good people, lay out the rules, communicate with your employees, motivate them, and reward them if they perform. If you do all those things effectively, you can't miss.

LEE IACOCCA (b. 1924), U.S. business-man. *Talking Straight* (chapter 4, "Good Business—More in Management") (1988).

11 The debit side of the balance sheet reflects incredibly hard work and self-sacrifice—with very little material return for the investment in the first few years. The credit side? It will be whatever you make it.

IRENE SMITH (b. ?1935), U.S. business-woman and writer. *Diary of a Small Business* (chapter 20, "If I Had It to Do Over Again . . . And Knew What I Know Now") (1982).

12 People say it takes so much courage to become an entrepreneur. I think it takes far more courage to work for somebody else, to get up each morning and go to work and not have something in your control.

HELEN VER STANDIG (b. ?1920), entrepreneur. Quoted in Edward A. Gazvoda, William M. Haney III, and John Greenya, *The Harvard Entrepreneurs Society's Guide to Making Money, or The Tycoon's Handbook* (book 4, "Entrepreneurism: Passing Fad? or Future?") (1983).

Ver Standig is "Madame Wellington," owner of The Wellington Stores, which sell simulated precious gemstones.

13 In games, many times there are prizes for effort. You can get second prize or third prize, and that is not bad at all. However, as in a battle, in the small business game it is winner take all. No reward for effort, no second prize. You try and you win or you lose. Please know this before you jump in. It is sink or swim.

WILLIAM A. DELANEY. *Why Small Businesses Fail—Don't Make the Same Mistake Once* ("What Exactly Are Your Chances") (1984).

14 YOUR OWN BUSINESS
Start small and grow big.
Start big and go broke.

MALCOLM FORBES (?–1990), U.S. businessman. *The Further Sayings of Chairman Malcolm* ("Boardroom Banter") (1986).

15 Most aspiring entrepreneurs believe that the key to success lies in developing an innovative and exciting product. After all, remember Emerson's adage "Build a better mousetrap, and the world will beat a path to your door." I'm here to tell you that if you believe in that adage, then you are doomed to failure. . . . The truth is, it's far better to aggressively market a mediocre mousetrap than to build a superior trap and wait for the phones to ring.

SCOTT A. CLARK, U.S. author. *Beating the Odds: Ten Smart Steps to Small Business Success* (chapter 1, "First Things First") (1991).

Sarah S. B. Yule and Mary S. Keene credit Emerson with the comment about the mousetrap, noting in their *Borrowings* (1889) that Emerson said, "If a man can write a better book, preach a better sermon, or make a better mousetrap than his neighbor, though he builds his house in the woods the world will make a beaten path to his door."

16 Benjamin Franklin discovered electricity, but the man who developed the electric meter made a lot more money from it.

E. JOSEPH COSSMAN (b. 1918) and WILLIAM A. COHEN, U.S. businessmen. *Making It!: Wealth-Building Secrets From Two Great Entrepreneurial Minds* ("Know How to Start a Business") (1994).

Promotion

1 The Master said, "Do not worry because you have no official position. Worry about your qualifications. Do not worry because no one appreciates your abilities. Seek to be worthy of appreciation."

CONFUCIUS (551?–479 B.C.), Chinese philosopher. *Analects* (Lun yü), book 4, section 14, trans. D. C. Lau (1979).

Confucius was writing before the era of downsizing, the hiring bonus, and 401k.

2 Winning promotion through Pull is a thing we all hate—in other people. Co-workers dislike the beneficiary of Pull (The Pullee) and usually express that dislike in comments on his incompetence.

RAYMOND HULL (b. 1919), U.S. author. *The Peter Principle* (chapter 4, "Pull and Promotion") (1969).

According to Hull, writing as Laurence J. Peter, the Peter Principle can be formulated as: "In a Hierarchy Every Employee Tends to Rise to His Level of Incompetence." The author restates the principle as: "In every hierarchy the cream rises until it sours." He defines "pull" as "an employee's relationship—by blood, marriage or acquaintance—with a person above him in the hierarchy."

3 Most managements complain about the lack of able people and go outside to fill key positions. Nonsense. Nobody inside an organization ever looked ready to move into a bigger job. I use the rule of 50 percent. Try to find somebody inside the company with a record of success (in any area) and with an appetite for the job. If he looks like 50 per cent of what you need, give him the job. In six months he'll have grown the other 50 per cent and everybody will be satisfied.

ROBERT TOWNSEND (b. 1920), U.S. author. *Up the Organization* ("Promotion, from Within") (1970).

4 People used to think at 45: *How do I prepare myself for the next promotion?* Now they have to think: *How do I prepare myself to make another start if/when I'm pitched over the* side? Companies today treat employees as disposable resources.

GAIL SHEEHY (b. 1937), U.S. author. *New Passages: Mapping Your Life Across Time* (part 2, "The Flourishing Forties"; chapter 3, "Men Redefining Success") (1995).

Becoming a Parent

1 Let not the fear of bad offspring deter you from having children; you must do your duty and God will do what pleases Him.

Berakoth 10a (Talmud).

2 A man without children is like a piece of wood, which though kindled does not burn or give out light.

Zohar, 1.187a, in *The Talmudic Anthology: Tales and Teachings of the Rabbis*, ed Louis I. Newman (1947).

3 Families, when a child is born
Want it to be intelligent.
I, through intelligence,
Having wrecked my whole life,
Only hope that the baby will prove
Ignorant and stupid.
Then he will crown a tranquil life
By becoming a Cabinet Minister.

SU SHIH (SU TUNG-PO) (1036–1101), Chinese poet. "On the Birth of His Son," trans. Arthur Waley in *170 Chinese Poems* (1977; originally published 1962).

4 Children sweeten labours, but they make misfortunes more bitter; they increase the cares of life, but they mitigate the remembrance of death.

FRANCIS BACON (1561–1626), English philosopher, essayist, and statesman. "Of Parents and Children," *Essays or Counsels, Civil and Moral* (1625), and reprinted in *The Essays of Francis Bacon*, ed. John Pitcher (1985).

5 He that hath children, all his mor-
sels are not his owne.

GEORGE HERBERT (1593–1633), English
poet and Anglican priest. *Outlandish Proverbs*,
no. 423 (1640).

6 Infants manners are moulded more
by the example of Parents, then by
stars at their nativities.

GEORGE HERBERT (1593–1633), English
poet and Anglican priest. *Jacula Prudentum, or
Outlandish Proverbs, Sentences, Etc.*, no. 1060
(1652).

7 You may love your children without
living in the Nursery, and you may
have a competent and discreet care
of them, without letting it break
out upon the company . . .

**GEORGE SAVILE, MARQUIS OF HALI-
FAX** (1633–1695), English courtier and author. *The Lady's New-Year's Gift; or, Advice to
a Daughter on Religion and Morality* (1688), in
*The Works of George Savile, Marquis of Hali-
fax*, ed. Mark N. Brown, vol. 2 (1989).

8 The Desire of having Children is as
much the Effect of Vanity as of
Good-nature. We think our Children a Part of ourselves, though as
they grow up they might very well
undeceive us.

**GEORGE SAVILE, MARQUIS OF HALI-
FAX** (1633–1695), English courtier and author. *Miscellaneous Thoughts and Reflections*
(1750), in *The Works of George Savile, Marquis of Halifax*, ed. Mark N. Brown, vol. 3
(1989).

9 As marriage produces children, so
children produce care and disputes;
and wrangling, as is said (at least by
old bachelors and old maids), is
one of the sweets of the conjugal
state.

MARY WORTLEY MONTAGU (1689–
1762), English author. Letter, 13 January

1715–16, *Letters* [Mary Wortley Montagu], ed.
Clare Brant (1992).

10 I wish either my father or my
mother, or indeed both of them, as
they were in duty both equally
bound to it, had minded what they
were about when they begot me;
had they duly considered how
much depended upon what they
were then doing;—that not only the
production of a rational Being was
concerned in it, but that possibly
the happy formation and tempera-
ture of his body, perhaps his genius
and the very cast of his mind;—
and, for aught they knew to the
contrary, even the fortunes of his
whole house might take their turn
from the humours and dispositions
which were then uppermost :—Had
they duly weighed and considered
all this, and proceeded accordingly,
——I am verily persuaded I should
have made a quite different figure
in the world from that in which the
reader is likely to see me.

LAURENCE STERNE (1713–1768), Anglo-
Irish author. *Tristram Shandy* (chapter 1, opening lines) (1760–67).

11 The parent who sedulously endeav-
ours to form the heart and enlarge
the understanding of his child, has
given that dignity to the discharge
of a duty, common to the whole
animal world, that only reason can
give. This is the parental affection
of humanity, and leaves instinctive
natural affection far behind. Such a
parent acquires all the rights of the
most sacred friendship, and his advice, even when his child is advanced in life, demands serious
consideration.

MARY WOLLSTONECRAFT (1759–
1797), English author and feminist. *A Vindica-*

tion of the Rights of Women (chapter 11, "Duty to Parents") (1792).

Wollstonecraft argues, however, that children should only be expected to follow parental advice slavishly while they are too young to reason for themselves.

12 O dearest, dearest boy! my heart
For better lore would seldom yearn,
Could I but teach the hundredth
 part
Of what from thee I learn.

WILLIAM WORDSWORTH (1770–1850), English poet. "An Anecdote for Fathers."

13 Our notion of the perfect society embraces the family as its centre and ornament. Nor is there a paradise planted till the children appear in the foreground to animate and complete the picture. Without these, the world were a solitude, houses desolate, hearts nameless; there are neither perspectives, nor prospects; ourselves are not ourselves, nor were there a future for us.

A. BRONSON ALCOTT (1799–1888), U.S. philosopher and educator. "Friendship," Tablets (1868).

14 Infancy conforms to nobody: all conform to it, so that one babe commonly makes four or five out of the adults who prattle and play to it.

RALPH WALDO EMERSON (1803–1882), U.S. author. "Self-Reliance," Essays, First Series (1841).

15 Respect the child. Wait and see the new product of Nature. Nature loves analogies, but not repetitions. Respect the child. Be not too much his parent. Trespass not on his solitude.

RALPH WALDO EMERSON (1803–1882), U.S. author and philosopher. "Education," Lectures and Biographical Sketches (1883).

16 It is a pleasant thing to reflect upon, and furnishes a complete answer to those who contend for the gradual degeneration of the human species, that every baby born into the world is a finer one than the last.

CHARLES DICKENS (1812–1870), English author. Nicholas Nickleby (chapter 36, "Private and confidential; relating to family matters. Showing how Mr. Kenwigs underwent violent Agitation, and how Mrs. Kenwigs was as well as could be expected") (1838–39).

17 When the mother's passionate welcome,
 Sorrow-like, bursts forth in tears,
And a sire's self-gratulation
 Prophesies of future years—
 It is well we cannot see
 What the end shall be.

FRANCES BROWNE (1816–1879), Irish poet. "What the End Shall Be," in Famous and Single Fugitive Poems, ed. Rossiter Johnson (1890).

Johnson notes: "This poem has been handed about for a quarter of a century. It is attributed to Frances Browne, the blind poetess (b. Stranolar, Ireland, 1816)."

18 Family likeness has often a deep sadness in it. Nature, that great tragic dramatist, knits us together by bone and muscle, and divides us by the subtler web of our brains; blends yearning and repulsion; and ties us by our heartstrings to the beings that jar us at every movement.

GEORGE ELIOT (MARY ANN OR MARIAN EVANS) (1819–1880), English author. Adam Bede (chapter 4, "Home and Its Sorrows") (1859).

19 If you would have your son to walk
honorably through the world, you
must not attempt to clear the
stones from his path, but teach him
to walk firmly over them—not insist upon leading him by the hand,
but let him learn to go alone.

ANNE BRONTË (1820–1849), English au-
thor. *The Tenant of Wildfell Hall* (chapter 3, "A
Controversy") (1848).

Advice given to a mother who is accused of
pampering her son.

20 Only a tender flower
  Sent us to rear;
Only a life to love
  While we are here;
Only a baby small,
  Never at rest;
Small, but how dear to us,
  God knoweth best.

MATTHIAS BARR (1831–?), Scottish
poet. "The Children's Laureate." "Only a Baby
Small."

21 . . . be aught you please, let all fulfil
All your pleasure; be your world
  your toy;
Mild or wild we love you, loud or
  still,
  Child or boy.

ALGERNON CHARLES SWINBURNE
(1837–1909), English poet. "Not a Child."

22 What does it matter, when you
come to think of it, whether a child
is yours by blood or not? All the little ones of our time are collectively
the children of us adults of the
time, and entitled to our general
care. That excessive regard of parents for their own children, and
their dislike of other people's, is,
like class-feeling, patriotism, save-
your-own soul-ism and other virtues, a mean exclusiveness at bottom.

THOMAS HARDY (1840–1928), English
author. *Jude the Obscure* (part 5, chapter 3)
(1896).

23 BABE or BABY, n. A misshapen
creature of no particular age, sex,
or condition, chiefly remarkable for
the violence of the sympathies and
antipathies it excites in others, itself
without sentiment or emotion.

AMBROSE BIERCE (1842–?1914), U.S.
author. *The Devil's Dictionary* (1881–1911).

24 Can you think of any service constituting a stronger claim on the
nation's gratitude than bearing and
nursing the nation's children? According to our view, none deserve
so well of the world as good parents. There is no task so unselfish,
so necessarily without return,
though the heart is well rewarded,
as the nurture of the children who
are to make the world for one another when we are gone.

EDWARD BELLAMY (1850–1898), U.S.
author and journalist. *Looking Backward*
(chapter 25) (1888).

Bellamy's utopian novel looks forward to a
time when this attitude about parenting and
the importance of the equality of men and
women is a reality.

25 Children begin by loving their parents; as they grow older they judge
them; sometimes they forgive them.

OSCAR WILDE (1854–1900), Irish author. *The Picture of Dorian Gray* (chapter 5)
(1890).

26 It's a strange thing, . . . but you
can't love a man till you've had a
baby by him. . . . If a woman's got
a baby and a husband she's got the
best things the Lord can give her.

OLIVE SCHREINER (1855–1920), South
African author. *The Story of An African Farm*
(part 2, chapter 14, "Waldo Goes Out to Sit in
the Sunshine") (1883).

27 They are a great deal of trouble, and they make a place untidy, and they cost a lot of money to keep; but still we would not have the house without them. It would not be home without their noisy tongues and their mischief-making hands. Would not the rooms seem silent without their pattering feet, and might not you stay apart if no prattling voices called you together?

JEROME K. JEROME (1859–1927), English actor and writer. "On Babies," *Idle Thoughts of an Idle Fellow* (1892).

28 Just when they sit down to enjoy in peace their evening meal of existence, the tables of most parents are pounced upon as by harpies, and pillaged by their children.

LOGAN PEARSALL SMITH (1865–1946), U.S. humorist. "Age and Death," *Afterthoughts* (1931) and *All Trivia: Trivia, More Trivia, Afterthoughts, Last Words* (1945).

29 The parents exist to teach the child, but they must learn what the child has to teach them; and the child has a very great deal to teach them. Chiefly the child has to teach them imagination, which is the source of justice and the foe of cruelty, conscious or unconscious.

ARNOLD BENNETT (1867–1931), English author. *How to Make the Best of Life* (chapter 8, "Children") (1923).

30 God, you have given me a boy:
      Now help me still my boy to rear;
    Too kind to quarrel, brave to fear,
    Too good for any sinful joy,
      Or, if temptation prove too strong,
    Too wise to follow folly long.

DOUGLAS MALLOCH (1877–1938), U.S. poet. "A Father's Prayer."

31 One of the most fascinating preoccupations when one has a child of one's own is watching for the appearance of hereditary traits and predispositions that can be attributed to—or blamed upon—one side of the family or the other. . . . The traits in which one takes pride and the traits of the other parent whom one loves are doubly endearing in the shared child.

MARGARET MEAD (1901–1978), U.S. anthropologist. *Blackberry Winter* ("Catherine, Born in Wartime") (1972).

Mead describes in her autobiography the birth of her daughter after she had been told she could not have children.

32 Everybody who has a baby thinks everybody who hasn't a baby ought to have a baby.

OGDEN NASH (1902–1971), U.S. poet. "Did Someone Say 'Babies?'"

33 Trust yourself. You know more than you think you do.

BENJAMIN SPOCK (1903–1998), U.S. psychologist. *Baby and Child Care* (opening chapter) (1977; originally published 1946 as *The Common Sense Book of Baby and Child Care*).

34 Loving a baby or child is a circular business, a kind of feedback loop. The more you give, the more you get, and the more you get, the more you feel like giving.

PENELOPE LEACH, English psychologist. *Your Baby & Child: From Birth to Age Five* (introduction) (1993).

35 Children do not need superhuman, perfect parents. They have always managed with good enough parents: the parents they happened to have.

PENELOPE LEACH, English psychologist. *Your Baby & Child: From Birth to Age Five* (introduction) (1993).

36 Getting advice on the best way to bring up children is like getting advice on the best way to breathe; sooner or later, you're probably going to forget it and go back to your regular old in-and-out.

CALVIN TRILLIN (b. 1935), U.S. author. *Family Man* (chapter 1, "No Advice Here") (1998).

37 Your responsibility as a parent is not as great as you might imagine. You need not supply the world with the next conqueror of disease or major motion-picture star. If your child simply grows up to be someone who does not use the word "collectible" as a noun, you can consider yourself an unqualified success.

FRAN LEBOWITZ (b. 1950), U.S. author. "Parental Guidance," *Social Studies* (1981).

38 [From a list of pros and cons for "prospective parents"]

[Pro:] Children ask better questions than do adults. "May I have a cookie?" "Why is the sky blue?" and "What does a cow say?" are far more likely to elicit a cheerful response than "Where's your manuscript?" "Why haven't you called?" and "Who's your lawyer?"

[Con:] Notoriously insensitive to subtle shifts in mood, children will persist in discussing the color of a recently sighted cement mixer long after one's own interest in the topic has waned.

FRAN LEBOWITZ (b. 1950), U.S. author. "Children: Pro or Con?" *Metropolitan Life* (1978).

Becoming a Grandparent

1 Babys i luv with all mi heart; they are mi sweetmeats, they warm up mi blood like a gin sling, they krawl into me and nestle by the side ov mi soul, like a kitten under a cook stove. . . . I have got grandchildren, and they are wuss than the first krop tew riot amung the feelings.

JOSH BILLINGS (HENRY W. SHAW) (1818–1885), U.S. humorist. "Babys," *The Complete Works of Josh Billings* (1876).

2 As grandparents, elders can *contribute to* the grandchildren's guidance and maintenance without being *responsible for* them. As grandparents, they can love, care for, and be helpful to the grandchildren—all without bearing the responsibility inherent in parental generativity. This freedom from middle age's responsibility for maintaining and perpetuating the world is central to the grand-generativity that characterizes old-age caring.

ERIK H. ERIKSON (1902–1994), American (German-born) psychoanalyst; **JOAN M. ERIKSON** (1902–1997), U.S. artist and therapist; and **HELEN Q. KIVNICK**, psychologist. *Vital Involvement in Old Age* (section II, "The Voices of Our Informants"; section 2, "Generativity and Stagnation: Care") (1986).

3 Because they are usually free to love and guide and befriend the young without having to take daily responsibility for them, they can often reach out past pride and fear of failure and close the space between generations.

JIMMY CARTER (b. 1924), U.S. president. Proclamation (9 September 1979) of National Grandparents' Day; quoted in Ruth K. Westheimer and Steven Kaplan, *Grandparenthood* (1998).

Moving House

1 The leaving a neighbourhood in which we had enjoyed so many hours of tranquility was not with-

out a tear, which scarce fortitude itself could suppress.

OLIVER GOLDSMITH (1730?–1774),
Anglo-Irish author. *The Vicar of Wakefield*
(chapter 3, "A Migration. The Fortunate Circumstances of Our Lives are Generally Found
at Last to Be of Our Own Procuring") (1766).

2   These annual migrations from farm
to farm were on the increase. . . .
With the younger families it was a
pleasant excitement which might
possibly be an advantage. The
Egypt of one family was the Land
of Promise to the family who saw it
from a distance, till by residence
there it became in turn their Egypt
also; and so they changed and
changed.

THOMAS HARDY (1840–1928), English
author. *Tess of the D'Urbervilles* (Phase the
Sixth, "The Convert"; chapter 51) (1891).

Hardy describes the annual custom of changing jobs and households on Lady Day. In the
story of Exodus, the Israelites suffered in Egypt
and anticipated a return to the Promised Land.

3   "I understand that inside of the
Pearly Gates, each Family has Permanent Quarters. There are no
Folding Beds to juggle down Back
Stairways, no Picture Cords to
shorten, no Curtain Poles to saw
off, no Book Cases to get jammed
in Stairways. I am sure there will be
no Piano Movers, for I have heard
their Language. Do you think you
can be happy in the Promised
Land?"

    "It will depend entirely on
whether or not the Rugs fit."

GEORGE ADE (1866–1944), U.S. humor-
ist and journalist. "The Search for the Right
House and How Mrs. Jump Had Her Annual
Attack"; in *The Permanent Ade: The Living
Writings of George Ade*, ed. Fred C. Kelly
(1947).

A dialogue between Mr. Jump and his wife,
who every spring looks for a "House that had

twice as many Closets as Rooms and a
Southern Exposure on All four sides."

4   O dear little cabin, I've loved you
        so long,
And now I must bid you good-bye!
I've filled you with laughter, I've
        thrilled you with song
And sometimes I've wished I could
        cry.
Your walls they have witnessed a
        weariful fight,
And rung to a won Waterloo:
But oh, in my triumph I'm dreary
        to-night—
Good-bye, little cabin, to you!

ROBERT W. SERVICE (1874–1958), Canadian poet. "Good-Bye, Little Cabin."

5   In the little houses the tenant people sifted their belongings and the
belongings of their fathers and of
their grandfathers. Picked over their
possessions for the journey to the
west. The men were ruthless because the past had been spoiled, but
the women knew how the past
would cry to them in the coming
days.

JOHN STEINBECK (1902–1968), U.S.
novelist. *The Grapes of Wrath* (chapter 9)
(1939).

Steinbeck describes the plight of farmers
forced to move from dust-bowl states like
Oklahoma to the "promised land" of California.

6   Without my twenty to forty years
of clutter, the lightness I feel here
in this new home is *good*. Come to
think of it, this move liberated me.
It refreshed and energized me
somehow, knowing I had to make
new friends here, start new projects,
plant my roots anew in journalist,
political, feminist, and writers'
groups (the interests of my past)—

even try something truly new for me.

BETTY FRIEDAN (b. 1921), U.S. author and feminist. *The Fountain of Age* (chapter 11, "To Move or to Stay?") (1993).

Friedan talks about a move made when she was in her mid-sixties, from New York to California, to teach. She argues: "Older, we must move, and stay, and move again, to keep our life-giving ties alive, for this movement *is* our fountain of age. And there's a freedom in realizing this, a new freedom to move or stay, new necessities and possibilities of choice."

7   Ah, I like the look of packing crates! A household in preparation for a journey! . . . Something full of the flow of life. . . . Movement, progress.

LORRAINE HANSBERRY (1930–1965), U.S. dramatist. *A Raisin in the Sun* (act 3) (1958).

Spoken by the character Asagai, who is a voice for change in the play.

8   The smell of fresh paint barely overlaid a fainter, more pungent odor, the accumulated fear and loneliness and terrified excitement of those who had lived here before me.

JOHN THORNE, U.S. author. "Learning to Eat" (1992), in *The Penguin Book of Food and Drink*, ed. Paul Levy (1996).

Thorne describes moving into his first New York City apartment, where the former tenant has left all her possessions.

Wedding Anniversary

1   To me, fair friend, you never can be old,
For as you were when first your eye I eyed,
Such seems your beauty still.

WILLIAM SHAKESPEARE (1564–1616), English poet and dramatist. Sonnet 104.

2   True and false fears let us refrain;
Let us love nobly, and live, and add again
Years and years unto years, till we attain
To write threescore; this is the second of our reign.

JOHN DONNE (1572–1631), English poet, clergyman, and courtier. "The Anniversary."

3   If ever two were one, then surely we.
If ever man were loved by wife, then thee;
If ever wife was happy in a man,
Compare with me, ye women, if you can.
I prize thy love more than whole mines of gold
Or all the riches that the East doth hold.

ANNE BRADSTREET (1612?–1672), U.S. (English-born) poet. "To My Dear and Loving Husband."

4   Frequent visits, presents, intimate correspondence, and intermarriages within allowed bounds, are means of keeping up the concern and affection that nature requires from relations.

WILLIAM PENN (1644–1718), English philosopher and statesman. *Fruits of Solitude: Reflections and Maxims Relating to the Conduct of Human Life* (part 1), "Marriage," no. 105 (1693).

Many couples may find Penn's advice interesting (what does he mean by "intermarriages"?) and inspiring (although for them probably only the presents would have a practical application).

5   Marriage is the beginning and the end of all culture. It makes the savage mild; and the most cultivated has no better opportunity for displaying his gentleness. Indissoluble

it must be, because it brings so much happiness that what small exceptional unhappiness it may bring counts for nothing in the balance.

JOHANN WOLFGANG VON GOETHE (1749–1832), German poet, novelist, and dramatist. *Elective Affinities* (book 1, chapter 9) (1809), trans. James Froude and R. Dillon Boylan (1962).

The passionate words of Mittler.

6 Dear Ellen, many a golden year
    May ripe, then dim, thy beauty's
      bloom
    But never shall the hour appear
    In sunny joy, in sorrow's gloom,
    When aught shall hinder me from
      telling
    My ardent love, all loves excelling.

RALPH WALDO EMERSON (1803–1882), U.S. author. "Dear Ellen" (1829).

Emerson wrote these lines during his engagement.

7 Ah, Lucy, life has swiftly sped
    From April to November;
    The summer blossoms all are shed
    That you and I remember;
    But while the vanished years we
      share
    With mingling recollections,
    How all their shadowy features
      wear
    The hue of old affections!

OLIVER WENDELL HOLMES (1809–1894), U.S. author and physician. "Lucy: for Her Golden Wedding, October 18, 1875."

8 Grow old along with me!
    The best is yet to be.

ROBERT BROWNING (1812–1889), English poet. "Rabbi Ben Ezra" (opening lines).

9 The noble lady's condition on these delightful occasions was one compounded of heroic endurance and heroic forgiveness. Lurid indica-
tions of the better marriages she might have made, shone athwart the awful gloom of her composure, and fitfully revealed the cherub as a little monster unaccountably favoured by Heaven, who had possessed himself of a blessing for which many of his superiors had sued and contended in vain. So firmly had this his position towards his treasure become established, that when the anniversary arrived, it always found him in an apologetic state.

CHARLES DICKENS (1812–1870), English author. *Our Mutual Friend* (book 3, chapter 4, "A Happy Return of the Day") (1864–65).

Describing the anniversary of the Wilfers, married more than 25 years. They celebrate the day "morally, rather as a Fast than a Feast." Mr. Wilfer is described as "cherubic" throughout the novel.

10 I have now been married ten years. . . . I am my husband's life as fully as he is mine. . . . To talk to each other is but a more animated and an audible thinking.

CHARLOTTE BRONTË (1816–1855), English author. *Jane Eyre* (chapter 38, "Conclusion") (1847).

11 The Silver Wedding! on some pensive ear
      From towers remote as sound the
        silvery bells,
    To-day from one far unforgotten
      year
      A silvery faint memorial music
        swells.

    And silver-pale the dim memorial
      light
      Of musing age on youthful joys is
        shed,
    The golden joys of fancy's dawning
      bright,

The golden bliss of, Woo'd, and won, and wed.

ARTHUR HUGH CLOUGH (1819–1861), English poet. "The Silver Wedding."

Written for the 25th wedding anniversary of Mr. and Mrs. Walrond.

12 True Love is but a humble, low-
    born thing,
    And hath its food served up in
    earthen ware;
    It is a thing to walk with, hand in
    hand,
    Through the every-dayness of this
    work-day world.

JAMES RUSSELL LOWELL (1819–1891), U.S. author. "Love."

13 Kissing don't last; cookery do!

GEORGE MEREDITH (1828–1909), English author. *The Ordeal of Richard Feverel* (chapter 28, "Preparations for Action") (1859).

Mrs. Berry, a woman whose husband left her after only nine months of marriage, gives this advice to a romantic young woman soon to be married herself.

14 Unto us all our days are love's an-
    niversaries, each one
    In turn hath ripen'd something of
    our happiness.

ROBERT BRIDGES (1844–1930), English poet. "Anniversary," *Poems in Classical Prosody.*

15 Do you know many wives . . . who
    respect and admire their husbands?
    And yet they and their husbands
    get on very well. How many brides
    go to the altar with hearts that
    would bear inspection by the men
    who take them there? And yet it
    doesn't end unhappily—somehow
    or other the nuptial establishment
    jogs on. The truth is, that women
    try marriage as a Refuge, far more

numerously than they are willing to admit; and, what is more, they find that marriage has justified their confidence in it.

WILKIE COLLINS (1848–1889), English author. *The Moonstone* (Second Period, "The Discovery of the Truth"; First Narrative, chapter 5) (1868).

16 Small is the trust when love is green
    In sap of early years;
    A little thing steps in between
    And kisses turn to tears.

    A while—and see how love be
    grown
    In loveliness and power!
    A while, it loves the sweets alone,
    But next it loves the sour.

ROBERT LOUIS STEVENSON (1850–1894), Scottish author. "Small is the Trust When Love is Green."

17 You've lived with me these fifty
    years,
    And all the time you loved me
    dearly:
    I may have given you cause for
    tears:
    I may have acted rather queerly.

    I ceased to love you long ago:
    I loved another for a season:
    As time went on I came to know
    Your worth, my wife. . . .

J. K. STEPHEN (1859–1892), English lawyer and journalist. "After the Golden Wedding (Three Soliloquies)."

Stephen's poem is a cynical juxtaposition of soliloquies. The wife indeed never loved the husband, although the minister who presides over this golden wedding anniversary sees them as a happy couple worthy of imitation.

18 Sometimes, I recollect, those twenty
    years with her had seemed long;

but that was because, firstly, twenty years were long, and secondly because we are none of us perfect, and thirdly, because a wife, unless she is careful, is apt to get on one's nerves.

MARY ANNETTE (BEAUCHAMP) RUSSELL, COUNTESS RUSSELL (MARY ELIZABETH BEAUCHAMP) (1866–1941), English novelist. *The Caravaners* (chapter 14) (1909).

Baron Von Ottringel, a Prussian army officer, remembers his experience with his first wife.

19 Wasn't marriage, like life, unstimulating and unprofitable and somewhat empty when too well ordered and protected and guarded. Wasn't it finer, more splendid, more nourishing, when it was, like life itself, a mixture of the sordid and the magnificent; of mud and stars; of earth and flowers; of love and hate and laughter and tears and ugliness and beauty and hurt.

EDNA FERBER (1887–1968), U.S. novelist. *Show Boat* (chapter 19) (1926).

Kim questions whether something is missing from marriage, although she relishes her "separate bedrooms and those lovely negligées" and her "personal liberty and privacy of thought and action."

20 Husbands are things that wives
   have to get used to putting up
   with,
And with whom they breakfast with
   and sup with.
They interfere with the discipline of
   nurseries,
And forget anniversaries.

OGDEN NASH (1902–1971), U.S. poet. "What Almost Every Woman Knows Sooner or Later."

21 For you wake one day,
Look around and say

Somebody wonderful
Married me.

FRED EBB, lyricist. "Married," from the musical *Cabaret* (act one) (1963).

22 That we arrived at fifty years together is due as much to luck as to love, and a talent for knowing, when we stumble, where to fall, and how to get up again.

RUBY DEE (b. 1924) and **OSSIE DAVIS** (b. 1917), U.S. actors. *Ossie and Ruby: In This Life Together* ("Sex Comes Out of the Closet") (1998).

23 A husband has many, many ways of making a wife feel loved, but he almost never does it with champagne and roses. . . . I will happily settle for love in its many oblique and unglamorous manifestations, for "I love you" can be translated into his willingness to lace my ski boots, and to listen to my discussion of infant diarrhea.

JUDITH VIORST (b. 1931), U.S. author. *Yes, Married* (chapter 14, "The Reason It's Worth It") (1972).

24 When I was . . . little, my mother once told me that if a married couple puts a penny in a pot for every time they make love in the first year, and takes a penny out every time after that, they'll never get all the pennies out of the pot.

ARMISTEAD MAUPIN (b. 1944), U.S. author. *Tales of the City* (1978).

Spoken by Mrs. Madrigal, who is explaining that sex is not the most binding or lasting element of marriage.

Family Reunion

1 For the hands that cannot clasp
   thee,

For the voices that are dumb,
For each and all I bid thee
A grateful welcome home!

JOHN GREENLEAF WHITTIER (1807–1892), U.S. poet. "A Welcome to Lowell."

In writing these lines to welcome James Russell Lowell, a fellow poet, Whittier also expresses the likely sentiment of someone speaking for any family that is understood to consist of the dead as well as the living.

2   To that dear home beyond the sea,
My Kathleen shall again return,
And when thy old friends welcome thee,
Thy loving heart will cease to yearn.

THOMAS P. WESTENDORF (1848–1923). "I'll Take You Home Again, Kathleen."

A husband here promises to take his wife back to their native Ireland.

3   Some human rôles are so fixed that it is too great a strain to act them in any but the accepted manner. Fathers ought to be tyrannical, and sons ungrateful; grandmothers must demoralize their children's children, and mothers-in-law make all the mischief they can.

LOGAN PEARSALL SMITH (1865–1946), U.S. humorist. "Other People," *Afterthoughts* (1931) and *All Trivia: Trivia, More Trivia, Afterthoughts, Last Words* (1945).

Smith's comments may remind us of the ways in which reunions may exaggerate our rôles within our families.

4   Home agin, an' home to stay—
Yes, it's nice to be away.
Plenty things to do an' see,
But the old place seems to me
Jest about the proper thing.
Mebbe 'ts 'cause the mem'ries cling
Closer 'round yore place o' birth
'N ary other spot on earth.

PAUL LAURENCE DUNBAR (1872–1906), U.S. poet. "Bein' Back Home."

5   People feel better when they gather together for the sake of love and fellowship. Their hearts are cleansed and kindled by the warm fire of eternal goodness.

JAMES FOLSON, U.S. politician, governor of Alabama. Christmas message, 25 December 1949, in *Lend Me Your Ears: Great Speeches in History*, ed. William Safire (1992).

6   We're all gonna be here forever
So Mama don't you make such a stir
Just put down that camera
And come on and join up
The last of the family reserve.

LYLE LOVETT (b. 1956), U.S. singer and songwriter. "Family Reserve."

The speaker urges his mother to join the living members of the family, though most of the verses of his song recall bizarre and tragic deaths.

School Reunion

1   I,—the man of middle years,
In whose sable locks appears
Many a warning fleck of gray,—
Looking back to that far day,
And thy primal lessons, feel
Grateful smiles my lips unseal,
As, remembering thee, I blend
Olden teacher, present friend.

JOHN GREENLEAF WHITTIER (1807–1892), U.S. poet. "To My Old Schoolmaster: An Epistle Not After the Manner of Horace."

Whittier writes in the headnote to this poem: "These lines were addressed to my worthy friend Joshua Coffin, teacher, historian, and antiquarian. He was one of the twelve persons who with William Lloyd Garrison formed the first anti-slavery society in New England."

2   We are older: our footsteps, so light in the play
Of the far-away school-time, move slower to-day;—

Here a beard touched with frost,
  there a bald, shining crown,
And beneath the cap's border gray
  mingles with brown.

But faith should be cheerful, and
  trust should be glad,
And our follies and sins, not our
  years, make us sad.

JOHN GREENLEAF WHITTIER (1807–1892), U.S. poet. "The Quaker Alumni: Read at the Friends' School Anniversary, Providence, R.I., 6th mo., 1860."

3 To-day our Reverend Mother welcomes back
  Her wisest Scholars, those who understood
  The deeper teaching of her mystic tome,
    And offered their fresh lives to make it good.

JAMES RUSSELL LOWELL (1819–1891), U.S. author. "Ode Recited at the Harvard Commemoration, July 21, 1865."

4 It takes some time to accept and realize that fact that while you have been growing old, your friends have not been standing still, in that matter.

MARK TWAIN (SAMUEL CLEMENS) (1835–1910), U.S. author. *Life on the Mississippi* (chapter 55, "A Vendetta and Other Things") (1883).

5 Whether we like it, or don't
    There's a sort of bond in the fact
  That we all by one master were taught,
    By one master were bullied and whackt.
  And now all the more when we see
    Our class in so shrunken a state
  And we, who were seventy-two,
    Diminished to seven or eight.

ROBERT LOUIS STEVENSON (1850–1894), Scottish author. "Poem for a Class Reunion."

Stevenson describes a reunion of the Edinburgh private school run by Mr. D'Arcy Wentworth Thompson. Stevenson attended the school from 1864 through 1867.

6 Is this the great campus that I remember so well from my freshman days? What was it? Half a mile long, I think, and broader even than its length. That football goal that stood some fifty or sixty feet in the air, has it shrunk to these poor sticks? These simple trees, can they be the great elms that reared themselves up to the autumn sky? And was the Tower no higher than this?

STEPHEN LEACOCK (1869–1944), Canadian (English-born) humorist. *College Days* ("My College Days: A Retrospect") (1923).

7 We'll love her as we loved the dear old school or very very near it,
For tho' she's thrown the dress away, she's kept the same old spirit;
And of her present boys and girls we'll each prove a believer
That every year she'll turn them out as good and bright as we were.

PAUL LAURENCE DUNBAR (1872–1906), U.S. poet. "The Old High School and the New."

Dunbar dedicates a new school building for both its current students and its alumni.

8 We have come back here, along with those we love, to see one another again. And by being together we shall remember that we are part of a great company, we shall remember that we are not mere individuals isolated in a tempest, but that we are members of a community—that what we have to do, we

shall do together, with friends beside us.

WALTER LIPPMANN (1889–1974), U.S. newspaper columnist. Speech (summer 1940) to Harvard class of 1910, in *Lend Me Your Ears: Great Speeches in History*, ed. William Safire (1992).

9   I never go to a college reunion that I don't come away feeling sorry for all those paunchy, balding jocks trying to hang onto youth. I feel sorry for the men, too.

ERMA BOMBECK (1927–1996), U.S. humorist and newspaper columnist. "College Reunion" (3 November 1977), in *Forever, Erma: America's Best-Loved Writing from America's Favorite Humorist* (1996).

10   The class reunion, known as a splendid opportunity to check out how we're doing in comparison to our age peers, is less often acknowledged for its temporal impact—for being a stark reminder of time's relativity. Returning for a reunion, we hear the same chorus of bedeviled reactions "Can you believe it's been a quarter of a century?" "Where has the time gone!" It seems like yesterday!" The decades since graduation have raced by like a jet stream, sucking us along and depositing us in the present before we realized what was happening. But the four years when we were in school were as leisurely as a stroll; they ambled, they meandered, they distinguished themselves one from the other . . . as if each were a separate country, and we a different person every year.

LETTY COTTIN POGREBIN (b. 1939), U.S. author. *Getting Over Getting Older: An Intimate Journey* (chapter 4, "Time Is All There Is") (1996).

Hospitals and Doctors

1   I do not deny that medicine is a gift of God, nor do I refuse to acknowledge science in the skill of many physicians; but, take the best of them, how far are they from perfection? . . . I have no objection to the doctors acting upon certain theories, but, at the same time, they must not expect us to be the slaves of their fancies.

MARTIN LUTHER (1483–1546), German leader of the Protestant Reformation. *The Table Talk of Martin Luther*, no. 471, trans. W. Hazlitt (1848), ed. Thomas S. Kepler (1952).

2   Physicians are some of them so pleasing and conformable to the humour of the patient, as they press not the true cure of the disease; and some are so regular in proceeding according to art for the disease, as they respect not sufficiently the condition of the patient. Take one of a middle temper; or if it may not be found in one man, combine two of either sort; and forget not to call, as well the best acquainted with your body, as the best reputed of for his faculty.

FRANCIS BACON (1561–1626), English philosopher, essayist, and statesman. "Of Regiment of Health," *Essays or Counsels, Civil and Moral* (1625), and reprinted in *The Essays of Francis Bacon*, ed. John Pitcher (1985).

3   When the artlesse Doctor sees
No one hope, but of his Fees,
And his skill runs on the lees,
    Sweet Spirit comfort me!

ROBERT HERRICK (1591–1674), English poet and clergyman. "His Letanie, to the Holy Spirit."

4   God heales, and the Physitian hath the thankes.

GEORGE HERBERT (1593–1633), English poet and Anglican priest. *Outlandish Proverbs*, no. 169 (1640).

5 When a doctor talks to you of aiding, succouring and relieving nature, of taking away from her what is injurious and of giving her what she lacks; of re-establishing her and restoring her to the full exercise of her functions; when he talks to you of purifying the blood, of regulating the bowels and the brain, of reducing the spleen, of strengthening the chest, of renovating the liver, of improving the action of the heart, of re-establishing and preserving natural heat, and being possessed of secrets which will prolong life for many years: he is beguiling you with the romance of physic. But, when you come to learn the truth of things by experience, you find there is nothing in it all, it is like those beautiful dreams which, when you wake, leave you nothing but the regret of having put faith in them.

MOLIÈRE (JEAN BAPTISTE POQUELIN) (1622-73), French dramatist. *The Hypochondriac* (La malade imaginaire) 3.3 (1673), in *The Plays of Molière in French*, trans. A. R. Waller, vol. 8 (1926).

The practical brother of the play's hypochondriac warns against putting faith in doctors.

6 God heals, and the doctor takes the fees.

BENJAMIN FRANKLIN (1706–1790), U.S. statesman, scientist, and author. *Poor Richard's Almanack* (1732–1757).

7 If you are making choice of a physician, be sure you get one, if possible, with a cheerful and serene countenance.

OLIVER WENDELL HOLMES (1809–1894), U.S. author and physician. *The Professor at the Breakfast Table* (chapter 6) (1872).

8 For everybody's family doctor was remarkably clever, and was understood to have immeasurable skill in the management and training of the most skittish or vicious diseases. The evidence of his cleverness was of the higher intuitive order, lying in his lady-patients' immovable conviction, and was unassailable by any objection except that their intuitions were opposed by others equally strong; each lady who saw medical truth in Wrench and "the strengthening treatment" regarding Toller and "the lowering system" as medical perdition. . . . The strengtheners and the lowerers were all "clever" men in somebody's opinion, which is really as much as can be said for any living talents.

GEORGE ELIOT (MARY ANN OR MARIAN EVANS) (1819–1880), English author. *Middlemarch* (chapter 15) (1872).

9 PHYSICIAN, n. One upon whom we set our hopes when ill and our dogs when well.

AMBROSE BIERCE (1842–?1914), U.S. author. *The Devil's Dictionar* (1881–1911).

10 It is the humdrum, day-in, day-out, everyday work that is the real satisfaction of the practice of medicine; the million and a half patients a man has seen on his daily visits over a forty-year period of weekdays and Sundays that make up his life. I have never had a money practice; it would have been impossible for me. But the actual calling on people, at all times and under all conditions, the coming to grips

with the intimate conditions of their lives, when they were being born, when they were dying, watching them die, watching them get well when they were ill, has always absorbed me.

William Carlos Williams (1883–1963), U.S. poet and physician. "The Practice," *Autobiography* (1951).

11 Have your own doctor, who answers to you. If you don't, when the time comes that you get mixed up with hospitals, they'll treat you like a fool. . . . You're bound to lose your health at some point, but you don't have to lose your dignity, too.

Sarah Delany (1889–1997) and **A. Elizabeth Delany** (1891–1995), U.S. authors. "A Word to Older Follks," *The Delany Sisters' Book of Everyday Wisdom* (1994).

12 Here in the hospital, I say,
that is not my body, not my body.
I am not here for the doctors
to read like a recipe.

Anne Sexton (1928–1974), U.S. poet. "August 17th," *Scorpio, Bad Spider, Die: The Horoscope Poems*.

13 Doctors need to give every patient a chance to talk with their clothes on after the examination is over.

Richard C. Reynolds (b. 1929), U.S. physician, educator and writer. "A Day in the Life of an Internist,"; in *On Doctoring: Stories, Poems, Essays*, ed. Richard Reynolds and John Stone (1991).

14 There is, of course, an ordinary medicine, an everyday medicine, humdrum, prosaic, a medicine for stubbed toes, quinsies, bunions and boils; but all of us entertain the idea of *another* sort of medicine, of a wholly different kind: something deeper, older, extraordinary, almost

sacred, which will restore to us our lost health and wholeness, and give us a sense of perfect well-being.

Oliver Sacks (b. 1933), English neurologist and author. *Awakenings* (introduction, "The Coming of L-dopa") (1974).

15 The first thing about being a patient is—you have to be patient.

Oliver Sacks (b. 1933), English neurologist and author. *A Leg to Stand On* (chapter 3, "Limbo") (1984).

Sacks, a neurologist, has injured his leg and finds himself in the unusual position of being a patient. This advice comes to him from a pilot who is transporting him from one hospital to another.

16 I like to see doctors cough.
What kind of human being
would grab all your money
just when you're down?
I'm not saying they enjoy this:

. . . .

they'd rather be playing golf
and swapping jokes about our
feet.

James Tate (b. 1943), U.S. poet and educator. "On the Subject of Doctors."

Illness (Mild)

1 For there was never yet philosopher
That could endure the toothache
patiently,
However they have writ the style of
gods
And made a push at chance and
sufferance.

William Shakespeare (1564–1616), English poet and dramatist. *Much Ado About Nothing* 5.1.35–38.

2 If a Child be sick, give it whatever it wants to eat or drink, although particularly forbid by the Doctor: For what we long for in Sickness,

will do us good; and throw the Physick out of the Window; the Child will love you the better; but bid it not tell. Do the same to your Lady when she longs for anything in Sickness, and engage it will do her good.

JONATHAN SWIFT (1667–1745), Anglo-Irish author. *Directions to Servants* (chapter 12, "Directions to the Children's Maid") (1745).

3 The best of remedies is a beefsteak
Against sea-sickness; try it, Sir, before
You sneer, and I assure you this is true,
For I have found it answer—so may you.

GEORGE GORDON, LORD BYRON (1788–1824), English poet. *Don Juan* (canto 2, stanza 13).

4 Laffing keeps oph sickness, and haz conquered az menny diseases az ever pills have, and at mutch less expense. —It makes flesh, and keeps it in its place. It drives away weariness and brings a dream ov sweeness to the sleeper.

JOSH BILLINGS (HENRY W. SHAW) (1818–1885), U.S. humorist. "Laughing," *The Complete Works of Josh Billings* (1899).

5 I reckon being ill as one of the great pleasures of life, provided one is not too ill and is not obliged to work till one is better.

SAMUEL BUTLER (1835–1902), English author. *The Way of All Flesh* (chapter 80) (1903).

Severe Illness

1 We study health, and we deliberate upon our meats and drink and air and exercises, and we hew and we

polish every stone that goes to that building; and so our health is a long and regular work. But in a minute a cannon batters all, overthrows all, demolishes all; a sickness unprevented for all our diligence, unsuspected for all our curiosity, nay, undeserved, if we consider only disorder, summons us, seizes us, possesses us, destroys us in an instant.

JOHN DONNE (1572–1631), English poet, clergyman, and courtier. Meditation 1 ("The first alteration, the first grudging of the sickness"), *Devotions Upon Emergent Occasions* (1624).

2 Now that the frequent pangs my frame assail,
Now that my sleepless eyes are sunk and dim,
And seas of Pain seem waving through each limb—
Ah what can all Life's gilded scenes avail?

SAMUEL TAYLOR COLERIDGE (1772–1834), English poet and critic. "Pain."

3 Long illness is the real vampyrism; think of living a year or two after one is dead, by sucking the life-blood out of a frail young creature at one's bedside! Well, souls grow white, as well as cheeks, in these holy duties; one that goes in a nurse may come out an angel.

OLIVER WENDELL HOLMES (1809–1894), U.S. author and physician. *The Autocrat of the Breakfast-Table* (chapter 9) (1858).

Holmes paints a grim picture of the caregiver's role.

4 The sick man in his apparent inactivity has a very grand human task to fulfil. He must of course never cease to aim at his own cure and recovery. Also he must of course

use all the strength that remains to him for the different kinds of sometimes extremely productive work that are within his powers. Christian resignation, in fact, is just the opposite of giving up. Once he has resolved to combat his sickness in this way, the sick man must realize that in proportion to his sickness he has a special function to perform, in which no one can replace him: the task of co-operating in the transformation (one might say conversion) of human suffering.

PIERRE TEILHARD DE CHARDIN (1881–1955), French philosopher, paleontologist, and Jesuit priest. In "Human Energy" (written 1933), trans. J. M. Cohen (1969), and included in *On Suffering* (1974).

5   In the last states of a final illness, we need only the absence of pain and the presence of family.

HELEN HAYES (b. 1900), U.S. actress. *Loving Life* ("A Stop Along the Way") (1987).

Written with Marion Glasserow Gladney.

6   I might have had a tough break; but I have an awful lot to live for!

LOU GEHRIG (1903–1941), U.S. baseball player. Speech at Yankee Stadium, Bronx, N.Y., 4 July 1939, in *Lend Me Your Ears: Great Speeches in History*, ed. William Safire (1992).

Having been diagnosed with the paralyzing illness that bears his name, Gehrig bid farewell to baseball, commenting, "I consider myself the luckiest man on the face of the earth."

7   To be sick brings out all our prejudices and primitive feelings. Like fear or love, it makes us a little crazy. Yet the craziness of the patient is part of his condition.

ANATOLE BROYARD (1920–1990), U.S. editor, critic, and essayist. "Doctor, Talk to Me," *The New York Times Magazine* (26 August 1990), and reprinted in *Intoxicated by My Illness: And Other Writings on Life and Death* (1992).

8   A man's illness is his private territory and, no matter how much he loves you and how close you are, you stay an outsider. You are healthy.

LAUREN BACALL (b. 1924), U.S. actress. *Lauren Bacall by Myself* (1978).

Bacall's husband, Humphrey Bogart, died from cancer.

9   Pain probably makes us a bit godly . . . as tender love does. It makes us rue and summarize; it makes us bend and yield up ourselves.

EDWARD HOAGLAND (b. 1932), U.S. essayist. "The Threshold and the Jolt of Pain," in *The Art of the Personal Essay: An Anthology from the Classical Era to the Present*, ed. Phllip Lopate (1994).

10   Grieve for a decent limited time over whatever parts of your old self you know you'll miss. . . . Then stanch the grief, by whatever legal means. Next find your way to be somebody else, the next viable you—a stripped down whole other clear-eyed person, realistic as a sawed-off shotgun and thankful for air, not to speak of the human kindness you'll meet if you get normal luck.

REYNOLDS PRICE (b. 1933), U.S. author. *A Whole New Life: An Illness and a Healing* (chapter 7) (1994).

Price here writes about his "recovery" from spinal cancer, which left him a paraplegic.

11   Cancer patients are lied to, not just because the disease is (or is thought to be) a death sentence, but because it is felt to be obscene—in the original meaning of the word: ill-omened, abominable, repugnant to the senses.

SUSAN SONTAG (b. 1933), U.S. author. *Illness as Metaphor* (chapter 1) (1977).

12 Illness is the night-side of life, a more onerous citizenship. Everyone who is born holds dual citizenship, in the kingdom of the well and in the kingdom of the sick.

SUSAN SONTAG (b. 1933), U.S. author. *Illness as Metaphor* (introduction) (1977).

13 Right there is the usefulness of migraine, there in that imposed yoga, the concentration on the pain. For when the pain recedes, ten or twelve hours later, everything goes with it, all the hidden resentments, all the vain anxieties. The migraine has acted as a circuit breaker, and the fuses have emerged intact. There is a pleasant convalescent euphoria.

JOAN DIDION (b. 1934), U.S. author. "In Bed," in *The Art of the Personal Essay: An Anthology from the Classical Era to the Present*, ed. Phillip Lopate (1994).

14 For a while she'd exist in that peculiar stage in her recovery in which she'd be too strong for the hospital, yet too weak for the world, able to repossess her body only enough to feel again the claims of those who loved and needed her, but not enough to feel that she could satisfy those claims.

ALAN SHAPIRO (b. 1952), U.S. poet and educator. *The Last Happy Occasion* ("Sittin' in a Funeral Place") (1996).

15 Night is when the patient imagines dying. It was at these moments that I was most acutely conscious of the stark truth that everyone faces in hospital: no amount of loving care and attention (and I was greatly blessed in this) can disguise the fact that a dramatic illness emphasizes our solitude and isolation.

ROBERT McCRUM (b. 1953), author and editor. *My Year Off: Rediscovering Life After a Stroke* (August 1–5) (1998).

Separation

1 How like a winter hath my absence been,
From Thee, the pleasure of the fleeting year!

WILLIAM SHAKESPEARE (1564–1616), English poet and dramatist. Sonnet 97.

2 Though seas and land betwixt us both
    Our faith and troth,
    Like separated souls,
    All time and space controls;
Above the highest sphere we meet
Unseen, unknown, and greet as angels greet.

RICHARD LOVELACE (1618–1657), English poet. "To Lucasta. Going Beyond the Seas."

3 There can never be any adequate ground for separation. The condition of man is pitched so high in its joys and in its sorrows, that the sum which two married people owe to each other defies calculation. It is an infinite debt, which can only be discharged through all eternity.

JOHANN WOLFGANG VON GOETHE (1749–1832), German poet, novelist, and dramatist. *Elective Affinities* (book 1, chapter 9) (1809), trans. James Anthony Froude and R. Dillon Boylan (1962).

4 For the sword outwears its sheath,
    And the soul wears out the breast,
And the heart must pause to breathe,
    And love itself have rest.

GEORGE GORDON, LORD BYRON (1788–1824), English poet. "So We'll Go No More A-Roving."

5 My dearest Mary, wherefore hast
    thou gone,
   And left me in this dreary world
    alone?
   Thy form is here indeed—a lovely
    one—
   But thou art fled, gone down the
    dreary road,
   That lead to Sorrow's most obscure
    abode.

PERCY BYSSHE SHELLEY (1792–1822),
English poet. "To Mary Shelley."

6 When two people are once
   parted—have abandoned a common domicile and a common environment—new growths insensibly
   bud upward to fill each vacated
   place; unforeseen accidents hinder
   intentions, and old plans are forgotten.

THOMAS HARDY (1840–1928), English
author. *Tess of the D'Urbervilles, A Pure
Woman* (Phase the Fifth, "The Woman Pays";
chapter 36) (1895).

7 Marriage is easy, and divorce difficult, because this is Nature's plan.
   The natural law of attraction brings
   men and women together, and it is
   difficult to separate them. . . . Most
   couples who desire freedom only
   think they do: what they really
   want is a vacation; but they would
   not separate for good if they could.
   It is hard to part—people who have
   lived together grow to need each
   other. They want someone to quarrel with.

ELBERT HUBBARD (1856–1915), U.S.
author, founder of the Roycroft community.
The Philosophy of Elbert Hubbard ("His
Thoughts about Marriage and Divorce")
(1930).

8 Let him lack for the million and
   one things that a wife has done so
   long for his comfort that he did not
   even know she had done them.
   Above all, let him have to turn to
   strangers who are not interested in
   him and his affairs and who have
   no common backgrounds or mutual interests with him, for society.
   Then he will find out the worth of
   a wife and the price of a divorce.

DOROTHY DIX (1861–1951), U.S. author.
How to Win and Hold a Husband (chapter 34,
"Trial Separation as a Divorce Cure") (1939).

Divorcing

1 When a divorced man marries a divorced woman, there are four natures with which to contend.

Pesahim 112, in *The Talmudic Anthology:
Tales and Teachings of the Rabbis,* ed. Louis I.
Newman (1947).

2 O Prophet! When ye (men) put
   away women, put them away for
   their (legal) period and reckon the
   period, and keep your duty to Allah, your Lord. Expel them not
   from their houses nor let them go
   forth unless they commit open im-
   morality. Such are the limits (imposed by) Allah; and whoso trans-
   gresseth Allah's limits, he verily
   wrongeth his soul. Thou knowest
   not: it may be that Allah will afterward bring some new thing to pass.
   Then, when they have reached their
   term, take them back in kindness
   or part from them in kindness, and
   call to witness two just men among
   you, and keep your testimony up-
   right for Allah.

Qur'an 65.1–2; *The Glorious Koran: An Explanatory Translation by Marmaduke Pickthall*
(1930; reprint 1992).

3 Weakness and incapacity legiti-
   mately break up a marriage.

MICHEL EYQUEM DE MONTAIGNE (1533–1592), French essayist. "On Some Verses of Virgil," book 3, essay 5 (1585–88), *The Complete Essays of Montaigne*, trans. Donald M. Frame (1976; originally published 1958).

4   Alas, sir,
In what have I offended you? What cause
Hath my behavior given to your displeasure,
That thus you should proceed to put me off
And take your good grace from me? Heaven witness,
I have been to you a true and humble wife,
At all times to your will conformable,
Ever in fear to kindle your dislike,
Yea, subject to your countenance—glad or sorry
As I saw it inclin'd.

WILLIAM SHAKESPEARE (1564–1616), English poet and dramatist. *King Henry VIII* 2.4.16–24.

Queen Katharine pleads with Henry VIII for justice as she fights the idea of divorce. Although he and his ministers proceed with the divorce, the king makes this acknowledgement: "That man i' th' world who shall report he has / A better wife, let him in nought be trusted / For speaking false in that."

5   Love in marriage cannot live nor subsist unless it be mutual; and where love cannot be, there can be left of wedlock nothing but the empty husk of an outside matrimony, as undelightful and unpleasing to God as any other kind of hypocrisy.

JOHN MILTON (1608–1674), English poet. "The Doctrine and Discipline of Divorce" (chapter 6, "The fourth Reason of this Law, that God regards Love and Peace in the family more than a compulsive performance of marriage, which is more broke by a grievous

continuance than by a needful divorce") (1643).

6   When a man receives no dowry [other] than that of beauty in his wife, he repents soon after the wedding ceremony is over, and the best-looking woman has but few means of defence against the indifference that soon takes the place of infatuation. I tell you again, these unbalanced raptures, these youthful longings and these transports may give us, at first, a few enjoyable nights, but this kind of happiness is not lasting, and, when our passion cools, disagreeable days follow the pleasant nights.

MOLIÈRE (JEAN BAPTISTE POQUELIN) (1622–1673), French dramatist. *The Blunderer* (L'Etourdi) 4.3 (first performed 1653 or 1655 and published 1658), in *The Plays of Molière in French*, trans. A. R. Waller, vol. 8 (1926).

Anselm's advice to the young gentleman Léandre, who has fallen in love with a young woman of a lower social class.

7   Why should a foolish marriage vow
       Which long ago was made,
Oblige us to each other now
       When passion is decayed?

JOHN DRYDEN (1631–1700), English poet and dramatist. *Marriage à la Mode* (act 1, opening song) (1672).

8   When they [the French] promise always to love a woman, they suppose that she, in turn, promises that she will always be lovable; if she breaks her word, they no longer feel bound to theirs.

CHARLES LOUIS DE SECONDAT, BARON DE LA BRÈDE ET DE MONTESQUIEU (1689–1755), French jurist and political philosopher. Letter 55 (Rica to Ibben, at Smyrna, Paris, the 7th of the moon of Zilcade, 1714), *The Persian Letters* (1721); trans. George R. Healy (1964).

9 It is quite difficult to understand clearly what reason led the Christians to abolish divorce. Marriage, in every nation on earth, is a contract sensitive to all conventions, and from it should be abolished only what could enfeeble its intended purpose. But the Christians do not regard it from this point of view and they go to considerable trouble to explain their attitude. Marriage to them does not consist in sensual pleasure; on the contrary . . . it seems they wish to banish that element from it as much as possible. Rather, it is to them an image, a symbol, and something mysteriously more, which I do not understand.

CHARLES LOUIS DE SECONDAT, BARON DE LA BRÈDE ET DE MONTESQUIEU (1689–1755), French jurist and political philosopher. Letter 116 (Usbek to Rhedi, at Venice, Paris, the 19th of the moon of Chahban, 1718), *Persian Letters* (1721); trans. George R. Healy (1964).

10 Divorce is probably of nearly the same date as marriage. I believe, however, that marriage is some weeks more ancient; that is to say, men quarrelled with their wives at the end of five days, beat them at the end of the month, and separated from them after six weeks' cohabitation.

VOLTAIRE (FRANÇOIS-MARIE AROUET) (1694–1778), French philosopher and author. "Divorce," *Philosophical Dictionary* (1764).

11 The only way to be reconciled to old friends is to part with them for good: at a distance we may chance to be thrown back (in a waking dream) upon old times and old feelings: or at any rate we should not think of renewing our intimacy, till we have fairly *spit our spite*, said, thought, and felt all the ill we can of each other.

WILLIAM HAZLITT (1788–1830), English essayist and critic. "On the Pleasure of Hating."

12 [Marriage] is never wholly happy. Two people can never literally be as one: there is, perhaps, a possibility of content under peculiar circumstances, such as are seldom combined; but it is as well not to run the risk: you may make fatal mistakes. . . . Let all the single be satisfied with their freedom.

CHARLOTTE BRONTË (1816–1855), English author. *Shirley* (chapter 21; or vol. 2, chapter 10) (1849).

Mrs. Pryor responds here to Caroline, who suggests: "Where affection is reciprocal and sincere, and minds are harmonious, marriage *must* be happy." She argues not for divorce but for the avoidance of marriage. Her comments nonetheless suggest why divorce is such a prevalent practice.

13 The sort of men and women that marriage enslaves would be vastly more wretched and mischievous, if they were set free. I believe that the hell people make for themselves isn't at all a bad place for them. It's the best place for them.

WILLIAM DEAN HOWELLS (1837–1920), U.S. author. *A Modern Instance* (chapter 26) (1882).

Atherton, a bachelor who considers marriage "the realm of unreason," explains his theories on the subject to his friend Halleck, who considers him "horrible" and "cold-blooded."

14 The instant, quick release by divorce from all troubles, great and small, between man and wife, is not better than that other instant, quick relief from bodily pain, which is

morphia. . . . We are a cowardly generation, and men shrink from pain.

FRANCES MARION CRAWFORD (1854–1909), U.S. author. *A Rose of Yesterday* (chapter 13) (1897).

15 When people are tied together for life they too often regard manners as a mere superfluity, and courtesy as a thing of no moment; but where the bond can be easily broken, its very fragility makes its strength, and reminds the husband that he should always try to please, and the wife that she should never cease to be charming.

OSCAR WILDE (1854–1900), Irish author. "The American Man," *Court and Society Review* 4 (13 April 1887), and reprinted in *The Artist as Critic: Critical Writings of Oscar Wilde*, ed. Richard Ellman (1968).

In this article Wilde describes the possibility of divorce as one of the strengths of American marriages.

16 Divorces are made in Heaven.

OSCAR WILDE (1854–1900), Irish author. *The Importance of Being Earnest* (act 1) (1895).

Algernon Moncrieff makes this statement in the course of discouraging his friend Jack Worthing from proposing to Gwendolyn Fairfax.

17 Divorce is a heroic remedy for an awful condition. It is the culmination of a fearful tragedy. I know of nothing worse than incompatibility. There is no hell equal to the hell of having to live with a person who is not your own.

ELBERT HUBBARD (1856–1915), U.S. author, founder of the Roycroft community. *The Philosophy of Elbert Hubbard* ("His Thoughts about Marriage and Divorce") (1930).

18 All young women begin by believing they can change and reform the men they marry. They can't.

GEORGE BERNARD SHAW (1856–1950), Irish dramatist and critic. *On the Rocks* (act 2) (1933).

19 Do you know, I always have a distinct feeling of pleasure when I hear of married people parting. . . . But it isn't a malicious pleasure; There's nothing personal in it. . . . But marriage in general is *such* a humbug—you forgive the word.

GEORGE GISSING (1857–1903), English author. *The Odd Women* (chapter 27) (1893).

Mrs. Cosgrove reacts to the breakup of the Widdowsons' unhappy and childless marriage.

20 Women are so used t' takin' things home on approval, an' makin' things over, an' exchangin' things, an' takin' things back, that they use th' same system with husbands. They jest reason that they kin take a man an' if they don't like him they kin dump him. Sometimes they try t' make him over. Men don't hanker fer divorces as much as women do. They hain't home much an' besides they kin get away with a double life better'n a woman.

KIN HUBBARD (1868–1930), U.S. humorist. "The Licklider Divorce Case," *The Best of Kin Hubbard: Abe Martin's Sayings and Wisecracks, Abe's Neighbors, His Almanack, Comic Drawings*, ed. David S. Hawes (1984).

21 *Alimony*— The ransom that the happy pay to the devil.

H. L. MENCKEN (1880–1956), U.S. author. "Sententiae," *A Book of Burlesques* (1920).

22 Each in a marriage must make a contribution. Of course. What was

that old song? "You're the cream in my coffee . . . You're the salt in my stew"? How great and how true. One has a right to expect such a complement. I was always eager to salt a good stew. The trouble was that I was expected to supply the meat and potatoes as well.

BETTE DAVIS, U.S. actress. *The Lonely Life: An Autobiography* (chapter 20) (1962).

One of Davis's husbands obtained a divorce on the grounds that "She reads in bed; she neglected me for her work." She reveals the blend of cynicism and lost innocence provoked by the end of one of her marriages when she writes: "I had no time to be shocked that my little white cottage was crumbling. Like a set that is struck after a performance, it seemed like the dream it was—a façade, a temporary scene for pointless arguments.

" . . . A boy and girl had adored each other, married and never dreamed of such an ending at all. It made me feel old and weary. The fact that I didn't care anymore that I was finding other men attractive was heartbreaking to me."

23   It is not the frequency of divorce which makes the times wicked; it is the wickedness of the times which increases divorce.

ROBERTSON DAVIES (1913–1995), Canadian author. "Of Divorce," *The Table Talk of Samuel Marchbanks* (1949).

24   Judaism regards divorce as a catastrophe that is bound to occur in a certain number of mistaken marriages. Rather than chain two unsuited and hating partners together for life, our law provides the machinery for dissolving such unions.

HERMAN WOUK (b. 1915), U.S. author. *This Is My God: The Jewish Way of Life* (chapter 11, "Love and Marriage: And Certain Elegant Variations") (1988).

25   I no longer believe that marriage means forever no matter how lousy

it is—or "for the sake of the children."

ANN LANDERS (EPPIE LEDERER) (b. 1918), U.S. advice columnist. Quoted in *U.S. News and World Report* (23 October 1995).

Ann Landers had been married to her husband for 35 years when they divorced.

26   I am still divorcing him,
adding up the crimes
Of how he came to me,
how he left me.

ANNE SEXTON (1928–1974), U.S. poet. "Divorce, Thy Name Is Woman."

27   I've been married too many times. How terrible to change children's affiliations, their affections—to give them the insecurity of placing their trust in someone when maybe that someone won't be there next year.

ELIZABETH TAYLOR (b. 1932), U.S. (English-born) actress. *Elizabeth Taylor: An Informal Memoir* (chapter 8) (1965).

28   The only hope I can see for the unhappiness of divorce is knowing that it is better than a bad marriage. The unhappiness of divorce ends, in time, for healthy people. Healthy people refuse to stay unhappy. Sooner or later they wake up and decide to be happy again. They lose weight and start exercising. They dye their hair or get a toupee. They buy a red dress and get to a party and start flirting. They redecorate their living quarters. They get out their address books and start looking for old lovers to recycle.

ELLEN GILCHRIST (b. 1935), U.S. author. "Meditations on Divorce," in *Women on Divorce: A Bedside Companion*, ed. Penny Kaganoff and Susan Spano (1995).

29 There is cruelty in divorce. There is cruelty in forced or unfortunate marriage. We will continue to cry at weddings because we know how bittersweet, how fragile is the troth. We will always need legal divorce just as an emergency escape hatch is crucial in every submarine. No sense, however, in denying that after every divorce someone will be running like a cat, tin cans tied to its tail: spooked and slowed down.

ANNE ROIPHE (b. 1935), U.S. author. "A Tale of Two Divorces," in *Women on Divorce: A Bedside Companion*, ed. Penny Kaganoff and Susan Spano (1995).

30 Divorce after sixty is likely to mean that one or both partners feel imprisoned—not enough space between them to breathe, too much togetherness, too much interdependence, and no separate hobbies, trips or learning experiences. Boredom from passivity; too *much* acceptance of limitations.

EDA LESHAN, U.S. author. *It's Better to Be Over the Hill Than Under It: Thoughts on Life Over Sixty* ("Divorce After Sixty") (1990).

31 There is rhythm to the ending of marriage just like the rhythm of courtship—only backward. You try to start again but get into blaming over and over. Finally, you are both worn out, exhausted, hopeless. Then lawyers are called in to pick clean the corpses.

ERICA JONG (b. 1942), U.S. novelist and poet. *How to Save Your Own Life* ("There is a rhythm to the ending . . .") (1977).

32 What we're asking when we ask about divorce is how people fall out of love. And if, as girls, we searched for answers about what boys really wanted, what we're asking, as adults, is what men and women *don't* want—what causes them to take a stand, to draw the line, to divorce.

FRANCINE PROSE (b. 1947), U.S. author. "Divorce as a Spectator Sport," in *Women on Divorce: A Bedside Companion*, ed. Penny Kaganoff and Susan Spano (1995).

33 Sometimes I dream of an eighth sacrament, the sacrament of divorce. Like communion, it is a slim white wafer on the tongue. Like confession, it is forgiveness. Forgiveness is important not so much for what we've done wrong, but for what we feel we need to be forgiven for. Family, friends, God, whoever loves us, forgives us, takes us in again. They are thrilled by our life, our possibilities, our second chances.

ANN PATCHETT (b. 1963), U.S. author. "The Sacrament of Divorce," *Women on Divorce: A Bedside Companion*, ed. Penny Kaganoff and Susan Spano (1995).

34 Nothing teaches children about our capacity for deception, for multiple selves, like divorce.

JONATHAN ROSEN (b. 1963), U.S. author and editor. "Pandora's Box, " in *Men on Divorce: The Other Side of the Story*, ed. Penny Kaganoff and Susan Spano (1997).

35 Truth be told, there is nothing like a divorce to make a Madonna out of a Tammy Wynette. Nothing like a divorce, that is, to make even the most accommodating and least politicized female sit up and take note of the fact that the judicial system is run primarily by men who tend on the whole to favor women who stay home and busy themselves

with *kinder* and *küche* —and to regard with punitive suspicion (however unconscious) those women who want it every which way, the career and the children and the divorce.

DAPHNE MERKIN, U.S. author and editor. "In the Country of Divorce," in *Women on Divorce: A Bedside Companion*, ed. Penny Kaganoff and Susan Spano (1995).

Reuniting

1   The course of true love never did run smooth.

WILLIAM SHAKESPEARE (1564–1616), English poet and dramatist. *A Midsummer Night's Dream* 1.1.134.

2   We fell out, my wife and I,
O we fell out I know not why,
    And kissed again with tears.
And blessings on the falling out
    That all the more endears,
When we fall out with those we love
        And kiss again with tears!

ALFRED, LORD TENNYSON (1809–1892), English poet. *The Princess* (section 1, concluding lyric) (1850).

3   I met my old lover on the street last night
She seemed so glad to see me, I just smiled
And we talked about some old times
And we drank ourselves some beers
Still crazy after all these years.

PAUL SIMON (b. 1941), U.S. singer and songwriter. "Still Crazy After All These Years" (1974).

Disasters

1   Man that is born of a woman is of few days, and full of trouble. He cometh forth like a flower, and is cut down; he fleeth also as a shadow, and continueth not.

Job 14.1–2.

2   The pencil of the Holy Ghost hath laboured more in describing the afflictions of Job, than the felicities of Solomon. Prosperity is not without many fears and distastes, and adversity is not without comforts and hopes. . . . Certainly, virtue is like precious odours, most fragrant, when they are incensed, or crushed; for prosperity doth best discover vice, but adversity doth best discover virtue.

FRANCIS BACON (1561–1626), English philosopher, essayist, and statesman. "Of Adversity," *Essays or Counsels, Civil and Moral* (1625), and reprinted in *The Essays of Francis Bacon*, ed. John Pitcher (1985).

3   I have often had occasion to remark the fortitude with which women sustain the most overwhelming reverses of fortune. Those disasters which break down the spirit of a man and prostrate him in the dust seem to call forth all the energies of the softer sex, and give such intrepidity and elevation to their character that at times it approaches to sublimity. Nothing can be more touching than to behold a soft and tender female, who had been all weakness and dependence and alive to every trivial roughness while treading the prosperous paths of life, suddenly rising in mental force to be the comforter and support of her husband under misfortune, and abiding with unshrinking firmness the bitterest blasts of adversity.

WASHINGTON IRVING (1783–1859), U.S. author. "The Wife," *The Sketch Book of Geoffrey Crayon, Gent.* (1819–20).

4   The petty misfortunes that vex us every hour may be regarded as intended to keep us in practice so that the strength to endure great misfortunes may not be wholly dissipated in prosperity.

ARTHUR SCHOPENHAUER (1788–1860), German philosopher. *Parerga and Paralipomena: Short Philosophical Essays* (chapter 5, "Counsels and Maxims") (1851), trans. E. F. J. Payne (1974).

5   God uses suffering as a whetstone, to make men sharp with.

HENRY WARD BEECHER (1813–1887), U.S. clergyman. "Sermon: Bearing, but Not Overbourne," *Beecher as a Humorist: Selections from the Published Works,* ed. Eleanor Kirk (1887).

6   Nothing ever happens but the *un*foreseen.

GEORGE DU MAURIER (1834–1896), English author. *Trilby* (part 4) (1894).

7   CALAMITY, n. A more than commonly plain and unmistakeable reminder that the affairs of this life are not of our own ordering.

AMBROSE BIERCE (1842–?1914), U.S. author. *The Devil's Dictionary* (1881–1911).

8   Life is terribly deficient in form. Its catastrophes happen in the wrong way and to the wrong people.

OSCAR WILDE (1854–1900), Irish author. "The Critic as Artist," *Intentions. A Dialogue: Part II* (1891).

9   He will be far less exposed to disaster who cherishes ideas within him that soar high above the indifference, selfishness, vanities of every-day life. And therefore, come happiness or sorrow, the happiest man will be he within whom the greatest idea shall burn the most ardently.

MAURICE MAETERLINCK (1862–1949), Belgian author. *Wisdom and Destiny* (section 16), trans. Alfred Sutro (1901).

10   We are perplexed to see misfortune falling upon decent, inoffensive, worthy people—on capable, hardworking mothers of families or diligent, thrifty, little trades-people, on those who have worked so hard, and so honestly, for their modest stock of happiness and now seem to be entering on the enjoyment of it with the fullest right. . . . Let me implore the reader to try to believe, if only for the moment, that God, who made these deserving people, may really be right when He thinks that their modest prosperity and the happiness of their children are not enough to make them blessed: that all this must fall from them in the end, and that if they have not learned to know Him they will be wretched.

C. S. LEWIS (1898–1963), English author. *The Problem of Pain* (chapter 6, "Human Pain") (1940).

Bereavement

1   Tzu-yu said, "When mourning gives full expression to grief nothing more can be required."

CONFUCIUS (551?–479), Chinese philosopher. *Analects* (Lun yü), book 19, section 12, trans. D. C. Lau (1979).

2   Jeremiah said: "Weep ye not for the dead, neither bemoan him" (Jeremiah 22.10). Weep not overmuch

and bemoan not beyond the measure. What is the measure? Three days for weeping; seven days for bemoaning; thirty days for not donning clothes that have been pressed, and for not having the hair cut. From now on, saith the Lord, ye may not feel more compassion over him than I do.

Moed Katon 27, in *The Talmudic Anthology: Tales and Teachings of the Rabbis*, ed. Louis I. Newman (1947).

3   I will instruct my sorrows to be
        proud,
    For grief is proud and makes his
        owner stoop.
    To me and to the state of my great
        grief
    Let kings assemble, for my grief's
        so great
    That no supporter but the huge
        firm earth
    Can hold it up.

WILLIAM SHAKESPEARE (1564–1616), English poet and dramatist. *King John* 3.1.68–73).

4   Moderate lamentation is the right of the dead, excessive grief the enemy to the living.

WILLIAM SHAKESPEARE (1564–1616), English poet and dramatist. *All's Well That Ends Well* (1.1.55–56).

Spoken by Lafew, an old lord who seems rather practical and cynical when it comes to emotions and matters of the heart.

5   It is the will of God and Nature that these mortal bodies be laid aside, when the soul is to enter into real life; 'tis rather an embrio state, a preparation for living; a man is not completely born until he be dead: Why then should we grieve that a new child is born among the immortals?

BENJAMIN FRANKLIN (1706–1790), U.S. statesman, scientist, and author. Letter to Elizabeth Hubbart, 22 February 1756, in *Letters of a Nation: A Collection of Extraordinary American Letters*, ed. Andrew Carroll (1997).

Franklin consoles Hubbart on the loss of her stepfather, his brother John Franklin.

6   Sorrow is a kind of rust of the soul, which every new idea contributes in its passage to scour away. It is the putrefaction of stagnant life, and it is remedied by exercise and motion.

SAMUEL JOHNSON (1709–1884), English author. "Means of Regulating Sorrow," *The Rambler*, no. 47 (28 August 1750).

7   Where there is leisure for fiction there is little grief.

SAMUEL JOHNSON (1709–1784), English author. *Milton* (preface).

Johnson criticizes Milton's elegy *Lycidas*, noting true passion would not run after "remote allusions and obscure opinions."

8   She lived unknown, and few could
        know
            When Lucy ceased to be;
    But she is in her grave, and oh,
        The difference to me!

WILLIAM WORDSWORTH (1770–1850), English poet. "She dwelt among the untrodden ways."

This is one of a group of poems about a girl named Lucy, whom some readers associate with Wordsworth's sister Dorothy.

9   The sorrow for the dead is the only sorrow from which we refuse to be divorced. Every other wound we seek to heal—every other affliction to forget; but this wound we consider it a duty to keep open—this affliction we cherish and brood over in solitude.

WASHINGTON IRVING (1783–1859), U.S. author. "Rural Funerals," *The Sketchbook of Geoffrey Crayon, Gent.* (1819–20).

10 Ah, woe is me! Winter is come and
    gone,
    But grief returns with the revolving
    year.

    PERCY BYSSHE SHELLEY (1792–1822),
    English poet. "Adonais" (section 18).

11 The persons on whom I have be-
    stowed my dearest love, lie deep in
    their graves; but, although the hap-
    piness and delight of my life lie
    buried there too, I have not made a
    coffin of my heart, and sealed it up,
    for ever, on my best affections.
    Deep affliction has but strength-
    ened and refined them.

    CHARLES DICKENS (1812–1870), En-
    glish novelist. Oliver Twist (chapter 14, "Com-
    prising further Particulars of Oliver's Stay at
    Mr. Brownlow's, with the remarkable Predic-
    tion which one Mr. Grimwig uttered concern-
    ing him, when he went out on an Errand")
    (1837–38).

    Mr. Brownlow tells young Oliver of the grief
    he has suffered.

12 Heaven knows we need never be
    ashamed of our tears, for they are
    rain upon the blinding dust of
    earth, overlying our hard hearts.

    CHARLES DICKENS (1812–1870), En-
    glish author. Great Expectations (chapter 19)
    (1860–61).

    Pip describes how he finally gave in to tears
    after parting from his family.

13 Only those whom we have never
    possessed can pass away. And we
    cannot even mourn not having
    truly possessed this person or
    that—we have neither time, nor
    strength nor right to do so, for the
    most fleeting experience of any real
    possession . . . casts us back into
    ourselves with so much force, gives
    us so much to do there, demands
    so much loneliest development

from us, that it suffices to absorb
our individual attention for ever.

RAINER MARIA RILKE (1857–1926),
German poet. Letter to Clara Rilke, 12 August
1904, Selected Letters: 1902–1926, trans. R. F.
C. Hull (1988).

14 When we lose one we love, our bit-
    terest tears are called forth by the
    memory of hours when we loved
    not enough.

    MAURICE MAETERLINCK (1862–
    1949), Belgian (writing in French) author. Wis-
    dom and Destiny (section 44) (1901), trans.
    Alfred Sutro (1901).

15 No one ever told me that grief felt
    so like fear. I am not afraid, but the
    sensation is like being afraid. The
    same fluttering in the stomach, the
    same restlessness, the yawning. I
    keep on swallowing. At other times
    it feels like being mildly drunk, or
    concussed. There is a sort of invisi-
    ble blanket between the world and
    me. I find it hard to take in what
    anyone says. Or perhaps, hard to
    want to take it in.

    C. S. LEWIS (1898–1963), English author.
    A Grief Observed (chapter 1) (1961).

16 . . . the body remains in a vacuum
    Gagged, bound, and sick with dread
    Knowing the words that can't be
    spoken
    Searching for words that must be
    said
    Dumb, inarticulate, heartbroken.

    NOËL COWARD (1899–1973), English
    dramatist, composer, and actor. "Condolence."

17 About suffering they were never
    wrong,
    The Old Masters; how well they
    understood
    Its human position; how it takes
    place

While someone else is eating or
  opening a window or just walking
  dully along.

W. H. AUDEN (1907–1973), English poet.
"Musée des Beaux Arts."

18 Life is very insistent; and it always
seems to be so when friends sadly
leave us.

ALEC GUINESS (b. 1914), English actor.
*My Name Escapes Me: The Diary of a Retiring
Actor* ("Monday, 22 May 1995") (1996).

19 You know it takes a year, a full turn
of the calendar, to get over losing
somebody. That's a true saying.

ANNIE PROULX (b. 1935), author. *The
Shipping News* (chapter 4, "Cast Away")
(1993).

20 I mourn in grey, grey as the sleeted
wind the bled shades of twilight,
gunmetal, battleships, industrial
paint.

MARGE PIERCY (b. 1936), U.S. poet.
"For mourning."

Piercy contrasts her color of mourning, the
"color of ash," with the traditional black of
mourning, which she associates with rare,
sleek, shining things.

Funeral

1 Formerly the deceased of the
wealthy were buried in fancy caskets, of the poor in cheap coffins.
This, too, was altered, and now all
who die, whether rich or poor, are
buried in inexpensive caskets.

Moed Katon 27, in *The Talmudic Anthology:
Tales and Teachings of the Rabbis*, ed. Louis I.
Newman (1947).

2 Not a flower, not a flower sweet,
  On my black coffin let there be
    strown;

Not a friend, not a friend greet
  My poor corpse, where my bones
    shall be thrown.
A thousand thousand sighs to save,
  Lay me, O where
Sad true lover never find my grave,
  To weep there!

WILLIAM SHAKESPEARE (1564–1616),
English poet and dramatist. *Twelfth Night*
(2.4.59–66).

The clown Feste sings for Duke Orsino to humor his melancholy mood.

3 I cannot choose but weep, to think
they would lay him i' th' cold
ground.

WILLIAM SHAKESPEARE (1564–1616),
English poet and dramatist. *Hamlet* (4.5.70–
71).

Ophelia, maddened by grief, mourns her father
Polonius.

4 Then cheerly to your work again
  With hearts new-brac'd and set
To run, untir'd, love's blessèd race,
  As meet for those, who face to face
Over the grave their Lord have
    met.

JOHN KEBLE (1792–1866), English clergyman and poet. "Burial of the Dead," *The
Christian Year* (1827).

5 Ah, with the Grape my fading Life
  provide,
And wash my Body whence the Life
  had died,
  And in a Windingsheet of Vine-
    leaf wrapt,
So bury me by some sweet Garden-
  side.

EDWARD FITZGERALD (1809–1883),
English author and translator. *Rubáiyát of
Omar Khayyám* (section 67) (1859).

6 No funeral gloom, my dears, when
  I am gone,

Corpse-gazing, tears, black raiment,
  graveyard grimness;
Think of me as withdrawn into the
  dimness,
Yours still, you mine; remember all
  the best
Of our past moments, and forget
  the rest.

WILLIAM ALLINGHAM (1824–1889),
Irish author. "A Poet's Epitaph."

7   Why is it that we rejoice at a birth
    and grieve at a funeral? Is it be-
    cause we are not the person in-
    volved?

MARK TWAIN (SAMUEL CLEMENS)
(1835–1910), U.S. author. *Pudd'nhead Wilson* ("Pudd'nhead Wilson's Calendar" at chapter 9) (1894).

8   It comes strangely over me in bid-
    ding you good-bye how a life is but
    a day and expresses mainly but a
    single note. It is so much like the
    act of bidding an ordinary good-
    night. Good night, my sacred old
    Father! If I don't see you again—
    Farewell! a blessed farewell!

WILLIAM JAMES (1842–1910), U.S. philosopher and psychologist. Letter to his father
Henry James Sr., 14 December 1882, in *Letters
of a Nation: A Collection of Extraordinary
American Letters*, ed. Andrew Carroll (1997).

Henry James Sr. died before he received his
son's farewell letter. It was read at the funeral
by Henry James Jr.

9   I know those are the conventional
    virtues that are inscribed on tomb-
    stones—but he is the one person in
    a million who deserves them. Per-
    haps these virtues are so common
    in cemeteries because they are so
    rare in life.

EUGENE O'NEILL (1888–1953), U.S.
dramatist. Letter to his wife Agnes, 10 August

1920, in *Letters of a Nation: A Collection of
Extraordinary American Letters*, ed. Andrew
Carroll (1997).

O'Neill describes watching his father die of intestinal cancer. He refers to his father as someone who was "well-liked" and a good husband and father.

10 Down, down, down into the dark-
      ness of the grave
    Gently they go, the beautiful, the
      tender, the kind;
    Quietly they go, the intelligent, the
      witty, the brave.
    I know. But I do not approve. And
      I am not resigned.

EDNA ST. VINCENT MILLAY (1892–
1950), U.S. poet. "Dirge Without Music."

11 Tell all my mourners
    To mourn in red—
    Cause there ain't no sense
    In my bein' dead.

LANGSTON HUGHES (1902–1967), U.S.
poet. "Wake."

12 Funerals are pretty compared to
    deaths. Funerals are quiet, but
    deaths—not always. Sometimes
    their breathing is hoarse, and some-
    times it rattles, and sometimes they
    even cry out to you, "Don't let me
    go!"

TENNESSEE WILLIAMS (1914–1983),
U.S. dramatist. *A Streetcar Named Desire*
(scene 1) (1947).

Blanche reproaches her sister Stella for being
present only for the "pretty flowers" of funerals
and not for the harsh reality of death.

13 O death, where is thy sting? O
    grave, where is thy victory? Where,
    indeed. Many a badly stung survi-
    vor, faced with the aftermath of
    some relative's funeral, has ruefully
    concluded that the victory has been
    won hands down by a funeral es-

tablishment—in a disastrously un-
equal battle.

JESSICA MITFORD (1917–1996), U.S.
author. *The American Way of Death Revisited.*
(chapter 2, "The American Way of Death")
(1998).

14   Every man in the chapel hoped that
when his hour came he, too, would
be eulogized, which is to say forgiven, and that all of his lapses,
greeds, errors, and strayings from
the truth would be invested with
coherence and looked upon with
charity. This was perhaps the last
thing human beings could give each
other, and it was what they de-
manded, after all, of the Lord.

JAMES BALDWIN (1924–1987), U.S. au-
thor. *Notes of a Native Son* (section 3) (1955).

Baldwin here comments on hearing a cleaned-
up version of his father's life in a funeral sermon.

15   I have no weddings or baptisms in
the funeral home and the folks that
pay me have maybe lost sight of the
obvious connections between the
life and the death of us. And how
the rituals by which we mark the
things that only happen to us once,
birth and death, or maybe twice in
the case of marriage, carry the same
emotional mail—a message of loss
and gain, love and grief, things
changed utterly.

THOMAS LYNCH (b. 1948), U.S. undertaker and author. *The Undertaking: Life Studies
from the Dismal Trade* ("Crapper") (1997).

Lynch comments throughout his work on the
disadvantages of the modern "out of sight, out
of mind" treatment of death. He says that only
a few "marginalized" people like "poets and
preachers, foreigners and undertakers" can appreciate "the 'good' in 'goodbye,' the 'sane' in
'sadness,' the 'fun' in 'funerals.'"

Recovery

1   The Physicians told me that yet
there was one help for me, if I
could constantly pursue it, to wit, *A
sober and orderly life* : for this had
every way great force for the recov-
ering and preserving of Health, as a
disorderly life to the overthrowing
of it; as I too wel by experience
found. For Temperance preserves
even old men and sickly men
sound: But Intemperance destroyes
most healthy and flourishing constitutions.

GEORGE HERBERT (1593–1633), English
poet and Anglican priest. *A Treatise of Temperance and Sobrietie: Written by Lud. Cornarus,
Translated into English by Mr. George Herbert*
(1634).

2   See the Wretch, that long has tost
On the thorny bed of pain,
At length repair his vigour lost,
And breathe, and walk again:
The meanest floweret of the vale,
The simplest note that swells the
  gale,
The common sun, the air, the skies,
To Him are opening Paradise.

THOMAS GRAY (1716–1771), English
poet. "Ode on the Pleasure Arising from Vicis-
situde."

3   The longer I abstained the higher
my spirits were, the keener my enjoyment—till the moment, the dire-
ful moment, arrived when my pulse
began to fluctuate, my heart to pal-
pitate, and such a dreadful falling
abroad, as it were, of my whole
frame, such intolerable restlessness,
and incipient bewilderment, that in
the last of my several attempts to
abandon the dire poison, I ex-
claimed in agony, which I now re-

peat in seriousness and solemnity, "I am too poor to hazard this."

SAMUEL TAYLOR COLERIDGE (1772– 1834), English poet and critic. Letter to Joseph Cottle, 26 April 1814, *A Second Treasury of the World's Great Letters*, ed. Wallace Brockway and Bart Winer (1941).

4   To promise not to do a thing is the surest way in the world to make a body want to go and do that very thing.

MARK TWAIN (SAMUEL CLEMENS) (1835–1910), English author. *The Adventures of Tom Sawyer* (chapter 22, "Tom's Confidence Betrayed—Expects Signal Punishment") (1876).

Tom here realizes the difficulty of keeping the vows, of the Cadets of Temperance, that he "abstain from smoking, chewing, and profanity."

5   It is difficult to live without opium after having known it because it is difficult, after knowing opium, to take earth seriously. And unless one is a saint, it is difficult to live without taking earth seriously.

JEAN COCTEAU (1889–1963), French author and filmmaker. *Opium: The Diary of a Cure* (1930), trans. Margaret Crosland and Sinclair Road (1958).

6   God grant me the serenity to accept the things I cannot change, courage to change the things I can and the wisdom to know the difference.

ANONYMOUS, Serenity Prayer.

This prayer is used in many twelve-step recovery programs.

7   I'm here to say that *you* can reel with your own heart and your own brain too once you quit believing that only alcohol or drugs can make you joyful. Sometimes, I'm almost sorry for people who *haven't* been alcoholic, because I know

things that a person who's never been sick doesn't know. I had to climb over hurdles. I had to experience the disease, be sick with it and then experience recovery.

BETTY FORD, U.S. author, former First Lady, and founder of the Betty Ford Clinic. *Betty: A Glad Awakening* (chapter 16) (1987).

Vacation

1   Keep moving! Steam, or Gas, or Stage,
Hold, cabin, steerage, hencoop's cage—
Tour, Journey, Voyage, Lounge, Ride, Walk,
Skim, Sketch, Excursion, Travel-talk—
For move you must! 'Tis now the rage,
The law and fashion of the Age.

SAMUEL TAYLOR COLERIDGE (1772– 1834), English poet and critic. "The Delinquent Travellers."

2   I must have leave, in the fulness of my soul, to regret the abolition, and doing away-with altogether, of those consolatory interstices and sprinklings of freedom, through the four seasons,—the *red-letter days*, now become, to all intents and purposes, *dead-letter days*. . . . These were bright visitations in a scholar's and clerk's life—"far off their coming shone."

CHARLES LAMB (1775–1834), English essayist. "Oxford in the Vacation," *Essays of Elia* (1823).

Lamb comments on the unusual peace of a university town when the students are on vacation.

3   He never took a vacation, and at sixty they read his will.

His day for "retiring from business"
Death wrote in a codicil;
And pinn'd on the door of his of-
fice
Was a notice which grimly read,
"Out of town—on a long vacation
Indefinite" it said.

JOHN WARREN HARPER. "He Never Took a Vacation."

4   The average wife does not get enough holidays. The average husband gets a day and a half every week, besides his annual holiday. The wife's working week consists of seven days; for there is no period in the week when she can throw off the burden of housekeeping. . . . Many wives have even to keep house during their so-called vacation, and thus obtain no real relief whatever. And so they continue without surcease for twenty years, thirty years, half a lifetime! At best the wife who always takes vacation in the company of her husband only achieves a partial holiday.

ARNOLD BENNETT (1867–1931), English author. *How to Make the Best of Life* (chapter 7, "The Continuation of Marriage") (1923).

5   I do not really like vacations; I much prefer an occasional day off when I do not feel like working. When I am confronted with a whole week in which I have nothing to do but enjoy myself I do not know where to begin. To me, enjoyment comes fleetingly and unheralded; I cannot determinedly enjoy myself for a whole week at a time.

ROBERTSON DAVIES (1913–1995), Canadian author. "Of Pleasure Too Determinedly Sought," *The Table Talk of Samuel Marchbanks* (1949).

Travel

1   The advantages of travel are many, such as recreation of the mind entailing profit; seeing of wonderful, and hearing of strange things; recreation in cities, associating with friends, acquisition of dignity, rank, property, the power of discriminating among acquaintances, and gaining experience of the world, as the travelers in the Tariqat have said: "As long as thou walkest about the shop or the house, thou wilt never become a man, O raw fellow! Go and travel in the world, before that day when thou goest from the world."

SHEIKH SA'DI (1184–1291), Persian author. *Tales from the Gulistân or Rose-Garden of the Sheikh Sa'di of Shirâz* (story 116) (1258) (1928), trans. and ed. Richard Burton (1928).

2   When a traveller returneth home, let him not leave the countries where he hath travelled altogether behind him, but maintain a correspondence by letters with those of his acquaintance which are of most worth. And let his travel appear rather in his discourse than in his apparel or gesture; and in his discourse let him be rather advised in his answers, than forward to tell stories.

FRANCIS BACON (1561–1626), English philosopher, essayist, and statesman. "Of Travel," *Essays or Counsels, Civil and Moral* (1625), and reprinted in *The Essays of Francis Bacon*, ed. John Pitcher (1985).

3   A traveler! By my faith, you have great reason to be sad. I fear you have sold your own lands to see other men's. Then to have seen much and to have nothing is to have rich eyes and poor hands.

WILLIAM SHAKESPEARE (1564–1616),
English poet and dramatist. *As You Like It*
4.1.20 ff.

Rosalind gently teases the melancholy Jacques,
who values his "experience" though it makes
him sad.

4   Walking has something that ani-
     mates and enlivens my ideas: I al-
     most cannot think when I stay in
     place; my body must be in motion
     to set my mind in motion . . .

     JEAN-JACQUES ROUSSEAU (1712–
     1778), French author. *Confessions* (book 4)
     (1781), trans. Christopher Kelly (1990).

5   The soul of a journey is liberty,
     perfect liberty, to think, feel, do,
     just as one pleases. We go on a
     journey chiefly to be free of all im-
     pediments and of all inconven-
     iences; to leave ourselves behind,
     much more to get rid of others.

     WILLIAM HAZLITT (1778–1830), En-
     glish essayist and critic. "On Going on a Jour-
     ney," *Table Talk; or Original Essays* (vol. 2)
     (1822).

6   Everything good is on the highway.

     RALPH WALDO EMERSON (1803–
     1882), U.S. author. "Experience," *Essays, Sec-
     ond Series* (1844).

7   Thare are hotels that are a joy upon
     earth, where a man pays hiz bill az
     cheerfully az he did the parson who
     married him, whare yu kant find
     the landlord unless yu hunt in the
     kitchen, whare servants glide
     around like angels ov mercy, whare
     the beds fit a man's back like the
     feathers on a goose, and whare the
     vittle taste just az tho yure wife, or
     yure mother had fried them. Theze
     kind ov hotels ought tew be bilt on
     wheels and travel around the coun-
     try; they are az phull ov real cum-
     fort az a thanksgiving pudding, but

alass! yes, alass! they are az un-
plenty az double-yelked eggs.

JOSH BILLINGS (HENRY W. SHAW)
(1818–1885), U.S. humorist. "Hotels," *The
Complete Works of Josh Billings* (1899).

8   We wish to learn all the curious,
     outlandish ways of all the different
     countries, so that we can "show
     off" and astonish people when we
     get home. We wish to excite the
     envy of our untraveled friends with
     our strange foreign fashions which
     we can't shake off. All our passen-
     gers are paying strict attention to
     this thing, with the end in view
     which I have mentioned. The gentle
     reader will never, never know what
     a consummate ass he can become
     until he goes abroad. I speak now,
     of course, in the supposition that
     the gentle reader has not been
     abroad, and therefore is not already
     a consummate ass.

     MARK TWAIN (SAMUEL CLEMENS)
     (1835–1910), U.S. author. *The Innocents
     Abroad, or, The New Pilgrims Progress* (chap-
     ter 23) (1869).

9   Travel is fatal to prejudice, bigotry,
     and narrow-mindedness, and many
     of our people need it sorely on
     these accounts. Broad, wholesome,
     charitable views of men and things
     cannot be acquired by vegetating in
     one little corner of the earth all
     one's lifetime.

     MARK TWAIN (SAMUEL CLEMENS)
     (1835–1910), U.S. author. *The Innocents
     Abroad, or, The New Pilgrims Progress* ("Con-
     clusion") (1869).

10   An adventure is only an inconven-
     ience rightly considered. An incon-
     venience is only an adventure
     wrongly considered.

G. K. Chesterton (1874–1936), English author. "On Running After One's Hat," *All Things Considered* (1908).

11 The traveller who has gone to Italy to study the tactile values of Giotto, or the corruption of the Papacy, may return remembering nothing but the blue sky and the men and women who live under it.

E. M. Forster (1879–1970), English novelist. *A Room With a View* (chapter 2, "In Santa Croce with No Baedeker") (1908).

Lucy Honeychurch leans out her window at the pension and watches the Italian crowds instead of preparing for a day of sightseeing.

12 And who would be a traveler
   And see the world afar,
What joys at Rome could equal home
   Where my two children are?

Edgar A. Guest (1881–1959), U.S. poet. "On Traveling."

13 Somewhere along the line I knew there'd be girls, visions, everything; somewhere along the line the pearl would be handed to me.

Jack Kerouac (1922–1969), U.S. author. *On the Road* (part 1, section 1) (1957).

Kerouac describes the attraction of his dream of taking "one great red line across America."

14 I didn't know who I was—I was far away from home, haunted and tired with travel, in a cheap hotel room I'd never seen, hearing the hiss of steam outside, and the creak of the old wood of the hotel, and footsteps upstairs, and all the sad sounds, and I looked at the cracked high ceiling and really didn't know who I was for about fifteen strange seconds. I wasn't scared; I was just somebody else, some stranger, and my whole life was a haunted life, the life of a ghost.

Jack Kerouac (1922–1969), U.S. author. *On the Road* (part 1, section 3) (1957).

Kerouac describes the reality of travelling across the country as a hitchhiker.

Writing a Report

1 True Ease in Writing comes from Art, not Chance,
As those move easiest who have learn'd to dance.

Alexander Pope (1688–1744), English poet. "An Essay on Criticism" (lines 362–63).

2 Sleep on your writing; take a walk over it; scrutinize it of a morning; review it of an afternoon; digest it after a meal; let it sleep in your drawer a twelvemonth; never venture a whisper about it to your friend, if he be an author especially. You may read selections to sensible women,—if young the better.

A. Bronson Alcott (1799–1888), U.S. philosopher and educator. *Concord Days* ("April: Scholarship. April 28") (1872).

3 What nuisance can be so great to a man busied with immense affairs, as to have to explain, or to attempt to explain, small details to men incapable of understanding them?

Anthony Trollope (1815–1882), English novelist. *The Way We Live Now* (chapter 37) (1875).

4 A little inaccuracy sometimes saves tons of explanation.

Saki (Hector Hugh Morton) (1870–1916), English author. "Clovis upon the Alleged Romance of Business," *The Square Egg* (1924).

5 Work expands so as to fill the time available for its completion.

C. Northcote Parkinson (1909–1993), historian, journalist, and novelist. *Parkinson's Law, and Other Studies in Administra-*

tion (chapter 1, "Parkinson's Law, or the Rising Pyramid") (1958).

Drinking

1   They question thee about strong drink and games of chance. Say: In both is great sin, and (some) utility for men; but the sin of them is greater than their usefulness.

Qur'an 2.219; *The Glorious Koran: An Explanatory Translation by Marmaduke Pickthall* (1930; reprint 1992).

2   A good sherris-sack . . . ascends me into the brain, dries me there all the foolish and dull and crudy vapors which environ it, makes it apprehensive, quick, forgetive, full of nimble, fiery and delectable shapes, which, deliver'd o'er to the voice, the tongue, which is the birth, becomes excellent wit.

WILLIAM SHAKESPEARE (1564–1616), English poet and dramatist. *The Second Part of King Henry IV* 4.3.95 ff.

Falstaff praises the benefits of his favorite libation, sack sherry. "Forgetive" means "inventive."

3   Good wine is a good familiar creature, if it be well us'd. Exclaim no more against it.

WILLIAM SHAKESPEARE (1564–1616), English poet and dramatist. *Othello* 2.3.303 ff.

Iago consoles Cassio, who regrets that through drunkenness he may have jeopardized his position.

4   Lechery, sir, it provokes, and unprovokes; it provokes the desire, but it takes away the performance. Therefore much drink may be said to be an equivocator with lechery: it makes him, and it mars him; it sets him on, and it takes him off; it persuades him, and it disheartens him; makes him stand to, and not

stand to; in conclusion, equivocates him in a sleep, and, giving him the lie, leaves him.

WILLIAM SHAKESPEARE (1564–1616), English poet and dramatist. *Macbeth* 2.3.28.

The porter here talks about the effects of drink, noting that it also provokes "nose-painting, sleep, and urine."

5   Old wine, and an old friend, are good provisions.

GEORGE HERBERT (1593–1633), English poet and Anglican priest. *Outlandish Proverbs*, no. 136 (1640).

6   How doth the earth bring forth *herbs, flowers,* and *fruits,* both for *physick* and the *pleasure* of mankind? and above all, to me at least, the fruitful *Vine,* of which when I drink moderately, it clears my brain, chears my heart, and sharpens my wit.

IZAAK WALTON (1593–1683), English author. *The Compleat Angler* (chapter 1, "A Conference betwixt an Angler, a Faulkner, and a Hunter, each commending his recreation") (1668).

7   Cupid and Bacchus my saints are;
    May drink and love still reign:
With wine I wash away my cares,
    And then to love again.

JOHN WILMOT, EARL OF ROCHESTER (1647–1680), English author. "Upon Drinking in a Bowl."

8   Who, by disgraces or ill fortune sunk,
Feels not his soul enlivened when he's drunk?

JONATHAN SWIFT (1667–1745), Anglo-Irish author. "Toland's Invitation to Dismal to Dine with the Calves' Head Club, Imitated from Horace Epistle 5, Liber 1."

The poem is a satire depicting a group of Whigs who have gathered to celebrate the anniversary of the execution of Charles I on 30 January 1649.

9   A facetious friend of mine used to say, the wine could not be bad, where the company is agreeable; a maxim which, however, ought to be taken *cum grano salis*.

TOBIAS SMOLLETT (1721–1771), Scottish novelist. *Humphry Clinker* (letter from Matthew Bramble to Dr. Lewis, dated June 8) (1771).

10   That's all that distinguishes us from the beasts, Madam—drinking when we aren't thirsty and making love whenever we feel like it.

PIERRE-AUGUSTIN CARON DE BEAUMARCHAIS (1732–1799), French dramatist. *The Marriage of Figaro* (act 2) (1874), trans. John Wood (1964).

11   O Whisky! soul o' plays an' pranks!
Accept a Bardie's gratefu' thanks!
When wanting thee, what tuneless cranks
    Are my poor verses!

ROBERT BURNS (1759–1796), Scottish poet. "Scotch Drink."

12   You women are always thinking of men's being in liquor. Why, you do not suppose a man is overset by a bottle? I am sure of *this* —that if everybody was to drink their bottle a day, there would not be half the disorders in the world there are now. It would be a famous good thing for us all. . . . There is not the hundredth part of the wine consumed in this kingdom that there ought to be. Our foggy climate wants help.

JANE AUSTEN (1775–1817), English novelist. *Northanger Abbey* (chapter 9) (1818).

Speaking to the heroine Catherine, Mr. Thorpe advances his theories on the benefits of drinking.

13   Gin! Gin! a Drop of Gin!
Oh! then its tremendous temptations begin,
    To take, alas!
    To the fatal glass,–
And happy the wretch that it does not win
    To change the black hue
    Of his ruin to blue—
While Angels sorrow, and Demons grin—
    And lose the rheumatic
    Chill of his attic
By plunging into the Palace of Gin!

THOMAS HOOD (1799–1845), English poet. "A Drop of Gin."

14   I rather like bad wine, . . . one gets so bored with good wine.

BENJAMIN DISRAELI (1804–1881), British statesman and author. *Sybil* (book 1, chapter 1) (1845).

15   Better is old wine than new, and old friends likewise.

CHARLES KINGSLEY (1819–1875), English author. *Hereward the Wake* (chapter 27, "How They Held a Great Meeting in the Hall of Ely") (1866).

16   ABSTAINER; n. A weak person who yields to the temptation of denying himself a pleasure. . . . BRANDY; n. A cordial composed of one part thunder-and-lightning, one part remorse, two parts bloody murder.

AMBROSE BIERCE (1842–?1914), U.S. author. *The Devil's Dictionary* (1881–1911).

17   The cocktail is a pleasant drink,
It's mild and harmless, I don't think.
When you've had one, you call for two,

And then you don't care what you
do.

GEORGE ADE (1866–1944), U.S. humorist and journalist. "R-E-M-O-R-S-E."

18 Say what you like and I'll be calm,
    No matter what I think;
But if you value blood and bones—
    No disrespect to Drink!

W. H. DAVIES (1871–1940), Welsh author. "Drink."

19 The harsh, useful things of the
    world, from pulling teeth to digging
    potatoes, are best done by men who
    are as starkly sober as so many convicts in the death-house, but the
    lovely and useless things, the
    charming and exhilarating things,
    are best done by men with, as the
    phrase is, a few sheets in the wind.

H. L. MENCKEN (1880–1956), U.S. author and journalist. *Prejudices, Fourth Series* (1924).

20 In some secluded rendez-vous
    That overlooks the avenue
with someone sharing a delightful
    chat
Of this and that
and cocktails for two.

ARTHUR JOHNSON and **SAM COSLOW** (1902–1982), U.S. songwriters. "Cocktails for Two" (1934), in *The World's Greatest Fake Book*, ed. Chuck Sher (1983).

21 Regular habits sweeten simplicity.
    In the middle of every morning I
    leave the kitchen and have a glass of
    sherry with Aunt. I can only say
    that *this is glorious*. There is a great
    deal of gloriousness in simplicity.

STEVIE SMITH (1902–1971), English poet and novelist. "Simply Living" (1964), in *Me Again: Uncollected Writings of Stevie Smith* (1981).

22 There is one thing I know I shall
    never get enough of—champagne. I
    cannot say when I drank my first,
    prickly, delicious glass of it. . . . I
    think I probably started my lifelong
    affair with Dom Pérignon's discovery in 1929, when I first went to
    France. It does not matter. I would
    gladly ask for the same end as a
    poor peasant's there, who is given a
    glass of champagne on his death
    bed to cheer him on his way.

M. F. K. FISHER (1908–1992), U.S. food writer. "Once a Tramp, Always . . . ," in *The Art of the Personal Essay: An Anthology from the Classical Era to the Present*, ed. Phillip Lopate (1995).

23 Do not allow your children to mix
    drinks. It is unseemly and they use
    too much vermouth.

FRAN LEBOWITZ (b. 1950), U.S. author. "Parental Guidance," *Social Studies* (1981).

Toasting

1 Now let them drink till they nod
    and wink
        Even as good fellows should do;
They shall not miss to have the
    bliss
        Good ale doth bring men to.

JOHN STILL (D. 1607), English prelate, bishop of Bath and Wells; **WILLIAM STEVENSON**. *Gammer Gurton's Needle* (17th cent.).

Authorship of *Gammer Gurton's Needle* is uncertain. It is attributed variously to Still, to Stevenson, to both, to "Mr S.," and to Anonymous.

2 Please ye we may contrive this afternoon
And quaff carouses to our mistress'
    health,
And do as adversaries do in law,

Strive mightily, but eat and drink as friends.

WILLIAM SHAKESPEARE (1564–1616), English poet and dramatist. *The Taming of the Shrew* 1.2.276–77.

The suitors of Baptista's daughters agree to enjoy one another's company despite their rivalry.

3 The best smell is bread, the best savour, salt, the best love that of children.

GEORGE HERBERT (1593–1633), English poet and Anglican priest. *Outlandish Proverbs*, no. 741 (1640).

4 Wine and beauty by turns great souls should inspire;
Present all together! and now, boys, give fire!

SIR GEORGE ETHEREGE (1634–1691), English author. *The Man of Mode; or, Sir Fopling Flutter* (4.2.494–95) (1676).

5 May you live as long as you are fit to live, but no longer! or, may you rather die before you cease to be fit to live than after!

PHILIP DORMER STANHOPE, FOURTH EARL OF CHESTERFIELD (1694–1773), English statesman and author. Letter to his son, 26 December 1749 OS, *The Letters of Philip Dormer Stanhope. Earl of Chesterfield*, ed. John Bradshaw, vol. 1 (1929).

6 I fill this cup to one made up
Of loveliness alone,
A woman, of her gentle sex
The seeming paragon,—
Her health! And would on earth there stood
Some more of such a frame,
That life might be all poetry,
And weariness a name.

EDWARD COATE PINKNEY (1802–1828), U.S. poet. "A Health."

Pinkney wrote only a few poems.

7 Think where man's glory most begins and ends
And say my glory was I had such friends.

WILLIAM BUTLER YEATS (1865–1939), Irish poet. "The Municipal Gallery Revisited."

Yeats imagines the portraits of the men who have shaped Ireland's history.

8 If Time, so fleeting, must like humans die, let it be filled with good food and good talk, and then embalmed in the perfumes of conviviality.

M. F. K. FISHER (1908–1992), food writer. "Meals for Me," *Serve It Forth* (1937).

Giving a Speech

1 The loud applause your speech received
    Was not at all deserved.
It was not the speech you gave we liked,
    But the dinner that you served.

MARTIAL (MARCUS VALERIUS MARTIALIS) (A.D. c. 40–c. 103), Roman poet. "To Pomponius" (6.48), *Selected Epigrams*, trans. Ralph Marcellino (1968).

2 A rhetorician of times past said that his trade was to make little things appear and be thought great. That's a shoemaker who can make big shoes for a small foot. They would have had him whipped in Sparta for professing a deceitful and lying art. . . . Those who mask and make up women do less harm, for it is a matter of small loss not to see them in their natural state; whereas the other men make a profession of deceiving not our eyes but our judgment, and of adulterating and corrupting the essence of things.

MICHEL EYQUEM DE MONTAIGNE (1533–1589), French essayist. "Of the Vanity of Words," book 1, essay 51 (1572–80), *The Complete Essays of Montaigne*, trans. Donald M. Frame (1976; originally published 1958).

3 Very good orators, when they are out, they will spit.

WILLIAM SHAKESPEARE (1564–1616), English poet and dramatist. *As Like You Like It* 4.1.71–72.

Posing as Ganymede, Rosalind urges Orlando to speak before he kisses when he goes to woo his beloved, who is Rosalind herself. She notes that he can kiss when he has run out of things to say, as "good orators" spit when they run out of "matter."

4 . . . since brevity is the soul of wit,
And tediousness the limbs and out-
    ward flourishes,
I will be brief.

WILLIAM SHAKESPEARE (1564–1616), English poet and dramatist. *Hamlet* 2.2.90.

In the midst of a rather long speech, Polonius announces his intention to be brief. He pro-vokes Gertrude, his impatient interlocutor, to request "more matter, with less art."

5 That is not good language which all understand not.

GEORGE HERBERT (1593–1633), English poet and Anglican priest. *Outlandish Proverbs*, no. 302 (1640).

6 To make oneself understood is good enough language for me; all your fine sayings don't do me no good.

MOLIÈRE (JEAN BAPTISTE POQUE-LIN) (1622–1673), French dramatist. *The Learned Ladies* (Les Femmes savantes) 2.6 (1672), in *The Plays of Molière in French*, trans. A. R. Waller, vol. 8 (1926).

A servant chides her betters.

7 The best foundation of eloquence, is the being master of the subject upon which a man is to speak. That is a root that will furnish sap to a discourse, so that it shall not go dry.

GEORGE SAVILE, MARQUIS OF HALI-FAX (1633–1695), English courtier and au-thor. *Maxims* (1750), in *The Works of George Savile, Marquis of Halifax*, ed. Mark N. Brown, vol. 3 (1989).

8 It is not enough to speak the lan-guage he speaks in, in its utmost purity, and according to the rules of grammar; but he must speak it ele-gantly; that is, he must choose the best and most expressive words, and put them in the best order. He should likewise adorn what he says by proper metaphors, similes and other figures of rhetoric; and he should enliven it, if he can, by quick and sprightly turns of wit.

PHILIP DORMER STANHOPE, FOURTH EARL OF CHESTERFIELD (1694–1773), English statesman and author. Letter to his son, Philip Stanhope, 1 November 1739 OS, *The Letters of Philip Dormer Stan-hope. Earl of Chesterfield*, ed. John Bradshaw, vol. 1 (1929).

The earl begins his advice by insisting on the importance of persuading and pleasing one's audience.

9 . . . true Expression, like th' un-
    changing Sun,
Clears, and improves whate'er it
    shines upon,
It gilds all Objects, but it alters
    none.
Expression is the Dress of Thought,
    and still
Appears more decent as more suit-
    able;
A vile Conceit in pompous Words
    exprest,
Is like a Clown in regal Purple
    drest;
For diff'rent Styles with diff'rent
    Subjects sort,

As several Garbs with Country,
    Town, and Court.

ALEXANDER POPE (1688–1744), English
poet. *An Essay on Criticism* (lines 315–23).

10 The *average* intellect of five hundred persons, taken as they come, is
not very high. It may be sound and
safe, so far as it goes, but it is not
very rapid or profound. A lecture
ought to be something which all
can understand, about something
which interests everybody.

OLIVER WENDELL HOLMES (1809–
1894), U.S. author and physician. *The Autocrat of the Breakfast-Table* (chapter 5) (1858).

11 A liberal use of wine makes after-
dinner speaking much easier. Men
will then laugh heartily at the oldest
kind of a chestnut.

HENRY WARD BEECHER (1813–1887),
U.S. clergyman. "Baptist Union: After-Dinner
Speech," *Beecher as a Humorist: Selections
from the Published Works*, ed. Eleanor Kirk
(1887).

Beecher does not specify whether the speaker
or the auditors are to make "liberal use of
wine."

12 Never be grandiloquent when you
want to drive home a searching
truth. Don't whip with a switch
that has the leaves on, if you want
it to tingle.

HENRY WARD BEECHER (1813–1887),
U.S. clergyman. *Yale Lectures on Preaching*,
first series; *The Personal Elements Which Bear
an Important Relation to Preaching* (section 9,
"Sermon-Making") (1872).

13 My heart goes out to anyone who is
making his first appearance before
an audience of human beings.

MARK TWAIN (SAMUEL CLEMENS),
1835–1910 author. Speech delivered after his
daughter made her singing debut, Norfolk,

Conn., 5 October 1906, in *Lend Me Your Ears:
Great Speeches in History*, ed. William Safire
(1992).

14 Once I was elected to membership
in a certain business organization. I
went to its dinners where there was
much speech-making. At first I re-
gretted that I could not hear those
often long orations. Then, one year,
they printed them after the dinner
and I read them. I haven't felt a
mite of sorrow since.

THOMAS ALVA EDISON (1847–1931),
U.S. inventor. *The Diary and Sundry Observations of Thomas Alva Edison* ("Sundry Observations"; chapter 1, "Autobiographical"; section 2 [1925]), ed. Dagobert D. Runes (1948).

Edison lost his hearing when he was twelve,
but in this chapter proves, with many exam-
ples, how his deafness relieved him from
noise, which he considered to be one of the
greatest sources of "nerve strain of our modern
life." In discussing speeches, he goes on to
say: "When the other day, I read that a certain
scientist had developed a short-term anesthetic, the first thought that came to me was
that it should be served out at banquets to people with good hearing."

15 I suppose that for every half-hour
speech that I make before a convention or over the radio, I put in
ten hours preparing it.

FRANKLIN D. ROOSEVELT (1882–
1945), U.S. president. Speech to the Daughters of the American Revolution, 20 April
1930, in *Lend Me Your Ears: Great Speeches
in History*, ed. William Safire (1992).

16 To read as if you were talking you
must first write as if you were talking. What you have on the paper in
front of you must be talk stuff, not
book stuff.

JOHN HILTON, U.S. broadcaster in Lon-
don, for BBC, before the Second World War.
BBC broadcast, 1 July 1937, in *Lend Me Your
Ears: Great Speeches in History*, ed. William
Safire (1992).

17 You can scrap, in writing a talk, most of what you've been told all your life was literary good form. You have to; if you want your talk to ring the bell and walk in and sit down by the hearth.

JOHN HILTON, U.S. broadcaster in London, for BBC, before the Second World War. BBC broadcast, 1 July 1937, in *Lend Me Your Ears: Great Speeches in History*, ed. William Safire (1992).

18 On the platform, as anyone used to public speaking knows, it is almost impossible not to take your tone from the audience. It is always obvious within a few minutes what they will respond to and what they will not, and in practice you are almost compelled to speak for the benefit of what you estimate as the stupidest person present, and also to ingratiate yourself by means of the ballyhoo known as "personality." If you don't do so, the result is always an atmosphere of frigid embarrassment.

GEORGE ORWELL (ERIC ARTHUR BLAIR) (1903–1950), English author. "Poetry and the Microphone" (1945), in *Collected Essays* (1961).

19 The man who writes only for the eye generally writes badly; the man who writes to be heard will write with some eloquence, some regard for the music of words, and will reach nearer to his reader's heart and mind.

ROBERTSON DAVIES (1913–1995), Canadian author. "The Inner Voice," *The Table Talk of Samuel Marchbanks* (1949).

20 I wonder whose after-dinner speeches, in history, have been most dreaded? Socrates went on and on but at least he kept his young fellow diners wide awake by catching them out with trick questions. . . . Of course you don't have to go back almost two thousand years to find people who bang on; they are right with us today.

ALEC GUINESS (b. 1914), English actor. *My Name Escapes Me: The Diary of a Retiring Actor* ("Monday, 5 February 1996") (1996).

Seeking a Favor

1 O, reason not the need! our basest beggars
   Are in the poorest thing superfluous.
   Allow not nature more than nature needs,
   Man's life is cheap as beast's.

WILLIAM SHAKESPEARE (1564–1616), English poet and dramatist. *King Lear* 2.4.264–67.

Lear's angry response when his daughter Regan refuses him a retinue of followers.

Financial Success

1 Let us not repine, or so much as think the gifts of God unequally dealt, if we see another abound with riches, when as God knows, the cares that are the keys that keep those riches hang often so heavily at the rich mans girdle, that they clog him with weary days and restless nights, even when others sleep quietly. We see but the outside of the rich mans happiness: few consider him to be like the Silk-worm, that, when she seems to play, is at the very same time spinning her own bowels, and consuming her self. And this many rich men do; loading themselves with the corrod-

ing cares, to keep what they have (probably) unconscionably got.

IZAAK WALTON (1593–1683), English author. *The Compleat Angler* (part 1; chapter 21, "Directions for making of a Line, and for the colouring of both Rod and Line") (1668).

2 Gold gives to the plainest a pleasing charm: without it all else is a miserable business.

MOLIÈRE (JEAN BAPTISTE POQUE-LIN) (1622–1673), French dramatist. *Sganarelle: The Husband Who Thought Himself Wronged* (Sganarelle ou, Le cocu imaginair) (scene 1) (1660), in *The Plays of Molière in French*, trans. A. R. Waller, vol. 2 (1926).

A father urges his daughter to marry a wealthy suitor rather than the man she has chosen because she loves him.

3 Billionism, or even millionism, must be a blessed kind of state, with health and clear conscience and youth and good looks,—but most blessed is this, that it takes off all the mean cares which give people the three wrinkles between the eyebrows, and leaves them free to have a good time and make others have a good time.

OLIVER WENDELL HOLMES (1809–1894), U.S. author and physician. *Elsie Venner* (chapter 7, "The Event of the Season") (1861).

4 I love money; just to be in the room with a millionaire makes me less forlorn. Wealthy people should be segregated like lepers to keep them from contaminating others.

LOGAN PEARSALL SMITH (1865–1946), U.S. humorist. "In the World," *Afterthoughts* (1931) and *All Trivia: Trivia, More Trivia, Afterthoughts, Last Words* (1945).

These comments which seem to contradict one another occur side by side in Smith's text.

5 Alas! old man, we're wealthy now, it's sad beyond a doubt;

We cannot dodge prosperity, success has found us out.
Your eye is very dull and drear, my brow is creased with care,
We realize how hard it is to be a millionaire.

ROBERT W. SERVICE (1874–1958), Canadian author. "The Joy of Being Poor."

6 Happiness lies not in the mere possession of money; it lies in the joy of achievement, in the thrill of creative effort. The joy and moral stimulation of work no longer must be forgotten in the mad chase of evanescent profits.

FRANKLIN D. ROOSEVELT (1882–1945), U.S. president. Inaugural address, March 1933, in *Lend Me Your Ears: Great Speeches in History*, ed. William Safire (1992).

Roosevelt delivered his speech at the height of the Depression, suggesting ways to handle the financial losses and burdens of the time.

Financial Loss

1 Poverty of goods is easy to cure, poverty of soul impossible.

MICHEL EYQUEM DE MONTAIGNE (1533–1589), French essayist. "Of Husbanding Your Will," book 3, essay 10 (1585–1588), *The Complete Essays of Montaigne*, trans. Donald M. Frame (1976; originally published 1958).

2 He that hath lost his credit is dead to the world.

GEORGE HERBERT (1593–1633), English poet and Anglican priest. *Outlandish Proverbs*, no. 357 (1640).

3 O fool! to think God hates the worthy mind,
The lover and the love of humankind,
Whose life is healthful, and whose conscience clear;

Because he wants a thousand
pounds a year.

ALEXANDER POPE (1688–1744), English
poet. *An Essay on Man: Or the First Book of
Ethnic Epistles to H. St. John L. Bolingbroke,*
Epistle 4, lines 189–92.

4   Unless I die, I shall beat [sic] up
against this foul weather. A penny I
will not borrow from any one. . . . I
am grieved for Lady Scott and
Anne, who cannot conceive adversity can have the better of them,
even for a moment. If it teaches a
little of the frugality which I never
had the heart to enforce when
money was plenty, and it seemed
cruel to interrupt the enjoyment of
it in the way they liked best, it will
be well.

SIR WALTER SCOTT (1771–1832), Scot-
tish author. Letter to John Gibson Lockhart, his
biographer and son-in-law, 20 January 1826, *A
Second Treasury of the World's Great Letters,*
ed. Wallace Brockway and Bart Keith Winer
(1941).

Scott ran up enormous debts by trying to manage his own publishing and printing firm and
by pouring money into the construction of his
estate, Abbotsford.

5   A man willing to work, and unable
to find work, is perhaps the saddest
sight that Fortune's inequality exhibits under this sun.

THOMAS CARLYLE (1795–1881), Scot-
tish author. *Chartism* (chapter 4, "Finest Peas-
antry in the World") (1839).

6   If success is rare and slow, everybody knows how quick and easy
ruin is.

WILLIAM MAKEPEACE THACKERAY
(1811–1863), English novelist. *Vanity Fair*
(chapter 18, "Who Played on the Piano Captain Dobbin Bought") (1847).

7   It is wonderful what an insight into
domestic economy being really hard

up gives one. If you want to find
out the value of money, live on fifteen shillings a week, and see how
much you can put by for clothes
and recreation. You will find that it
is worthwhile to wait for the far-
thing change, that it is worthwhile
to walk a mile to save a penny, that
a glass of beer is a luxury to be in-
dulged in only at rare intervals, and
that a collar can be worn for four
days.

JEROME K. JEROME (1859–1927), English actor and writer. "On Being Hard Up,"
Idle Thoughts of an Idle Fellow (1892).

8   Bein' poor never holds stylish people back.

KIN HUBBARD (1868–1930), U.S. humorist. *52 Weeks of Abe Martin* (1924).

9   Pity those in Mammon's thrall,
        Poor, misguided souls are they,
Money's nothing, after all—
        Make the grocer think that way!

DOROTHY PARKER (1893–1967), U.S.
author. "Song for the First of the Month."

*M*eals

1   Regard thy table as the table before
the Lord. Chew well, and hurry
not.

Zohar 4.246a, in *The Talmudic Anthology:
Tales and Teachings of the Rabbis,* ed. Louis I.
Newman (1947).

2   Dry bread at home is better than
roast meate abroad.

GEORGE HERBERT (1593–1633), English
poet and Anglican priest. *Outlandish Proverbs,*
no. 681 (1640).

3   When I am hungry the least disappointment seizes me and pulls me
down, but when I have had a

hearty meal I can face the world, and the greatest misfortunes do not matter a snap. Take my advice, drink freely to support yourself against the blows of fortune; twenty glasses of wine round your heart will prevent sorrow entering it.

MOLIÈRE (JEAN BAPTISTE POQUE-LIN) (1622–1673), French dramatist. *Sganarelle: The Husband Who Thought Himself Wronged* (Sganarelle ou, Le cocu imaginair) (scene 7) (1660), in *The Plays of Molière in French*, trans. A. R. Waller, vol. 2. (1926).

The advice of a valet to his master.

4   Why, to eat and drink together, and to promote kindness; and Sir, this is better done when there is no solid conversation; for when there is, people differ in opinion, and get into bad humour, or some of the company who are not capable of such conversation, are left out, and feel themselves uneasy. It was for this reason, Sir Robert Walpole said, he always talked bawdy at his table, because in that all could join.

SAMUEL JOHNSON (1709–1784), English author. Quoted in James Boswell, *Life of Johnson* ("May 1776") (1791).

Boswell has complained about a dinner party where there was no memorable conversation and asks why men should meet at all during a meal if there is not to be discussion. Johnson replies.

5   A breakfast, a lunch, a tea, is a circumstance, an occurrence, in social life, but a dinner is an event. It is the full-blown flower of that cultivated growth of which those lesser products are the buds.

OLIVER WENDELL HOLMES (1809–1894), U.S. author and physician. *One Hundred Days in Europe* (chapter 1) (1891).

6   Fill up the lonely glass, and drain it
    In memory of dear old times.

Welcome the wine, whate'er the
    seal is;
        As sit you down and say your
        grace
With thankful heart, whate'er the
    meal is.

WILLIAM MAKEPEACE THACKERAY (1811–1863), English author. "The Ballad of Bouillabaisse."

7   Even to this hour, the first acquaintance with oysters is with much hesitation and squeamish apprehension. Who, then, first gulped the dainty thing, and forever after called himself blessed?

HENRY WARD BEECHER (1813–1887), U.S. clergyman. "Food Discoveries," *Eyes and Ears* (1866).

8   The best of the tables and the best
    of the fare—
And as for the others, the devil may
    care;
It isn't our fault if they dare not afford
To sup like a prince and be drunk
    as a lord.
    So pleasant it is to have money,
    heigh ho!
So pleasant it is to have money.

ARTHUR HUGH CLOUGH (1819–1861), English poet. *Dipsychus* (scene 4, lines 161–65) (1850).

The Spirit here gives voice to the worldly side of Dipsychus's nature.

9   Great was the clatter of knives and pewter-plates and tin-cans when Adam entered the house-place, but there was no hum of voices to this accompaniment: the eating of excellent roast-beef, provided free of expense, was too serious a business to those good farm-labourers to be performed with a divided attention,

even if they had had anything to say to each other, —which they had not.

GEORGE ELIOT (MARY ANN OR MARIAN EVANS) (1819–1880), English author. *Adam Bede* (chapter 53, "The Harvest Supper") (1859).

The Poyser family in the novel provides this meal for their laborers who seldom have the treat of "hot roast-beef and fresh-drawn ale."

10 A good dinner brings out all the softer side of a man. Under its genial influence, the gloomy and morose become jovial and chatty. Sour, starchy individuals, who all the rest of the day go about looking as if they lived on vinegar and Epsom salts, break out into wreathed smiles after dinner, and exhibit a tendency to pat small children on the head, and talk to them— vaguely —about sixpences. Serious young men thaw, and become mildly cheerful; and snobbish young men, of the heavy moustache type, forget to make themselves objectionable.

JEROME K. JEROME (1859–1927), English actor and writer. "On Eating and Drinking," *Idle Thoughts of an Idle Fellow* (1892).

11 We are all reared in a traditional belief that what we get to eat at home is, by virtue of that location, better than what we get to eat anywhere else. The expression, "home-cooking," carries a connotation of assured excellence, and the popular eating-house advertises "pies like those your mother used to make," as if pie-making were a maternal function. Economy, comfort, and health are supposed to accompany our domestic food supply, and danger to follow the footsteps of those

who eat in a hotel, a restaurant, or a boarding house.

CHARLOTTE PERKINS GILMAN (1860–1935), U.S. author. *The Home: Its Work and Influence* (chapter 7, "Home-Cooking") (1903; reprint 1972).

Gilman questions the truth of this old belief and shows the severe limitations placed on women who must struggle daily to feed families and have little time to experiment or improve the kinds of food they offer.

12 When I think of Etiquette and Funerals; when I consider the euphemisms and conventions and various costumes with which we invest the acts of our animal existence; when I bear in mind how elegantly we eat our victuals, and remember all the ablutions and preparations and salutations and exclamations and manipulations I performed when I dined out last evening, I reflect what creatures we are of ceremony; how elaborately polite a simian Species.

LOGAN PEARSALL SMITH (1865–1946), U.S. humorist. "Dining Out," *More Trivia* (1931) and *All Trivia: More Trivia, Afterthoughts, Last Words* (1945).

13 The dinner table was the intellectual, spiritual, and social center of our lives. It was where the day was headed and it was about as close to heavenly satisfaction as a poor man could expect to get.

OSSIE DAVIS (b. 1917), U.S. actor. *Ossie and Ruby: In This Life Together* ("The Waycross Years") (1998).

Davis and his wife alternate chapters describing their lives before they met. This is Davis's description of meals in his boyhood.

Parties

1 I sent out invitations
To summon guests.

I collected together
All my friends.
Loud talk
And simple feasting.

CH'ENG-KUNG SUI (D. A.D. 273), Chinese poet. "Inviting Guests," *One Hundred and Seventy Chinese Poems*, trans. Arthur Waley (1977; originally published 1962).

2   To what end the house, if not for conversation, kindly manners, the entertainment of friendships, and cordialities that render the house large, and the ready receptacle of hosts and guests?

A. BRONSON ALCOTT (1799–1888), U.S. philosopher and educator. "Fellowship," *Tablets* (1868).

3   More fascinating at a party, than any other music is the rushing sound of fashionable voices;—the vociferation of all those fairies, each faintly blowing its own trumpet.

LOGAN PEARSALL SMITH (1865–1946), U.S. humorist. "In the World," *Afterthoughts* (1931) and *All Trivia: Trivia, More Trivia, Afterthoughts, Last Words* (1945).

4   Every time she gave a party she had this feeling of being something not herself, and that every one was unreal in one way; much more real in another. It was, she thought, partly their clothes, partly being taken out of their ordinary ways, partly the background, it was possible to say things you couldn't say anyhow else, things that needed an effort; possible to go much deeper.

VIRGINIA WOOLF (1882–1941), English novelist. *Mrs. Dalloway* (1925).

5   Superior people never make long visits.

MARIANNE MOORE (1887–1972), U.S. poet. "Silence."

6   I like large parties. They're so intimate. At small parties there isn't any privacy.

F. SCOTT FITZGERALD (1896–1940), U.S. author. *The Great Gatsby* (chapter 3) (1925).

Jordan Baker, a bored socialite, comments on the large, elaborate parties given by Jay Gatsby.

7   Many times my heart has bled for the hostess who has slaved for hours to produce four kinds of sandwiches and two kinds of cake, and who is so exhausted by her labours that she casts a gloom over her own party. Far, far better to offer something simple and good, in a spirit of revelry, than to toil to produce pretentious mediocrity. It is the spirit which makes a party, and not dainty sandwiches, cut in the form of hearts and tasting like spades.

ROBERTSON DAVIES (1913–1995), Canadian author. "Of Wasted Effort," *The Table Talk of Samuel Marchbanks* (1949).

8   To entertain at home is both a relief and a rediscovery—of rooms and settings, of your favorite things, and particularly of your own tastes and ideas.

MARTHA STEWART, U.S. author and television personality. *Entertaining* (introduction) (1987).

9   Most importantly, one must never go to a party without a clear objective: whether it be to "network," thereby adding to your spread of contacts to improve your career; to make friends with someone specific; or simply "clinch" a top deal. Understand where have been going wrong by going to parties armed

only with objective of not getting too pissed.

HELEN FIELDING, English author. *Bridget Jones's Diary* ("Tuesday 11 April") (1998).

Bridget here plans her strategy according to an article on how to make parties "work" for one.

Meetings

1 The more we enquire, the less we can resolve.

SAMUEL JOHNSON (1709–1784), English author. *The History of Rasselas, Prince of Abisinnia* (chapter 26, "The Princess Continues Her Remarks Upon Private Life") (1759).

2 If you want a piece of work well and thoroughly done, pick a busy man. The man of leisure postpones and procrastinates, and is ever making preparations and "getting things in shape"; but the ability to focus on a thing and do it is the talent of the man seemingly o'erwhelmed with work.

ELBERT HUBBARD (1856–1915), U.S. author, founder of the Roycroft community. *The Philosophy of Elbert Hubbard* ("His Thoughts about Business") (1930).

Interviews

1 It seems odd to me that in our present educational system, in which virtually everything else is taught or half-taught, nobody teaches these young hopefuls how to behave when looking for a job. I do not ask for groveling humility, but some hint of modesty, and some offer of honest service, would be welcome.

ROBERTSON DAVIES (1913–1995), Canadian author. "Of Getting a Job," *The Table-Talk of Samuel Marchbanks* (1945).

The speaker describes the tiresome task of having to interview applicants who state quite

openly that they ultimately want to move on to other jobs.

2 Walk in very serious. You are not applying for a boy's job. Money is to pass. Be quiet, fine, and serious. Everybody likes a kidder, but nobody lends him money. . . .

Walk in with a big laugh. Don't look worried. Start off with a couple of your good stories to lighten things up. It's not what you say, it's how you say it—because personality always wins the day.

ARTHUR MILLER (b. 1915), U.S. dramatist. *Death of a Salesman* (act 1) (1949).

Willy Loman's seemingly contradictory advice to his son Biff, who has just proposed going to ask an old friend for a job.

3 You have an interviewer pretending to be a person, and an applicant pretending to be what he is not. They are both talking past each other to the Mt. McKinley Business School.

ALAN HARRINGTON (1919–1997), U.S. author. *Life in the Crystal Palace* (chapter 4, "The Tyranny of Forms") (1959).

Introductions

1 Alice—Mutton: Mutton—Alice.

LEWIS CARROLL (CHARLES LUTWIDGE DODGSON) (1832–1898), English author and mathematician. *Through the Looking Glass* (chapter 9, "Queen Alice") (1871).

Here the Red Queen introduces a rather shy "queen" Alice to the mutton brought to a dinner party table. The Red Queen warns that "it isn't etiquette to cut any one you've been introduced to," and the meat is taken away uneaten.

2 If you really want to hear about it, the first thing you'll probably want to know is where I was born, and what my lousy childhood was like,

and how my parents were occupied and all before they had me, and all the David Copperfield kind of crap, but I don't feel like going into it, if you want to know the truth.

J. D. SALINGER (b. 1919), U.S. author. *The Catcher in the Rye* (chapter 1) (1951).

3 Usually, I forget first meetings, excepting always those solemn audiences granted by the old and famous when I was young and green.

GORE VIDAL (b. 1925), U.S. author. "Some Memories of the Glorious Bird and an Earlier Self," *United States: Essays 1952–1992* (1993).

Vidal here writes about meeting Tennessee Williams.

Consolation

1 Sweet are the uses of adversity,
Which, like the toad, ugly and venomous,
Wears yet a precious jewel in his head;
And this our life, exempt from public haunt,
Finds tongues in trees, books in the running brooks,
Sermons in stones, and good in everything.

WILLIAM SHAKESPEARE (1564–1616), English poet and dramatist. *As You Like It* 2.1.12.

2 There is nothing so distressing as the consolations to be drawn from the necessity of evil, the uselessness of remedies, the inevitability of fate, and the wretchedness of the human condition. It is a mockery to try to lessen an evil by recalling that man is miserable; how much better it is to raise the mind away from such reflections and to treat man as a feeling, rather than a reasoning being.

CHARLES LOUIS DE SECONDAT, BARON DE LA BRÈDE ET DE MONTESQUIEU (1689–1755), French jurist and political philosopher. Letter 33 (Usbek to Rhedi, at Venice, Paris, the 25th of the moon of Zilcade, 1713), *The Persian Letters* (1721), trans. George R. Healy (1964).

3 Human life is every where a state in which much is to be endured, and little to be enjoyed.

SAMUEL JOHNSON (1709–1784), English author. *The History of Rasselas, Prince of Abissinia* (chapter 11, "Imlac's Narrative Continued. A Hint on Pilgrimage") (1759).

4 Before an affliction is digested,—consolation ever comes too soon;—and after it is digested, it comes too late.

LAURENCE STERNE (1713–1768), Anglo-Irish author. *Tristram Shandy* (vol. 3, chapter 28) (1760-67).

5 It would be a poor result of all our anguish and our wrestling, if we won nothing but our old selves at the end of it—if we could return to the same blind loves, the same self-confident blame, the same light thoughts of human suffering, the same frivolous gossip over blighted human loves, the same feeble sense of that Unknown towards which we have sent forth irrepressible cries in our loneliness. Let us rather be thankful that our sorrow lives in us as an indestructible force, only changing its form, as forces do, and passing from pain into sympathy—the one poor word which includes all our best insight and our best love.

GEORGE ELIOT (MARY ANN OR MARIAN EVANS) (1819–1890), English author. *Adam Bede* (chapter 50, "In the Cottage") (1859).

6   This World is not Conclusion.
    A Species stands beyond—
    Invisible, as Music—
    But positive, as Sound.

EMILY DICKINSON (1830–1886), U.S. poet. "This World is not Conclusion."

7   Sorrow comes in great waves . . . but it rolls over us, and though it may almost smother us it leaves us on the spot and we know that if it is strong we are stronger, inasmuch as it passes and we remain. It wears us, uses us, but we wear it and use it in return; and it is blind, whereas we after a manner see.

HENRY JAMES (1843–1916), U.S. author. Letter to Grace Norton, 28 July 1883, in *Letters of a Nation: A Collection of Extraordinary American Letters*, ed. Andrew Carroll (1997).

James, who himself often suffered from depression, was writing to Norton, also a writer, to console her in a time of emotional distress.

8   The test of a first-rate intelligence is the ability to hold two opposed ideas in the mind at the same time, and still retain the ability to function. One should, for example, be able to see that things are hopeless and yet be determined to make them otherwise.

F. SCOTT FITZGERALD (1896–1940), U.S. author. "The Crack-Up," *Esquire* magazine (1936) and *The Crack-Up* (1945).

9   A man cannot despair if he can only imagine a better life, and if he can enact something of its possibility.

WENDELL BERRY (b. 1934), U.S. poet and essayist. "An Entrance to the Woods."

Awards, Rewards, and Congratulation

1   Whoever is a good man only because people will know it, and because they will esteem him better for it after knowing it, whoever will do well only on condition that his virtue will come to the knowledge of men, that man is not one from whom one can derive much service.

MICHEL EYQUEM DE MONTAIGNE (1533–1592), French essayist. "Of Glory," book 2, essay 16 (1578–80), *The Complete Essays of Montaigne*, trans. Donald M. Frame (1976; originally published 1958).

2   It might perhaps be excusable for a painter or another artisan, or even for a rhetorician or a grammarian, to toil to acquire a name by his works; but the actions of virtue are too noble in themselves to seek any other reward than from their own worth, and especially to seek it in the vanity of human judgments.

MICHEL EYQUEM DE MONTAIGNE (1533–1592), French essayist. "Of Glory," book 2, essay 16 (1578–80), *The Complete Essays of Montaigne*, trans. Donald M. Frame (1976; originally published 1958).

3   Certainly, Fame is like a river, that beareth up things light and swollen and drowns things weighty and solid. But if persons of quality and judgement concur, then it is, (as the Scripture saith) *Nomen bonum instar unguenti fragrantis* : it filleth all round about, and will not easily away. For the odours of ointments are more durable than those of flowers.

FRANCIS BACON (1561–1626), English philosopher, essayist, and statesman. "Of Praise," *Essays or Counsels, Civil and Moral*

(1625), and reprinted in *The Essays of Francis Bacon*, ed. John Pitcher (1985).

The Latin phrase refers to Ecclesiastes 7.1 and is translated: "A good name is like a fragrant ointment."

4 The winning of honour is but the revealing of a man's virtue and worth without disadvantage. For some in their actions do woo and affect honour and reputation, which sort of men are commonly much talked of, but inwardly little admired. And some, contrariwise, darken their virtue in the show of it, so as they be undervalued in opinion. . . . Envy, which is the canker of honour, is best extinguished by declaring a man's self in his ends, rather to seek merit than fame, and by attributing a man's successes, rather to divine Providence and felicity, than to his own virtue or policy.

FRANCIS BACON (1561–1626), English philosopher, essayist, and statesman. "Of Honour and Reputation," *Essays or Counsels, Civil and Moral* (1625), and reprinted in *The Essays of Francis Bacon*, ed. John Pitcher (1985).

5 How many things by season season'd are
To their right praise and true perfection!

WILLIAM SHAKESPEARE (1564–1616), English poet and dramatist. *The Merchant of Venice* 5.1.107.

Portia here notes that many times we praise by comparison or because of context. If a nightingale, for example, were heard during the day instead of during the still of the night, it "would be thought / No better a musician than the wren."

6 Good and evil, reward and punishment, are the only motives to a rational creature: these are the spur

and reins whereby all mankind are set on work, and guided.

JOHN LOCKE (1632–1704), English philosopher. *Some Thoughts Concerning Education* (section 54) (1693).

7 The reward of a thing well done, is to have done it.

RALPH WALDO EMERSON (1803–1882), U.S. author. "New England Reformers," *Essays, Second Series* (1844).

8 The reward of labor is *life*. Is that not enough? . . . If you are going to ask to be paid for the pleasure of creation, which is what excellence in work means, the next thing we shall hear of will be a bill sent in for the begetting of children.

WILLIAM MORRIS (1834–1896), English author, artist, and social reformer. *News from Nowhere* (chapter 15, "On the Lack of Incentive to Labour in a Communist Society") (1891).

Hammond replies to the question as to how one gets people to "work strenuously" when there is "no reward of labour."

Inspiring

1 Great works are performed, not by strength, but perseverance: yonder palace was raised by single stones, yet you see its height and spaciousness. He that shall walk with vigour three hours a day will pass in seven years a space equal to the circumference of the globe.

SAMUEL JOHNSON (1709–1784), English author. *The History of Rasselas, Prince of Abissinia* (chapter 13, "Rasselas Discovers the Means of Escape") (1759).

2 There is no allurement or enticement, actual or imaginary, which a well-disciplined mind may not surmount. The *wish* to resist more than half accomplishes the object.

CHARLOTTE DACRE (1782–?1841), English author. *The Passions* (vol. 2, letter 41) (1811).

3 Nothing contributes so much to tranquilize the mind as a steady purpose—a point on which the soul may fix its intellectual eye.

MARY SHELLEY (1797–1851), English author. *Frankenstein* (letter 1) (1816).

4 Insist on yourself; never imitate.

RALPH WALDO EMERSON (1803–1882), U.S. author. "Self-Reliance," *Essays, First Series* (1841).

5 Preach! Write! Act! Do any thing, save to lie down and die!

NATHANIEL HAWTHORNE (1804–1864), U.S. author. *The Scarlet Letter* (chapter 17, "The Pastor to His Parishioner") (1850).

6 If you have built castles in the air, your work need not be lost; that is where they should be. Now put the foundations under them.

HENRY DAVID THOREAU (1817–1862), U.S. author. *Walden* (Conclusion) (1854).

7 Make no little plans; they have no magic to stir men's blood and probably will not be realized. Make big plans; aim high in hope and work, remembering that a nobler, logical diagram once recorded will never die, but long after we are gone will be a living thing, asserting itself with ever growing insistency.

DANIEL HUDSON BURNHAM (1846–1912), U.S. architect and city planner, master architect of the 1893 World's Columbian Exposition. In *Introduction to Planning History in the United States*, ed. Donald A. Krueckeberg (1983).

8 The world is full of people giving good advice to others, but I have thought we should all be better off if we would advise ourselves more, and others less. If I could take the good advice I am capable of giving, I should have no occasion to accept it from others.

E. W. HOWE (1853–1937), U.S. author. *The Story of a Country Town* (chapter 10, "Jo Erring Makes a Full Confession") (1883).

9 We are all in the gutter, but some of us are looking at the stars.

OSCAR WILDE (1854–1900), Irish author. *Lady Windermere's Fan* (act 3) (1893).

10 Always give your best. Never get discouraged. Never be petty. Always remember: others may hate you. Those who hate you don't win unless you hate them. And then you destroy yourself. . . .

Only if you have been in the deepest valley can you ever know how magnificent it is to be on the highest mountain.

RICHARD NIXON (1913–1994), U.S. president. Nixon's farewell to the White House staff (August 1973); in Robert Ramsay and Randall Toye, *The Goodbye Book* (1979).

11 Know whence you came. If you know whence you came, there is really no limit to where you can go.

JAMES BALDWIN (1924–1987), U.S. author. "My Dungeon Shook: Letter To My Nephew on the One Hundredth Anniversary of the Emancipation," *The Fire Next Time* (1962).

12 The best remedy for those who are frightened, lonely or unhappy is to go outside, somewhere they can be alone, alone with the sky, nature and God. For then and only then can you feel that everything is as it

should be and that God wants people to be happy amid nature's beauty and simplicity.

Anne Frank (1929–1945), Dutch diarist. *The Diary of a Young Girl: The Definitive Edition* (Wednesday, 23 February 1944), trans. Susan Massotty (1995).

13 If you cultivate a healthy poverty and simplicity, so that finding a penny will literally make your day, then, since the world is in fact planted in pennies, you have with your poverty bought a lifetime of days.

Annie Dillard (b. 1945), U.S. author. "Seeing," *Pilgrim at Tinker Creek* (1974).

Invitation

1 Tonight, grave sir, both my poor house and I
  Do equally desire your company;
Not that we think us worthy such a guest,
  But that your worth will dignify our feast
With those that come, whose grace may make that seem
  Something, which else could hope for no esteem.

Ben Jonson (1572/3–1637), English poet and dramatist. "Inviting a Friend to Supper," *Epigrams*, no. 101 (1616).

2 I happened to start a question of propriety, whether, when a man knows that some of his intimate friends are invited to the house of another friend, with whom they are all equally intimate, he may join them without an invitation. JOHNSON. "No, Sir; he is not to go when he is not invited. They may be invited on purpose to abuse him" (smiling).

James Boswell (1740–1795), Scottish author. *Life of Johnson* ("18 April 1775") (1791).

3 Best and brightest, come away!
  . . . .
Away, away, from men and towns,
To the wild wood and the downs—
To the silent wilderness
Where the soul need not repress
Its music lest it should not find
An echo in another's mind.

Percy Bysshe Shelley (1792–1822), English poet. "To Jane: The Invitation."

4 "I didn't know I was to have a party at all," said Alice; "but, if there *is* to be one, I think *I* ought to invite the guests."

Lewis Carroll (Charles Lutwidge Dodgson) (1832–1898), English author and mathematician. *Through the Looking Glass* (chapter 9, "Queen Alice") (1871).

In this chapter Alice has been made a queen, but she puzzles over the manners and customs of the Looking Glass world.

5 No one should consider a last-minute invitation an insult. . . . . A neighbor or close friend should not feel diffident about offering last-minute invitations. It is a pleasant thing at the end of a long day to find that you have plenty of food and energy to entertain a guest or two who may well feel equally delighted to put aside dinner plans and join you. This kind of spontaneous entertainment is much more attractive than the planned kind.

Amy Vanderbilt (1908–1974), U.S. author. *Amy Vanderbilt's Etiquette* (chapter 38, "Hosts and Guests") (1972).

6 So come, and slowly we will walk through green gardens and marvel at this strange and sweet world.

SYLVIA PLATH (1932–1963), U.S. author. Letter to her mother, 23 April 1956, in *Letters of a Nation: A Collection of Extraordinary American Letters*, ed. Andrew Carroll (1997).

In this letter Plath invites her mother Aurelia to visit her in England in order to recuperate from an operation.

Welcome

1   For I was hungry, and ye gave me food; I was thirsty, and ye gave me drink; I was a stranger, and ye took me in. . . . Verily I say unto you, Inasmuch as ye have done it unto one of the least of these my brethren, ye have done it unto me.

Matthew 25.35, 25.40.

2   . . . unbidden guests
   Are often welcomest when they are gone.

WILLIAM SHAKESPEARE (1564–1616), English poet and dramatist. *The First Part of King Henry VI* 2.2.55–56.

3   I can express no kinder sign of love Than this kind kiss.

WILLIAM SHAKESPEARE (1564–1616), English poet and dramatist. *The Second Part of King Henry VI* 1.1.18–19

King Henry VI greets Queen Margaret.

4   Small cheer and great welcome makes a merry feast.

WILLIAM SHAKESPEARE (1564–1616), English poet and dramatist. *The Comedy of Errors* 3.1.26.

5   As a long-parted mother with her child
   Plays fondly with her tears and smiles in meeting,
   So, weeping, smiling, greet I thee, my earth,
   And do thee favors with my royal hands.

WILLIAM SHAKESPEARE (1564–1616), English poet and dramatist. *Richard II* 3.2.8–10.

King Richard expresses his gratitude on returning to his home after a difficult voyage by sea.

6   Th' appurtenance of welcome is fashion and ceremony.

WILLIAM SHAKESPEARE (1564–1616), English poet and dramatist. *Hamlet* 2.2.371.

Hamlet indicates to Rosencrantz and Guildenstern that he will put on the proper formalities to welcome the players.

7   It gives me wonder great as my content
   To see you here before me. O my soul's joy!
   If after every tempest come such calms
   May the winds blow till they have waken'd death!
   . . . If I were now to die,
   'Twere now to be most happy; for, I fear,
   My soul hath her content so absolute
   That not another comfort like to this
   Succeeds in unknown fate.

WILLIAM SHAKESPEARE (1564–1616), English poet and dramatist. *Othello* 2.1.181–89.

Othello greets his wife Desdemona on her safe arrival in Cyprus.

8   True friendship's laws are by this rule express'd,
   Welcome the coming, speed the parting guest.

HOMER (9th?–8th? cent. B.C.), Greek poet. *Odyssey* 15.83–84, trans. Alexander Pope (1725–26).

Pope also makes reference to this passage *in The Second Satire of the Second Book of Horace Paraphrased*, written in 1733 and published in 1734. There he writes: "For I, who hold sage Homer's rule the best, / Welcome the coming, speed the going guest" (l.159–60).

9   In a commercial country, a busy country, time becomes precious, and therefore hospitality is not so much valued. No doubt there is still room for a certain degree of it; and a man has a satisfaction in seeing his friends eating and drinking around him. But promiscuous hospitality is not the way to gain real influence. You must help some people at table before others; you must ask some people how they like their wine oftener than others. You therefore offend more people than you please.

SAMUEL JOHNSON (1709–1784), English author. Quoted in James Boswell, *Life of Johnson* ("31 March 1772") (1791).

10 Hospitality is one of the first Christian duties. The beast retires to its shelter, and the bird flies to its nest; but helpless man can only find refuge from his fellow creature. The greatest stranger in this world was he that came to save it. He never had an house, as if willing to see what hospitality was left remaining amongst us.

OLIVER GOLDSMITH (1728–1774), Anglo-Irish author. *The Vicar of Wakefield* (chapter 6, "The Happiness of a Country Fire-Side") (1764).

11 There is an emanation from the heart in genuine hospitality which cannot be described but is immediately felt and puts the stranger at once at his ease.

WASHINGTON IRVING (1783–1859), U.S. author. "Christmas Eve," *The Sketch Book of Geoffrey Crayon, Gent.* (1819–20).

12 'Tis an honour to see me, a favour to hear:
'Tis a privilege high to have dinner and tea

Along with the Red Queen, the White Queen, and me!

LEWIS CARROLL (CHARLES LUTWIDGE DODGSON) (1832–1898), English author and mathematician. *Through the Looking Glass* (chapter 9, "Queen Alice") (1871).

As she listens to this shrill song, Alice thinks to herself, "I'm glad they've come without waiting to be asked. . . . I should never have known who were the right people to invite."

13 Hail, guest, and enter freely! All you see
    Is, for your momentary visit, yours; and we
Who welcome you, are but the guests of God
And know not our departure.

ROBERT LOUIS STEVENSON (1850–1894), Scottish author. "Hail, Guest, and Enter Freely!"

The lines were a proposed inscription for Stevenson's new house, Skerryvore.

14 Good morning, Life—and all
Things glad and beautiful.
My pockets nothing hold,
But he that owns the gold,
The Sun, is my great friend—
His spending has no end.

W. H. DAVIES (1871–1940), Welsh author. "A Greeting."

Saying Goodbye

1   Eyes, look your last!
Arms, take your last embrace! And, lips, O you
The doors of breath, seal with a righteous kiss
A dateless bargain to engrossing death.

WILLIAM SHAKESPEARE (1564–1616), English poet and dramatist. *Romeo and Juliet* 5.3.112–15.

2   After three days men grow weary,
     of a wench, a guest, and weather
     rainy.

     BENJAMIN FRANKLIN (1706–1790),
     U.S. statesman, scientist, and author. *Poor
     Richard's Almanack*, June 1733.

3   Go, fetch to me a pint o' wine,
         And fill it in a silver tassie,
     That I may drink before I go
         A service to my bonnie lassie.

     ROBERT BURNS (1759–1796), Scottish
     poet. "The Silver Tassie."

4   It is a far, far better thing that I do,
     than I have ever done; it is a far, far
     better rest that I go to than I have
     ever known.

     CHARLES DICKENS (1812–1870), En-
     glish author. *A Tale of Two Cities* (book 3;
     chapter 15, "The Footsteps Die out For Ever")
     (1859).

     Sydney Carton's final words and the final
     words of the novel.

5   I still remember the refrain of one
     of the most popular barrack ballads
     of the day which proclaimed most
     proudly that old soldiers never die;
     they just fade away. And, like the
     old soldier of that ballad, I now
     close my military career and just
     fade away, an old soldier who tried
     to do his duty as God gave him the
     light to see that duty. Goodbye.

     DOUGLAS MACARTHUR (1880–1964),
     U.S. general. Address to a joint meeting of
     Congress, 19 April 1951, in *Lend Me Your
     Ears: Great Speeches in History*, ed. William
     Safire (1992).

6   What I was really hanging around
     for, I was trying to feel some kind
     of a good-by. I mean I've left
     schools and places I didn't even
     know I was leaving them. I hate
     that. I don't care if it's a sad good-
     by or a bad good-by, but when I
     leave a place I like to *know* I'm
     leaving it. If you don't, you feel
     even worse.

     J. D. SALINGER (b. 1919), U.S. author.
     The Catcher in the Rye (chapter 1) (1951).

7   It is easy to see the beginnings of
     things, and harder to see the ends.

     JOAN DIDION (b. 1934), U.S. author.
     "Goodbye to All That" (1967), in *Slouching to-
     wards Bethlehem* (1968).

     Didion writes about falling in and out of love
     with New York City.

8   Farewells and separations never, I
     find, quite live up to the drama
     they promise to afford. Human be-
     ings (I find again) have a tendency
     to feel the wrong quantity of emo-
     tion, or indeed the wrong emotion,
     so that life is an endless procession
     of liquid being poured into and ex-
     changed between badly designed
     containers, the wrong color, the
     wrong shape, the wrong size.

     JOHN LANCHESTER, English novelist and
     journalist. *The Debt to Pleasure* (section "Au-
     tumn," subsection "An Omelette") (1996).

Concluding a Deal

1   But the olde saying is, hast maketh
     waste, and bargains made in speede,
     are commonly repented at leisure.

     GEORGE PETTIE (c. 1548–1589), En-
     glish author. "Cephalus and Procris," *A Petite
     Pallace of Pettie His Pleasure* (1576).

2   In dealing with cunning persons,
     we must ever consider their ends,
     to interpret their speeches; and it is
     good to say little to them, and that
     which they least look for. In all ne-
     gotiations of difficulty, a man may
     not look to sow and reap at once,

but must prepare business, and so ripen it by degrees.

FRANCIS BACON (1561–1626), English philosopher, essayist, and statesman. "Of Negotiating," *Essays or Counsels, Civil and Moral* (1625), and reprinted in *The Essays of Francis Bacon,* ed. John Pitcher (1985).

3 The most eminent negotiators have always been the politest and best-bred men in company; even what the women call the *prettiest men.* For God's sake, never lose view of these your two capital objects; bend everything to them, try everything by their rules, and calculate everything by their purposes.

PHILIP DORMER STANHOPE, FOURTH EARL OF CHESTERFIELD (1694–1773), English statesman and author. Letter, 26 September 1752 OS, *The Letters of Philip Dormer Stanhope, Earl of Chesterfield,* ed. John Bradshaw, vol. 2 (1929).

4 Win/Win is a frame of mind and heart that constantly seeks mutual benefit in all human interactions. Win/Win means that agreements or solutions are mutually beneficial, mutually satisfying. With a Win/Win solution, all parties feel good about the decision and feel committed to the action plan.

STEPHEN R. COVEY (b. 1932), U.S. author. *The Seven Habits of Highly Effective People: Restoring the Character Ethic* ("Habit 4: Principles of Interpersonal Leadership") (1989).

5 The worst thing you can possibly do in a deal is seem desperate to make it. That makes the other guy smell blood, and then you're dead. The best thing you can do is deal from strength, and leverage is the biggest strength you can have. Leverage is having something the other guy wants.

DONALD J. TRUMP, U.S. businessman. *The Art of the Deal* (chapter 2, "Trump Cards: The Elements of the Deal") (1982).

Thanks

1 Sweet is the breath of vernal shower,
The bee's collected treasures sweet,
Sweet music's melting fall, but sweeter yet
The still small voice of Gratitude.

THOMAS GRAY (1716–1771), English poet. "Ode for Music."

2 Gratitude is a fruit of great cultivation; you do not find it among gross people.

JAMES BOSWELL (1740–1795), Scottish author. *Boswell's Journal of a Tour to the Hebrides,* 20 September 1773 (1785).

Boswell attributes the remark to Samuel Johnson.

3 I suppose all phrases of mere compliment have their turn to be true. A man is occasionally grateful when he says "Thank you."

GEORGE ELIOT (MARY ANN OR MARIAN EVANS) (1819–1890), English author. *The Mill on the Floss* (book 6, "The Great Temptation"; chapter 2, "First Impressions") (1860).

4 For all the gifts you give
Me, dear, each day you live,
    Of thanks above
All thanks that could be spoken
Take not my song in token,
    Take my love.

ALGERNON CHARLES SWINBURNE (1837–1909), English poet. "A Child's Battles."

5 God give you pardon from gratitude
and other mild forms of servitude—

and make peace for all of us
with what is easy.

ROBERT CREELEY (b. 1926), U.S. poet.
"Song ['God give you pardon from gratitude']."

6   A talent for receiving gifts is far, far
     more rare than a talent for giving
     them—one concedes so much
     more, in the act of reception,
     whereas to be in the position of the
     giver is to retain all the psychic ap-
     purtenances of power, patronage,
     and control.

JOHN LANCHESTER, English novelist and
journalist. The Debt to Pleasure (section
"Spring," subsection "Roast Lamb") (1996).

Apology

1   The commonest way of softening
     the hearts of those we have of-
     fended, when, vengeance in hand,
     they hold us at their mercy, is by
     submission to move them to com-
     miseration and pity. However, au-
     dacity and steadfastness—entirely
     contrary means—have sometimes
     served to produce the same effect.

MICHEL EYQUEM DE MONTAIGNE
(1533–1589), French essayist. "By Diverse
Means We Arrive at the Same End," book 1,
essay 1 (1578–1580), The Complete Essays of
Montaigne, trans. Donald M. Frame (1976;
originally published 1958).

2   Reconciliations are the cement of
     friendship. Therefore friends should
     quarrel to strengthen their attach-
     ment, and offend each other for the
     pleasure of being reconciled.

MARIA EDGEWORTH (1768–1849),
Irish author. "The Noble Science of Self-Justification," Letters for Literary Ladies (1795).

3   Apologizing. —A very desperate
     habit,—one that is rarely cured.
     Apology is only egotism wrong side

out. Nine times out of ten, the first
thing a man's companion knows of
his shortcoming is from his apology. It is mighty presumptuous on
your part to suppose your small
failures of so much consequence
that you must make a talk about
them.

OLIVER WENDELL HOLMES (1809–
1894), U.S. author and physician. The Professor at the Breakfast-Table (chapter 6).

4   All of us . . . are subject to making
     mistakes; so that the chief art of
     life, is to learn how best to remedy
     mistakes. Now one remedy for mis-
     takes is honesty.

HERMAN MELVILLE (1819–1891), U.S.
author. Israel Potter (chapter 7, "After a Curious Adventure Upon the Pont Neuf, Israel Enters the Presence of the Renowned Sage, Dr.
Franklin, Whom He Finds Right Learnedly and
Multifariously Employed") (1855).

Advice attributed to Benjamin Franklin.

5   APOLOGIZE, v. to lay the founda-
     tion for a future offense.

AMBROSE BIERCE (1842–?1914), U.S.
author. The Devil's Dictionary (1881–1911).

6   He also told me that a hostess
     should never apologise for any fail-
     ure in her household arrangements,
     if there is a hostess there is insofar
     as there is a hostess no failure.

GERTRUDE STEIN (1874–1946), U.S.
author. The Autobiography of Alice B. Toklas
(chapter 1, "Before I Came to Paris") (1933).

This sentiment is attributed to Alice's father
who is described as "a quiet man who took
things quietly."

7   Never apologize and never ex-
     plain—it's a sign of weakness.

LAURENCE STALLINGS (1894–1968),
U.S. screenwriter. She Wore a Yellow Ribbon
(1949).

Spoken by John Wayne.

8 Anybody who has ever tried to rectify an injustice or set a record straight comes to feel that he is going mad. And from a social point of view, he *is* crazy, for he is trying to undo something that is finished, to unravel the social fabric.

MARY MCCARTHY (1912–1989), U.S. author. "My Confession," *On the Contrary* (1976).

Praise

1 Certainly nothing gratifies us like . . . applause. But you can't live on applause; praise alone won't pay the rent. We need something a bit more solid; the best hand people can give us is a hand with cash in it.

MOLIÈRE (JEAN BAPTISTE POQUE-LIN) (1622–1673), French dramatist. *Le Bourgeois Gentilhomme* 1.1 (1670), in *Eight Plays by Molière*, trans. Morris Bishop (1957).

A music teacher tells a dancing teacher that he appreciates their pupil M. Jourdain, a Parisian merchant, because he pays well, although he has little taste or ability.

2 Praise, like gold and diamonds, owes its value only to its scarcity.

SAMUEL JOHNSON (1709–1784), English author. *The Rambler* (6 June 1751).

3 Praise everybody: . . . never be squeamish, but speak out your compliment both point-blank in a man's face, and behind his back, when you know there is a reasonable chance of his hearing it again. Never lose a chance of saying a kind word.

WILLIAM MAKEPEACE THACKERAY (1811–1863), English novelist. *Vanity Fair* (chapter 19, "Miss Crawley at Nurse") (1847–48).

4 Flattery iz like ice-cream—to relish good we want it a little at a time, and often. The more yu praze a man who don't deserve it, the more yu abuze him. Yu kan't flatter a truly wize man—he knows just how much praze iz due him; that he takes, and charges over all the balance tew the proffit and loss ackount.

JOSH BILLINGS (HENRY W. SHAW) (1818–1885), U.S. humorist. "Fust Impreshuns," *The Complete Works of Josh Billings* (1899).

5 I don't go in for that stuff. . . . Compliments to women about their looks. I never met a woman that didn't know if she was good-looking or not without being told, and some of them give themselves credit for more than they've got.

TENNESSEE WILLIAMS (1914–1983), U.S. dramatist. *A Streetcar Named Desire* (scene 2) (1947).

This is Stanley Kowalski's response when his sister-in-law Blanche DuBois informs him that she has been "fishing for a compliment."

Forgiving

1 The quality of mercy is not strained.
It droppeth as the gentle rain from heaven
Upon the place beneath. It is twice blest:
It blesseth him that gives and him that takes.

WILLIAM SHAKESPEARE (1564–1616), English poet and dramatist. *The Merchant of Venice* 4.1.184–87.

In a discussion with Shylock and Antonio about the nature of the law, Portia reflects on the quality of mercy.

2 If thou hast done an injury to another, rather own it than defend it.

One way thou gainest forgiveness;
the other thou doublest the wrong
and reckoning.

WILLIAM PENN (1644–1718), English
philosopher and statesman. *The Fruits of Solitude: Reflections and Maxims Relating to the
Conduct of Human Life* (part 1), "Reparation,"
no. 121 (1693).

3   To Err is Humane; to Forgive, Divine.

ALEXANDER POPE (1688–1744), English
poet. *An Essay on Criticism* (line 525).

4   We are taught to believe that forgiveness is never denied to sincere
repentance.

ANN RADCLIFFE (1764–1823), English
author. *A Sicilian Romance* (chapter 1) (1821).

The consolation of Madame de Menon to Vincent, who seeks to unburden himself of a guilt
"beyond remedy in this world, . . . and without
pardon in the next."

5   If we should deal out justice only,
in this world, who would escape?
No, it is better to be generous, and
in the end more profitable, for it
gains gratitude for us, and love.

MARK TWAIN (SAMUEL CLEMENS)
(1835–1910), U.S. author. *The Autobiography
of Mark Twain*, vol. 1 (1925).

6   Nothing human disgusts me unless
it's unkind, violent.

TENNESSEE WILIAMS (1914–1983),
U.S. dramatist. *The Night of the Iguana* (act 3)
(1961).

Spoken by Hannah Jelkes to Reverend Shan-
non.

Vowing

1   Give me chastity and continence,
but not just now.

**SAINT AUGUSTINE (AURELIUS AU-
GUSTINUS)** (354–430), theologian, bishop

of Hippo, and doctor of the Roman Catholic
Church. *Confessions* (8.7) (397–401).

2   'Tis not the many oaths that makes
the truth,
But the plain single vow that is
vow'd true.
What is not holy, that we swear not
by,
But take the High'st to witness.

WILLIAM SHAKESPEARE (1564–1616),
English poet and dramatist. *All's Well That
Ends Well* 4.2.21–24.

Diana tries to educate Bertram, whom she mis-
trusts, in the proper way of swearing and keeping a vow.

3   I hate to promise; what we do then
is expected from us and wants
much of the welcome it finds when
it surprises.

SIR GEORGE ETHEREGE (1634?–1691),
English dramatist. *The Man of Mode: or Sir Fopling Flutter* 5.2.183 (1676).

4   Rarely promise; but if lawful, constantly perform.

WILLIAM PENN (1644–1718), English
philosopher and statesman. *Fruits of Solitude:
Reflections and Maxims Relating to the Conduct of Human Life* (part 1), "Promising," no.
186 (1693).

5   Any overt act, above all, is felt to be
alchemic in its power to change. A
drunkard takes the pledge; it will be
strange if that does not help him.
For how many years did Mr. Pepys
continue to make and break his little vows? And yet I have not heard
that he was discouraged in the end.

ROBERT LOUIS STEVENSON (1850–
1894), English author. "Virginibus Puerisque
II," *Virginibus Puerisque* (1881).

6   I'm going to live through this, and
when it's all over, I'll never be hungry again—no, nor any of my

folks!—if I have to lie, steal, cheat or kill! As God is my witness, I'll never be hungry again!

SIDNEY HOWARD, U.S. screenwriter. *Gone with the Wind* (1939).

*P*raying

1   Only that man's prayer is answered who lifts his hands with his heart in them.

Tannit 8a, in *The Talmudic Anthology: Tales and Teachings of the Rabbis*, ed. Louis I. Newman (1947).

2   O ye who believe! When ye rise up for prayer, wash your faces, and your hands up to the elbows, and lightly rub your heads and (wash) your feet up to the ankles. And if ye are unclean, purify yourselves. . . . Allah would not place a burden on you, but He would purify you and would perfect His grace upon you, that ye may give thanks.

Qur'an 5.6; *The Glorious Koran: An Explanatory Translation by Marmaduke Pickthall* (1930; reprint 1992).

3   From needing danger to be good, From owing thee yesterday's tears today,
  From trusting so much to thy blood
That in that hope we wound our souls away,
  From bribing thee with alms to excuse
  Some sin more burdenous,

. . . .
. . . Lord, deliver us.

JOHN DONNE (1572–1631), English poet, clergyman, and courtier. "A Litany" (stanza 16).

4   Teach me to feel another's Woe;
    To hide the Fault I see;
  That Mercy I to others show,
    That Mercy show to me.

ALEXANDER POPE (1688–1744), English poet. "The Universal Prayer" (lines 37–40).

Printed as a pendant to the *Essay on Man*.

5   Work as if you were to live a hundred years, Pray as if you were to die tomorrow.

BENJAMIN FRANKLIN (1706–1790), U.S. statesman, scientist, and author. *Poor Richard's Almanac*, May 1757.

6   To Mercy, Pity, Peace, and Love
All pray in their distress;
And to these virtues of delight
Return their thankfulness.

WILLIAM BLAKE (1757–1827), English poet and artist. "The Divine Image," *Songs of Innocence* (1789).

7   He prayeth best, who loveth best
All things both great and small;
For the God who loveth us,
He made and loveth all.

SAMUEL TAYLOR COLERIDGE (1772–1834), English poet and critic. "The Rime of the Ancient Mariner" (part 7, lines 613–16).

8   I own that I am disposed to say grace upon twenty other occasions in the course of the day besides my dinner. I want a form for setting out upon a pleasant walk, for a moonlight ramble, for a friendly meeting, or a solved problem. Why have we none for books, these spiritual repasts—a grace before Milton—a grace before Shakespeare—a devotional exercise proper to be said before reading *The Fairie Queene*?

CHARLES LAMB (1775–1834), English essayist. "Grace Before Meat, " *London Magazine* (1821) and *Essays of Elia* (1823).

9 Almost every human being, however vague his notions of the Power addressed, is capable of being lifted and solemnized by the exercise of public prayer.

OLIVER WENDELL HOLMES (1809–1894), U.S. author and physician. *The Poet at the Breakfast Table* (chapter 7) (1872).

10 Prayer is often an argument of laziness: "Lord, my temper gives me a vast deal of inconvenience, and it would be a great task for me to correct it; and wilt thou be pleased to correct it for me, that I may get along easier?" If prayer was answered under such circumstances, independent of action of natural laws, it would be paying a premium on indolence.

HENRY WARD BEECHER (1813–1887), U.S. clergyman. *Lecture Room Talks: Answers to Prayers,* in *Beecher as a Humorist: Selections from the Published Works,* ed. Eleanor Kirk (1887).

11 Prayer draws us near to our own souls, and purifies our thoughts.

HERMAN MELVILLE (1819–1891), U.S. author. *Mardi and A Voyage Thither* (chapter 111, "The Visit the Lake of Yammo") (1849).

12 There's something in it when a body like the widow or the parson prays, but it don't work for me, and I reckon it don't work for only just the right kind.

MARK TWAIN (SAMUEL CLEMENS) (1835–1910), U.S. author. *Adventures of Huckleberry Finn* (chapter 8) (1885).

13 PRAY, v. To ask that the laws of the universe be annulled in behalf of a single petitioner confessedly unworthy.

AMBROSE BIERCE (1842–?1914), U.S. author. *The Devil's Dictionary* (1881–1911).

14 I added that he said we ought to pray for things we needed and that I needed the humming top a great deal more than I did the conversion of the heathen or the restitution of Jerusalem to the Jews, two objects of my nightly supplication which left me very cold.

EDMUND GOSSE (1849–1928), English author. *Father and Son* (chapter 2) (1907).

Gosse here expresses his confusion as a child about his parents' belief that God answers all needs.

15 Prayer, among sane people, has never superseded practical efforts to secure the desired end.

GEORGE SANTAYANA (1863–1952), American (Spanish-born) philosopher and poet. *The Life of Reason: Reason in Religion* (chapter 4) (1905–1906).

16 Prayer is not an old woman's idle amusement. Properly understood and applied, it is the most potent instrument of action. . . .
. . . Prayer is the first and the last lesson in learning the noble and brave art of sacrificing self in the various walks of life culminating in the defence of one's nation's liberty and honour.

MOHANDAS K. GANDHI (1869–1948), Indian political and spiritual leader. *Non-Violence in Peace and War* (vol. 2, section 77) (1949).

17 Scientific research is based on the idea that everything that takes place is determined by laws of nature, and therefore this holds for the actions of people. For this reason, a research scientist will hardly be in-

clined to believe that events could be influenced by a prayer, i. e. by a wish addressed to a supernatural Being.

ALBERT EINSTEIN (1879–1955), American (German-born) theoretical physicist. Letter to Phyllis Wright, 24 January 1936, in *Letters of a Nation: A Collection of Extraordinary American Letters*, ed. Andrew Carroll (1997).

Einstein responds to Wright, a sixth-grader, who wrote to ask if scientists pray.

18   Peter said "Lord, I believe. Help my unbelief." It is the most natural and most human and most agonizing prayer in the gospels, and I think it is the foundation prayer of faith.

FLANNERY O'CONNOR (1925–1964), U.S. author. Letter to Alfred Corn, 30 May 1962, in *Letters of a Nation: A Collection of Extraordinary American Letters*, ed. Andrew Carroll (1997).

O'Connor responds to Corn, a college freshman, who had heard the author speak at the University of Atlanta and wrote to tell her about his crisis of faith.

19   You know I ain't never prayed before
'Cause it always seemed to me
That prayin's the same as beggin'
       Lord,
I don't take no charity.

STEVE EARLE, U.S. songwriter. "Tom Ames' Prayer" (1994).

Celebrating

1   If all the year were playing holidays,
To sport would be as tedious as to
       work;
But when they seldom come, they
       wish'd for come,
And nothing pleaseth but rare accidents.

WILLIAM SHAKESPEARE (1564–1616), English poet and dramatist. *The First Part of Henry IV* 1.2.198–201.

The young prince here vows ultimately to throw off the unrestrained life of Falstaff and Eastcheap and to take on the duties of his kingdom.

2   Give me women, wine, and snuff
Until I cry out "hold, enough!"
You may do so sans objection
Till the day of resurrection.

JOHN KEATS (1795–1821), English poet. "Give Me Women, Wine and Snuff."

Confessing

1   Boldness in sinning is somewhat compensated and bridled by boldness in confession. Whoever would oblige himself to tell all, would oblige himself not to do anything about which we are constrained to keep silent.

MICHEL EYQUEM DE MONTAIGNE (1533–1592), French essayist. "On Some Verses of Virgil," book 3, essay 5 (1585–88), *The Complete Essays of Montaigne*, trans. Donald M. Frame (1976; originally published 1958).

2   There is a luxury in self-reproach. When we blame ourselves we feel that no one else has a right to blame us. It is the confession, not the priest, that gives us absolution.

OSCAR WILDE (1854–1900), Irish author. *The Picture of Dorian Gray* (chapter 8) (1891).

Winning

1   All successful men have agreed in one thing,—they were causationists. They believed that things went not by luck, but by law; that there was not a weak or a cracked link in the chain that joins the first and last of things.

RALPH WALDO EMERSON (1803–1882), U.S. author. "Power," *The Conduct of Life* (1860).

2 A minute's success pays the failure
of years.

ROBERT BROWNING (1812–1889), English poet. "Apollo and the Fates."

3 Success is counted sweetest
By those who ne'er succeed.

EMILY DICKINSON (1830–1886), U.S. poet. "Success is Counted Sweetest."

4 Nothing succeeds like excess.

OSCAR WILDE (1854–1900), Irish author. *A Woman of No Importance* (act 3) (1893).

5 I dread success. To have succeeded is to have finished one's business on earth, like the male spider, who is killed by the female the moment he has succeeded in his courtship. I like a state of continual becoming, with a goal in front and not behind.

GEORGE BERNARD SHAW (1856–1950), Irish dramatist and critic. Letter to Ellen Terry, 28 August 1896, *Collected Letters*, ed. Dan H. Laurence, vol. 1 (1965).

6 People are utterly wrong in their slant upon things. They see the successes that men have made and somehow they appear to be easy. But that is a world away from the facts. It is failure that is easy. Success is always hard. A man can fail in ease; he can succeed only by paying out all that he has and is. It is this which makes success so pitiable a thing if it be in lines that are not useful and uplifting.

HENRY FORD (1863–1947), U.S. industrialist. In *My Life and Work* (1922; reprint 1973) and reprinted in *Ford on Management: Harnessing the American Spirit* (chapter 8, "Why Charity?") (1991).

7 I had trouble as a competitor because I kept wanting to fight the other player every time I started to lose a match. . . . After a while I began to understand that you could walk out on the court like a lady, all dressed up in immaculate white, be polite to everybody, and still play like a tiger and beat the liver and lights out of the ball.

ALTHEA GIBSON DARBEN (b. 1927), U.S. tennis player. *I Always Wanted to Be Somebody* (chapter 2, "Between Two Worlds"), ed. Ed Fitzgerald (1958).

8 To be a great champion you must believe you are the best. If you're not, pretend you are.

MUHAMMAD ALI (b. 1942), U.S. boxer. Quoted in Eric V. Copage, *Black Pearls: Daily Meditations, Affirmations, and Inspirations for African-Americans* ("February 17") (1993).

Losing

1 I would prefer even to fail with honor
than win by cheating.

SOPHOCLES (c. 496–406 B.C.), Greek dramatist. *Philoctetes* (lines 92–93), trans. David Grene, in *The Complete Greek Tragedies*, ed. David Grene and Richard Lattimore, vol. 2 (1957).

2 One is always more vexed at losing a game of any sort by a single hole or ace, than if one has never had a chance of winning it.

WILLIAM HAZLITT (1778–1830), English essayist and critic. "On Great and Little Things," *Literary Remains* (1836).

3 There is not a fiercer hell than the failure in a great object.

JOHN KEATS (1795–1821), English poet. *Endymion* (preface).

4 The *probability* that we may fall in the struggle *ought not* to deter us from the support of a cause we be-

lieve to be just; it *shall not* deter
me.

ABRAHAM LINCOLN (1809–1865), U.S.
president. "Speech on the Sub-Treasury" (26
December 1839), *Collected Works of Abraham
Lincoln*, ed. Roy Prentice Basler (1953, 1990).

5   The victor shall soon be the vanquished, if he relax in his exertion;
and that the vanquished this year,
may be victor the next, in spite of
all competition.

ABRAHAM LINCOLN (1809–1865), U.S.
president. "Address Before the Wisconsin State
Agricultural Society, Milwaukee, Wisconsin"
(30 September 1859), *Collected Works of
Abraham Lincoln*, ed. Roy Prentice Basler
(1953, 1990).

6   Failure after long perseverance is
much grander than never to have a
striving good enough to be called a
failure.

**GEORGE ELIOT (MARY ANN OR
MARIAN EVANS)** (1819–1880), English
author. *Middlemarch* (book 2, "Old and
Young"; chapter 22) (1872).

7   In all failures, the beginning is certainly the half of the whole.

**GEORGE ELIOT (MARY ANN OR
MARIAN EVANS)** (1819–1880), English
author. *Middlemarch* (book 3, "Waiting for
Death"; chapter 31) (1872).

8   How fascinating all failures are!

OSCAR WILDE (1854–1900), Irish au-
thor. Letter to Julia Ward Howe, 6 July 1882,
The Letters of Oscar Wilde, ed. Rupert Hart-
Davis (1962).

Wilde refers specifically to the American soldier and statesman Jefferson Davis.

9   Do not mistake your objection to
defeat for an objection to fighting,
your objection to being a slave for
an objection to slavery, your objection to not being as rich as your
neighbor for an objection to pov-

erty. The cowardly, the insubordi-
nate, and the envious share your
objections.

GEORGE BERNARD SHAW (1856–
1950), Irish dramatist and critic. "Maxims for
Revolutionists," *The Revolutionist's Handbook*
in *Man and Superman* (1903).

10   There may be a few things about a
success that haint generally known,
but ther's never no secrets about a
failure.

KIN HUBBARD (1868–1930), U.S. humorist. *Fifty-Two Weeks of Abe Martin* (1924).

11   Look, victory and defeat ain't
bound to be same for the big shots
up top as for them below, not by
any means. Can be times the bottom lot find a defeat really pays
them. Honour's lost, nowt else. . . .
As a rule you can say victory and
defeat both come expensive to us
ordinary folk. Best thing for us is
when politics get bogged down
solid.

BERTOLT BRECHT (1898–1956), German poet and dramatist. *Mother Courage and
Her Children* (scene 3) (1941), trans. John Wil-
lett (1994).

12   I coulda had class! I coulda been a
contender! I coulda been somebody! Instead of a bum which is
what I am! Let's face it! . . . He gets
the title shot outdoors in the ball
park and whadda I get? A one-way
ticket to Palookaville.

BUD SCHULBERG, U.S. screenwriter. *On
the Waterfront* (1954).

Spoken by Marlon Brando, blaming his brother
(Rod Steiger) for an abortive boxing career. The
film was directed by Elia Kazan and written by
Bud Schulberg.

13   In a game, just losing is almost as
satisfying as just winning. . . . In
life the loser's score is always zero.

W. H. AUDEN (1907–1973), Anglo-American poet. "Postscript: The Frivolous and the Earnest," *The Dyer's Hand* (1962).

14 All men are mortal, and therefore all men are losers; our profoundest loyalty goes out to the failed.

JOHN UPDIKE (1932-), U.S. author. "The Boston Red Sox, As of 1986," *Odd Jobs* (1991).

Reconciliation

1 There are more quarrels smothered by just shutting your mouth, and holding it shut, than by all the wisdom in the world.

HENRY WARD BEECHER (1813–1887), U.S. clergyman. "Sermon: Peaceable Living," *Beecher As a Humorist: Selections from the Published Works,* ed. Eleanor Kirk (1887).

Once in a Lifetime

Birth

1   Whate'er is Born of Mortal Birth
Must be consumed with the Earth
To rise from Generation free.

WILLIAM BLAKE (1757–1827), English poet and artist. "To Tirzah," *Songs of Experience.*

"Tirzah" in Blake's cosmology approximates Mother Nature. Here she figures as the mother of "my Mortal part," by which Blake means particularly the five senses.

2   But when I saw it on its mother's
arm,
    And hanging at her bosom (she
    the while
    Bent o'er its features with a tear-
    ful smile)
Then I was thrill'd and melted, and
most warm
Impressed a father's kiss.

SAMUEL TAYLOR COLERIDGE (1772–1834), English poet and critic. "Sonnet: To a Friend Who Asked, How I Felt When the Nurse First Presented My Infant to Me."

3   Out of the dark sweet sleep
        Where no dreams laugh or
        weep
            Borne through bright gates of
            birth
        Into the dim sweet light
        Where day still dreams of
        night
            While heaven takes form on
            earth
White rose of spirit and flesh, and
lily of love,
            What note of song have we
            Fit for the birds and thee,
        Fair nestling couched beneath the
        mother-dove?

ALGERNON CHARLES SWINBURNE (1837–1909), English poet. "Birth-Song: For Olivia Frances Madox Rossetti, Born September 20, 1875."

4   Birth, and copulation, and death.
I've been born, and once is enough.
You dont remember, but I remem-
ber,
Once is enough.

T. S. ELIOT (1888–1965), Anglo-American poet. "Sweeney Agonistes."

5   I woke up out of the ether with an
utterly abandoned feeling, and
asked the nurse right away if it was
a boy or a girl. She told me it was a
girl, and so I turned my head away
and wept. "All right," I said, "I'm
glad it's a girl. And I hope she'll be
a fool—that's the best thing a girl
can be in this world, a beautiful little fool."

F. SCOTT FITZGERALD (1896–1940), U.S. author. *The Great Gatsby* (chapter 1) (1925).

Spoken by Daisy Buchanan.

6   The cradle rocks above an abyss,
and common sense tells us that our
existence is but a brief crack of
light between two eternities of
darkness. Although the two are
identical twins, man, as a rule,
views the prenatal abyss with more
calm than the one he is heading for
(at some forty-five hundred heart-
beats an hour).

VLADIMIR NABOKOV (1899–1977), American (Russian-born) novelist. *Speak, Memory: An Autobiography Revisited* (chapter 1, part 1) (1951).

7   And I was fascinated to discover
that far from being "ten times
worse than the worst pain you ever
had" (as our childless woman doctor had told us in college) or
"worse than the worst cramps you
ever had, but at least you get something out of it" (as my mother had

said), the pains of childbirth were altogether different from the enveloping effects of other kinds of pain. These were pains one could follow with one's mind; they were like a fine electric needle outlining one's pelvis.

MARGARET MEAD (1901–1978), U.S. anthropologist. *Blackberry Winter* ("Catherine, Born in Wartime") (1972).

8   Your birth is not an accident; G-d chooses each of us to fulfill a specific mission in this world, just as a composer arranges each musical note. Take away even one note, and the entire composition is affected. Each person matters; each person is irreplaceable.

MENACHEM MENDEL SCHNEERSON (1902–1994), U.S. rabbi. *Toward a Meaningful Life: The Wisdom of the Rebbe* (chapter 2, "Birth: The Mission Begins") (1995).

9   Women perceive the child's first movement with varied feelings, this kick delivered at the portals of the world, against the uterine wall that shuts him off from the world. One woman is lost in wonder at this signal announcing the presence of an independent being; another may feel repugnance at containing a stranger.

SIMONE DE BEAUVOIR (1908–1986), French author and philosopher. *The Second Sex* (part 5, "Situation"; chapter 17, "The Mother") (1949); trans. H. M. Parshley (1979).

Later in the text, Beauvoir notes, "Every woman wants to give birth to a hero, a genius; but all the mothers of actual heroes and geniuses have at first complained that their sons were breaking their hearts."

10   We are *not to talk about* having babies, because that is not part of the experience of men and so nothing to do with reality, with civilization, and no concern of art.—A rending scream in another room.

URSULA K. LeGUIN (b. 1929), U.S. author. Commencement address at Brywn Mawr College (1986); in *Dancing at the Edge of the World: Thoughts on Words, Women and Places* (1987).

First Baby

1   I wish him good and constant health,
His father's learning, but more wealth,
And that to use, nor hoard; a purse
Open to bless, not shut to curse.
May he have many and fast friends,
Meaning good will, not private ends,
Such as scorn to understand
When they name love, a piece of land.

WILLIAM CARTWRIGHT (1611–1643), English poet and dramatist. "To Mr. W. B., at the Birth of his First Child."

2   If in the whole course of a woman's sensitive life there is one moment of happiness more keen, blissful, bright, than another, it is that in which the husband of her choice thanks her for his firstborn child.

EMILY EDEN (1797–1869), English author. *The Semi-Detached House* (chapter 18) (1859).

3   Tew look upon the trak that life takes—tew see the sunshine and shower—tew plead for the best, and shrink from the wust—tew shudder when sikness steals on, and tew be chastened when death comes—tiz this—oh! tiz this that makes the fust baby a hope upon arth, and a gem up in heaven.

JOSH BILLINGS (HENRY W. SHAW) (1818–1885), U.S. humorist. "The Fust Baby," *The Complete Works of Josh Billings* (1876).

Shaw also notes the way a new father sees his wife differently after the birth of a child: "Tew find the pale Mother again bi yure side, more luvly than when she was wooed—tew see a new tenderness in her eye, and tew hear the chastened sweetness of her laff, as she tells you something new about 'Willie'—tew luv her far more than ever, and tew find oftimes a prayer on yure lips—tiz this that makes the first baby a fountain or sparkling plezure."

4   For some reason the most important thing to me was actually seeing the baby come out of you yourself and making sure it was yours. I thought if you had to have all that pain anyway you might just as well stay awake. I had always imagined myself hitching up on to my elbows on the delivery table after it was all over—dead white, of course, with no makeup and from the awful ordeal, but smiling and radiant, with my hair down to my waist, and reaching out for my first little squirmy child and saying its name, whatever it was.

SYLVIA PLATH (1932–1963), U.S. author. *The Bell Jar* (chapter 6) (1962).

The nineteen-year-old narrator's reaction to seeing birth first-hand.

5   Oh, I wish I could completely explain how I feel about having a baby. It's that procreation is the greatest miracle of all, and you are participating in it, contributing to it—as animals must do, as the grizzly bears must do because they kill to protect their cubs. You feel an affinity with all the vast things in the world since time began. And you feel so small. Procreation is like the tide, it's like the planets it's like everything inexplicable. And yet it's so utterly personal.

ELIZABETH TAYLOR (b. 1932), U.S. (English-born) actress. *Elizabeth Taylor: An Informal Memoir* (chapter 3) (1965).

Second Baby

1   Most innovations in science, especially radical ones, have been initiated and championed by laterborns. Firstborns tend to reject new ideas, especially when the innovation appears to upset long-accepted principles.

FRANK J. SULLOWAY, U.S. historian of science. *Born to Rebel: Birth Order, Family Dynamics, and Creative Lives* (chapter 2, "Birth Order and Scientific Revolutions") (1996).

2   It is so difficult to anticipate bringing home an invader of the love affair that one has created with the first child.

T. BERRY BRAZELTON (b. 1918), U.S. pediatrician and author. *Touchpoints: The Essential Reference* (chapter 36) (1992).

Third Baby

1   Studies made on first children say they're not all that bad. They are usually shy, serious and sensitive, are academically superior and are more likely to be an Einstein. Second children, on the other hand, are relaxed, independent, cheerful, learn toward creativity and are more likely to be Picasso. No one has had the courage to find—let alone study—child Number 3 and the ones who follow, whom I call et ceteras.

ERMA BOMBECK (1927–1996), U.S. humorist and newspaper columnist. "Third Child" (5 November 1981), in *Forever, Erma: America's Best-Loved Writing from America's Favorite Humorist* (1996).

Death of a Child

1   Grief fills the room up of my ab-
    sent child,
    Lies in his bed, walks up and down
    with me,
    Puts on his pretty looks, repeats his
    words,
    Remembers me of all his gracious
    parts,
    Stuffs out his vacant garments with
    his form;
    Then, have I reason to be fond of
    grief?
    Fare you well! Had you such a loss
    as I,
    I could give better comfort than
    you do.

WILLIAM SHAKESPEARE (1564–1616),
English poet and dramatist. *The Life and Death
of King John* 3.4.93–100.

Constance speaks about her son Arthur.

2   More fool than I to look on that
    was lent,
    As if mine own, when thus imper-
    manent.

ANNE BRADSTREET (1612?–1672), U.S.
(English-born) poet. "In Memory of My Dear
Child, Anne Bradstreet."

3   Oh tell, rude stone! the passer by,
    That here the pretty babe doth lie,
    Death sang to sleep with Lullaby.

SAMUEL TAYLOR COLERIDGE (1772–
1834), English poet and critic. "Epitaph on an
Infant."

4   Riddle of destiny, who can show
    What thy short visit meant, or
    know
    What thy errand here below?
    Shall we say, that Nature blind
    Check'd her hand, and changed her
    mind,
    Just when she had exactly wrought
    A finish'd pattern without fault?

CHARLES LAMB (1775–1834), English essayist. "On an Infant Dying As Soon As Born."

5   Still mine! maternal rights serene
        Not given to another!
    The crystal bars shine faint between
        The souls of child and mother.

ELIZABETH BARRETT BROWNING
(1806–1861), English poet. "A Child's Grave
at Florence (A. A. E. C. Born July 1848. Died
November 1849)."

6   One young life lost, two happy
    young lives blighted,
        With earthward eyes we see;
    With eyes uplifted, keener, farther-
    sighted,
        We look, O Lord, to Thee.

CHRISTINA ROSSETTI (1830–1894),
English poet. "A Death of a First-Born."

7   Perfect little body, without fault or
    stain on thee,
        With promise of strength and
        manhood full and fair!
            Though cold and stark
            and bare,
    The bloom and the charm of life
    doth awhile remain on thee.

ROBERT BRIDGES (1844–1930), English
poet. "On a Dead Child."

8   For the old, it is a never-ending
    grief to lose those who are younger
    than themselves and whom they as-
    sociate with their own future, above
    all if they are their children, or if
    they have brought them up: the
    death of a child, of a small child, is
    the sudden ruin of a whole under-
    taking; it means that all the hopes
    and sacrifices centred upon him are
    pointless, utterly in vain.

SIMONE DE BEAUVOIR (1908–1986),
French author and philosopher. *The Coming of
Age* (part 2, "The Being in the World"; chapter

6, "Time, Activity, History") (1970), trans. Patrick O'Brian (1972).

First Day of School

1 Those that do teach young babes
Do it with gentle means and easy
tasks.

WILLIAM SHAKESPEARE (1564–1616),
English poet and dramatist. *Othello* 4.2.112–
13.

Desdemona is not speaking of sending a child
to school, but the words may reassure young
pupils or their caretakers.

2 A good village primary school
ought to be a cross between a nursery and a play-room; and the
teacher ought to be playmate,
nurse, and mother, all combined.

HENRY WARD BEECHER (1813–1887),
U.S. clergyman. "Going to School," *Star Papers; or, Experiences of Art and Nature*, new
edition (1873), and reprinted in *Beecher As a
Humorist: Selections from the Published
Works*, ed. Eleanor Kirk (1887).

3 And this was the cause of my suffering when I was sent to school.
For all of a sudden I found my
world vanishing from around me,
giving place to wooden benches and
straight walls staring at me with the
blank stare of the blind. But the
legend is that eating of the fruit of
knowledge is not consonant with
dwelling in paradise. Therefore
men's children have to be banished
from their paradise into a realm of
death dominated by the decency of
a tailoring department. So my mind
had to accept the tight-fitting encasement of the school which, being like the shoes of a mandarin
woman, pinched and bruised my
nature on all sides and at every
movement.

RABINDRANATH TAGORE (1861–1941),
Indian author and philosopher. "My School,"
in *A Tagore Reader*, ed. Amiya Chakravarty
(1961).

4 Why, she asked, pressing her chin
on James's head, should they grow
up so fast? Why should they go to
school? She would have liked always
to have had a baby.

VIRGINIA WOOLF (1882–1941), English
novelist. *To the Lighthouse* ("The Window,"
section 10) (1927).

The thoughts of Mrs. Ramsay, a 50-year-old
woman who has had eight children. She is not
specifically sending a child off to school but
captures the feeling of many parents in doing
so.

5 The idea of entering upon a life of
my own intoxicated me. Until now
I had been growing up on the
fringe of adult life, as it were; from
now on I should have my satchel,
my textbooks, my exercise books
and my homework.

SIMONE DE BEAUVOIR (1908–1986),
French author and philosopher. *Memoirs of a
Dutiful Daughter* (part 1) (1958), trans. James
Kirkup (1959).

This is Beauvoir's memory of her first day of
school at the age of five.

6 I don't remember my first day at
school, who the teacher was, or
how I behaved. It was only during
my second year that school and
books and a beautiful teacher
named Mary Lee Hall, brought it
all alive. I loved it all because I
thought she did.

OSSIE DAVIS (b. 1917), U.S. actor. *With
Ossie and Ruby: In This Life Together* ("The
Way Cross Years") (1998).

Davis and his wife, actress Ruby Dee, take
turns in this memoir writing about their experiences before and after they met. Davis indicates that the first day is not so important as
one good experience.

7   Surely there were other important Julys scattered throughout those many years. For instance, that month of my fifth year was when I realized I had to go to school in September. It was a prospect I dreaded, believing in my heart that I was already sufficiently educated by Central Park, by the books I had read since I was three and a half, and by the disruptive arrival that year of a baby sister who taught me terrible lessons in displacement, resentment, hatred.

DORIS GRUMBACH (b. 1918), U.S. novelist and memoirist. *Coming into the End Zone* (1991).

Grumbach here remembers "Julys," other than the one of her seventieth birthday, that were significant to her.

8   What if they mispronounce my last name and everyone laughs?
     What if my teacher doesn't make her D's like Mom taught me?
     What if I spend the whole day without a friend?

ERMA BOMBECK (1927–1996), U.S. humorist and newspaper columnist. "The First Day of School" (3 September 1981), in *Forever, Erma: America's Best-Loved Writing from America's Favorite Humorist* (1996).

9   we pray
     you will learn easily
     in this new place
     you will laugh and share
     loving people other than us.

LUCY TAPAHANSO, U.S. poet. "For Misty Starting School," in *Multicultural Voices: Literature from the United States* (1995).

Puberty

1   There are three things the gentleman should guard against. In youth when the blood and *ch'i* are still unsettled he should guard against the attraction of feminine beauty. In the prime of life when the blood and *ch'i* have become unyielding, he should guard against bellicosity. In old age when the blood and *ch'i* have declined, he should guard against acquisitiveness.

CONFUCIUS (551?–479 B.C.), Chinese philosopher. *Analects* (Lun yü), book 16, section 7, trans. D. C. Lau (1979).

2   I would there were no age between ten and three-and-twenty, or that you would sleep out the rest; for there is nothing in the between but getting wenches with child, wronging the ancientry, stealing, fighting.

WILLIAM SHAKESPEARE (1564–1616), English poet and dramatist. *The Winter's Tale* 3.3.59–63.

One of the shepherds complains of young men scaring away his sheep.

3   The happiest time in my life was when I was twelve years old. I was just old enough to have a good time in the world, but not old enough to understand any of its troubles.

THOMAS ALVA EDISON (1847–1931), U.S. inventor. *The Diary and Sundry Observations of Thomas Alva Edison* ("Sundry Observations"; chapter 1, "Autobiographical"; section 5 [1930]), ed. Dagobert D. Runes (1948).

Edison also noted the downside of adolescence when he commented: "Somewhere between the ages of eleven and fifteen, the average child begins to suffer from this atrophy, the paralysis of curiosity and the suspension of the power to observe" ("Sundry Observations"; section 19, "Education and Work: The Habit of Forgetting" [1921]).

4   Don't laugh at a youth for his affectations; he's only trying on one face after another till he finds his own.

LOGAN PEARSALL SMITH (1865–1946), U.S. humorist. "Age and Death," *After-*

thoughts (1931) and *All Trivia: Trivia, More Trivia, Afterthoughts, Last Words* (1945).

5 The principal of our adolescents' difficulties are the presence of conflicting standards and the belief that every individual should make his or her own choices, coupled with a feeling that choice is an important matter.

MARGARET MEAD (1901–1978), U.S. anthropologist. *Coming of Age in Samoa: A Psychological Study of Primitive Youth for Western Civilisation* (chapter 14, "Education for Choice") (1928).

6 Anything can happen in adolescence. It is always a risky time. Ugly ducklings can sometimes change into swans. The reverse is equally possible. The best-brought-up child is taken over by powers as divorced from daily habits as earthquakes.

AGNES DE MILLE (1909–1993), U.S. dancer and choreographer. *Dance to the Piper* (chapter 10, "Adolescence") (1952).

7 My body was changing, and my life was changing too: my past was being left behind.

SIMONE DE BEAUVOIR (1908–1986), French author and philosopher. *Memoirs of a Dutiful Daughter* (part 2) (1958), trans. James Kirkup (1959).

8 When Jeffrey turned fourteen and Matilda twelve, they had begun to change; to grow rude, coarse, selfish, insolent, nasty, brutish, and tall. It was as if she were keeping a boarding house in a bad dream, and the children she had loved were turning into awful lodgers—lodgers who paid no rent, whose leases could not be terminated.

ALISON LURIE (b. 1926), U.S. author. *The War Between the Tates* (chapter 1) (1974).

9 The curse had come upon me. My friend Isobel said I would die if I had a bath. I got pulsating spots on my chin, my back was solid with acne, and you had to buy sanitary towels from men in chemists. How did St. Joan manage? All that armour. How did Pavlova, when she danced *Swan Lake* in that plate-like tutu? Who invented tampons? Have they been knighted?

PHYLLIDA LAW (b. 1932), English (Scottish-born) actress. "Much Thanks," *A Certain Age: Reflecting on the Menopause*, ed. Joanna Goldsworthy (1993).

10 Are you there God? It's me, Margaret. I just told my mother I want a bra. Please help me grow God. You know where. I want to be like everyone else.

JUDY BLUME (b. 1938), U.S. author. *Are You There, God? It's Me, Margaret* (1970).

11 If you are a girl, worry that your breasts are too round. Worry that your breasts are too pointed. Worry that your nipples are the wrong color. Worry that your breasts point in different directions. If you are a boy, worry that you will get breasts.
. . . If you are a boy, worry that you'll never be able to grow a mustache. . . .
If you are a girl, worry that you have a mustache.

DELIA EPHRON (b. 1944?), U.S. humorist. *Teenage Romance; or How to Die of Embarrassment* ("How to Worry") (1981).

12 There is perhaps, for all concerned, no period of life as unpleasant, so unappealing, so downright unpalatable, as that of adolescence. And while pretty much everyone who comes into contact with him is disagreeably affected, certainly no one is in for a ruder shock than the actual teenager himself. Fresh from twelve straight years of uninterrupted cuteness, he is singularly unprepared to deal with the harsh consequences of inadequate personal appearance.

FRAN LEBOWITZ (b. 1950), U.S. author. "Tips for Teens," *Social Studies* (1981).

Lebowitz adds: "Remember that as a teenager you are at the last stage in your life when you will be happy to hear that the phone is for you."

13 My adolescence progressed normally: enough misery to keep the death wish my usual state, an occasional high to keep me from actually taking the gas-pipe.

FAYE MOSKOWITZ (b. 1930), U.S. essayist and teacher. *And the Bridge Is Love: Life Stories* (1991).

14 Something dramatic happens to girls in early adolescence. Just as planes and ships disappear mysteriously into the Bermuda Triangle, so do the selves of girls go down in droves. They crash and burn in a social and developmental Bermuda Triangle.

MARY PIPHER (b. 1948), U.S. author. *Reviving Ophelia: Saving the Selves of Adolescent Girls* (chapter 1, "Saplings in the Storm") (1994).

High School

1 ACADEME, n. An ancient school where morality and philosophy were taught.

ACADEMY, n. (from academe). A modern school where football is taught.

AMBROSE BIERCE (1842–?1914), U.S. author. *The Devil's Dictionary* (1881–1911).

2 It's full of phonies, and all you do is study so that you can learn enough to be smart enough to be able to buy a goddam Cadillac some day, and you have to keep making believe you give a damn if the football team loses, and all you do is talk about girls and liquor and sex all day, and everybody sticks together in these dirty little goddam cliques.

J. D. SALINGER (b. 1919), U.S. author. *The Catcher in the Rye* (chapter 17) (1951).

Holden Caulfield describes a boys' school.

3 In this quiet little pond, encouraged by doting teachers, we felt successful and shining in *some* way, but once graduated we would disappear into the crowd of faceless adults and be like everyone else, old, a little tired, disappointed, and things not work out. College would be too hard and flunk us; the Army would unmask us as cowards; marriage would turn sour and love would die. One way or another, we would find disgrace, as others had.

GARRISON KEILLOR (b. 1942), U.S. author and radio personality. *Lake Wobegon Days* (1985).

Turning 16

1 A man at sixteen, will prove a child at sixty.

THOMAS FULLER (1608–1661), English clergyman and author. *Gnomologia: Adages and Proverbs, Wise Sentences, and Witty Sayings. Ancient and Modern, Foreign and British*, no. 273 (1660).

2 People are, in general, what they are made, by education and company, from fifteen to five-and-twenty.

**PHILIP DORMER STANHOPE,
FOURTH EARL OF CHESTERFIELD**
(1694–1773), English statesman and author.
Letter to his son, 1 April 1748 OS, *The Letters
of Philip Dormer Stanhope. Earl of Chesterfield*, ed. John Bradshaw, vol. 1 (1929).

3 To look *almost* pretty is an acquisition of higher delight to a girl who
has been looking plain the first fifteen years of her life than a beauty
from her cradle can ever receive.

JANE AUSTEN (1775–1817), English novelist. *Northanger Abbey* (chapter 1) (1818).

4 Although I was sixteen years of age,
and although I was treated with indulgence and affection, I was still
but a bird fluttering in the network of my Father's will and incapable of the smallest independent
action.

EDMUND GOSSE (1849–1928), English
author. *Father and Son* (chapter 12) (1907).

5 You are sixteen, going on seventeen,
   Baby, it's time to think!
Better beware, be canny and care-
ful,
   Baby, you're on the brink!

OSCAR HAMMERSTEIN (1895–1960),
U.S. lyricist and librettist. "Sixteen Going on
Seventeen," from the musical *The Sound of
Music* (1959).

6 Most people . . . fix the prime of a
man's life somewhere about thirty
or thirty-five. Personally . . . I
should place it at between fifteen
and sixteen. It is then, it always
seems to me, that his vitality is at its
highest; he has greatest sense of the
ludicrous and least sense of dignity.
After that time, decay begins to set
in. Possibly he attains to the "un-
gainly wisdom" of the Sixth Form
and in that languorous atmosphere
drinks deep of the opiate of spe-

cialization; possibly he attains to
some abnormal form of muscular
development and in his gyrations
upon the football field loses his
sense of the ludicrous; possibly he
attains to an official position in the
school and loses that still greater
gift, his sense of humor.

EVELYN WAUGH (1903–1966), English
author. Debate at Lancing School, September
1920, *The Diaries of Evelyn Waugh*, ed.
Michael Davie (1976).

Waugh was 16 at the time he advanced these
arguments.

7 After sixteen—this is it—for life.
The chances are good you won't
like it.

AGNES DE MILLE (1909–1993), U.S.
dancer and choreographer. *Dance to the Piper*
(chapter 10, "Adolescence") (1952).

8 American youth attributes much
more importance to arriving at
driver's-license age than at voting
age.

MARSHALL MCLUHAN (1911–1980),
Canadian author and educator. *Understanding
Media: The Extensions of Man* (1964).

9 You're sixteen,
you're beautiful
and you're mine.

RICHARD M. SHERMAN (b. 1928) and
ROBERT B. SHERMAN (b. 1925), songwriters. "You're Sixteen" (1960), in *The
World's Greatest Fake Book*, ed. Chuch Sher
(1983).

10 I hope you come to find that which
gives life a deep meaning for you
. . . something worth living for,
maybe even worth dying for . . .
something that energizes you, en-
thuses you, enables you to keep
moving ahead.

ITA FORD (1940–1980), U.S. nun and missionary in El Salvador. Letter to her niece, 18 August 1980, in *Letters of a Nation: A Collection of Extraordinary American Letters*, ed. Andrew Carroll (1997).

Ford wrote this letter for her niece, Jennifer Sullivan (living in Brooklyn), on her sixteenth birthday. She explains the importance of finding purpose and commitment in one's life whether one lives in a war-torn country like El Salvador or in Brooklyn. Three months after writing this letter, Ford and three other American nuns were found murdered.

11 Sweet sixteen ain't that peachy keen.

BOB GELDOF (b. 1954), Irish singer and songwriter. "I Don't Like Mondays" (1980).

Geldof and the Boomtown Rats based their song "I Don't Like Mondays" on the experiences of 16-year-old Brenda Spencer, who, shooting into a crowd at her high school, killed two people and injured eight others.

Coming Out (Socially)

1 Give a girl an education, and introduce her properly into the world, and ten to one but she has the means of settling well, without farther expense to anybody.

JANE AUSTEN (1775–1817), English novelist. *Mansfield Park* (vol. 1, chapter 1) (1814).

2 What causes young people to "come *out*," but the noble ambition of matrimony? What sends them trooping to watering-places? What keeps them dancing till five o'clock in the morning through a whole mortal season? . . . What causes respectable parents to take up their carpets, set their houses topsy-turvy, and spend a fifth of their year's income in ball suppers and iced champagne? Is it sheer love of their species, and an unadulterated wish to see young people happy and dancing? Psha! they want to marry their daughters.

WILLIAM MAKEPEACE THACKERAY (1811–1863), English novelist. *Vanity Fair* (chapter 3, "Rebecca is in Presence of the Enemy") (1848).

3 In Victorian days, when young girls up to the age of about eighteen were closely guarded at home, their debuts or formal introduction to their parents' friends in society had real meaning. . . . Today, however, with most girls going on to college, the debut when it occurs is merely a break in the educational procedure. It is rather meaningless now as an announcement that the girl is on the marriage market, for with four years ahead of her of increasingly difficult college courses, the girl, if she is sensible, awaits the completion of her education before marrying.

AMY VANDERBILT (1908–1974), U.S. author. *Amy Vanderbilt's Etiquette* (chapter 2, "Debuts") (1971).

College

1 When first the college rolls receive
       his name,
    The young enthusiast quits his ease
       for fame;
    Through all his veins the fever of
       renown
    Burns from the strong contagion of
       the gown.
    . . . .
    Deign on the passing world to turn
       thine eyes,
    And pause awhile from letters, to
       be wise;
    There mark what ills the scholar's
       life assail,

Toil, envy, want, the patron, and
the jail.

SAMUEL JOHNSON (1709–1784), English
author. "The Vanity of Human Wishes: The
Tenth Satire of Juvenal Imitated" (lines 135–38,
157–60).

2   An assemblage of learned men,
zealous for their own sciences, and
rivals of each other, are brought, by
familiar intercourse and for the
sake of intellectual peace, to adjust
together the claims and relations of
their respective subjects of investi-
gation. They learn to respect, to
consult, to aid each other. Thus is
created a pure and clear atmosphere of thought, which the student also breathes, though in his
own case he only pursues a few sciences out of the multitude.

JOHN HENRY NEWMAN (1801–1890),
English author and Roman Catholic cardinal,
founder of the Oxford Movement. *The Idea of
a University* (discourse 5, part 1) (1873).

3   Colleges . . . have their indispensable office,—to teach elements. But
they can highly serve us when they
aim not to drill, but to create; when
they gather from far every ray of
various genius to their hospitable
halls, and by the concentrated fires,
set the hearts of their youth on
flame.

RALPH WALDO EMERSON (1803–
1882), U.S. author. "The American Scholar"
(31 August 1837).

4   There is only one valid reason for
sending a boy to college, and that
is, so he can discover for himself
that there is nothing in it. A college
degree, as matters now stand, is like
a certificate of character—useful
only to those who need it. However, there must surely come a time
when degrees will be given only to
those who can earn a living—and
this degree will be signed by the
young man's employer.

ELBERT HUBBARD (1856–1915), U.S.
author, founder of the Roycroft community.
The Philosophy of Elbert Hubbard ("His
Thoughts about Business") (1930).

5   *And* we all praise famous men—
        Ancients of the College;
For they taught us common
        sense—
Tried to teach us common sense—
Truth and God's Own Common
        Sense
        Which is more than knowledge!

RUDYARD KIPLING (1865–1936), English author. "A School Song."

6   Would I send a boy to college?
Well, at the age when a boy is fit to
be in college I wouldn't have him
around the house.

PHILIP DUNNE (1867–1936), U.S. humorist. "Some Observations by Mr. Dooley,"
*Mr. Dooley Remembers: The Informal Memoirs
of Finley Peter Dunne* (1963).

7   The function of the Negro college,
then, is clear: it must maintain the
standards of popular education, it
must seek the social regeneration of
the Negro, and it must help in the
solution of problems of race contact and co-operation. And finally,
beyond all this, it must develop
men. . . . There must come a loftier
respect for the sovereign human
soul that seeks to know itself and
the world about it; that seeks a
freedom for expansion and self-de-
velopment; that will love and hate
and labor in its own way, untram-
meled alike by old and new.

W. E. B. Du Bois (1868–1963), U.S. civil-rights leader and author. *The Souls of Black Folk* (chapter 6, "Of the Training of Black Men") (1903).

8   What an Oxford tutor does is to get a little group of students together and smoke at them. Men who have been systematically smoked at for four years turn into ripe scholars. If anybody doubts this, let him go to Oxford and he can see the thing actually in operation. A well-smoked man speaks and writes English with a grace that can be acquired in no other way.

STEPHEN LEACOCK (1869–1944), Canadian (English-born) humorist. *My Discovery of England* ("Oxford As I See It") (1922).

Later in the essay Leacock notes that if he were founding a university he would create first a smoking room, then a dorm.

9   The old college is no doubt gone and we could not bring it back if we would. But it would perhaps be well for us if we could keep alive something of the intimate and friendly spirit that inspired it.

STEPHEN LEACOCK (1869–1944), Canadian (English-born) humorist. "The Old College and the New University," *College Days* (1923).

10   I approached the idea of college with the expectation of taking part in an intellectual feast. . . . In college, in some way that I devoutly believed in but could not explain, I expected to become a person.

MARGARET MEAD (1901–1978), U.S. anthropologist. *Blackberry Winter: My Earlier Years* (1972).

Mead's expectations of college life were disappointed when she discovered at DePauw University an emphasis on snobbery and affectation instead of intellectual feasting. She found a better banquet later at Barnard College.

11   I learned three important things in college—to use a library, to memorize quickly and visually, to drop asleep at any time given a horizontal surface and fifteen minutes. What I could not learn was to think creatively on schedule.

AGNES DE MILLE (1909–1993), U.S. dancer and choreographer. *Dance to the Piper* (chapter 11, "Decision") (1952).

Although it took her away from her intensive training as a dancer, De Mille loved college. She writes: "I was intoxicated by all the learning available and regularly signed up for more courses than I was permitted."

12   College ain't so much where you been as how you talk when you get back.

OSSIE DAVIS (b. 1917), U.S. actor. *Purlie Victorious* (act 1, scene 1) (1961).

13   People will come up to you on the street and say, "Does a paramecium beat its flagella?" or "How many wheels has a fiacre?" or "When does an oryx mate?" and if you have not been to college, you simply cannot answer them.

MAX SHULMAN (1919–1988), U.S. author. *Barefoot Boy with Cheek* (chapter 3) (1943).

Faculty advisor Mr. Ingelbretsvold gives this advice to the novel's hero, Asa Hearthrug, on his first day at college. This comment on the value of a college education follows Ingelbretsvold's story of a friend who took a job straight out of high school and made $75 million but was embarrassed when he could not name the eighth avatar of Vishnu.

14   Demand of your teachers and yourself not merely information but a way of learning that you can use every day for the rest of your life. It is what we professors promise, and sometimes even deliver: the secret of how to learn by discovering

things on your own—learn not by asking but by finding out on your own.

JACOB NEUSNER (b. 1932), U.S. educator. Speech at the convocation for incoming students, Elizabethtown College, Penn., 25 September 1991, in *Lend Me Your Ears: Great Speeches in History*, ed. William Safire (1992).

15 When I climbed down from the bus in front of the Student Union I realized that there were 30,000 students at the University of Michigan and I did not know one.

RUTH REICHL (b. 1948), U.S. author and restaurant critic. *Tender at the Bone* ("Serafina") (1999).

Graduation

1 You have but to hold forth in cap and gown, and any gibberish becomes learning, all nonsense passes for sense.

MOLIÈRE (JEAN BAPTISTE POQUELIN) (1622–1673), French dramatist. *The Hypochondriac* (La malade imaginaire) 3.4 (1673), in *The Plays of Molière in French*, trans. A. R. Waller, vol. 8 (1926).

The hypochondriac's brother here discusses the privilege accorded to physicians by deferential patients, but graduates may hope to enjoy the same privilege.

2 The great object of Education should be commensurate with the object of life. It should be a moral one; to teach self-trust: to inspire the youthful man with an interest in himself; with a curiosity touching his own nature; to acquaint him with the resources of his mind, and to teach him that there is all his strength, and to inflame him with a piety towards the Grand Mind in which he lives. Thus would education conspire with the Divine Providence.

RALPH WALDO EMERSON (1803–1882), U.S. author. "Education," *Lectures and Biographical Sketches* (1883).

3 Gambol and song and jubilee are done,
Life's motley pilgrimage must be begun;—
Another scene is crowding on the last,—
Perhaps a darkened picture of the past;
And we, who leave Youth's fairy vales behind,
Where Joy hath hailed us on the summer wind,
Would fain, with fond delay, prolong the hour,
Which sternly strikes at Friendship's golden power.

RALPH WALDO EMERSON (1803–1882), U.S. author. "Valedictory Poem" (delivered 17 July 1821, at Harvard College Class Day).

4 Remember that a man is valuable in our day for what he *knows* and that his company will always be desired by others in exact proportion to the amount of intelligence and instruction he brings with him.

JAMES RUSSELL LOWELL (1819–1891), U.S. author. Letter to his 14-year-old nephew Charlie, 11 June 1849, in *Letters of a Nation: A Collection of Extraordinary American Letters*, ed. Andrew Carroll (1997).

5 Training is everything. The peach was once a bitter almond; cauliflower is nothing but cabbage with a college education.

MARK TWAIN (SAMUEL CLEMENS) (1835–1910), U.S. author. *Pudd'nhead Wilson* ("Pudd'nhead Wilson's Calendar" at chapter 5) (1894).

6 For the development of the race depends on the development of the
individual, and where self-culture
has ceased to be the ideal, the intellectual standard is instantly low-
ered, and, often, ultimately lost. If
you meet at dinner a man who has
spent his life in educating himself—
a rare type in our time, I admit, but
still one occasionally to be met
with—you rise from table richer,
and conscious that a high ideal has
for a moment touched and sancti-
fied your days.

OSCAR WILDE (1854–1900), Irish author. "The Critic as Artist," *Intentions* (1891).

Wilde's comments suggest the importance of
continuing education after the time of graduation.

7 For it must be known, Reader, that
when the Gentle Youth break out of
High School they not only Launch
on the Tempestuous Sea, but they
also begin to climb the ladder of
Fame and hike up the toilsome
Mountain-side and go into the
waiting Harvest Field, all at the
same time. . . .
    I will now ask you to come up
and get your Sheepskins. Take this
precious Certificate home and put
it in a Dark, Cool Place. A few
Years hence when you are less Experienced, it will give you a Melancholy Pleasure to look at it and
Hark back to the Time when you
knew it all. Just one Word in Parting. Always count your Change,
and if you can't be Good, be Careful.

GEORGE ADE (1866–1944), U.S. humor-
ist and journalist. "The Fable of the Last Day of
School and the Tough Trustee's Farewell to the
Young Voyagers," *Forty Modern Fables* (1902).

The first passage reflects the typical commencement address that speakers are expected
to give. The second represents the impromptu
speech of a "political boss."

8 Year after year stereotyped, perfunctory commencements which are
projects of the administration
rather than of the graduates themselves point to the schools that are
not utilizing the unique opportunity presented by the commencement season to bring secondary
education to an inspiring climax.
That the seniors do not compre-
hend the full significance of their
graduation is revealed by their
questioning the application of the
word "Commencement" to an
event which, to them, symbolizes
something completed and terminated.

GERTRUDE JONES, U.S. eduator. *Commencement* (1929).

9 The mistake that others make, and
that I trust you will never make, is
to treat education as a chore instead of a joy; to treat graduation as
an end of education rather than as
a beginning.

ARTHUR BURNS (1904–1987), U.S.
(Austrian-born) economist. Commencement
address, Hebrew University, Jerusalem, 6 July
1970, in *Lend Me Your Ears: Great Speeches
in History*, ed. William Safire (1992).

10 Now, I could have said something
very profound today, but you
would have forgotten it in ten minutes; so I chose to give this kind of
speech instead so that in twenty
years from now when your children
ask you what you did on graduation day, you can proudly say, "I
laughed."

ART BUCHWALD (b. 1925), U.S. humorist
and journalist. Commencement address at Columbus School of Law, Catholic University,

Washington, D.C., 7 May 1977, in *Lend Me Your Ears: Great Speeches in History*, ed. William Safire (1992).

11 "Commencement speakers," said Father Flynn, "should think of themselves as the body at an old-fashioned Irish wake. They need you in order to have the party, but nobody expects you to say very much."

MARIO CUOMO (b. 1932), U.S. politician, former governor of New York. Commencement address, Iona College, New Rochelle, N.Y., 3 June 1984, in *Lend Me Your Ears: Great Speeches in History*, ed. William Safire (1992).

12 Summing up, it is clear the future holds great opportunities. It also holds pitfalls. The trick will be to avoid the pitfalls, seize the opportunities, and get back home by six o'clock.

WOODY ALLEN (b. 1935), U.S. filmmaker, actor, and author. "My Speech to the Graduates," *Side Effects* (1980).

13 The commencement oratory which floods the land every June may be an effective anesthetic which youth may take at its second birth, out of the solid, unyielding, factual environment of childhood and of books, out of the substantial fabric of the curriculum with its sure reward of grade, class standing, and satisfying compensation, into the bewildering, hazy and altogether ironic mockeries that we call, in humorous euphony, real life.

WILLIAM ALLEN WHITE (1868–1944), U.S. journalist. Commencement address, Northwestern University, Evanston, Ill., June 1936, in *Lend Me Your Ears: Great Speeches in History*, ed. William Safire (1992).

14 You're leaving college now, and going out into real life. And you have to realize that real life is not like college. Real life is like high school.

MERYL STREEP (b. 1949), U.S. actress. Speech to the graduating class of Vassar College, Poughkeepsie, N.Y.; quoted by Roy Blount Jr., *Be Sweet: A Conditional Love Story* (1998).

First Sex

1 I find it much easier to bear a suit of armor all one's life than a virginity; and the vow of virginity is the most noble of all vows, as being the hardest.

MICHEL EYQUEM DE MONTAIGNE (1533–1592), French essayist. "On Some Verses of Virgil," book 3, essay 5 (1585–1588), *The Complete Essays of Montaigne*, trans. Donald M. Frame (1976; originally published 1958).

2 It is not politic in the commonwealth of nature to preserve virginity. Loss of virginity is rational increase, and there was never virgin got till virginity was first lost. That you were made of is metal to make virgins. Virginity by being once lost may be ten times found; by being ever kept, it is ever lost. 'Tis too cold a companion; away with 't!

WILLIAM SHAKESPEARE (1564–1616), English poet and dramatist. *All's Well That Ends Well* 1.1.126–28.

Parolles's answer to the young Helena, who has asked how women might set up barricades when men assault their virginity.

3 Against diseases here the strongest fence
Is the defensive vertue, Abstinence.

ROBERT HERRICK (1591–1674), English poet and clergyman. "Abstinence."

4 So putting the Purse into my Bosom, I made no more Resistance to him, but let him do just what he

pleas'd; and as often as he pleas'd; and thus I finish'd my own Destruction at once, for from this Day, being forsaken of my Virtue, and my Modesty, I had nothing of Value left to recommend me, either to God's Blessing, or Man's Assistance.

DANIEL DEFOE (1660?–1731), English author. *Moll Flanders* (1722).

5 No, no; for my virginity,
   When I lose that, says Rose, I'll
      die:
Behind the elms, last night, cried
   Dick,
   Rose, were you not extremely
      sick?

MATTHEW PRIOR (1664–1721), English poet. "A True Maid."

6 Have you the assurance to pretend, that when a lady demeans herself to throw aside the rules of decency, in order to honour you with the highest favour in her power, your virtue should resist her inclination? That when she had conquer'd her own virtue, she should find an obstruction in yours?

HENRY FIELDING (1707–1754), English author. *Joseph Andrews* (book 1, chapter 8) (1742).

The amorous and experienced widow Lady Booby chides her footman Joseph Andrews for refusing her favors and trying to protect his own chastity.

7 A little still she strove, and much
      repented,
And whispering, "I will ne'er consent"—consented.

GEORGE GORDON, LORD BYRON (1788–1824), English poet. *Don Juan* (canto 1, stanza 117).

8 Instruction in sex is as important as instruction in food; yet not only are our adolescents not taught the physiology of sex, but never warned that the strongest sexual attraction may exist between persons so incompatible in tastes and capacities that they could not endure living together for a week much less a lifetime.

GEORGE BERNARD SHAW (1856–1950), Irish dramatist and critic. *Everybody's Political What's What* (chapter 21) (1944).

9 Too chaste an adolescence makes for a dissolute old age. It is doubtless easier to give up something one has known than something one imagines. It is not what one has done that one regrets here; but rather what one has not done and might have done.

ANDRÉ GIDE (1869–1951), French author. *Journals 1889–1949* ("21 January 1929"), trans. and ed. Justin O'Brien (1967).

10 This majesty of passion is possessed by nearly every man once in his life, but it is usually an attribute of youth and conduces to the first successful mating.

THEODORE DREISER (1871–1945), U.S. author. *Sister Carrie* (chapter 23) (1900).

It is said of Hurstwood, an older suitor attracted to the younger Carrie, that he lacks this "majesty of passion."

11 The whole edifice of female government is based on that foundation stone; chastity is their jewel, their centre piece, which they run mad to protect, and die when ravished of.

VIRGINIA WOOLF (1882–1941), English novelist. *Orlando* (chapter 4) (1928).

Orlando, in this fantastic journey through time and personalities, has been transformed from a man into a woman. Having "been a man for thirty years or so, and an Ambassador into the bargain," the character has a "very complicated" start on the issue of preserving virginity.

12 He closed his eyes, surrendering himself to her, body and mind, conscious of nothing in the world but the dark pressure of her softly parting lips. They pressed upon his brain as upon his lips, as though they were the vehicle of a vague speech, and between them he felt an unknown and timid pressure, darker than the swoon of sin, softer than sound or odour.

JAMES JOYCE (1882–1941), Irish author. *A Portrait of the Artist as a Young Man* (section 2) (1916).

Joyce describes Stephen's first sexual encounter, with a prostitute.

13 We had read so many books written by the sex specialists of the 1920s, who believed that sex was a matter of proper technique—that men should learn to play on women's bodies as if they were musical instruments, but without including in their calculations the idea that women must be very good musical instruments in order to please the men who played on them.

MARGARET MEAD (1901–1978), U.S. anthropologist and writer. *Blackberry Winter: My Earlier Years* (chapter 10, "Student Marriage and Graduate School") (1972).

Although Mead does not say in her autobiography whether or not she and her husband had had sex before their marriage, this comment indicates that her firsthand experience was not extensive.

14 However deferential and polite the man may be, the first penetration is always a violation. Because she desires caresses on lips or breasts, or even longs for a known or imag-

ined pleasure more specifically sexual, what happens is that a man's sex organ tears the young girl and penetrates into regions where it has not been desired.

SIMONE DE BEAUVOIR (1908–1986), French author and philosopher. *The Second Sex* (part 4, "The Formative Years"; chapter 14, "Sexual Initiation") (1949), trans. H. M. Parshley (1979).

15 In my first year at Annie Wright Seminary, I lost my virginity. I am not sure whether this was an "educational experience" or not. The act did not lead to anything and was not repeated for two years. But at least it dampened my curiosity about sex and so left my mind free to think about other things.

MARY MCCARTHY (b. 1912), U.S. author. *How I Grew* (chapter 3) (1986).

16 If you really want to know the truth, I'm a virgin. I really am. I've had quite a few opportunities to lose my virginity and all, but I've never got around to it yet. Something always happens.

J. D. SALINGER (1919-), U.S. author. *The Catcher in the Rye* (chapter 13) (1951).

17 Boys and girls in America have such a sad time together; sophistication demands that they submit to sex immediately without proper preliminary talk. Not courting talk—real straight talk about souls, for life is holy and every moment is precious.

JACK KEROUAC (1922–1969), U.S. author. *On the Road* (part 1, chapter 10) (1957).

18 Sexual intercourse began
In nineteen sixty-three
(Which was rather late for me)—

Between the end of the *Chatterley* ban
And the Beatles' first LP.

Philip Larkin (1922–1985), English poet and critic. "Annus Mirabilis."

19   They lay as if paralyzed by what they had done. Congealed in sin, frozen with delight. Charles—no gentle postcoital sadness for him, but an immediate and universal horror—was like a city struck out of a quiet sky by an atom bomb. All lay razed; all principle, all future, all faith, all honorable intent. Yet he survived, he lay in the sweetest possession of his life, . . . but already the radioactivity of guilt crept, crept through his nerves and veins.

John Fowles (b. 1926), English author. *The French Lieutenant's Woman* (chapter 47) (1969).

The passage describes the mixed feelings of Charles after having his first sexual encounter, with Sarah Woodruff, a woman he believed to be experienced and discovers to be a virgin. Although the novel is set in Victorian times, the passage's reference to atomic explosions reflects the anachronistic imagery that characterizes the work.

20   Love is understanding someone, caring for him, sharing his joys and sorrows. This eventually includes physical love. You've shared something, given something away and received something in return, whether or not you're married, whether or not you have a baby. Losing your virtue doesn't matter, as long as you know that for as long as you live you'll have someone at your side who understands you, and who doesn't have to be shared with anyone else!

Anne Frank (1929–1945), Dutch diarist. *The Diary of a Young Girl: The Definitive Edition* (Thursday, 2 March 1944) trans. Susan Massotty (1995).

21   Virginity is now a mere preamble or waiting room to be got out of as soon as possible; it is without significance.

Ursula K. LeGuin (b. 1929), U.S. author. "The Space Crone" (1976), *Dancing at the Edge of the World: Thoughts on Words, Women, Places* (1989).

22   Instead of the world being divided up into Catholics and Protestants or Republicans and Democrats or white men and black men or even men and women, I saw the world divided into people who had slept with somebody and people who hadn't, and this seemed the only really significant difference between one person and another. I thought a spectacular change would come over me the day I crossed the boundary line. I thought it would be the way I'd feel if I ever visited Europe. I'd come home, and if I looked closely into the mirror I'd be able to make out a little white Alp at the back of my eye. Now I thought that if I looked into the mirror tomorrow I'd see a doll-size Constantin sitting in my eye and smiling out at me.

Sylvia Plath (1932–1963), U.S. author. *The Bell Jar* (chapter 7) (1962).

Plath's 19-year-old narrator describes her anticipation of her first sexual experience.

23   I have never fully shaken that adolescent boy's insecurity that there was more to it than I could ever imagine, and that I needed a full-time instructress. For my first sexual experiences, in fact, I chose older women.

PHILLIP LOPATE (b. 1943), U.S. essayist. "Against Joie de Vivre," in *The Art of the Persona Essay: An Anthology from the Classical Era to the Present*, ed. Phillip Lopate (1994).

24 He talks to me very softly, and when he enters my body, I feel a single moment of sharp pain. But it is not the old terrible agony of the locked door and the banging crowbar.

JOYCE MAYNARD (b. 1953), U.S. author. *At Home in the World* (1998).

Maynard had been unable to consummate an affair with J. D. Salinger and sought medical treatment for her sexual dysfunction. Here she describes her first successful sexual intercourse (with a man other than Salinger).

25 I kept telling myself, He's been with other women, he knows what he's doing—relax, trust him. But when he got down to it, there were no bells, no stars, no flashing lights, no colors, and not a lot of affection or skill, either.

MARTINA NAVRATILOVA (b. 1956), Czech tennis player. *Martina* ("First Boyfriend") (1985).

Navratilova expresses regret that she did not wait until she was in love to have sex, but denies that this first experience had any effect on her sexual preference.

26 You don't need me to tell you, I'm sure, that you don't learn about sex from doing it with boys, but from talking about it with girls.

SUZANNE MOORE (b. 1958), English journalist. "Labour of Love," *Guardian* (1995), and reprinted in *The Idler's Companion: An Anthology of Lazy Literature*, ed. Tom Hodgkinson and Matthew De Abaitua (1997).

In this passage, Moore talks about her friend Janice initiating her into the aphrodisiac power of the singer Barry White. Moore continues to wonder whether the more appropriate approach to sex is "lying on your back and thinking of England."

First Car

1 So he bought the automobile, and Boon found his soul's lily maid, the virgin's love of his rough and innocent heart. It was a Winton Flyer.

WILLIAM FAULKNER (1897–1962), U.S. author. *The Reivers* (chapter 2) (1962).

Boon Hogganbeck drives one of the very few cars in this small Mississippi town in the early part of the century.

2 There is talk of lowering the driving age. It might be a good idea. There was a time when I had more patience. But whoever heard of a five-year-old behind the wheel of a car?

ERMA BOMBECK (1927–1996), U.S. humorist and newspaper columnist. "Daughter Learning to Drive" (18 July 1969), in *Forever, Erma: America's Best-Loved Writing from America's Favorite Humorist* (1996).

3 I happen to feel an almost visceral connection to the cars of my youth, a passionate nostalgia for certain models that carry very personal meanings—automobile as autobiography, you might say. A road sighting of a 1948 Dodge with Fluid Drive gives me palpitations because I *know* the car, I know the dials on the dashboard and the smell of the upholstery and where I was in life the last time I rode in one. It's the car in which I learned to drive.

LETTY COTTIN POGREBIN (b. 1939), U.S. author. *Getting Over Getting Older: An Intimate Journey* (part 2, "Keeping Time"; chapter 5, "Forgetting and Remembering") (1996).

First Love

1 In her first passion Woman loves her lover
In all others, all she loves is Love.

GEORGE GORDON, LORD BYRON
(1788–1824), English poet. *Don Juan* (canto
3, stanza 3).

2   We are all very much alike when we
are in our first love.

GEORGE ELIOT (MARY ANN *OR*
MARIAN EVANS) (1819–1880), English
author. *Adam Bede* (chapter 26, "The Dance")
(1859).

3   Men always want to be a woman's
first love. That is their clumsy vanity. We women have a more subtle
instinct about things. What we like
is to be a man's last romance.

OSCAR WILDE (1854–1900), Irish author. *A Woman of No Importance* (act 2)
(1893).

4   First love is only a little foolishness
and a lot of curiosity.

GEORGE BERNARD SHAW (1856–
1950), Irish dramatist and critic. *John Bull's
Other Island* (act 4) (1904).

5   I whispered, "I am too young"
And then, "I am old enough";
Wherefore I threw a penny
To find out if I might love.

WILLIAM BUTLER YEATS (1865–1939),
Irish poet. "Brown Penny."

6   At twenty a man is rash in love,
and again, perhaps at fifty; a man
of middle-age enamoured of a
young girl is capable of sublime follies. But the man of thirty who
loves for the first time is usually the
embodiment of cautious discretion.
He does not fall in love with a violent descent, but rather lets himself
gently down, continually testing the
rope. His social value, especially if
he have achieved worldly success, is
at its highest, and, without conceit,
he is aware of it. He has lost many

illusions concerning women; he had
seen more than one friend wrecked
in the sea of foolish marriage; he
knows the joys of a bachelor's freedom, without having wearied of
them; he perceives risks where the
youth perceives only ecstasy, and
the oldster only a blissful release
from solitude. Instead of searching,
he is sought for; accordingly he is
selfish and exacting. All these things
combine to tranquillize passion at
thirty.

ARNOLD BENNETT (1867–1931), English
novelist and dramatist. *Anna of the Five Towns*
(chapter 10, "The Isle") (1902).

The successful 30-year old potter Mynors feels
this very qualified sort of love for the miser's
daughter Anna.

7   But that mimosa grove—the haze
of stars, the tingle, the flame, the
honeydew, and the ache remained
with me, and that little girl with her
seaside limbs and ardent tongue
haunted me ever since—until at
last, twenty-four years later, I broke
her spell by incarnating her in another.

VLADIMIR NABOKOV (1899–1977),
U.S. (Russian-born) novelist. *Lolita* (part 1,
chapter 5) (1958).

The narrator Humbert Humbert describes his
first trysting place, in his adolescence, with his
first love.

8   In first love a choice is seldom and
blinding.

ROBERT LOWELL (1917–1977), U.S.
poet. "First Love."

First Job

1   Lao said, "The Master said, 'I have
never been proved in office. That is
why I am a Jack of all trades.'"

CONFUCIUS (551?–479 B.C.), Chinese philosopher. *Analects* (Lun yü), book 9, section 7, trans. D. C. Lau (1979).

2 A man should pray for the welfare of him who gives him employment.

Tanhuma, Wayyesheb 13, in *The Talmudic Anthology: Tales and Teachings of the Rabbis*, ed. Louis I. Newman (1947).

3 Our work keeps us free of three great evils: boredom, vice, and poverty.

VOLTAIRE (FRANÇOIS-MARIE AROUET) (1694–1778), French philosopher and author. *Candide* (chapter 30, "Conclusion") (1759), trans. Lowell Bair (1959).

Candide and his philosophical entourage consult an old man about tragedies in the world; he claims to want to know about nothing except cultivating his 20 acres of land.

4 Employment is a source of happiness, especially when you are usefully employed. An industrious person is always a happy person, provided he is not obliged to work too hard; and even where you have cause for unhappiness, nothing makes you forget it so soon as an occupation.

FREDERICK MARRYAT (1792–1848), English author and naval captain. *Masterman Ready* (vol. 2, chapter 6) (1842).

5 A little integrity is better than any career.

RALPH WALDO EMERSON (1803–1882), U.S. author. "Behavior," *The Conduct of Life* (1860).

6 I have found out that whatever a man is during the first six weeks after he gets a job, he will be the same after 60 years and no amount of advice will have any effect whatsoever in changing him. When he is 21 years of age, he is set for life and if a dullard then he will continue so through life. The main quality for success in my estimation is ambition and a will for work.

THOMAS ALVA EDISON (1847–1931), U.S. inventor. *The Diary and Sundry Observations of Thomas Alva Edison* ("Sundry Observations"; chapter 19, "Education and Work"; section 24, "The Will to Work" [1922]), ed. Dagobert D. Runes (1948).

7 No, I don't like work. I had rather laze about and think of all the fine things that can be done. I don't like work—no man does—but I like what is in work—the chance to find yourself. Your own reality—for yourself, not for others—what no other man can ever know.

JOSEPH CONRAD (1858–1924), English (Polish-born) novelist. *The Heart of Darknesss* (section 1) (1902).

8 Most of us are doing two things—that by which the body is kept alive, and that by which the higher part of our nature lives. We go to the job to pay expenses and then we indulge ourselves in what we like to do and maybe are meant to do. The whole secret of a successful life is to find out what it is one's destiny to do, and then do it.

HENRY FORD (1863–1947), U.S. industrialist. *My Philosophy of Industry: An Authorized Interview by Fay Leone Faurotes* (1929).

9 The natural thing to do is to work—to recognize that prosperity and happiness can be obtained only through honest effort. Human ills flow largely from attempting to escape from this natural course. . . . I take it for granted that we must work. All that we have done comes as the result of a certain insistence that since we must work it is better

to work intelligently and forehand-
edly; that the better we do our
work the better off we shall be.

HENRY FORD (1863–1947), U.S. industrialist and automobile manufacturer. In *My Life
and Work* (1922; reprint 1973) and reprinted
in *Ford on Management: Harnessing the American Spirit* ("Introduction: What Is the Idea?")
(1991).

10   The test of a vocation is the love of
the drudgery it involves.

LOGAN PEARSALL SMITH (1865–
1946), U.S. humorist. "Arts and Letters," *Afterthoughts* (1931) and *All Trivia: Trivia, More
Trivia, Afterthoughts, Last Words* (1945).

11   Nearly all young people who go
into the world in order to exchange
their talents for a livelihood begin
as employees. And most of them
remain employees to the end of
their working days. That is to say,
the great majority of us are depen-
dent upon the approval and the
goodwill of somebody else for the
safety of our existence in that dangerous and shifting piece of human
mechanism we call society.

ARNOLD BENNETT (1867–1931), English
author. *How to Make the Best of Life* (chapter
4, "Starting in Life") (1923).

12   I spent six or seven years after high
school trying to work myself up.
Shipping clerk, salesman, business
of one kind or another. And it's a
measly manner of existence. To get
on that subway on the hot morn-
ings in summer. To devote your
whole life to keeping stock, or making phone calls, or selling or buying. To suffer fifty weeks of the year
for the sake of a two-week vacation,
when all you really desire is to be
outdoors, with your shirt off. And
always to have to get ahead of the

next fella. And still—that's how you
build a future.

ARTHUR MILLER (b. 1915), U.S. dramatist. *The Death of a Salesman* (act 1) (1949).

Biff describes the difficulty of making his way
in the world, feeling, at age 34, that since he is
not married or in business he is "like a boy."

13   I don't think earning a living is half
as difficult as going to school, doing
homework, and getting through
college. By the time you've survived
growing up and educating your
parents on how to raise children,
just going out and earning a living
is a comparative breeze, the freedom exhilarating.

MALCOLM FORBES (? –1990), U.S.
businessman. *More Than I Dreamed* (chapter
1) (1989).

14   A corporation prefers to offer a job
to a man who already has one, or
doesn't immediately need one. The
company accepts you if you are already accepted. To obtain entry
into paradise in terms of employment, you should be in a full state
of grace.

ALAN HARRINGTON (1919–1997), U.S.
author. *Life in the Crystal Palace* (chapter 4,
"The Tyranny of Forms") (1959).

Marriage (First)

1   Every man receives the wife he de-
serves.

*Sotah 2, in The Talmudic Anthology: Tales and
Teachings of the Rabbis*, ed. Louis I. Newman
(1947).

2   And of His signs is this: He created
for you helpmeets from yourselves
that ye might find rest in them, and
He ordained between you love and
mercy.

Qur'an 30.21; *The Glorious Koran: An Explanatory Translation by Marmaduke Pickthall* (1930; reprint 1992).

3 *Bachelers boast, how they will teach*
their wives good;
But *many a man speaketh of Robin*
Hood,
That never shot in his bow. When
all is sought,
Bachelers wives, and maides children
bee well tought.
And this with this I also begin to
gather,
Every man can rule a shrew, save he
that hath her.

JOHN HEYWOOD (1497?–?1580), English author and musician. *The Proverbs of John Heywood* (part 2, chapter 6) (1874; originally published 1564).

4 A good marriage, if there be such, rejects the company and conditions of love. It tries to reproduce those of friendship. It is a sweet association in life, full of constancy, trust, and an infinite number of useful and solid services and mutual obligations.

MICHEL EYQUEM DE MONTAIGNE (1533–1592), French essayist. "On Some Verses of Virgil," book 3, essay 5 (1585–1588), *The Complete Essays of Montaigne*, trans. Donald M. Frame (1976; originally published 1958).

5 In this stately state of Matrimonie, there is nothing fearefull, nothing fayned, all things are done faithfully without doubting, truely without doublyng, willingly without constraint, joyfully without complaint.

GEORGE PETTIE (c. 1548–1589), English author. "Sinorix and Camma," *A Petite Pallace of Pettie His Pleasure* (1576).

6 Marrye whyle you are young, that you may see your fruite florish be-

fore your selves fade, that you bee not in doubt or dispayre of having children, or in daunger of your lyves in having children, that you may have great tyme to rid a great many of husbandes, that no day may passe without dalliance, that you be not thought unwise in refusing good offers . . .

GEORGE PETTIE (c. 1548–1589), English author. "Coriatus and Horatia," *A Petite Pallace of Pettie His Pleasure* (1576).

7 Wives are young men's mistresses; companions for middle age; and old men's nurses. So as a man may have a quarrel to marry when he will.

FRANCIS BACON (1561–1626), English philosopher, essayist, and statesman. "Of Marriage and Single Life," *Essays or Counsels, Civil and Moral* (1625), and reprinted in *The Essays of Francis Bacon*, ed. John Pitcher (1985).

"Quarrel" in this case means a "reason" or "pretext."

8 When I said I would die a bachelor, I did not think I should live till I were married.

WILLIAM SHAKESPEARE (1564–1616), English poet and dramatist. *Much Ado About Nothing* (2.3.234–35).

Benedick has railed against marriage throughout the play, but is finally won by the charms of the beautiful and witty Beatrice.

9 Men are April when they woo, December when they wed. Maids are May when they are maids, but the sky changes when they are wives.

WILLIAM SHAKESPEARE (1564–1616), English poet and dramatist. *As You Like It* (4.1.140–42).

Rosalind here speaks in the disguise of Ganymede and discusses marriage with Orlando, the man she will eventually wed.

10 It is the Man and Woman united that make the compleat human Being. Separate, she wants his Force of Body and Strength of Reason; he, her Softness, Sensibility and acute Discernment. Together they are more likely to succeed in the World. A single Man . . . resembles the odd Half of a Pair of Scissors. If you get a prudent, healthy Wife, your industry in your Profession, with her good Economy, will be a Fortune sufficient.

BENJAMIN FRANKLIN (1706–1790), U.S. statesman, scientist, and author. "Advising a Young Man as to the Selection of a Mistress," 1745, in *Letters of a Nation: A Collection of Extraordinary American Letters*, ed. Andrew Carooll (1997).

In the same letter Franklin advises men to choose older women as wives because "They are so grateful!"

11 Marriage has many pains, but celibacy has no pleasures.

SAMUEL JOHNSON (1709–1784), English author. *The History of Rasselas, Prince of Abissinia* (chapter 26, "The Princess Continues Her Remarks Upon Private Life") (1759).

12 Wedded love supplies the want of every other blessing in life; and as no condition can be truly happy without it, so none can be absolutely miserable with it.

CHARLOTTE LENNOX (1720–1804), Anglo-American author. *Henrietta* (chapter 1) (1758).

13 It is a truth universally acknowledged, that a single man in possession of a good fortune, must be in want of a wife.

JANE AUSTEN (1775–1817), English novelist. *Pride and Prejudice* (vol. 1, chapter 1; opening lines) (1813).

14 What is marriage, but the most sordid of bargains, the most cold and

slavish of all the forms of commerce?

THOMAS LOVE PEACOCK (1785–1866), English author. *Melincourt* (chapter 7) (1817).

15 Marriage is . . . a lottery, and the less choice and selection a man bestows on his ticket the better; for if he has incurred considerable pains and expense to obtain a lucky number, and his lucky number proves a blank, he experiences not a simple, but a complicated disappointment; the loss of labour and money being superadded to the disappointment of drawing a blank, which, constituting simply and entirely the grievance of him who has chosen his ticket at random, is, from its simplicity, the more endurable.

THOMAS LOVE PEACOCK (1785–1866), English author. *Nightmare Abbey* (chapter 1) (1818).

16 Marriage means tyranny on one side and deceit on the other.

ANTHONY TROLLOPE (1815–1882), English novelist. *Barchester Towers* (chapter 15, "The Widow's Suitors") (1857).

This comment is part of a debate between the sisters Madeleine and Charlotte about the nature of marriage.

17 Two pure souls fused into one by an impassioned love—friends, counselors—a mutual support and inspiration to each other amid life's struggles, must know the highest human happiness;—this is marriage; and this is the only cornerstone of an enduring home.

ELIZABETH CADY STANTON (1815–1902), U.S. suffragist. *History of Woman Suffrage* (1881).

18 Thare aint no resipee for a perfekt wife, enny more than there iz for a

perfekt husband. There iz just az menny good wifes az thare iz good husbands, and i never knew two people, married or single, who were determined tew make themselfs agreeable to each other, but what they suckceeded.

JOSH BILLINGS (HENRY W. SHAW) (1818–1885), U.S. humorist. "How to Pick Out a Wife," *The Complete Works of John Billings* (1899).

19 What greater thing is there for two human souls, than to feel that they are joined for life—to strengthen each other in all labor, to rest on each other in all sorrow, to minister to each other in all pain, to be one with each other in silent unspeakable memories at the moment of the last parting?

GEORGE ELIOT (MARY ANN *or* MARIAN EVANS) (1819–1890), English author. *Adam Bede* (chapter 54, "The Meeting on the Hill") (1859).

20 My bride hath need of no disguise.—
But rather, let her come to me
In such a form as bent above
    My pillow when, in infancy,
I knew not anything but love.—
O let her come from out the lands
    Of Womanhood—not fairy isles,
And let her come with Woman's hands
And Woman's eyes of tears and smiles,—
With Woman's hopefulness and grace
Of patience lighting up her face.

JAMES WHITCOMB RILEY (1849–1916), U.S. poet. "My Bride That Is To Be."

The speaker here imagines the perfect woman.

21 For there is something in marriage so natural and inviting, that the step has an air of great simplicity and ease; it offers to bury forever many aching preoccupations; it is to afford us unfailing and familiar company through life; it opens up a smiling prospect of the blest and passive kind of love, rather than the blessing and active; it is approached not only through the delights of courtship, but by a public performance and repeated legal signatures. A man naturally thinks it will go hard with him if he cannot be good and fortunate and happy within such august circumvallations.

ROBERT LOUIS STEVENSON (1850–1894), Scottish author. "Virginibus Puerisque II," *Virginibus Puerisque* (1881).

22 The one charm of marriage is that it makes a life of deception absolutely necessary for both parties.

OSCAR WILDE (1854–1900), Irish author. *The Picture of Dorian Gray* (chapter 1) (1891).

Lord Henry to Basil.

23 Men marry because they are tired; women, because they are curious: both are disappointed.

OSCAR WILDE (1854–1900), Irish author. *The Picture of Dorian Gray* (chapter 4) (1891) and *A Woman of No Importance* (act 3) (1893).

24 Marriage is popular because it combines the maximum of temptation with the maximum of opportunity.

GEORGE BERNARD SHAW (1856–1950), Irish dramatist and critic. "Maxims for Revolutionists," *The Revolutionist's Handbook* in *Man and Superman* (1903).

25 It is the duty of every man, who has sufficient means, to maintain a wife. The life of unmarried women

is a wretched one; every man who is able ought to save one of them from that fate.

GEORGE GISSING (1857–1903), English author. *The Odd Women* (chapter 9, "The Simple Faith") (1893).

An older man, who has waited to attain a respectable income for marriage, advises a younger man, who is more privileged and has declared his intention not to marry.

26 If they lost the incredible conviction that they can change their wives or their husbands, marriage would collapse at once.

LOGAN PEARSALL SMITH (1865–1946), U.S. humorist. "Other People," in *Afterthoughts* (1931) and *All Trivia: Trivia, More Trivia, Afterthoughts, Last Words* (1945).

27 A man wants a wife who sits still, and not only still but on the same chair every day so that he knows where to find her should he happen to want anything.

MARY ANNETTE (BEAUCHAMP) RUSSELL, COUNTESS RUSSELL (MARY ANNETTE BEAUCHAMP) (1866–1941), English novelist. *The Caravaners* (chapter 14) (1909).

This passage conveys the sentiments of Baron Von Ottringel, a Prussian army officer, reflecting on the merits of his first wife.

28 O my love O my love we dance under the chuppah standing over us
like an animal on its four legs,
like a table on which we set our love
as a feast, like a tent
under which we work
not safe but no longer solitary
in the searing heat of our time.

MARGE PIERCY (b. 1936), U.S. author. "The Chuppah," *The Art of Blessing the Day: Poems with a Jewish Theme* (1999).

29 You must make it plain to your husband right at the start what you

expect of him. That is what a wife is for—to scold her husband into becoming a good man.

MAXINE HONG KINGSTON (b. 1940), U.S. author. *The Woman Warrior* (1976).

30 Our marriage was the recognition that we suited one another remarkably well as company—could walk and talk and share insights all day, work side by side like Chinese peasants, read silently together like graduate students, tease each other like brother and sister, and when at night we found our bodies tired, pull the covers over ourselves and become lovers.

PHILLIP LOPATE (b. 1943), U.S. essayist. "Against Joie de Vivre," in *The Art of the Personal Essay: An Anthology from the Classical Era to the Present*, ed. Phllip Lopate (1994).

First Home

1 Through wisdom is an house builded, and by understanding it is established; and by knowledge shall the chambers be filled with all precious and pleasant riches.

Proverbs 24.3–4.

2 Eat less than you can afford, dress less fittingly, but have a fine dwelling.

Bereshit Rabbah 20.12, in *The Talmudic Anthology: Tales and Teachings of the Rabbis*, ed. Louis I. Newman (1947).

3 Houses are built to live in, and not to look on; therefore let use be preferred before uniformity, except where both may be had. Leave the goodly fabrics of houses, for beauty only, to the enchanted palaces of the poets; who build them with small cost.

Francis Bacon (1561–1626), English philosopher, essayist, and statesman. "Of Building," *Essays or Counsels, Civil and Moral* (1625), and reprinted in *The Essays of Francis Bacon*, ed. John Pitcher (1985).

4   Lord, Thou hast given me a cell
        Wherein to dwell;
    And little house, whose humble
        Roof
            Is weather-proof.

Robert Herrick (1591–1674), English poet and clergyman. "A Thanksgiving to God, for His House."

5   Ah! happy is the man whose early
        lot
    Hath made him master of a fur-
        nished cot.

Joanna Baillie (1762–1851), Scottish poet and dramatist. "A Reverie" (stanza 3) (1790).

6   We need not power or splendor;
    Wide hall or lordly dome;
    The good, the true, the tender,
    These form the wealth of home.

Sarah Josepha Hale (1788–1879), U.S. author and editor. "Home."

7   A house, like a person, invites by amiable reserves, as if it loved to be introduced in perspective and reached by courteous approaches. Let it show bashfully behind shrubberies, screen its proportions decorously in plain tints, not thrust itself rudely, like an inn, upon the street at cross-roads. A wide lawn in front, sloping to the road gracefully, gives it the stately air and courtly approach.

A. Bronson Alcott (1799–1888), U.S. philosopher and educator. "April: My House," *Concord Days* (1872).

8   I was married when I was twenty-five years old to a man rich in Greek and Hebrew, Latin and Ara-

bic, and, alas! rich in nothing else. When I went to housekeeping, my entire stock of china for parlor and kitchen was bought for eleven dollars. That lasted very well for two years, till my brother was married and brought his bride to visit me. I then found, on review, that I had neither plates nor teacups to set a table for my father's family; wherefore I thought it best to reinforce the establishment by getting me a tea-set that cost ten dollars more, and this, I believe, formed my whole stock in trade for some years.

Harriet Beecher Stowe (1811–1896), U.S. author. Letter to Mrs. Follen, apparently a writer of children's books, 16 February 1853, in *A Second Treasury of The World's Great Letters*, ed. Wallace Brockway and Bart Keith Winer (1941).

Stowe recounts the details of her life to an Englishwoman, emphasizing the details of her household; elsewhere in the letter she refers to her work, recently begun, on *Uncle Tom's Cabin*.

9   Let a little preliminary exultation of a new man in a new place be forgiven, ye who are now established! Remember your own household fervor on first setting up, while we recount our economic joy, and anticipations of modern conveniences that would take away all human care, and speed life upon a downhill path, where it was to be easier to move than to stand still!

Henry Ward Beecher (1813–1887), U.S. clergyman. "Modern Conveniences," *Eyes and Ears* (1866).

These remarks are included in a description of the headaches caused by the "conveniences" of a modern house.

10 People are not expected to be large in proportion to the houses they live in, like snails.

GEORGE ELIOT (MARY ANN *or* MARIAN EVANS) (1819–1880), English author. *The Mill on the Floss* (book 6, "The Great Temptation"; chapter 2, "First Impressions") (1860).

Maggie Tulliver counsels her cousin Lucy, who worries that after her marriage she will shrink into insignificance by moving into a grand house.

11   Let us celebrate the soil. Most men toil that they may own a piece of it; they measure their success in life by their ability to buy it. It is alike the passion of the *parvenu* and the pride of the aristocrat. Broad acres are a patent of nobility; and no man but feels more of a man in the world if he have a bit of ground that he can call his own. However small it is on the surface, it is four thousand miles deep; and that is a very handsome property.

CHARLES DUDLEY WARNER (1829–1900), U.S. author. *My Summer in a Garden* ("Preliminary") (1870).

12   HOUSE, n. A hollow edifice erected for the habitation of man, rat, mouse, beetle, cockroach, fly, mosquito, flea, bacillus, and microbe.

AMBROSE BIERCE (1842–?1914), U.S. author. *The Devil's Dictionary* (1881–1911).

13   Is the house not homely yet?
There let pleasant thoughts be set:
With bright eyes and hurried feet,
There let severed friendships meet,
There let sorrow learn to smile,
And sweet talk the nights beguile.

ROBERT LOUIS STEVENSON (1850–1894), Scottish author. "The New House."

14   The home should offer to the individual rest, peace, quiet, comfort, health, and that degree of personal expression requisite; and these conditions should be maintained by the best methods of the time. The home should be to the child a place of happiness and true development; to the adult a place of happiness and that beautiful reinforcement of the spirit needed by the world's workers.

CHARLOTTE PERKINS GILMAN (1860–1935), U.S. author. *The Home: Its Work and Influence* (chapter 1, "Introductory") (1903).

15   Man is but mildly interested in his immediate surroundings because he can find self-expression in projects. Whereas woman is confined within the conjugal sphere; it is for her to change that prison into a realm.

SIMONE DE BEAUVOIR (1908–1986), French author and philosopher. *The Second Sex* (part 5, "Situation"; chapter 16, "The Married Woman") (1949), trans. H. M. Parshley (1971).

Beauvoir sees the homemaker as one who collects knickknacks, who "eagerly seeks self-realization in what she *has*" because "she *does* nothing."

16   An old house is a nuisance, but it is obviously intended for men and women to live in. Much modern housing would be better called kenneling.

ROBERTSON DAVIES (1913–1995), Canadian author. "Of Modern Houses," *The Table Talk of Samuel Marchbanks* (1949).

17   Willy: To weather a twenty-five-year mortgage is—
Linda: It's an accomplishment.

ARTHUR MILLER (b. 1915), U.S. dramatist. *Death of a Salesman* (act 2) (1949).

Willy and Linda are one payment away from paying off their house.

Baptism

1   Reason in no way contributes to faith. Nay, in that children are des-

titute of reason, they are all the more fit and proper recipients of baptism. For reason is the greatest enemy that faith has. . . . If God can communicate the Holy Ghost to grown persons, he can, *a fortiori,* communicate it to young children. Faith comes of the Word of God, when this is heard; little children hear that Word when they receive baptism, and therewith they receive also faith.

MARTIN LUTHER (1483–1546), German leader of the Protestant Reformation. *The Table Talk of Martin Luther,* no. 303, trans. W. Hazlitt (1848), ed. Thomas Kepler (1952).

2   Baptism is not only a sign of profession, and mark of difference, whereby Christian men are discerned from others that be not christened, but it is also a sign of Regeneration or New-Birth, whereby, as by an instrument, they that receive Baptism rightly are grafted into the Church; the promises of the forgiveness of sin, and of our adoption to be the sons of God by the Holy Ghost, are visibly signed and sealed; Faith is confirmed, and Grace increased by virtue of prayer unto God.

The Book of Common Prayer (article 27) (Episcopal Church, 1945).

3   Hee says that prayer with great devotion, where God is thanked for calling us to the knowledge of his grace, Baptisme being a blessing, that the world hath not the like. He willingly and cheerfully crosseth the child, and thinketh the Ceremony not onely innocent, but reverend. He instructeth the God-fathers, and God-mothers, that it is no complementall or light thing to sustain

that place, but a great honour, and no less burden, as being done both in the presence of God, and his Saints, and by way of undertaking for a Christian soul. He adviseth all to call to minde their Baptism often; for if wise men have thought it the best way of preserving a state to reduce it to its principles by which it grew great; certainly, it is the safest course for Christians to meditate on the Baptisme often (being the first step into their great and glorious calling) and upon what termes, and with what vowes they are Baptized.

GEORGE HERBERT (1593–1633), English poet and Anglican priest. "The Parson in Sacraments," *A Priest to the Temple, or The Country Parson* (1632).

4   When the Child is Christened, you may have God-fathers enough.

JOHN TRUSLER (1735–1820), English clergyman. *Proverbs Exemplified and Illustrated by Pictures from Real Life* (1790).

Trusler explains that "The moment a man is independent of the favours of the world, that moment he will find it more ready to bestow them; when we no longer need a friend, we find enough ready to assist us."

5   Array'd—a half-angelic sight—
In vests of pure Baptismal white,
The Mother to the Font doth bring
The little helpless nameless thing,
With hushes soft and mild caressing,
At once to get—a name and blessing.

CHARLES LAMB (1775–1834), English essayist. "The Christening."

6   A few calm words of faith and prayer,
   A few bright drops of holy dew,
   Shall work a wonder there

Earth's charmers never knew.

JOHN KEBLE (1792–1866), English clergyman and poet. "Holy Baptism," *The Christian Year* (1827).

7 Now to christen the infant Kilmansegg,
   For days and days it was quite a
   plague,
      To hunt the list in the Lexicon:
   And scores were tried like coin by
   the ring,
   Ere names were found just the
   proper thing
      For a minor rich as a Mexican.

THOMAS HOOD (1799–1845), English poet. "Her Christening," *Miss Kilmansegg and Her Precious Leg*

The poem pursues the notion that a name "has more than nominal worth, / And belongs to good or bad luck at birth."

8 Though little Paul was said, in
   nursery phrase, "to take a deal of
   notice for his age," he took as little
   notice of all this as of the preparations for his christening on the next
   day but one. . . . Neither did he, on
   the arrival of the appointed morning, show any sense of its importance; being, on the contrary, unusually inclined to sleep, and
   unusually inclined to take it ill in
   his attendants that they dressed him
   to go out.

CHARLES DICKENS (1812–1870), English author. *Dombey and Son* (chapter 5) (1847–48).

Little Paul is the heir of a wealthy and unfeeling head of a shipping house. His mother has died in childbirth. The elder Dombey places all his hope and love in the son, who unfortunately dies while away at school.

9 Under my platform in Brooklyn I
   have a baptistery; and if anybody's
   son or daughter, brought up in
   Baptist ideas, wants to be im-
   mersed, you won't catch me reasoning with them: I baptize them.
   So it is that I immerse, I sprinkle,
   and I have in some instances
   poured; and I never saw there was
   any difference in the Christianity
   that was made.

HENRY WARD BEECHER (1813–1887), U.S. clergyman. Address to the London Congregational Board, *Beecher as a Humorist: Selections from the Published Works,* ed. Eleanor Kirk (1887).

10 Tess then stood erect with the in-
    fant on her arm beside the basin,
    the next sister held the Prayer-Book
    before her, as the clerk at church
    held it before the parson; and thus
    the girl set about baptizing her
    child.

THOMAS HARDY (1840–1928), English author. *Tess of the D'Urbervilles, A Pure Woman* (Phase the Second, "Maiden No More"; chapter 14) (1891).

Tess's child Sorrow is born out of wedlock. Since the church will not recognize the child, Tess sets out to care for its immortal soul by baptizing the child herself.

11 BAPTISM, n. A sacred rite of such
    efficacy that he who finds himself
    in heaven without having under-
    gone it will be unhappy forever. It
    is performed with water in two
    ways—by immersion, or plunging,
    and by aspersion, or sprinkling.
       But whether the plan of immer-
       sion
       Is better than simple aspersion
          Let those immersed
          And those aspersed
       Decide by the Authorized Ver-
       sion,
       And by matching their agues ter-
       tian. (G.J.)

AMBROSE BIERCE (1842–?1914), U.S. author. *The Devil's Dictionary* (1881–1911).

Many of Bierce's definitions include "poems" by the fictitious Father Gassalasca Jape, S.J.

12 Writer or painter god-parents are notoriously unreliable. That is, there is certain before long to be a cooling of friendship.

GERTRUDE STEIN (1874–1946), U.S. author. *The Autobiography of Alice B. Toklas* (chapter 7, "After the War—1919–1932") (1933).

Alice B. Toklas and Stein were asked to be godmothers ("an English war comrade of Hemingway's was to be godfather") of Ernest Hemingway's son, baptized in the Episcopal Church.

13 It should be kept in mind that this is a celebration in honor of the baby, following a formal religious ceremony. It has a character quite different from a cocktail party and should be kept on such a plane that even the most conservative baby could not object to the behavior and bearing of his elders.

AMY VANDERBILT (1908–1974), U.S. author. *Amy Vanderbilt's Etiquette* (chapter 1, "Christenings") (1971).

Vanderbilt urges decorum at the party following the religious ceremony of christening.

Confirmation

1 Do ye here, in the presence of God, and of this congregation, renew the solemn promise and vow that ye made, or that was made in your name, at your Baptism; ratifying and confirming the same; and acknowledging yourselves bound to believe and to do all those things which ye then undertook or your Sponsors then undertook for you?

"The Order of Confirmation or Laying on of Hands Upon Those That Are Baptized, and Come to Years of Discretion," *The Book of Common Prayer* (Episcopal Church, 1945).

2 I allowed myself to be prepared for confirmation, and confirmed, and to make my first Communion, in

total disbelief, acting a part, eating and drinking my own condemnation. As Johnson points out, where courage is not, no other virtue can survive except by accident. Cowardice drove me into hypocrisy and hypocrisy into blasphemy. It is true that I did not and could not then know the real nature of the thing I was doing: but I knew very well that I was acting a lie with the greatest possible solemnity.

C. S. LEWIS (1898–1963), English author. *Surprised by Joy* (chapter 10, "Fortune's Smile") (1955).

3 Mr. O'Dea's eyes roll in his head when he tells us that with Confirmation we will become part of Divinity. We will have the Gifts of the Holy Ghost: Wisdom, Understanding, Counsel, Fortitude, Knowledge, Piety, the Fear of the Lord. Priests and masters tell us Confirmation means you're a true soldier of the church and that entitles you to die and be a martyr in case we're invaded by Protestants or Mahommedans or any other class of a heathen.

FRANK McCOURT, U.S. (Irish-born) memoirist. *Angela's Ashes* (chapter 8) (1996).

4 You got a nice white dress and a party on your Confirmation. You got a brand new soul and a cross of gold.

BILLY JOEL (b. 1949), U.S. singer and songwriter. "Only the Good Die Young" (1974).

First Communion

1 The Lord Jesus himself declares: "This is my body"(Matt. 26.26). Before the blessing of heavenly words occurs it is a different thing that is

referred to, but after the consecration it is called a body. He himself
says that it is his blood (cf. Matt.
26-28). Before the consecration it
has another name, but after the
consecration it is designated blood.
And you say: "Amen," which
means: "It is true." What the
mouth speaks, let the mind confess
within: what the word says, let love
acknowledge.

SAINT AMBROSE (340?–397), bishop of
Milan and doctor of the Roman Catholic
Church. "On the Mysteries" (4th century),
trans. Boniface Ramsey (1997).

2   The time of every ones first receiving is not so much by yeers, as by
understanding: particularly, the rule
may be this: When any one can distinguish the Sacramentall from
common bread, knowing the Institution, and the difference, hee
ought to receive of what age soever.
Children and youths are usually de-
ferred too long, under pretence of
devotion to the Sacrament, but it is
for want of Instruction; their un-
derstandings being ripe enough for
ill things, and why not then for better? But Parents and Masters should
make hast in this, as to a great pur-
chase for their children, and servants, which while they deferr, both
sides suffer; the one, in wanting
many excitings of grace; the other,
in being worse served and obeyed.

GEORGE HERBERT (1593–1633), English
poet and Anglican priest. "The Parson in Sacraments," A Priest to the Temple, or the Country Parson (1632).

3   Welcome sweet, and sacred feast;
welcome life!
Dead I was, and deep in trouble;
But grace, and blessings came with
thee so rife,

That they have quickened even dry
stubble.

HENRY VAUGHAN (1622–1695), English
(Welsh-born) poet. "The Holy Communion."

4   The little children sweetly grouped
Before the altar rail;
Yea, even the ancient saints, aligned
In shadows vaguely dim
Beneath the cumbering dust of
years,
In silence seemed to smile!

JOSÉ ASUNCIÓN SILVA (1865–1896),
Colombian poet. "First Communion," The
Catholic Anthology: The World's Great Catho-
lic Poetry, ed. Thomas Walsh (1947).

Translated from the Spanish by Thomas Walsh.

5   The day of your first communion
was the happiest day of your life.
And once a lot of generals had
asked Napoleon what was the happiest day of his life. They thought
he would say the day he won some
great battle or the day he was made
an emperor. But he said:
—Gentlemen, the happiest day
of my life was the day on which I
made my first holy communion.

JAMES JOYCE (1882–1941), Irish author.
The Portrait of the Artist as a Young Man (section 1) (1916).

6   It stood to reason that a fellow confessing after seven years would have
more to tell than people that went
every week. The crimes of a lifetime.

FRANK O'CONNOR (MICHAEL
O'DONOVAN) (1903–1966), Irish author.
"First Confession," The Stories of Frank
O'Connor (1952).

This story describes a young man's fear of his
first confession and communion and his relief
at finding a sympathetic priest.

7　At the Cours Désir, on the eve of our First Communion, we were exhorted to go and cast ourselves at our mothers' feet and ask them to forgive our faults; not only had I not done this, but when my sister's turn came I persuaded her not to do so either.

SIMONE DE BEAUVOIR (1908–1986), French author and philosopher. *Memoirs of a Dutiful Daughter* (part 2) (1958), trans. James Kirkup (1959).

8　When I was still a teenager, I received Christ. The scripture says that he clothed me in a robe of righteousness because of the cross, and when God looks at me, he does not see my sins. He sees the blood of Christ, and we celebrate that blood when we take communion.

BILLY GRAHAM (b. 1918), U.S. evangelist. Sermon in Novosibirsk (in Siberia), U.S.S.R., 18 September 1984, in *Lend Me Your Ears: Great Speeches in History*, ed. William Safire (1992).

9　He tells us that next to a relic of the True Cross the Communion wafer is the holiest thing in the world and our First Communion is the holiest moment in our lives. Talking about First Communion makes the master all excited. He paces back and forth, waves his stick, tells us we must never forget that the moment the Holy Communion is placed on our tongues we become members of that most glorious congregation, the One, Holy, Roman, Catholic and Apostolic Church, that for two thousand years men, women, and children have died for the Faith, that the Irish have nothing to be ashamed of in the martyr department.

FRANK McCOURT, U.S. (Irish-born) memoirist. *Angela's Ashes* (chapter 4) (1996).

10　When the priest actually placed the round wafer on my outstretched tongue, it was almost redundant. I had already received my first communion. My mother was my priest, the flowers were my Eucharist, and I was the stumbling, sorry recipient, overwhelmed at my own unworthiness, shaky in my faith, but loved completely in spite of it.

MARTHA MANNING (b. 1952), U.S. author. *Chasing Grace: Reflections of a Catholic Girl, Grown Up* ("Eucharist: Lilies of the Valley") (1996).

Having had a run-in with a nun during preparations for her First Holy Communion, Manning is lovingly prepared for the ceremony by her mother, who gives her a homemade bouquet and gold religious medals.

Bar, Bat Mitzvah

1　Today you have joined the covenant of God and our people. You are taking upon yourself the holy duty of keeping the words of this Torah and walking in the path of your parents and forefathers. You have chosen it willingly. May you follow it all the days of your life.

A. A. KABAK, *Solomon Molkho* ("Bar Mitzvah in Spain") (1927), trans. Sora I. Eisenberg (1952).

The author describes the bar mitzvah of a young man during the fifteenth entury, the time of the Spanish Inquisition, which had made the ceremony punishable by death.

2　When I place my hands upon your head in benediction, I will be the humble instrument through which will flow the stream of history and memories of the great and the good in Israel, the ideals and aspirations of our people, the strength and the life of our faith. It is something which places upon you a solemn responsibility to be worthy of its precepts, to be loyal to its ideals, and to express them in a life of service.

PHILIP BERNSTEIN (b. 1901), U.S. rabbi and advisor on Jewish affairs to the American military government. *What the Jews Believe* (1950).

The author addresses his son Stephen, in 1947, at the first bar mitzvah in Frankfurt, Germany, since 1940.

3   My God, God of my fathers, in truth and single-heartedness I lift my eyes to Thee on this great and solemn day. I have been a Jew from my birth, but on this day I voluntarily reenter Thy community of Israel. Henceforth it is my duty to keep Thy commandments, and I now become responsible for my own actions and I alone am answerable for them to Thee.

HAHAM BENJAMIN ARTOM , In *Book of Prayer*, ed. David de Sola Pool (1941).

4   I was signaled to step forward to a place below the bimah [synagogue platform] at a very respectable distance from the scroll of the Torah, which had already been rolled up and garbed in its mantle. I pronounced the first blessing and from my own humash [Five Books of Moses] read the selection which Father had chosen for me, continued with the reading of the English translation, and concluded with the closing brachah [blessing]. That was it. The scroll was returned to the ark with song and procession, and the service was resumed. No thunder sounded, no lightning struck. The institution of Bat Mitzvah had

been born without incident and the rest of the day was all rejoicing.

JUDITH KAPLAN EISENSTEIN, U.S.; first woman to have a bas mitzvah (1922); daughter of Mordechai M. Kaplan, founder of the Reconstructionist movement. Quoted in *Judaism: The Key Spiritual Writings of the Jewish Tradition*, ed. Arthur Herzberg, rev. edition (1991).

5   This religion was a masculine thing . . . and Seth was coming into his own. The very Hebrew had a rugged male sound to it, all different from the bland English comments of the rabbi.

HERMAN WOUK (b. 1915), U.S. author. *Marjorie Morningstar* (chapter 9, "The Bar-Mitzva") (1955).

These are the reflections of the novel's title character at her brother Seth's bar mitzvah.

6   The Dickensian Christmas is the nearest thing in literature I know to an American bar-mitzva. It has in much the same degree the fantastic preparations, the incredible eating, the enormous wassailing, the swirl of emotions and of family mixups, all superimposed with only partial relevance on a religious solemnity. Christmas in the books of Dickens bursts with extravagant vitality, and so does our bar-mitzva.

HERMAN WOUK (b. 1915), U.S. author. *This is My God: The Jewish Way of Life* (chapter 10, "Birth and Beginnings") (1988).

7   It has been said, with the kind of wry humor which contains a kernel of truth, that the modern Bar Mitzvah is celebrated with too much Bar and too little Mitzvah.

ERWIN L. HERMAN, U.S. rabbi. Introduction to *Bar Mitzvah with Ease*, by Hattie Eisenberg (1966).

8 I didn't feel like a man, really, or know how I was supposed to feel, but it was nice for a thirteen-year-old boy to hear others say that I was a man now.

ELI N. EVANS (b. 1936), U.S. historian and foundation president. *The Provincials: A Personal History of Jews in the South* (chapter 11, "Mr. Jew") (1997).

9 It was vulgar, crass, thoroughly un-spiritual, and my parents spent far too much money for all the wrong reasons. And yet—something happened in spite of that. Through the long process of preparing for my bar mitzvah, I learned that I was Jewish and received the barest taste of what that might mean. Years later, I would come to know more, much more.

HOWARD BERKOWITZ (b. 1948), U.S. psychiatrist. Quoted in Eric A. Kimmel, *Bar Mitzvah: A Jewish Boy's Coming of Age* (1995).

10 Stretching back centuries and deeply rooted in history, bar mitz-vah constituted an enduring link with the past; moreover, it seemed to provide an organically Jewish opportunity for sentimental expres-sion and ritual celebration.

JENNA WEISSMAN JOSELIT, U.S. author. *The Wonders of America: Reinventing Jewish Culture 1880–1950* (1994).

11 Where the male puberty rite, an es-tablished tradition of long standing, needed a jolt of consumerism, some "Hollywood ballyhoo," to render it attractive and meaningful to American Jews of the interwar years, its female analogue satisfied on its own modest terms. Mediat-ing between the need of the folk, the mandate of the clergy, the plas-

ticity of Jewish ritual and the rigid-ity of gender, the new female pu-berty rite fit perfectly with the tenor of the times.

JENNA WEISSMAN JOSELIT, U.S. author. *The Wonders of America: Reinventing Jewish Culture: 1880–1950* (chapter 3, "Red Letter Days") (1994).

Bat mitzvah is a twentieth-century invention, in part a way to provide an equivalent to bar mitzvah.

12 In Jewish law, a boy becomes an adult, responsible for carrying out the *mitzvot* (religious command-ments) at thirteen years and a day old. A girl reaches the same status, although she has far fewer positive commandments to carry out, tradi-tionally speaking, at twelve years old.

JULIA NEUBERGER (b. 1950), English author and rabbi. *On Being Jewish* (chapter 1) (1995).

13 I have met women in their seventies who still cry because they were de-nied the chance to study Torah, or prepare for Bat Mitzvah as young girls, or become rabbis though it was clearly their calling. My Bat Mitzvah was not only for me, but for generations of females denied permission or encouragement to do this.

NINA PERLMUTTER, U.S. teacher. "Better Late than Early: A Forty-Eight-Year-Old's Bat Mitzvah Saga"; in Rachel Josefowitz Siegel and Ellen Cole, eds., *Celebrating the Lives of Jew-ish Women: Patterns in a Feminist Sampler* (1997).

14 As the bar mitzvah grew in impor-tance in affluent post-World War II America, the accompanying meal did as well, all too often turning into an excessive and pretentious affair, stereotyped in popular cul-

ture by chopped liver sculptures, exotic dancers and marching bands.

G<small>IL</small> M<small>ARKS</small> (b. 1952), U.S. author. *The World of Jewish Entertaining* (1998).

Coming Out

1 At some point I believe one has to stop holding back for fear of alienating some imaginary reader or real relative or friend, and come out with personal truth.

M<small>AY</small> S<small>ARTON</small> (1912–1995), U.S. author. *Journal of a Solitude* ("January 5th") (1973).

2 The passion of debating ideas with women was an erotic passion for me, and the risking of self with women that was necessary in order to win some truth out of the lies of the past was also erotic.

A<small>DRIENNE</small> R<small>ICH</small> (b. 1929), U.S. poet. "Split at the Root" (1982), in *The Art of the Personal Essay: An Anthology from the Classical Era to the Present,* ed. Phillip Lopate (1997).

Rich writes about the process of coming to terms with being what she calls a "Jewish lesbian raised to be a heterosexual gentile."

3 I am both gay and conservative and don't find a contradiction. There shouldn't be any "shame" in being gay. Moreover, the conservative view, based as it is on the inherent rights of the individual over the state, is the logical political home of gay men and women. The conservative movement must reject the bigots and the hypocrites and provide a base for gays as well as others.

M<small>ARVIN</small> L<small>IEBMAN</small> (1923–1997), U.S. author and editor. Letter, *National Review* (9 July 1990), and reprinted in *Coming Out Conservative: An Autobiography* (1992.)

Liebman had worked for conservative publications for years and was a longtime friend of

William F. Buckley Jr., the editor of the *National Review.* Buckley published the letter and replied that, while the magazine would not condone "gay bashing," they could not support the "repeal of convictions that are more, much more, than mere accretions of bigotry."

4 In Czechoslovakia they call male homosexuals "warm people," which is not as nice as it sounds, and I don't even think they have a word for lesbians. Women just don't come out of the closet. In Czechoslavakia they think that all lesbians are women who are so ugly they can't get a man. I tried to tell my parents it's a bit more complex than that.

M<small>ARTINA</small> N<small>AVRATILOVA</small> (b. 1956), Czech tennis player. *Martina* ("Family Visit") (1985).

5 I think one of the greatest things we have to do still is just to increase the ability of Americans who do not yet know that gays and lesbians are their fellow Americans in every sense of the word to feel that way.

B<small>ILL</small> C<small>LINTON</small> (b. 1946), U.S. president. Speech at a dinner honoring actress Ellen DeGeneres, 8 November 1997; quoted by Andrew Tobias, *The Best Little Boy in the World Grows Up* (1998).

6 Unlike losing your virginity, coming out is something you can do over and over. Not because you want to bore the world to tears, but because there always seems to be a new audience to whom it remains, even today, unexpected.

A<small>NDREW</small> T<small>OBIAS</small> (J<small>OHN</small> R<small>EID</small>) (b. 1947), U.S. author. *The Best Little Boy in the World Grows Up* (1998).

7 I *planned* to tell my parents I was gay, and I *expected* they'd say that as far as they were concerned, I was still the best little boy in the world.

ANDREW TOBIAS (JOHN REID) (b. 1947), U.S. author. *The Best Little Boy in the World Grows Up* (1998).

8 As the university's pastor and preacher, as a Christian, and as a homosexual, I decided to reclaim by proclaiming a vision of the gospel that was inclusive rather than exclusive, and to do so as a Christian who was more than the sum of the parts of which I was made. I did so. I did so because I wanted all and sundry, but particularly these young homosexuals and their polemic antagonists, to see that there was more than one way to read the Bible and to understand the imperatives of the Christian faith.

PETER J. GOMES (b. 1942), U.S. clergyman and theologian. *The Good Book: Reading the Bible with Heart and Mind* (chapter 8, "The Bible and Homosexuality: The Last Prejudice") (1996).

Gomes describes coming out at a rally, in Harvard Yard, to defend gays against attacks made by an undergraduate publication.

9 Coming out has been described as an earthquake that shakes the world not only of the person coming out but of everyone around him or her. It has also been described as less a declaration of sexuality to the rest of the world than a personal act of self-love. It is, without a doubt, a discovery of self and a rite of passage that should be celebrated—not only because your daughter or son has taken this courageous step toward being her or his own person, but because you are being given an opportunity to do the same. Coming out is a gift.

BETTY DEGENERES, U.S. author. *Love, Ellen: A Mother/Daughter Journey* (prologue) (1999).

DeGeneres is the mother of actress Ellen DeGeneres, who announced her homosexuality and incorporated it into the plot of her TV show.

10 I am the woman who lost herself but now is found, the lesbian, outside the law of church and man, the one who has to love herself or die. If you are not as strong as I am, what will we make together? I am all muscle and wounded desire, and I need to know how strong we both can be.

DOROTHY ALLISON (b. 1949), U.S. author. *Two or Three Things I Know for Sure* (1995).

Allison is not coming out here, but she clearly defines her position in relation to her society and to her lover.

11 There's something I've been wanting to tell you for a while. I am a L-L-L-L-awrence Welk fan.

K. D. LANG (b. 1961), Canadian singer and songwriter. Concert (26 August 1992) at Radio City Music Hall, New York City; reported in the *New York Times* (28 August 1992).

Turning 18

1 "Just wait till we can vote," I said, bursting with 10-year-old fervor, ready to fast, freeze, march and die for peace and freedom as Joan Baez, barefoot, sang "We Shall Overcome." Well, now we can vote, and we're old enough to attend rallies and knock on doors and wave placards, and suddenly it doesn't seem to matter any more.

JOYCE MAYNARD (b. 1953), U.S. author. "An 18-Year-Old Looks Back at Life," *New York Times Magazine* (23 April 1972).

Turning 20 or 21

1 If you're a child at twenty, you're a jackass at twenty-one.

Jewish proverb, in Leo Rosten, *Leo Rosten's Treasury of Jewish Quotations* (1972).

2   In delay there lies no plenty,
Then come kiss me, sweet and
   twenty.
Youth's a stuff will not endure.

WILLIAM SHAKESPEARE (1564–1616),
English poet and dramatist. *Twelfth Night*
(2.3.50–52).

This is the song of the clown Feste.

3   He that is not handsome at 20, nor
strong at 30, nor rich at 40, nor
wise at 50, will never bee handsome, strong, rich, or wise.

GEORGE HERBERT (1593–1633), English
poet and Anglican priest. *Outlandish Proverbs*,
no. 349 (1640).

4   Long-expected one and twenty
    Ling'ring year at last is flown;
Pomp and Pleasure, Pride and
   Plenty,
    Great Sir John, are all your
      own.

SAMUEL JOHNSON (1709–1784), English
author. "A Short Song of Congratulation."

5   How swift have flown
To me thy girlish times, a woman
   grown
Beneath my heedless eyes! in vain I
   rack
My fancy to believe the almanac,
That speaks thee Twenty-One.

CHARLES LAMB (1775–1834), English essayist. "To a Young Friend: On Her Twenty-
First Birthday."

6   To justify the festive cup
What horrors here are conjured up!
What things of bitter bite and sup,
   Poor wretched Twenty-One's!
No landed lumps, but frumps and
   humps,
(Discretion's Days are far from
   trumps)

Domestic discord, dowdies, dumps,
   Death, dockets, debts, and duns!

THOMAS HOOD (1799–1845), English
poet. "Stanzas on Coming of Age."

The speaker notes that, while a rich man's son
may look forward to coming to his majority,
the poor man turning 21 is required to recognize his lowly place in the world of men.

7   The lad who talks at twenty as men
should talk at thirty, has seldom
much to say worth the hearing
when he is forty; and the girl who
at eighteen can shine in society
with composure, has generally
given over shining before she is a
full-grown woman.

ANTHONY TROLLOPE (1815–1882), English novelist. *He Knew He Was Right* (chapter
97, "Mrs. Brooke Burgess") (1869).

The narrator praises late bloomers, noting that
"The flower that blows the quickest is never
the sweetest. The fruit that ripened tardily has
ever the finest flavour."

8   The youth of twenty-one who has
health, hope, ambition, and anima-
tion is not to be pitied. Poverty is
only for the people who think poverty.

ELBERT HUBBARD (1856–1915), U.S.
author, founder of the Roycroft community.
The Philosophy of Elbert Hubbard ("His
Thoughts about Business" (1930).

9   When a man is tired of life at 21 it
indicates that he is rather tired of
something in himself.

F. SCOTT FITZGERALD (1896–1940),
U.S. author. Letter, 29 November 1940, *Scott
Fitzgerald: Letters to His Daughter*, ed. Andrew
Turnbull (1965).

10   One's life has a natural defining
frame. One knows who one is; in
childish egotism, one supposes people have a relationship only with
oneself. But after the age of twenty,
the frame is uncertain, change is

hard to pin down, one is less and less sure of who one is, and other egos with their court of adherents invade one's privacy with theirs. One's freedom is inhibited by their natural insistence on themselves.

V. S. PRITCHETT (b. 1905), English author. *The Midnight Oil* (chapter 1) (1971).

11 That's a hell of a good age to be. I wish I was that age again. Because Ben, you'll never be young again.

BUCK HENRY (B. ZUCKERMAN) (b. 1930), U.S. actor and screenwriter. *The Graduate* (1967).

The comments of Mr. Robinson to Benjamin Braddock, his wife's 21-year-old lover.

Second Marriage / Remarriage

1 A man can find contentment only in his first wife.

Yebamot 63, in *The Talmudic Anthology: Tales and Teachings of the Rabbis*, ed. Louis I. Newman (1947).

2 If a man's wife has died, and she has left him grown-up children, he should not take another wife before he has married off his children.

Bereshit Rabbah 60, in *The Talmudic Anthology: Tales and Teachings of the Rabbis*, ed. Louis I. Newman (1947).

3 Marry a widdow before she leave mourning.

GEORGE HERBERT (1593–1633), English poet and Anglican priest. *Outlandish Proverbs*, no. 252 (1640).

4 A good season for courtship is, when the widow returns from the funeral.

THOMAS FULLER (1608–1661), English clergyman and author. *Gnomologia: Adages and Proverbs, Wise Sentences, and Witty Say-*

ings. *Ancient and Modern, Foreign and British*, no. 175 (1660).

5 After all this, to marry a widow, a kind of chewed meat! What a fantastical stomach hast thou, that canst not eat of a dish till another man hath cut of it! Who would wash after another, when he might have fresh water enough for asking?

SIR JOHN SUCKLING (1609–1642), English courtier and writer. "A letter to a friend to dissuade him from marrying a widow which he formerly had been in love with, and quitted" (1758), in *Seventeenth-Century Prose and Poetry*, 2d. ed., ed. Alexander M. Witherspoon and Frank J. Warnke (1963).

6 Torments of suspicion will often follow on a second marriage.

JEAN RACINE (1630–1699), French dramatist. *Phèdre* (2.5) (1677), trans. Paul Landis (1931).

Hippolytus says this to Phaedra, who worries about the effect of her marriage on her children.

7 Marriage is always bad then [when one chooses the wrong man], first or second. Priority is a poor recommendation in a husband if he has got no other. I would rather have a good second husband than an indifferent first.

GEORGE ELIOT (MARY ANN OR MARIAN EVANS) (1819–1880), English author. *Middlemarch* (book 6, "The Widow and the Wife"; chapter 55) (1872).

8 Marriage will not content me, nor will single life. . . . I have tried both, and I cannot recommend either. It is a choice between two evils, and one does not know to say which is the least.

JOHN W. DEFOREST (1826–1906), U.S. author. *Miss Ravenel's Conversion from Secession to Loyalty* (chapter 13) (1867).

Words of a widow to a man who is considering her as a possible wife.

9   When a woman marries again, it is because she detested her first husband. When a man marries again, it is because he adored his first wife. Women try their luck; men risk theirs.

OSCAR WILDE (1854–1900), Irish author. *The Picture of Dorian Gray* (chapter 15) (1890).

10   Many a man owes his success to his first wife, and his second wife to his success.

JIM BACKUS (1913–1989), U.S. actor. *Morrow's International Dictionary of Contemporary Quotations*, ed. Jonathon Green (1982).

11   When the bride is a widow and the groom is a widower; when the former has lived in Our Great Little Town for hardly two years, and the latter for hardly a month; when Monsieur wants to get the whole damned thing over with as quickly as possible, and Madam gives in with a tolerant smile; then, my reader, the wedding is generally a "quiet affair." The bride may dispense with a tiara of orange blossoms securing her finger-tip veil, nor does she carry a white orchid in a prayer book.

VLADIMIR NABOKOV (1899–1977), U.S. (Russian-born) novelist. *Lolita* (part 1, chapter 18) (1955).

Humbert Humbert describes his hasty marriage to Charlotte Haze, his landlady and the mother of his beloved Lolita.

Third Marriage

1   We were married as soon as a twelvemonth and a day had passed from the death of the second Mrs. Balwhidder; and neither of us have had occasion to rue the bargain. It is, however, but a piece of justice due to my second wife to say, that this was not a little owing to her good management; for she had left such a well plenished house, that her successor said, we had nothing to do but to contribute to one another's happiness.

JOHN GALT (1779–1839), Scottish author. *Annals of the Parish* (1821).

Turning 30

1   It has . . . been asserted, by some naturalists, that men do not attain their full growth and strength till thirty; but that women arrive at maturity by twenty. I apprehend that they reason on false ground, led astray by the male prejudice, which deems beauty the perfection of woman . . . whilst male beauty is allowed to have some connection with the mind. Strength of body, and that character of countenance, which the French term a *physionomie*, women do not acquire before thirty, any more than men. The little artless tricks of children, it is true, are particularly pleasing and attractive; yet, when the pretty freshness of youth is worn off, these artless graces become studied airs, and disgust every person of taste.

MARY WOLLSTONECRAFT (1759–1797), English writer and feminist. *A Vindication of the Rights of Woman* (chapter 4, "Observations on the State of Degradation to Which Woman is Reduced by Various Causes") (1792).

2   After thirty a man wakes up sad every morning excepting perhaps five or six until the day of his death.

RALPH WALDO EMERSON (1803–1882), U.S. author. *The Journals and Miscellaneous Notebooks of Ralph Waldo Emerson*, 1 August 1835 (vol. 5, 1835–38), ed. Merton M. Sealts (1965).

3 In America, Newman reflected, lads of twenty-five and thirty have old heads and young hearts, or at least young morals; here [in Europe] they have young heads and very aged hearts, morals the most grizzled and wrinkled.

HENRY JAMES (1843–1916), U.S. author. *The American* (chapter 7) (1877).

4 The age of thirty is, for the workingman, just the beginning of a period of some stability, and as such one feels young and full of energy. But, at the same time, a period of life has passed, which makes one melancholy, thinking that some things will never come back.

VINCENT VAN GOGH (1853–1890), Dutch painter. Letter to his brother Theo, 8 February 1883, *Dear Theo: The Autobiography of Vincent Van Gogh*, ed. Irving Stone (1946.)

5 I have never admitted that I am more than twenty-nine, or thirty at the most. Twenty-nine when there are pink shades, thirty when there are not.

OSCAR WILDE (1854–1900), Irish author. *Lady Windermere's Fan* (act 4) (1892).

Mrs. Erlynne comments on the embarrassment of claiming her 21-year-old daughter, since that would destroy the image of relative youth that she has upheld.

6 One's thirtieth birthday and one's seventieth are days that press their message home with iron hand. With his seventieth milestone past, a man feels that his work is done, and dim voices call to him from across the Unseen. His work is done, and so illy, compared with what he had wished and expected! But the impressions made upon his heart by the day are no deeper than those his thirtieth birthday inspires. At thirty, youth, with all it palliates

and excuses, is gone forever. The time for mere fooling is past; the young avoid you, or else look up to you and tempt you to grow reminiscent. You are a man and must give an account of yourself.

ELBERT HUBBARD (1856–1915), U.S. author, founder of the Roycroft community. *The Philosophy of Elbert Hubbard* ("His Thoughts about Business") (1930).

7 Thirty-one or fifty-one is much the same for a woman who has made up her mind to live alone and work steadily for a definite object.

GEORGE GISSING (1857–1903), English author. *The Odd Women* (chapter 4, "Monica's Majority") (1893).

8 Is your own character, at thirty, the same as it was when you were ten years younger? It will be better or worse in the measure that you have believed that disloyalty, wickedness, hatred and falsehood have triumphed in life, or goodness, and truth, and love.

MAURICE MAETERLINCK (1862–1949), Belgian author. *Wisdom and Destiny* (section 19) (1898), trans. Alfred Sutro (1910).

9 people in their thirties, and the
    older ones, have gotten
      bad inside, like fruit
that nobody eats and nobody
wants, so it rots, but is not forgotten.

D. H. LAWRENCE (1885–1930), English author. "Beware, O My Dear Young Men."

Lawrence's speaker disdains the "small obscenities and village-idiot minds of young men in their 20s and 30s."

10 Thirty—the promise of a decade of loneliness, a thinning list of single men to know, a thinning briefcase of enthusiasm, thinning hair.

F. SCOTT FITZGERALD (1896–1940),
U.S. author. *The Great Gatsby* (chapter 7)
(1925).

The reflections of Nick Carraway, the narrator
of the story, on his thirtieth birthday.

11 Miranda in Miranda's sight
Is old and gray and dirty;
Twenty-nine she was last night;
This morning she is thirty.

OGDEN NASH (1902–1971), U.S. poet.
"A Lady Thinks She is Thirty."

12   It was my thirtieth
Year to heaven stood there then in
the summer noon
Though the town below lay leaved
with October blood.
        O may my heart's truth
            Still be sung
    On this high hill in a year's turn-
    ing.

DYLAN THOMAS (1914–1953), Welsh
poet. "Poem in October."

13 I believe that as many women over
thirty marry out of fear of being
alone someday—not necessarily
now but *some* day—as for love of
or compatibility with a particular
man. The plan seems to be to get
someone while the getting's good
and by the time you lose your looks
he'll be too securely glued to you to
get away. Isn't it silly? A man can
leave a woman at fifty (though it
may cost him some dough) as
surely as you can leave dishes in the
sink. . . . Then you have it all to do
over again as if you hadn't gobbled
him up in girlish haste.

HELEN GURLEY BROWN (b. 1922),
U.S. author and editor. *Sex and the Single Girl*
(chapter 1, "Women Alone? Oh Come Now!")
(1962).

14 I am only thirty.
And like the cat I have nine times
    to die.

SYLVIA PLATH (1932–63), U.S. author.
"Lady Lazarus."

This poem was written after Plath's third sui-
cide attempt.

15 Impatient with devoting ourselves
to the "shoulds," a new vitality
springs from within as we approach
30. Men and women alike speak of
feeling too narrow and restricted.
They blame all sorts of things, but
what the restrictions boil down to
are the outgrowth of career and
personal choices of the twenties.
They may have been choices perfectly suited to that stage. But now
the fit feels different. Some inner
aspect that was left out is striving to
be taken into account. Important
new choices must be made, and
commitments altered or deepened.
The work involves great change,
turmoil, and often crisis—a simul-
taneous feeling of rock bottom and
the urge to bust out.

GAIL SHEEHY (b. 1937), U.S. author. *Passages: Predictable Crises of Adult Life* (part 1,
"Mysteries of the Life Cycle"; chapter 2, "Predictable Crises of Adulthood") (1976).

16 Looking at ourselves in cold, hard
evolutionary terms, we are all rela-
tively useless after 30. All a species
needs to survive is to reproduce itself, which is easily possible at the
age of 15, and fifteen years more to
raise the next generation to reproductive age. Certainly by 40, when
both the male testes and the female
ovaries begin to show the changes
of age, we are, from an evolutionary point of view, thoroughly disposable.

Gail Sheehy (b. 1937), U.S. author. *Passages: Predictable Crises of Adult Life* (part 6, "Deadline Decade"; chapter 22, "The Sexual Diamond") (1976).

17   I remember the day I turned thirty. I was getting out of the shower and I stood in front of the mirror and stared at myself for a long time. I examined every inch of my body and appreciated the fact that I finally looked like a grown woman. I also assumed that this was how I was going to look for the rest of my life. The way I saw it, I was never going to *age* ; I'd just look up one day and be old.

Terry McMillan (b. 1951), U.S. author. *Waiting to Exhale* (1992).

Turning 40

1   Food is better for a man up to the age of forty; after forty drink is better.

Shabbat 152, in *The Talmudic Anthology: Tales and Teachings of the Rabbis*, ed. Louis I. Newman (1947).

2   When Nature first created man, monkey, and bull, she endowed the man with forty years of life, the monkey with forty, and the bull with twenty. The man wanted more, and the monkey and the bull volunteered to help him out. "Twenty's enough for me," said the monkey. "Man can have my other twenty." "And I'll give him ten of mine," said the bull. And thus it came about that man's life runs to seventy years, on the average, and is divided into these three periods: first forty years, normal living; next twenty, monkey business; last ten, shooting the bull.

Anonymous. *Anything for a Laugh: A Collection of Jokes and Anecdotes That You, Too, Can Tell and Probably Have,* ed. Bennett Cerf (1946).

3   When forty winters shall besiege
     thy brow,
   And dig deep trenches in thy
     beauty's field,
   Thy youth's proud livery, so gazed
     on now,
   Will be a tattered weed, of small
     worth held.

William Shakespeare (1564–1616), English poet and dramatist. Sonnet 2.

4   I am resolved to grow fat, and look young till forty, and then slip out of the world, with the first wrinkle, and the reputation of five-and-twenty.

John Dryden (1631–1700), English poet and dramatist. *The Maiden Queen* (act 3) (1667).

5   A woman, till five and thirty, is only looked upon as a raw girl, and can possibly make no noise in the world till about forty. I don't know what your ladyship may think of this matter, but 'tis a considerable comfort to me to know there is upon earth such a paradise for old women, and I am content to be insignificant at present, in the design of returning when I am fit to appear nowhere else.

Mary Wortley Montagu (1689–1762), English author. Letter to Lady Rich, 20 September 1716, *Letters [Lady Mary Wortley Montagu]*, ed. Clare Brant (1992).

The author refers to Vienna as a paradise for the middle-aged woman.

6   At twenty years of age, the will reigns, at thirty, the wit; and at forty, the judgment.

BENJAMIN FRANKLIN (1706–1790), U.S. statesman, scientist, and author. *Poor Richard's Almanac*, May 1733.

7 The true period of human existence may be reasonably estimated as forty years.

SAMUEL JOHNSON (1709–1784), English author. *The History of Rasselas, Prince of Abissina* (chapter 4, "The Prince Continues to Grieve and Muse") (1759).

8 After his fortieth year, any man of merit, anyone who is not just one of five-sixths of humanity so grievously and miserably endowed by nature, will hardly be free from a certain touch of misanthropy. For, as is natural, he has inferred the characters of others from his own and has gradually become disappointed.

ARTHUR SCHOPENHAUER (1788–1860), German philosopher. *Parerga and Paralipomena* (chapter 6, "On the Different Periods of Life") (1851), trans. E. F. J. Payne (1974).

9 When life, once past its fortieth
   year,
   Wheels up its evening hemisphere,
   The mind's own shadow, which the
   boy
   Saw onward point to hope and joy,
   Shifts round, irrevocably set
   Tow'rd morning's loss and vain re-
   gret,
   And, argue with it as we will,
   The clock is unconverted still.

JAMES RUSSELL LOWELL (1819–1891), U.S. author. "A Familiar Epistle to a Friend."

10 I'm now forty, and after all forty is an entire lifetime, it really is extreme old age. It isn't done to live beyond forty, it's vulgar and immoral. Who lives beyond forty, give me an honest answer? I'll tell you

who does: fools and good-for-nothings. . . . I've got the right to speak thus because I myself will live to be sixty. I'll live to be seventy! I'll live to be eighty!

FEDOR DOSTOEVSKY (1821–1881), Russian novelist. *Notes from the Underground* (chapter 1) (1864), trans. Jane Kentish (1991).

The comments of a man who opens his narrative by declaring himself sick, spiteful, unattractive, and possibly suffering from a liver ailment.

11 At the age of forty, men that love love rootedly. If the love is plucked from them, the life goes with it.

GEORGE MEREDITH (1828–1909), English author. *The Tragic Comedians: A Study in a Well-Known Story* (chapter 16) (1898).

12 To hold the same views at forty as we hold at twenty is to have been stupefied for a score of years, and take rank, not as a prophet, but as an unteachable brat, well birched and none the wiser.

ROBERT LOUIS STEVENSON (1850–1894), Scottish author. "Crabbed Age and Youth" (1878), *Virginibus Puerisque* (1881).

13 As if a man's soul were not too small to begin with, they have dwarfed and narrowed theirs by a life of all work and no play; until here they are at forty, with a listless attention, a mind vacant of all material of amusement, and not one thought to rub against another, while they wait for the train.

ROBERT LOUIS STEVENSON (1850–1894), Scottish author. "An Apology for Idlers," (1877), *Virginibus Puerisque* (1881).

14 Every man over 40 is a scoundrel.

GEORGE BERNARD SHAW (1856–1950), Irish dramatist and critic. "Maxims for Revolutionists," *The Revolutionist's Handbook* in *Man and Superman* (1903).

15 Men at forty
Learn to close softly
The doors to rooms they will not
  be
Coming back to.

DONALD JUSTICE (b. 1925), U.S. poet. "Men at Forty."

Justice describes this period of transition when men are "more fathers than sons themselves," as they live out their lives in their "mortgaged houses."

16 The womb is not a clock
nor a bell tolling,
but in the eleventh month of its life
I feel the November
of the body as well as of the calendar.
In two days it will be my birthday
and as always the earth is done
  with its harvest.

ANNE SEXTON (1928–1974), U.S. poet. "Menstruation at Forty."

17 It is almost universal to have a hurry-up feeling as we hit 40. The first little fissures appear in our physical shells. Damn, why is the type in the phone book so small? Students start calling you "mister." (Behind your back you know they're probably calling you "that old fart.")

GAIL SHEEHY (b. 1937), U.S. author. *New Passages: Mapping Your Life Across Time* (part 2, "The Flourishing Forties"; chapter 2, "The Vietnam Generation Hits Middlescence") (1995).

18 If life really begins at 40, it's be-cause that's when women finally get it. The guts to take back their lives. Seize the day. Glorify the season and seasoning.

LAURA B. RANDOLPH (b. 1957), U.S. journalist. "The Top 40," *Ebony* (August 1997).

This quotation appears in an article about tele-vision personality Oprah Winfrey on her forti-eth birthday.

19 Thanks to modern medical ad-vances such as antibiotics, nasal spray, and Diet Coke, it has become routine for people in the civilized world to pass the age of 40, some-times more than once.

DAVE BARRY (b. 1947), U.S. humorist and newspaper columnist. *Dave Barry Turns 40* (chapter 2, "Your Disintegrating Body") (1990).

20 When they used to say "Life begins at forty," I did the same "yeah, right" that you, if you're under forty, still do. But of course if you play your cards right (study hard! work hard! buy in bulk! live be-neath your means!) and if you have your share of good luck—it's true.

ANDREW TOBIAS (JOHN REID) (b. 1947), U.S. author. *The Best Little Boy in the World Grows Up* (1998).

Middle Age

1 If the characteristic feature of the first half of life is an unsatisfied longing for happiness, that of the second is a dread of misfortune.

ARTHUR SCHOPENHAUER (1788–1860), German philosopher. *Parerga and Par-alipomena: Short Philosophical Essays* (chapter 6, "On the Different Periods of Life") (1851), trans. E. F. J. Payne (1974).

2 The useful man never leads the easy, sheltered, knockless, un-shocked life. At thirty-six he ought to be prepared to deal with realities and after about that period in his life, until he is sixty, he should be able to handle them with a steadily increasing efficiency. Subsequently, if he has not injured his body by

excess indulgence in any of the narcotics (and by this term I mean, here, liquor, tobacco, tea, and coffee), and if he has not eaten to excess, he very likely may continue to be achievingly efficient up to his eightieth birthday and in exceptional cases until ninety.

THOMAS ALVA EDISON (1847–1931), U.S. inventor. *The Diary and Sundry Observations of Thomas Alva Edison* ("Sundry Observations"; chapter 6, "Man and Machine"; section 34, "Age and Achievement" [1927]), ed. Dagobert D. Runes (1948).

3   We advance in years somewhat in the manner of an invading army in a barren land; the age that we have reached, as the saying goes, we but hold with an outpost, and still keep open communications with the extreme rear and first beginnings of the march.

ROBERT LOUIS STEVENSON (1850–1894), Scottish author. "Virginibus Puerisque II," *Virginibus Puerisque* (1881).

4   Beyond doubt, other things being equal, a man will turn to a woman of twenty-five rather than to a woman of thirty-five, and to a woman of thirty-five rather than to a woman of forty-five—even though the one is by miracle as attractive as the other. You may protest that it is unjust. It may be, but it is so.

ARNOLD BENNETT (1867–1931), English author. *How to Make the Best of Life* (chapter 9, "Not for the Young") (1923).

5   Cares seem to crowd on us—so much to do;
New fields to conquer, and time's on the wing.
Grey hairs are showing, a wrinkle or two;

Somehow our footstep is losing its spring.
Pleasure's forsaken us, Love ceased to smile;
Youth has been funeralled; Age travels fast.
Sometimes we wonder: is it worth while?

ROBERT W. SERVICE (1874–1958), Canadian author. "A Song of Success."

6   She had the oddest sense of being herself invisible; unseen; unknown; there being no more marrying, no more having of children now, but only this astonishing and rather solemn progress with the rest of them, up Bond Street, this being Mrs. Dalloway; not even Clarissa any more; this being Mrs. Richard Dalloway.

VIRGINIA WOOLF (1882–1941), English novelist. *Mrs. Dalloway* (1925).

7   You are not half so beautiful
Since middle-age befell you;
But since this is your birthday
I suppose I mustn't tell you.

ALINE KILMER (1888–1941), U.S. poet. "For the Birthday of a Middle-Aged Child."

8   Middle age is when you go to bed at night and think you're going to feel better in the morning. Old age is when you go to bed at night and hope you wake up in the morning.

GROUCHO MARX (1890?–1977), U.S. comic and actor. Quoted in Arthur Marx, "Still the Best Player at the Club," in *The Courage to Grow Old*, ed. Phillip C. Berman (1989).

Arthur Marx is Groucho's son.

9   How to put an age label on true middle age is a hot potato. Working-class men describe themselves as middle-aged at 40 and old by 60.

Business executives and professionals, by contrast, do not see themselves as reaching middle age until 50, and old age means 70 to them.

GAIL SHEEHY (b. 1937), U.S. author. *Passages: Predictable Crises* (part 6, "Deadline Decade"; chapter 18, "You Are in Good Company") (1976).

10 The old write memoirs, the young do résumés. In midlife we keep a kind of diary that always begins with a discussion of the weather. The present is where we live, equidistant from our birth and death.

THOMAS LYNCH (b. 1948), U.S. undertaker and author. *The Undertaking: Life Studies from the Dismal Trade* ("Sweeney") (1997).

Turning 50

1 Said Nestor, to his pretty wife, quite
sorrowful one day,
"Why, dearest, will you shed in
pearls those lovely eyes away?
You ought to be more fortified;"
"Ah, brute, be quiet, do,
I know I'm not so fortyfied, nor fiftyfied, as you!"

THOMAS HOOD (1799–1845), English poet. "December and May."

The wife is a tradesman's widow who agreed to marry an old man after taking him at his word that he would "die" for her. She weeps because he has not kept his promise soon enough.

2 Love is lame at fifty years.

THOMAS HARDY (1840–1928), English author. "The Revisitation" [poem].

3 . . . now that I have come to fifty
years
I must endure the timid sun.

WILLIAM BUTLER YEATS (1865–1939), Irish poet. "Lines Written in Dejection."

4 When she looked in the glass and saw her hair grey, her cheek sunk, at fifty, she thought, possibly she might have managed things better—her husband; money; his books. But for her own part she would never for a single second regret her decision, evade difficulties, or slur over duties.

VIRGINIA WOOLF (1882–1941), English novelist. *To the Lighthouse* ("The Window," section 1) (1927).

5 What changed her was what changes all women at fifty: the transfer from the active service of life—with a pension or the honors of war, as the case may be—to the mere passive state of a looker-on. A weight fell away from her; she flew up to a higher perch and cackled a little. Her fortune helped her only in so far as it provided the puff of air under her wings that enabled her to fly a little higher and cackle a little louder, although it also did away with all criticism from her surroundings. In her laughter of liberation there certainly was a little madness.

ISAK DINESEN (KAREN CHRISTENCE DINESEN, BARONESS BLIXEN-FINECKE) (1885–1962), Danish author. "The Deluge at Nordenerney," *Seven Gothic Tales* (1934).

6 All normal children (however much we discourage them) look forward to growing up. "Except ye become as little children," except you can wake on your fiftieth birthday with the same forward-looking excitement and interest in life that you enjoyed when you were five, "ye cannot see the Kingdom of God." One must not only die daily, but every day one must be born again.

Dorothy L. Sayers (1893–1957), English author. "Strong Meat," *Creed or Chaos?* (1949).

Sayers argues that Christ's exhortation to "become as little children" is too often "quoted to justify the flight into infantilism." She sees Christianity as "a religion for adult minds."

7 Norma, you're a woman of 50. Now, grow up! There's nothing tragic about being 50—not unless you try to be 25.

Charles Brackett, D. M. Marshman Jr., and **Billy Wilder**, screenwriters. *Sunset Boulevard* (1950).

Spoken by a young hack screenwriter, played by William Holden, to Norma Desmond, a faded silent-film star played by Gloria Swanson. The film was directed by Wilder.

8 I spent my second quarter-century
Losing what I had learnt at university

And refusing to take in what had happened since.

Philip Larkin (1922–1985), English poet and critic. "The Winter Palace."

9 Be glad you're fifty—and
That you got there while things were nice,
In a world worth looking at twice.
So here's wishing you many more years,
But not all that many. Cheers!

Kingsley Amis (1922–1995), English author. "Ode to Me."

10 This turning point of fifty, I had become convinced, ought to form as vital a milestone in a woman's life as graduation, promotion, marriage or the birth of a child. At fifty, I had concluded, a woman might celebrate a rite of passage, a ritual as regularly marched as a confirmation.

Carolyn G. Heilbrun (b. 1926), U.S. author. *The Last Gift of Time: Life Beyond Sixty* (1997).

11 Fifty was the end of this long familiar plateau that you enter at 13—you know, the country of the female stereotype. And when I got to 50, which is the edge of this territory—indeed the edge used to be 35, 40, we've *pushed* it to 50—then it was like falling off a cliff. There was no map. Now it's true that I had been fighting with the map. But you're enmeshed in it either way, whether you're obeying it or fighting with it.

Gloria Steinem (b. 1934), U.S. author and feminist. Interview with Cynthia Gorney in *Mother Jones* (November–December 1995).

12 The age of 50 seems to represent a sort of tollgate, beyond which, having chosen the route and the traveling companions, one expects to be on the same road for a long, long time. Thus people who find themselves approaching 50, unattached—either divorced or never married—are particularly prone to playing out a perpetual middlescence.

Gail Sheehy (b. 1937), U.S. author. *New Passages: Mapping Your Life Across Time* (part 2, "The Flourishing Forties"; chapter 6, "Perpetual Middlescence") (1995).

"Middlescence" is a sort of middle-aged adolescence.

13 An attractive woman friend confided that when she turned 50, she felt like one of those park statues that turn green, weather-streaked, and crumbly, the kind that no one, not even the people on the benches right in front of it, notices anymore.

GAIL SHEEHY (b. 1937), U.S. author. *New Passages: Mapping Your Life Across Time* (part 4, "Flaming Fifties: Women"; chapter 8, "Women: Pits to Peak") (1995).

14 Irreparable physical damage aside, being fifty or sixty is surely no more of a "problem" than being ten, twenty, thirty or forty. However old you are, you're mortal. Isn't that exactly what makes life as interesting, precious, cruel, unjust and altogether extraordinary as it is?

SHEILA MACLEOD (b. 1939), English (Scottish-born) author. "Drunken Drowning," in *A Certain Age: Reflecting on the Menopause*, ed. Joanna Goldsworthy (1993).

15 "Fifty is halftime," said Joe Namath when his big birthday rolled around. I appreciate sports metaphors as much as the next guy, but this one won't make the cut. Few fifty-year-olds can expect to play two more full quarters of the game of life.

LETTY COTTIN POGREBIN (b. 1939), U.S. author. *Getting Over Getting Older: An Intimate Journey* (chapter 2, "Feeling Out Fifty") (1996).

16 If someone could guarantee that I'll live to be a healthy, vigorous ninety, I'm not sure I'd have been so upset about turning fifty, but without that assurance I felt vulnerable and pressed for time. Suddenly, death seemed imminent and eminently possible.

LETTY COTTIN POGREBIN (b. 1939), U.S. author. *Getting Over Getting Older: An Intimate Journey* (chapter 2, "Feeling Out Fifty") (1996).

17 It happens in America about eleven thousand times a day now—someone turning 50—far outstripping the casualty rate for hunting accidents and car wrecks combined.

BILL GEIST (b. 1945), U.S. journalist. *The Big Five-Oh!: Fearing, Facing, and Fighting Fifty* ("The Birthday") (1999).

18 Fifty is not "just another birthday." It is a reluctant milepost on the way to wherever it is we are meant to wind up. It can be approached in only two ways. First, it can be a ball of snakes that conjures up immediate thoughts of mortality and accountability. ("What have I done with my life?") Or, it can be a great excuse to reward yourself for just getting there. ("He who dies with the most toys wins.") I instinctively choose door number two.

JIMMY BUFFETT (b. 1946), U.S. singer and songwriter. *A Pirate Looks at Fifty* (section 1, "Questions and Answers") (1998).

Losing a Parent

1 The Master said: "Observe what a man has in mind to do when his father is living, and then observe what he does when his father is dead. If, for three years, he makes no changes to his father's ways, he can be said to be a good son."

CONFUCIUS (551?–479 B.C.), Chinese philosopher. *Analects* (Lun yü), book 1, section 12, trans. D. C. Lau (1979).

2 I have now lost my barrier between me and death; God grant I may live to be as well prepared for it, as I confidently believe her to have been! If the way to Heaven be through piety, truth, justice and charity, she is there.

JONATHAN SWIFT (1667–1745), Anglo-Irish author. *Miscellaneous and Autobiogrphical Pieces, Fragments and Marginalia* in *Prose*

Works of Jonathan Swift (10 May 1710), vol. 5 (1962)

Swift reflects on his mother's death.

3   I imbibed commiseration, remorse, and an unmanly gentleness of mind, which has since ensnared me into ten thousand calamities; and from whence I can reap no advantage, except it be, that, in such a humour as I am now in, I can the better indulge myself in the softnesses of humanity, and enjoy that sweet anxiety which arises from the memory of past afflictions.

RICHARD STEELE (1672–1729), Anglo-Irish author. "An Hour or Two Sacred to Sorrow," in *The Art of the Personal Essay: An Anthology from the Classical Era to the Present*, ed. Phillip Lopate (1994).

Steele describes the effects of losing his father at the age of 5 and growing up around a mournful mother.

4   With my mother's death all settled happiness, all that was tranquil and reliable, disappeared from my life. There was to be much fun, many pleasures, many stabs of Joy; but no more of the old security. It was sea and islands now; the great continent had sunk like Atlantis.

C. S. LEWIS (1898–1963), English author. *Surprised by Joy: The Shape of My Early Life* (chapter 1, "The First Years") (1955).

5   *No one glancing into our car can possibly imagine my grief. In a few hours, people at the funeral will hug me and say how sorry they are, but no one will ever know how it feels for this child to lose this mother. I am alone. My mother is dead. And life has dared to go on without me.*

LETTY COTTIN POGREBIN (b. 1939), U.S. author. *Getting Over Getting Older: An Intimate Journey* (chapter 5, "Forgetting and Remembering") (1996).

Reassessing her life at the age of 50, Pogrebin recalls the loss of her mother, 35 years earlier, as one of her first "frozen moments."

6   I was forty-two when . . . my mother died and it felt as though I had been left in the world alone. Although I was myself a mother, although I had a husband, two sons, two brothers and many friends, with whom my relations were passionate and often complicated, my relation to my mother was the most passionate and complicated of all. So intense was our bond that I was never sure what belonged to whom, where I ended, and she began.

HELEN EPSTEIN (b. 1947), U.S. author. *Where She Came From: A Daughter's Search for Her Mother's History* (chapter 1) (1997).

Losing a Spouse

1   The widower lives in a darkened world.

Sanhedrin 22a, in *The Talmudic Anthology: Tales and Teachings of the Rabbis*, ed. Louis I. Newman (1947).

2   My wife, my wife! What wife? I have no wife.
O insupportable! O heavy hour!
Methinks it should be now a huge eclipse
Of sun and moon, and that th' affrighted globe
Should yawn at alteration.

WILLIAM SHAKESPEARE (1564–1616), English poet and dramatist. *Othello* (5.2.101–105).

Othello's grief is particularly intense because he is responsible for his wife's death.

3   From those bright regions of eternal day,
Where now thou shin'st amongst thy fellow saints,

Array'd in purer light, look down
  on me!
In pleasing visions and delusive
  dreams.
O! sooth my soul, and teach me
  how to lose thee.

SAMUEL JOHNSON (1709–1784), English
author. *Irene* (written in 1736, first performed
in 1749).

In his *Life of Johnson*, James Boswell cites this
passage as proof that, long before Johnson's
wife died, in 1752, Johnson had considered
the "state of mind in which a man must be
upon the death of a woman whom he sincerely loves" ("17 March 1752").

4 Although he probably was not oftener in the wrong than she was, in
the little disagreements which
sometimes troubled his married
state, during which, he owned to
me, that the gloomy irritability of
his existence was more painful to
him than ever, he might very naturally, after her death, be tenderly
disposed to charge himself with
slight omissions and offences, the
sense of which would give him
much uneasiness.

JAMES BOSWELL (1740–1795), Scottish
author. *Life of Johnson* ("17 March 1752")
(1791).

Boswell describes Johnson's distress after losing his wife.

5 Ay, go to the grave of buried love
and meditate! There settle the account with thy conscience for every
past benefit unrequited—every past
endearment unregarded, of that de-
parted being, who can never, never,
never return to be soothed by thy
contrition.

WASHINGTON IRVING (1783–1859),
U.S. author. "Rural Funerals," *The Sketch Book
of Geoffrey Crayon, Gent.* (1819–20).

6 I hold it true, whate'er befall;
    I feel it when I sorrow most;
    'Tis better to have loved and lost
Than never to have loved at all.

ALFRED, LORD TENNYSON (1809–
1892), English poet. *In Memoriam A.H.H.* 27
(1850).

Although Tennyson does not mourn a spouse
here, many critics have noted that he treats the
death of Arthur Henry Hallam as if it were the
death of a beloved woman.

7 Woman much missed, how you call
  to me, call to me,
Saying that now you are not as you
  were
When you had changed from the
  one who was all to me,
But as at first, when our day was
  fair.

THOMAS HARDY (1840–1928), English
author. "The Voice."

"The Voice" is one of a series of poems (*Poems of 1912–13*) that Hardy composed soon
after the death of his first wife, Emma.

8 Masses of flowers
loaded the cherry branches
and color some bushes
yellow and some red
but the grief in my heart
is stronger than they
for though they were my joy
formerly, today I notice them
and turned away forgetting.

WILLIAM CARLOS WILLIAMS (1883–
1963), U.S. poet and physician. "The Widow's
Lament in Springtime."

Williams wrote this poem in tribute to his
mother.

9 There is one place where her absence comes locally home to me,
and it is a place I can't avoid. I
mean my own body. It had such a
different importance while it was

the body of H.'s lover. Now it's like an empty house.

C. S. LEWIS (1898–1963), English author. *A Grief Observed* (chapter 1) (1961).

10 Bereavement is not the truncation of married love but one of its regular phases—like the honeymoon. What we want is to live our marriage well and faithfully through that phase too. If it hurts (and it certainly will) we accept the pains as a necessary part of this phase. . . . We were one flesh. Now that it has been cut in two, we don't want to pretend that it is whole and complete.

C. S. LEWIS (1898–1963), English author. *A Grief Observed* (chapter 3) (1961).

11 Most widows want their loss acknowledged, not glossed over, and the name of their dead husband spoken, not avoided. They would like to tell callers not to bother if they are going to talk about the weather or how terribly funny their new poodle puppy is.

GENEVIEVE DAVIS GINSBURG (1917–1996), U.S. author. *To Live Again: Rebuilding Your Life After You've Become a Widow* ("The Dumb Things People Say") (1987).

*M*enopause

1 In this country it is more despicable to be married and not fruitful, than it is with us to be fruitful before marriage. They have a notion, that, whenever a woman leaves off bringing children, it is because she is too old for that business, whatever her face says to the contrary, and this opinion makes the ladies here so ready to make proofs of their youth . . . that they do not content themselves with using the natural means, but fly to all sorts of quackeries, to avoid the scandal of being past child-bearing, and often kill themselves by them.

MARY WORTLEY MONTAGU (1689–1762), English author. Letter to Mrs. Thistlethwayte, 4 January 1718 OS, *Letters* [Mary Wortley Montagu], ed. Clare Brant (1992).

Montagu's letter suggests that the fear of menopause (or of seeming to be no longer of childbearing age) is a universal one.

2 The crisis of the menopause rudely cuts the life of woman in two; the resulting discontinuity is what gives woman the illusion of a "new life"; it is *another* time that opens before her, so she enters upon it with the fervor of a convert; she is converted to love, to the godly life, to art, to humanity; in these entities she loses herself and magnifies herself.

SIMONE DE BEAUVOIR (1908–1986), French author and philosopher. *The Second Sex* (part 5, "Situation"; chapter 20, "From Maturity to Old Age") (1949), trans. H. M. Parshley (1971).

3 Menopause Manor is not merely a defensive stronghold. . . . It is a house or household, fully furnished with the necessities of life. In abandoning it, women have narrowed their domain and impoverished their souls. There are things the Old Woman can do, say, and think that the Woman cannot do, say, or think. The Woman has to give up more than her menstrual periods before she can do, say, or think them. She has got to change her life.

URSULA K. LEGUIN (b. 1929), U.S. author. "The Space Crone" (1976), *Dancing at the Edge of the World: Thoughts on Words, Women, Places* (1989).

4 Menopause would be celebrated as a positive event, the symbol that men had accumulated enough years of cyclical wisdom to need no more.

GLORIA STEINEM (b. 1934), U.S. author and feminist. "If Men Could Menstruate," *Outrageous Acts and Everyday Rebellions* (1983).

Steinem lists changes that would occur in attitudes toward menstruation if menstruation were a male phenomenon.

5 In the South of my childhood, no woman could weather the "Change" completely unscathed; it was femininity's Appomattox and you had to milk it for every possible drop of theater.

FLORENCE KING (b. 1936), U.S. author. *Lump or Leave It* ("Fifty something") (1990).

6 Menopause—word used as an insult:
a menopausal woman, mind or
  poem
as if not to leak regularly or on the
  caprice
of the moon, the collision of egg
  and sperm,
were the curse we first learned to
  call that blood.

MARGE PIERCY (1936-), U.S. author. "Something to look forward to."

Piercy concludes the poem by saying that she "will secretly dance / and pour out a cup of wine on the earth / when time stops that leak permanently."

7 The best gift for making a conscious, disciplined trip through menopause is *postmenopausal zest.* This is a special, buoyant sort of energy, fueled in part by the change in ratio of testosterone to estrogen. . . . Once a woman has come through the menopausal passage, she can say good-bye to pregnancy fears and monthly mood swings.

Now that she is no longer confined by society's narrow definition of woman as sex object and breeder, she is freer to integrate the masculine and feminine aspects of her nature. She can now claim the license to *say what she truly thinks.*

GAIL SHEEHY (b. 1937), U.S. author. *New Passages: Mapping Your Life Across Time* (part 4, "Flaming Fifties: Women"; chapter 9, "Wonder Woman Meets Menopause") (1995).

Sheehy explains that Margaret Mead coined the term "postmenopausal zest" and observed its presence in women in different cultures.

8 The central myth is that menopause is a time in a woman's life when she goes batty for a few years—subject to wild rages and deep depressions—and after it she mourns her lost youth and fades into the woodwork. In truth, menopause is a bridge to the most vital and liberated period in a woman's life.

GAIL SHEEHY (b. 1937), U.S. author. *The Silent Passage: Menopause* (1998).

9 Though there is no public rite of passage for the woman approaching the end of her reproductive years, there is evidence that women devise their own private ways of marking the irrevocability of the change. . . . The climacteric is a time of stocktaking, of spiritual as well as physical change, and it would be a pity to be unconscious of it.

GERMAINE GREER (b. 1939), Australian author and feminist. *The Change: Women, Ageing and the Menopause* (introduction) (1991).

10 To be precise, the word "menopause" applies to a non-event, the menstrual period that does not happen. It is the invisible Rubicon

that a woman cannot know she is crossing until she has crossed it.

GERMAINE GREER (b. 1939), Australian author and feminist. *The Change: Women, Ageing and the Menopause* (chapter 1, "The Undescribed") (1991).

11   Menopause is a time when, if we have not already done so, we should learn to take as good care of ourselves as we do of others. Many women become more self-confident and assertive and less interested in pleasing others. Increasingly, women are writing about the change of life, or menopause, as a time of preparing for later life through emotional and spiritual transformation. . . .

. . . Women at midlife may be subject to overtreatment when physicians view the normal changes of menopause as a deficiency disease requiring medication, or they may suffer from undertreatment and misdiagnosis of real symptoms of disease. Some physicians attribute to menopause almost anything reported by women at midlife, overlooking what might be symptoms of gallbladder disease, hypertension, and other serious conditions.

PAULA B. DORESS-WORTERS and **DIANA LASKIN SIEGAL**, U.S. authors. *The New Ourselves, Growing Older: Women Aging with Knowledge and Power*, ed. Paula B. Doress-Worters and Diana Laskin Siegal (chapter 10, "Experiencing Our Change of Life: Menopause") (1994).

Doress-Worters and Siegal have served as project coordinators for the Boston Women's Health Book Collective and the Greater Boston Older Women's League.

12   Pregnancy and childbirth are pretty rotten jokes to play on the female, but I cannot help suspecting that the menopause may be nature's

last—and most outrageous—grand belly laugh.

ELIZABETH BUCHAN (b. 1948), English author and editor. "Rite of Passage," in *A Certain Age: Reflecting on the Menopause*, ed. Joanna Goldsworthy (1993).

Turning 60

1   Spring still makes spring in the mind,
        When sixty years are told;
    Love wakes anew this throbbing heart,
        And we are never old.

RALPH WALDO EMERSON (1803–1882), U.S. author. "The World-Soul" (1847).

2   You've got t' be fifty-nine years ole t'believe a feller is at his best at sixty.

KIN HUBBARD (1868–1930), U.S. humorist. *Abe Martin's Primer* (1914).

3   Picasso once said, "One starts to get young at the age of sixty, and then it's too late."

HENRY MILLER (1891–1980), U.S. author. "On Turning 80" (1972), *A Henry Miller Reader*, ed. John Calder (1985).

Miller in his essay writes about his friendship with Picasso and the artist's continuing vitality.

4   It comes as a surprise, even at first almost a feeling of guilt: after a long time of being afraid, of not wanting to think about it, of pretending everything's the same, the delight, the sheer excitement of coming into a new place after sixty, after it's all supposed to be over. And it may not have come easily.

BETTY FRIEDAN (b. 1921), U.S. author and feminist. *The Fountain of Age* (chapter 10, "Coming into a New Place") (1993).

Friedan also notes (chapter 18, "Age as Adventure") that, despite her final sense of excitement at turning 60, she and her "feminist women friends" had a hard time coming up with a ceremony or ritual to commemorate the milestone birthdays after 60. She said they tried to create a celebration but "somehow couldn't get beyond the discomfort and the rage: 'When Sleeping Beauty woke up, she was sixty years old!' "

5   For those of us over sixty, high on the list of gratitude should be that we are still alive! Even if it hurts. Even if we feel thirty-five inside of our heads and can no longer even count the wrinkles.

EDA LESHAN (b. 1922), U.S. author. *It's Better to Be Over the Hill Than Under It: Thoughts on Life Over Sixty* ("Thanksgiving Thoughts") (1997).

6   I'm sixty years of age. That's 16 Celsius.

GEORGE CARLIN (b. 1937), U.S. comic and author. *Brain Droppings* (1997).

Turning 65

1   Let others Sing of Youth and
    Spring, still will it seem to me
    The golden time's the olden time,
    some time round Sixty-five.

ROBERT W. SERVICE (1874–1958), Canadian poet. "A Song of Sixty-Five."

2   I determined that at sixty-five business properly speaking should know me no more. On my sixty-fifth birthday—or, to put it more correctly, on my sixty-sixth—I woke a free man. For my practice had always been a discipline rather than an inclination.

VICTORIA (OR VITA) SACKVILLE-WEST (1892–1962), English novelist and poet. *All Passion Spent* (part 1) (1931).

While Mr. Bucktrout now avoids any activity that breaks his repose and retirement, he argues that, in his day, he was "fierce," quickly realizing that in business "modesty, moderation, consideration, and nicety" never pay.

3   At sixty-five one is not merely twenty years older than one was at forty-five. One has exchanged an indefinite future—and one had a tendency to look upon it as infinite—for a finite future. In earlier days we could see no boundary-mark upon the horizon: now we do see one.

SIMONE DE BEAUVOIR (1908–1986), French author and philosopher. *The Coming of Age* (part 2, "The Being-in-the-World"; chapter 6, "Time, Activity, History") (1970), trans. Patrick O'Brian (1972).

4   I discovered when I began to look into the whole question of retirement, our society exactly pinpoints the onset of that decline at age sixty-five. No one would presume to date so precisely the onset of childhood, adolescence, or adulthood, and reward—or punish—those who don't arrive or depart on time.

BETTY FRIEDAN (b. 1921), U.S. author and feminist. *The Fountain of Age* (chapter 6, "The Retirement Paradox") (1993).

5   Presents and parties disappear,
    The cards grow fewer year by year,
    Till, when one reaches sixty-five,
    How many care we're still alive?

PHILIP LARKIN (1922–1985), English poet and critic. "Dear CHARLES, My Muse, Asleep or Dead.'"

Retirement

1   He may not do what the young men are doing, but he is really do-

ing much greater and better things: great affairs are not accomplished by strength or speed or swiftness of bodies, but by planning, authority, deliberation, things which old age is not deprived of, but which even then increase.

CICERO, MARCUS TULLIUS (106–43 B.C.), Roman author, orator, and statesman. *De Senectute* (On Old Age) (c. 44 B.C.), trans. Harry G. Edinger (1967).

2   . . . 'tis our fast intent
     To shake all cares and business
        from our age,
     Conferring them on younger
        strengths, while we
     Unburden'd crawl toward death.

WILLIAM SHAKESPEARE (1564–1616), English poet and dramatist. *King Lear* 1.1.38–41.

3   Great men have a dark chimerical prospect of retiring, which their circumstances will seldom permit them to execute, till they are forced to it.

GEORGE SAVILE, MARQUIS OF HALIFAX (1633–1695), English courtier and author. *Maxims* ("Retire") (1750), in *The Works of George Savile, Marquis of Halifax*, ed. Mark N. Brown, vol. 3 (1989.)

4   The love of Retirement has, in all ages, adhered closely to those minds which have been most enlarged by knowledge, or elevated by genius. Those who enjoyed every thing generally supposed to confer happiness have been forced to seek it in the shades of privacy.

SAMUEL JOHNSON (1709–1784), English author. *The Rambler* (10 April 1750).

5   Nothing is more incumbent on the old, than to know when they shall get out of the way, and relinquish

to younger successors the honors they can no longer earn and the duties they can no longer perform.

THOMAS JEFFERSON (1743–1826), U.S. president. Letter to John Vaughan, 5 February 1815, *The Writings of Thomas Jefferson*, Memorial edition, ed. Andrew A. Lipscomb et al. (1903–1904).

6   It was like passing out of Time into Eternity—for it is a sort of Eternity for a man to have his Time all to himself.

CHARLES LAMB (1775–1834), English essayist. "The Superannuated Man" *London Magazine* (1825) and *Last Essays of Elia* (1833).

7   When you will have worked hard and faithfully, there will come a day when you will wish to rest, when you will wish to give to her whom you love and whom you will love the more as years pass, your own time, your own self, that you two may go hand in hand into the winter, unafraid and unburdened by cares and sorrows.

CHARLES ADAMS , Letter to his son Ansel Adams, 30 January 1928, in *Letters of a Nation: A Collection of Extraordinary American Letters*, ed. Andrew Carroll (1997).

Adams offers advice on the occasion of Ansel's marriage.

8   I noticed a tendency among many men in business to feel that their lot was hard—they worked against a day when they might retire and live on an income—get out of the strife. Life to them was a battle to be ended as soon as possible. That was another point I could not understand, for as I reasoned, life is not a battle except with our own tendency to sag with the downpull of "getting settled." . . . Life, as I see

it, is not a location, but a journey. Even the man who most feels himself "settled" is not settled—he is probably sagging back. Everything is in flux, and was meant to be. Life flows. We may live at the same number of the street, but it is never the same man who lives there.

HENRY FORD (1863–1947), U.S. industrialist and automobile manufacturer. *My Life and Work* (1922), and reprinted in *Ford on Management: Harnessing the American Spirit* (chapter 2, "What I Learned About Business") (1991).

9   The argument for retirement is an erroneous one. It assumes that our goal in life is to amass the right amount of wealth so that we can shut down our productivity at a certain age and revel in our material success and free time. . . . We should never abandon the world of work and productivity for a world of inactivity, a world that doesn't challenge us, a world that isolates us from our spiritual quest.

MENACHEM MENDEL SCHNEERSON (1902–1994), U.S. rabbi. *Toward a Meaningful Life: The Wisdom of the Rebbe* (chapter 13, "Aging and Retirement: Regeneration and Dignity") (1995).

10   Ages of compulsory retirement are fixed at point varying from 55 to 75, all being equally arbitrary and unscientific. Whatever age has been decreed by accident and custom can be defended by the same argument. Where the retirement age is fixed at 65 the defenders of this system will always have found, by experience, that the mental powers and energy show signs of flagging at the age of 62. This would be a most useful conclusion to have reached had not a different phe-

nomenon been observed in organizations where the age of retirement has been fixed at 60. There, we are told, people are found to lose their grips, in some degree, at the age of 57.

C. NORTHCOTE PARKINSON (1909–1993), historian, journalist, and novelist. *Parkinson's Law, and Other Studies in Administration* (chapter 10, "Pension Point or the Age of Retirement") (1958).

11   Soon, I think, public-relations offices will find a new word for "retirement." This new word will undoubtedly project the image of continuing activity and participation in life on a person's own terms, rather than the image of rest (white-thatched oldster fishing) that we still have before us today.

ALAN HARRINGTON (1919–1997), U.S. author. *Life in the Crystal Palace* (chapter 11, "Life Begins at 65") (1959).

12   Early retirement is . . . sound, to take care of people who, like '51 and '54 vintages, didn't work out.

ROBERT TOWNSEND (b. 1920), U.S. author. *Up the Organization* ("Retirement, Mandatory") (1970).

13   You can't put off being young until you retire.

PHILIP LARKIN (1922–1985), English poet and critic. "Money" [poem].

14   It is a time when we can, by default, live a passive and inactive life. But there is a wonderful, if riskier, alternative. We can take advantage of our newfound freedom and embark on new and exciting adventures. We now have time to fulfill some earlier ambitions. If we make a mistake, there are plenty of fallbacks. We need not be too cautious.

JIMMY CARTER (b. 1924), U.S. president. *The Virtues of Aging* (chapter 10, "What is Successful Aging?") (1998).

15   We do not actually know how competent and industrious people between seventy and eighty years old can be in our society. In an agricultural economy, when they are healthy, they are able to bear a considerable portion of the necessary workload. Old men and women have continued to perform their customary chores until they were physically unable to do so. They sometimes did so of necessity, but more often they seem to have done so by choice. They not only felt useful and needed but actually were.

ERIK H. ERIKSON (1902–1990), U.S. (German-born) psychoanalyst; JOAN M. ERIKSON (1902–1997), U.S. artist and therapist; and HELEN Q. KIVNICK, psychologist, *Vital Involvement in Old Age* (section 4, "Old Age in Our Society, 'Retirement'") (1986).

The authors go on to say that it is "responsible" to care for retired people in "organized ways" but that "entertaining them with bingo games and concerts is . . . patronizing."

16   People who were never too crazy about their jobs look forward to retirement, as do people who know exactly what they'd like to do, at long last. People who have no idea what they will do with retirement dread it. And then there are the rest of us, who had this crazy idea that we would have enough money to quit working at sixty or sixty-five and could then pick up all the unfulfilled dreams of things we'd always longed to do.

EDA LeSHAN (b. 1922), U.S. author. *It's Better To Be Over the Hill Than Under It* ("The *No* Retirement Blues") (1990).

17   Retirement used to be the square that one landed on in the playing board of life roughly five years before one expired, the reward for thirty-five or more years of hard work, when a pencil pusher could enjoy a paid mortgage, a cruise or two, and a golden wedding anniversary while waiting around to die. Today the question is not so much *when* is ideal retirement age as how does one *define* retirement.

GAIL SHEEHY (b. 1937), U.S. author. *New Passages: Mapping Your Life Across Time* (part 6, "Passage to the Age of Integrity"; chapter 17, "Men: Make My Passage") (1995).

18   Like many men, he gave up his identity along with his job. One day he was a boss at the factory, with a brass plate on his door and a reputation to uphold; the next day he was a nobody at home.

SCOTT RUSSELL SANDERS (b. 1945), U.S. essayist. "Under the Influence" (1989), in *The Art of the Personal Essay: An Anthology from the Classical Era to the Present*, ed. Phillip Lopate (1994).

Sanders writes here about his alcoholic father.

19   We want retirement to mean that we have chosen to leave paid work for something else, and not survival on a pittance because we are no longer welcome at work.

EDITH STEIN, PAULA B. DORESS-WORTERS, and MARY D. FILMORE, U.S. authors. *The New Ourselves, Growing Older: Women Aging with Knowledge and Power*, ed. Paula B. Doress-Worters and Diana Laskin Siegal (chapter 13, "Work and Retirement") (1994).

20   Retirement places more time on your hands. Indeed, it is one of the enjoyments of retirement that you are able to drift through the day at your own pace, easy in the knowl-

edge that you have put hard work and achievement behind you.

KAZUO ISHIGURO (b. 1954), *An Artist of the Floating World* ("October 1948") (1986).

Old Age

1 Cast me not off in the time of my old age; forsake me not when my strength faileth.

Psalms 71.9.

2 Old age puts more wrinkles in our minds than on our faces; and we never, or rarely, see a soul that in growing old does not come to smell sour and musty.

MICHEL EYQUEM DE MONTAIGNE (1533–1589), French essayist. "Of Repentance," book 3, essay 2 (1585–88), in *The Complete Essays of Montaigne*, trans. Donald M. Frame (1976; originally published 1958).

3 If you will be cherished when you be old, be curteous while you be young; if you look for comfort in your hoary hairs, be not coy when you have your golden locks.

JOHN LYLY (1554?–1606), English author. *Euphues: The Anatomy of Wit* (1578).

4 If to be old and merry be a sin, then many an old host that I know is damn'd.

WILLIAM SHAKESPEARE (1564–1616), English poet and dramatist. *The First Part of King Henry IV* 2.4.466.

Falstaff tries to justify himself to the Prince.

5 Though I look old, yet I am strong and lusty,
For in my youth I never did apply
Hot and rebellious liquors in my blood,
Nor did not with unbashful forehead woo

The means of weakness and debility.
Therefore my age is as a lusty winter,
Frosty, but kindly.

WILLIAM SHAKESPEARE (1564–1616), English poet and dramatist. *As You Like It* 2.3.47–52.

Spoken by Adam, one of the servants of Oliver, one of the sons of Sir Rowland de Boys.

6 . . . when thou are old and rich,
Thou hast neither heat, affection, limb, nor beauty,
To make thy riches pleasant.

WILLIAM SHAKESPEARE (1564–1616), English poet and dramatist. *Measure for Measure* 3.1.36–38.

The Duke addresses Claudio, urging him to "be absolute for death," since life is a good that "none but fools would keep."

7 I have liv'd long enough. My way of life
Is fall'n into the sear, the yellow leaf,
And that which should accompany old age,
As honor, love, obedience, troops of friends,
I must not look to have.

WILLIAM SHAKESPEARE (1564–1616), English poet and dramatist. *Macbeth* 5.3.22.

Spoken by Macbeth as his crimes close in on him.

8 When a man cometh by age to bee of no use, the respect given to him is only out of compassion, which is a very slender tenure in this ill natured Age. When a man is no more usefull to the world, the respect given him is a kind of almes; hee must not clayme it.

GEORGE SAVILE, MARQUIS OF HALIFAX (1633–1695), English courtier and writer. *Maxims* ("Age") (1750), in *The Works of*

George Savile, Marquis of Halifax, ed. Mark N. Brown, vol. 3 (1989).

9 Many a man is seen to the best advantage in old age when he is more lenient and indulgent because he is more experienced, unruffled, and resigned.

ARTHUR SCHOPENHAUER (1788–1860), German philosopher. *Parerga and Paralipomena: Short Philosophical Essays* (chapter 6, "On the Different Periods of Life") (1851), trans. E. F. J. Payne (1974).

10 The surest sign of age is loneliness. While one finds company in himself and his pursuits, he cannot be old, whatever his years may number.

A. BRONSON ALCOTT (1799–1888), U.S. philosopher and educator. "Fellowship," *Tablets* (1868).

11 We have settled when old age begins. Like all Nature's processes, it is gentle and gradual in its approaches, strewed with illusions, and all its little griefs are soothed by natural sedatives. But the iron hand is not less irresistible because it wears the velvet glove.

OLIVER WENDELL HOLMES (1809–1894), U.S. author and physician. *The Autocrat of the Breakfast-Table* (chapter 7) (1858).

12 What is it to grow old?
. . . .
It is to spend long days
And not once feel that we were ever young;
It is to add, immured
In the hot prison of the present, month
To month with weary pain.

MATTHEW ARNOLD (1822–1888), English poet and critic. "Growing Old."

13 Love is always young and fair.
What to us is silver hair,
Faded cheeks or steps grown slow,
To the heart that beats below?

EBEN E. REXFORD (1848–1916), U.S. poet and editor. "Silver Threads among the Gold."

In *The Fireside Book of Favorite American Songs*, ed. Margaret Bradford Boni (1952), Boni notes that H. P. Dunks, who composed the music for this song, bought a number of poems from Rexford for three dollars apiece.

14 There's many a good tune played on an old fiddle.

SAMUEL BUTLER (1835–1902), British author. *The Way of All Flesh* (chapter 61) (1903).

Mrs. Jupp, a talkative woman, responds to an insensitive comment about her age.

15 AGE, n. That period of life in which we compound for the vices that we still cherish by reviling those that we have no longer the enterprise to commit.

AMBROSE BIERCE (1842–?1914), U.S. author. *The Devil's Dictionary* (1881–1911).

16 Oh, dear, this living and eating and growing old; these doubts and aches in the back, and want of interest in Nightingales and Roses . . . [and]
Growing old is no gradual decline, but a series of tumbles, full of sorrow, from one ledge to another. Yet when we pick ourselves up we find that our bones are not broken; while not unpleasing is the new terrace which lies unexplored before us.

LOGAN PEARSALL SMITH (1856–1946), U.S. humorist. "Last Words," *All Trivia: Trivia, More Trivia, Afterthoughts, Last Words* (1945).

17 There are people who, like houses, are beautiful in dilapidation.

LOGAN PEARSALL SMITH (1865–1946), U.S. humorist. "Age and Death," *Afterthoughts* (1931) and *All Trivia: Trivia, More Trivia, Afterthoughts, Last Words* (1945).

18 Many a man that couldn't direct you to the drugstore on the corner when he was thirty will get a respectful hearing when age has further impaired his mind.

FINLEY PETER DUNNE (1867–1936), U.S. humorist. "Some Observations by Mr. Dooley," *Mr. Dooley Remembers: The Informal Memoirs of Finley Peter Dunne* (1963).

19 It seems like th' only way t' reach a ripe an' peaceful ole age is just t' be downright an' everlastin'ly worthless.

KIN HUBBARD (1868–1930), U.S. humorist. *Fifty Weeks of Abe Martin* (1924).

20 Yes, the truth is that unless old men possess some deep interior life of their own they are almost bound to hang like millstones round the necks of their children and their children's children. Nor is it to be supposed, though he possesses all the natural vanity in the world, that this state of things can be completely concealed from an old man. He is really alone in an unsympathetic world and in his heart he knows that he is. He knows that in spite of all the care that surrounds him his death will be a relief if not an unspeakable comfort to his survivors.

JOHY COWPER POWYS (1872–1963), English author. *The Art of Growing Old* (chapter 9, "Old Age and Literature") (1974).

21 Age wins and one must learn to grow old. As I learnt with the loss of a nurse to put childish things behind me, as I learnt when the joys of dependence were over to embrace with fear the isolation of independence, so now I must learn to walk this long unlovely wintry way, looking for spectacles, shunning the cruel looking-glass, laughing at my clumsiness before others mistakenly condole, not expecting gallantry yet disappointed to receive none, apprehending every ache of shaft of pain, alive to blinding flashes of mortality, unarmed, totally vulnerable.

LADY DIANA COOPER (1892–1986), English author, actor, and nurse. *Trumpets from the Steep* (chapter 8, "Winter and Journey's End") (1860).

22 I have never come across one single woman, either in life or in books, who has looked upon her own old age cheerfully.

SIMONE DE BEAUVOIR (1908–1986), French author and philosopher. *The Coming of Age* (part 2, "The Being-in-the-World"; chapter 5, "The Discovery and Assumption of Old Age: The Body's Experience") (1970); trans. Patrick O'Brian (1972).

23 If we face now the reality, at sixty-five or seventy, seventy-five, eighty, ninety, that we will indeed, sooner or later, die, then the only big question is how are we going to *live* the years we have left, however many or few they may be? What adventures can we now set out on to make sure we'll be alive when we die? Can age itself be such an adventure?

BETTY FRIEDAN (b. 1921), U.S. author and feminist. *The Fountain of Age* (chapter 17, "Dying with Life") (1993).

24 Continuing to live—that is, repeat
A habit formed to get necessaries—

Is nearly always losing, or going
without.

PHILIP LARKIN (1922–1985), English
poet and critic. "Continuing to Live."

Turning 70

1   The Master said, "At fifteen I set
my heart on learning; at thirty I
took my stand; at forty I came to
be free from doubts; at fifty I understood the Decree of Heaven; at
sixty my ear was attuned; at seventy
I followed my heart's desire without
overstepping the line."

CONFUCIUS (551?–479 B.C.), Chinese philosopher. Analects (Lun yü), book 2, section 4,
trans. D. C. Lau (1979).

2   Approaching, nearing, curious,
Thou dim, uncertain spectre—
   bringest thou life or death?
Strength, weakness, blindness, more
   paralysis and heavier?
Or placid skies and sun?

WALT WHITMAN (1819–1892), U.S.
poet. "Queries to My Seventieth Year."

3   I have been asked what a man over
seventy can do to keep occupied.
The trouble is, that a man who
can't keep busy didn't take interest
in a great number of things when
he was mentally active in his
younger years. If he had done so,
he would find plenty to occupy his
time in reading, observing and
watching people. There are a great
many hobbies he can work with
and keep busy until his death. . . .
   . . . Men are not as active at seventy as they were at fifty because
they hurt their machinery too
much. If they like a certain thing,
they will overdo it. They eat too
much, or drink too much, or if

they like sleeping they will sleep too
much.

THOMAS ALVA EDISON (1847–1931),
U.S. inventor. The Diary and Sundry Observations of Thomas Alva Edison ("Sundry Observations"; chapter 1, "Autobiographical"; section 4 [1927]), ed. Dagobert D. Runes (1948).

Edison claimed he would be unwilling to retire
from work until "the doctor brings in the oxy-
gen cylinder."

4   I can scarcely, nowadays, endure
the company of anybody under seventy. Young people compel one to
look forward on a life full of effort.
Old people permit one to look
backward on a life whose effort is
over and done with. That is repose-
ful.

VICTORIA (OR VITA) SACKVILLE-
WEST (1892–1962), English novelist and
poet. All Passion Spent (part 1) (1931).

Mr. Bucktrout comments to Lady Slade that
most people do not appreciate or achieve repose until old age "imposes" it upon them,
and even then "half of them still sigh for the
energy which once was theirs."

5   This is the year of my seventieth
birthday, a fact that bewilders me. I
find it hard to believe. I understand
now the look of affront I often saw
in my father's face after this age
and that I see in the faces of my
contemporaries. We are affronted
because, whatever we may feel, time
has turned us into curiosities in
some secondhand shop. We are
haunted by the suspicion that the
prayers we did not know we were
making have been only too bla-
tantly answered.

V. S. PRITCHETT (b. 1905), English author. The Midnight Oil (chapter 1) (1971).

6   Being over seventy is like being engaged in a war. All our friends are
going or gone and we survive

amongst the dead and the dying as on a battlefield.

MURIEL SPARK (b. 1918), Scottish author. *Memento Mori* (chapter 4) (1959).

7 To realize that I've touched seventy was absolutely devastating. [*Very long pause.*] I'm disturbed by my concern in undertaking new commitments—as if my time is limited. I never had that feeling before. I don't want to take responsibility for something that I may not be able to complete. It's a very worrisome thing. Being seventy made me angry. Being sixty-nine did not. [*Laughs.*]

JUDITH VLADEK (b. 1925), U.S. lawyer. Interview with Studs Terkel in *Coming of Age: The Story of Our Century by Those Who've Lived It* (1995).

Vladek speaks here as senior partner in a 30-member law firm and as someone who still meets daily with clients.

Turning 80

1 When Rabbi Hanina was eighty years old, he was still able to stand on one foot and remove the shoe from the other. He said: "My strength in old age comes from the frequent warm baths and anointing in oil given my body during infancy."

Hullin 24, in *The Talmudic Anthology: Tales and Teachings of the Rabbis*, ed. Louis I. Newman (1947).

2 I am a very foolish fond old man, Fourscore and upward, not an hour more nor less; And, to deal plainly, I fear I am not in my perfect mind.

WILLIAM SHAKESPEARE (1564–1616), English poet and dramatist. *King Lear* 4.7.62–65.

King Lear in a poignant understatement.

3 By the time a man gets to be eighty he learns that he is compassed by limitations, and that there has been a natural boundary set to his individual powers. As he goes on in life, he begins to doubt his ability to destroy all evil and to reform all abuses, and to suspect that there will be much left to do after he has done.

CHARLES DUDLEY WARNER (1829–1900), U.S. author. *My Summer in a Garden* ("What I Know About Gardening") (1870).

4 . . . they who nobly fail will find The peace of the heroic mind, Will taste life's sacred joy, the joy Earth cannot give nor earth destroy. These things I see as the cloud clears, Here at the height of eighty years.

EDWIN MARKHAM (1852–1940), poet. "At Eighty Years."

5 If at eighty you're not a cripple or an invalid, if you have your health, if you still enjoy a good walk, a good meal (with all the trimmings), if you can sleep without first taking a pill, if birds and flowers, mountains and sea still inspire you, you are a most fortunate individual and you should get down on your knees morning and night and thank the good Lord for savin' and keepin' his power.

HENRY MILLER (1891–1980), U.S. author. "On Turning 80," *A Henry Miller Reader*, ed. John Calder (1985).

6 The new octogenarian feels as strong as ever when he is sitting back in a comfortable chair. He ruminates, he dreams, he remembers. He doesn't want to be disturbed by others. It seems to him that old age

is only a costume assumed for those others; the true, the essential self is ageless. In a moment he will rise and go for a ramble in the woods, taking a gun along, or a fishing rod, if it is spring. Then he creaks to his feet, bending forward to keep his balance, and realizes that he will do nothing of the sort. The body and its surroundings have their messages for him, or only one message: "You are old."

MALCOLM COWLEY (1898–1989), U.S. author and literary critic. *The View From 80* (chapter 1), (1980).

7   Once you reach 80, everyone wants to carry your baggage and help you up the steps. If you forget your name or anybody else's name, or an appointment, or your own telephone number, or promise to be three places at the same time, or can't remember how many grandchildren you have, you need only explain that you are 80.

FRANK LAUBACH, U.S. "Life Begins at 80," quoted in Ann Landers, *Wake Up and Smell the Coffee! Advice, Wisdom and Uncommon Good Sense* (1996).

Turning 90

1   A man over ninety is a great comfort to all his elderly neighbors: he is a picket-guard at the extreme outpost; and the young folks of sixty and seventy feel that they enemy must get by him before he can come near their camp.

OLIVER WENDELL HOLMES (1809–1894), U.S. author and physician. *The Guardian Angel* (chapter 2, "Great Excitement") (1895).

2   The riders in a race do not stop short when they reach the goal.

There is a little finishing canter before coming to a standstill. There is time to hear the kind voices of friends and to say to oneself, "The work is done." But just as one says that, the answer comes: "The race is over, but the work never is done while the power to work remains." The canter that brings you to a standstill need not be only coming to rest. It cannot be, while you still live. For to live is to function. That is all there is to living.

OLIVER WENDELL HOLMES (1841–1935), U.S. Supreme Court justice. Speech at his ninetieth-birthday tribute, 7 March 1931, in *Lend Me Your Ear: Great Speeches in History*, ed. William Safire (1992).

Turning 100

1   Grandpa Cartmell was celebrating his 100th birthday and everybody complimented him on how athletic and well preserved he appeared. "I will tell you the secret of my success," he cackled. "My wife and I were married 75 years ago. On our wedding night we made a solemn pledge that whenever we had a fight, the one who was proved wrong would go out and take a walk. Gentlemen, I have been in the open air practically continuously for 75 years."

ANONYMOUS. *Anything For a Laugh: A Collection of Jokes and Anecdotes That You, Too, Can Tell and Probably Have*, ed. Bennett Cerf (1946).

2   I shouldn't mind . . . living to my hundredth year, like Fontenelle, who never wept nor laughed, never lost his temper; to whom all the science of his day was known, but who all his life adored three things—music, painting and

women—about which he said he understood absolutely nothing.

LOGAN PEARSALL SMITH (1865–1946), U.S. humorist. "Myself," *Afterthoughts* (1931) and *All Trivia: Trivia, More Trivia, Afterthoughts, Last Words* (1945).

3 A parrot nears a hundred years (or
     so the legend goes),
  So were I he this century I might
     see to its close.
  Then I might swing within my ring
     while revolutions roar,
  And watch a world to ruin
     hurled—and find it all a bore.

ROBERT W. SERVICE (1874–1958), Canadian author. "Longevity."

4 Turning one hundred was the worst birthday of my life. I wouldn't wish it on my worst enemy. Turning 101 was not so bad. Once you're past that century mark, it's just not as shocking.

A. ELIZABETH DELANY (1891–1995), U.S. author. *Having Our Say: The Delany Sisters' First 100 Years* (section 32, "Outliving the Rebby Boys") (1993).

The remark is attributed to Bessie; the book was written with her sister Sarah.

5 Other characteristics of healthy centenarians, garnered from a number of studies, are these: Most have high native intelligence, a keen interest in current events, a good memory, and few illnesses. They tend to be early risers, sleeping on average between six and seven hours. Most drink coffee, follow no special diets, but generally prefer diets high in protein, low in fat. There is no uniformity in their drinking habits, but they use less medication in their lifetimes than many old people use in a week. They prefer living in the present,

with changes, and are usually religious in the broad sense.

GAIL SHEEHY (b. 1937), U.S. author. *New Passages: Mapping Your Life Across Time* (part 6, "Passage to the Age of Integrity"; chapter 19, "Two Species of Aging") (1995).

Death

1 Lord, make me to know mine end, and the measure of my days, what it is, that I may know how frail I am.

Psalm 39.4.

2 The mystics conceived of the body as an encumbering garment which falls away at death and leaves the true man free to rise into the light of the heavenly life.

Zohar to Terumah, in *The Talmudic Anthology: Tales and Teachings of the Rabbis*, ed. Louis I. Newman (1947).

3 To be dead is the same as never to
     have been born,
  And better far than living on in
     wretchedness.
  The dead feel nothing; evil then can
     cause no pain.

EURIPIDES (c. 485-406 B.C.), Greek dramatist. *The Women of Troy* (lines 634–36).

Andromache, Hector's widow, speaks, tr. Philip Vellacott (1972).

4 No one knows whether death is really the greatest blessing a man can have, but they fear it is the greatest curse, as if they knew well.

PLATO (427-347 B.C.), Greek philosopher. *The Apology*, in *Great Dialogues of Plato*, trans. W. H. D. Rouse and ed. Eric H. Warmington and Philip G. Rouse (1956).

5 My ancestors are turned to clay,
     And many of my mates are gone,
  My youngers daily drop away,

And can I think to 'scape alone?
No, no, I know that I must die,
And yet my life amend not I.

ROBERT SOUTHWELL (1561–1595), English poet, Jesuit priest, and martyr. "Upon the Image of Death."

Gardner indicates that the attribution of this poem to Southwell is frequent and traditional but disputed by modern scholars.

6   It is as natural to die as to be born; and to a little infant, perhaps, the one is as painful as the other. He that dies in an earnest pursuit, is like one that is wounded in hot blood; who for the time scarce feels the hurt; and therefore a mind fixed and bent upon somewhat that is good, doth aver the dolours of death.

FRANCIS BACON (1561–1626), English philosopher, statesman, and essayist. "Of Death," *Essays or Counsels, Civil and Moral* (1625), and reprinted in *The Essays of Francis Bacon*, ed. John Pitcher (1985).

7   . . . they say the tongues of dying men
Enforce attention like deep harmony.
Where words are scarce, they are seldom spent in vain,
For they breathe truth that breathe their words in pain.

WILLIAM SHAKESPEARE (1564–1616), English poet and dramatist. *Richard II* 2.1.5–8.

8   Death, be not proud, though some have callèd thee
Mighty and dreadful, for thou art not so;
For those whom you think'st thou dost overthrow
Die not, poor Death, nor yet canst thou kill me.

JOHN DONNE (1572–1631), English poet, clergyman, and courtier. *Holy Sonnets* 10.

9   Though since thy first sad entrance by
      Just Abel's blood,
'Tis now six thousand years well nigh,
And still thy sovereignty holds good:
Yet by none art thou understood.

HENRY VAUGHAN (1622–1695), Welsh-born English poet. "Death."

10 Death in itself is nothing; but we fear,
To be we know not what, we know not where.

JOHN DRYDEN (1631–1700), English poet and dramatist. *Aureng-Zebe* 4.1 (1676).

11 Vital spark of heav'nly flame!
Quit, oh quit this mortal frame:
Trembling, hoping, ling'ring, flying,
Oh the pain, the bliss of dying!

ALEXANDER POPE (1688–1744), English poet. "The Dying Christian to His Soul, Ode," *Adaptations of the Emperor Hadrian*.

12 Life is sweet, let me tell you, and never sweeter than when we are near losing it.

HENRY FIELDING (1707–1754), English novelist. *Amelia* (book 1; chapter 10, " 'Table Talk' Consisting of a Facetious Discourse that Passed in the Prison") (1751).

13 The death of a dear friend, wife, brother, lover, which seemed nothing but privation, somewhat later assumes the aspect of a guide or genius; for it commonly operates revolutions in our way of life, terminates an epoch of infancy or of youth which was waiting to be closed, breaks up a wonted occupation, or a household, or style of living, and allows for the formation of

new ones more friendly to the growth of character.

RALPH WALDO EMERSON (1803–1882), U.S. author. "Compensation," *Essays: First Series* (1841).

14 It is the secret of the world that all things subsist and do not die, but only retire from sight and afterwards return again.

RALPH WALDO EMERSON (1803–1882), U.S. author. "Nominalist and Realist," *Essays, Second Series* (1844).

15 So far as I have observed persons nearing the end of life, the Roman Catholics understand the business of dying better than Protestants. They have an expert by them, armed with spiritual specifics, in which they both, patient and priestly ministrant, place implicit trust. Confession, the Eucharist, Extreme Unction,—these all inspire a confidence which without this symbolism is too apt to be wanting in over-sensitive natures.

OLIVER WENDELL HOLMES (1809–1894), U.S. author and physician. *Over the Tea Cups* (chapter 10) (1891).

16 God waits only the separation of spirit from flesh to crown us with a full reward. Why, then, should we ever sink overwhelmed with distress, when life is soon over, and death is so certain an entrance to happiness—to glory?

CHARLOTTE BRONTË (1816–1855), English author. *Jane Eyre* (chapter 8) (1847).

Helen Burns tries to console the young Jane here after she has been publicly called a liar.

17 Death is beautiful when seen to be a law, and not an accident—It is as common as life.

HENRY DAVID THOREAU (1817–1862), U.S. author. Letter to Ralph Waldo Emerson, 11 March 1842, in *Letters of a Nation: A Collection of Extraordinary American Letters*, ed. Andrew Carroll (1997).

Thoreau wrote after the unexpected deaths, within two weeks, of Thoreau's brother John and Emerson's son Waldo.

18 We've wholly forgotten how to die. But be sure you do die nevertheless. Do your work, and finish it. If you know how to begin, you will know when to end.

HENRY DAVID THOREAU (1817–1862), U.S. author. "A Plea for John Brown" (1859).

19 . . . to die is different from what any one supposed, and luckier.

WALT WHITMAN (1819–1892), U.S. poet. "Song of Myself" (section 6).

20 Every life, no matter if its hour is rich with love and every moment jewelled with joy, will, at its close, become a tragedy as sad and deep and dark as can be woven of the warp and woof of mystery and death.

ROBERT GREEN INGERSOLL (1833–1899), U.S. orator, known as the "great agnostic." Tribute to his brother Clark at his death, 1879, in *Lend Me Your Ears: Great Speeches in History*, ed. William Safire (1992).

21 Old and young, we are all on our last cruise.

ROBERT LOUIS STEVENSON (1850–1894), Scottish author. "Crabbed Age and Youth" (1878), *Virginibus Puerisque* (1881).

22 Life does not cease to be funny when people die any more than it ceases to be serious when people laugh.

GEORGE BERNARD SHAW (1856–1950), Irish dramatist and critic. *The Doctor's Dilemma* (act 5) (1906).

23   Upon the eyes, the lips, the feet,
     On all the passages of sense,
     The atoning oil is spread with sweet
     Renewal of lost innocence.

ERNEST DOWSON (1867–1900), English poet. "Extreme Unction."

24   Death has been treated too much as a subject for melancholy reflection, or as an occasion for self-discipline, or as a rather hazy theological entity. . . . What we have to do is to see it in its true context, see it as an active reality, as one more phase, in a world and a "becoming" that are those of our own experience.

PIERRE TEILHARD DE CHARDIN (1881–1955), French philosopher, paleontologist, and Jesuit priest. "The Making of a Mind" (written 1916), trans. René Hague (1974), and included in *On Suffering* (1974).

25   Hooray for the last grand adventure! I wish I had won, but it was worthwhile anyway.

AMELIA EARHART (1897–1937), U.S. aviator. "Popping Off Letter," 20 May 1928, in *Letters of a Nation: A Collection of Extraordinary American Letters,* ed. Andrew Carroll (1997).

Earhart wrote the letter to her father and requested that it be opened in the event that she died in her attempt to be the first woman passenger on a transatlantic crossing. In 1937, Earhart's plane disappeared during her attempt at a solo flight around the world.

26   Do not go gentle into that good
     night,
     Old age should burn and rave at
     close of day;
     Rage, rage against the dying of the
     light.

DYLAN THOMAS (1914–1953), Welsh poet. "Do Not Go Gentle into That Good Night."

27   This is the end, the redemption from Wilderness, way for the Wanderer, House sought for All, black handkerchief washed clean by weeping.

ALLEN GINSBERG (1926–1998), U.S. poet. "Kaddish" (section 1).

28   What is it about death that bothers me so much? Probably the hours. Melnick says the soul is immortal and lives on after the body drops away, but if my soul exists without my body, I am convinced all my clothes will be loose-fitting.

WOODY ALLEN (b. 1935), U.S. film director, writer, and actor. *Without Feathers* ("Selections from the Allen Notebooks") (1975).

29   Being dead is one—the worst, the last—but only one in a series of calamities that afflicts our own and several other species. The list may include, but is not limited to, gingivitis, bowel obstruction, contested divorce, tax audit, spiritual vexation, cash flow problems, political upheaval, and on and on and on some more. There is no shortage of misery.

THOMAS LYNCH (b. 1948), U.S. author and undertaker. *The Undertaking: Life Studies from the Dismal Trade* ("The Undertaking") (1997).

Lynch here explains the undertaker's relation to death, arguing that undertakers have no more stomach for death or other miseries than anyone else does.

Index of Sources

The numbers refer to the pages.

Van Gogh, Vincent
TURNING 30, 219
Vanderbilt, Amy
BAPTISM, 209; COMING OUT (SOCIALLY), 188;
INVITATION, 162; WEDDING, 106
Vaughan, Henry
DEATH, 244; EASTER, 18; FIRST COMMUNION, 210
Ver Standig, Helen
STARTING A BUSINESS, 108
Verhovek, Sam Howe
LABOR DAY, 35
Vidal, Gore
INTRODUCTIONS, 158
Viorst, Judith
WEDDING ANNIVERSARY, 119
Vladek, Judith
TURNING 70, 241
Voltaire (François-Marie Arouet)
DIVORCING, 130; FIRST JOB, 199
von Arnim, Elizabeth
See Russell, Mary Annette (Beauchamp),
Countess Russell
von Goethe, Johann Wolfgang
WEDDING ANNIVERSARY, 116
von Grunebaum, Gustav Edmund
ISLAMIC NEW YEAR, 22
Walton, Izaak
DRINKING, 145; FINANCIAL SUCCESS, 151
Warner, Charles Dudley
AUGUST, 69; FIRST HOME, 206; JULY, 69; TURNING
80, 241
Washington, George
THANKSGIVING, 45
Watts, Isaac
EASTER, 18
Waugh, Evelyn
TURNING 16, 187
West, Mae
WEDNESDAY, 61
Westendorf, Thomas P.
FAMILY REUNION, 120
Wharton, Edith
ENGAGEMENT, 97
White, E. B.
CHRISTMAS, 54
White, William Allen
GRADUATION, 193
Whitfield, Norman
BREAKING UP, 93
Whitman, Walt
DEATH, 245; INDEPENDENCE DAY, 33; TURNING 70,
240
Whittier, John Greenleaf
AUTUMN, 77; DECEMBER, 71; FAMILY REUNION, 119;
INDEPENDENCE DAY, 32; JUNE, 68; NOVEMBER, 71;
SCHOOL REUNION, 120; SEPTEMBER, 70; SUNDAY,
58; THANKSGIVING, 46; WINTER, 81
Wiesel, Elie
FRIDAY, 62; ROSH HASHANAH, 37; YOM KIPPUR, 41
Wilbur, Richard
WEDDING, 106

Wilcox, Ella Wheeler
BREAKING UP, 92; FRIDAY, 61; MONDAY, 60; NEW
YEAR, 5; SUNDAY, 59; WEDNESDAY, 61
Wilde, Oscar
BECOMING A PARENT, 112; BIRTHDAY, 3;
CONFESSING, 172; DISASTERS, 135; DIVORCING, 131;
ENGAGEMENT, 97; FIRST LOVE, 198; GRADUATION,
192; INSPIRING, 161; LOSING, 174; MARRIAGE
(FIRST), 203; PROPOSALS, 95; QUITTING SMOKING,
99; SECOND MARRIAGE/REMARRIAGE, 218; TURNING
30, 219; WINNING, 173
Wilder, Billy
TURNING 50, 226
Wilhelm, Richard
CHINESE NEW YEAR, 9
Williams, Paul
MONDAY, 60
Williams, Tennessee
FORGIVING, 169; FUNERAL, 139; PRAISE, 168
Williams, William Carlos
HOSPITALS AND DOCTORS, 123; LOSING A SPOUSE,
229
Wilmot, Earl of Rochester, John
BREAKING UP, 92; DRINKING, 145
Winterrowd, Wayne
JULY, 69
Wolfe, Charles
MEMORIAL DAY, 28
Wollstonecraft, Mary
BACK TO SCHOOL, 87; BECOMING A PARENT, 110;
TURNING 30, 218
Wonder, Stevie (Stevelund Judkins)
MARTIN LUTHER KING DAY, 8
Woodward, Kenneth L.
KWANZAA, 51
Woolf, Virginia
FIRST DAY OF SCHOOL, 183; FIRST SEX, 194; MIDDLE
AGE, 224; PARTIES, 156; TURNING 50, 225
Wordsworth, William
BECOMING A PARENT, 111; BEREAVEMENT, 136;
MARCH, 64; MAY, 67
Wouk, Herman
BAR, BAT MITZVAH, 212; DIVORCING, 132;
HANUKKAH, 49; PASSOVER, 21; ROSH HASHANAH,
37; YOM KIPPUR, 40
Wright, A. R.
APRIL FOOL'S DAY, 17; HALLOWEEN, 42
Wright, Frances (Fanny)
INDEPENDENCE DAY, 32
Wyatt, Thomas
BREAKING UP, 92
Xun, Lu
CHINESE NEW YEAR, 9
Yeats, William Butler
FIRST LOVE, 198; HALLOWEEN, 42; OCTOBER, 70;
TOASTING, 148; TURNING 50, 225
Yee, Chiang
CHINESE NEW YEAR, 9
Yonge, Charlotte M.
SUNDAY, 58
Young, Grace
CHINESE NEW YEAR, 11
Zuckerman, B.
See Henry, Buck